Joseph Henry Allen

Hebrew Men and Times

From the patriarchs to the Messiah

Joseph Henry Allen

Hebrew Men and Times
From the patriarchs to the Messiah

ISBN/EAN: 9783337317850

Printed in Europe, USA, Canada, Australia, Japan

Cover: Foto ©Lupo / pixelio.de

More available books at **www.hansebooks.com**

HEBREW

MEN AND TIMES,

FROM

THE PATRIARCHS TO THE MESSIAH.

BY

JOSEPH HENRY ALLEN.

BOSTON:

WALKER, WISE, AND COMPANY,

245 WASHINGTON STREET.

LONDON: CHAPMAN AND HALL.

1861.

University Press, Cambridge :
Stereotyped and Printed by Welch, Bigelow, & Co.

TO

MY HONOURED TEACHER AND FRIEND,

PRESIDENT WALKER,

LATE OF HARVARD UNIVERSITY, CAMBRIDGE,

AND TO THE

REV. JAMES MARTINEAU,

OF MANCHESTER NEW COLLEGE, LONDON,

𝕿𝖍𝖎𝖘 𝖁𝖔𝖑𝖚𝖒𝖊

IS, BY PERMISSION, GRATEFULLY INSCRIBED.

PREFACE.

ABOUT ten years ago, in undertaking a course of lectures on portions of the Jewish and Christian annals, I felt very much the want of some such guide as I have tried to furnish here. The singular interest of the Hebrew history, — its epical unity and completeness, — its place and connection among other memorials of the ancient world, — the unique literature which contains it, and the peculiarly sacred relation it bears to the religious life and faith of men, — these, of course, have not escaped the attention of scholars. And the body of literature that has gathered about this topic is perhaps equal in richness and breadth to that in any other field. But there seemed room and need of a clear, brief sketch, or outline; — one that should spare the details and give the results of scholarship; that should trace the historical sequences and connections, without being entangled in questions of mere erudition, or literary discussions, or theological polemics; that should preserve the honest independence of scholarly thought, along with the temper of

a*

Christian faith ; that should not lose from sight the broad perspective of secular history, while it should recognize at each step the hand of " Providence as manifest in Israel."

Such have been the aim and purpose of this volume. I wish that it may be taken for no more than what it claims. It is a Sketch, not a History. It does not supersede, it assumes, knowledge of the Scripture narrative. To be rightly judged, its rapid outline should be followed Bible in hand. I disclaim once for all the pretension, as I have not had the means, of original research. Other cares and occupations have forbidden me the attempt to master the vast learning of the subject. Of scholars by profession I can only crave indulgence. To those who are not I may say that I have used the best guides within my reach, and have spared no pains to trace with all possible fidelity the real character of each epoch, or train of events, or literary monument that records it.

It should in justice be said at the outset, that the conception of this task, or a single step in its execution, would have been quite impossible without the masterly and admirable work of Ewald,* to which I wish to express my constant indebtedness, — throughout the earlier portion especially, where the general tone is his, and where, in many matters of detail, his opinion is silently assumed. At the same time, there are cardinal points of history and criticism where I have found myself unable to follow him, and where, with all

* Geschichte des Volkes Israel.

deference and reluctantly, a different view has been adopted.
I desire, also, here to express my obligations to the very
fine ability and scholarship of Mr. Newman's "Hebrew
Monarchy," and to the portions which I have been able to
consult of Bunsen's unfinished "Bibelwerk." Such acknowl-
edgment as seems due to other authorities will be found in
the course of the volume. But in all cases requiring the
exercise of independent judgment, the statements and the
opinions are my own.

Some portions under the titles "The Law" and "The
Messiah" are probably most open to the charge of novelty
or mistake. As to these, — involving as they do the rudiments, or immediate antecedents, of the Hebrew and Christian faith, — I can only say that they have cost the most
anxious care of all in preparation, and that no assertion has
been ventured without being duly weighed. And, while
there is much to protest against in the spirit, method, and
results of such writers as Ghillany and Gfrörer, whom I
have freely consulted on these portions, it seems to me that
it is right to use such of their investigations as we honestly can, where they may help us to simple truth of fact.

To the affluent learning, and the constant, most generous
kindness of the late Theodore Parker, and to the personal
encouragement or counsel received from others, — among
whom I am proud to reckon so illustrious a theologian and
critic as Mr. Martineau, and the historian Ewald, — I would
express my grateful sense of obligation.

I am well aware of the risk I run in attempting metrical versions of a few of the earlier and more striking specimens of the Hebrew national poetry. But it is the only way I know of exhibiting one very essential feature of the genius of that people, without marring, by literary discussions, the work in hand. And, with deference to the opinion of critics, I venture to think that the formality of Hebrew "parallelism" is best represented to our minds by the formality of English rhyme and rhythm. In these versions I have retained where I could the phrases of the common English Bible ; and, where I have varied from its sense, it has generally been for more accurate rendering of the original.

I have conscientiously sought to avoid entangling this little work with any sort of dogmatism, literary or theological, and to keep it true to its strictly historical intention. Not that I can claim to have succeeded perfectly. Indeed, where materials at first hand are so fragmentary and few, no reconstruction can possibly be had without the open or tacit assumption of some guiding idea. But, whatever personal prepossession may have been betrayed, or judgment of matters in controversy, I trust it has been kept so far in reserve as not to interfere seriously with the main purpose of the book, or to impair such value as it may have to readers of whatever creed.

I would submit, further, that in the way above hinted we may best approach the true and unexhausted sense of an historic Revelation. The divine or supernatural element is shown under terrestrial limitations and conditions. Events must be seen on their human side to enable us to judge truly of their Divine side. The philosophy of History, rightly apprehended, plays into the hands of the philosophy of Faith. The results of a genuine scientific criticism will be taken up and appropriated by that higher criticism which deals with the interior principles of a nation's life and the grand laws of historical evolution; which traces events from their "first great Cause, least understood,"— the fountain-head of special revelations, and the governing Force in human affairs.

JAMAICA PLAIN, Massachusetts,
  January, 1861.

CONTENTS.

HEBREW MEN AND TIMES.

I. THE PATRIARCHS.

THE little country of Palestine is a slender strip
of rugged land, lying between the desert and the
sea, divided about midway from north to south by
the river Jordan, and making the natural highway
between Asia and Africa. Its dimensions are about
those of Vermont, or Belgium. It was once very
populous and fertile. In the fond language of Hebrew Scripture, it was " a land flowing with milk
and honey ; a land of hills and valleys, drinking
water of the rain of heaven : the glory of all lands."
Now, it is mostly sterile and desolate. Its forests
are hewn down, its soil washed by the torrents of a
thousand winters, its river-courses dried, its cities
ravaged by centuries of war, its prosperity blasted by
centuries of misrule. Bare limestone hills, glens
infested by robbers, scattered ruins of towns and
villages, regions of lovely but forsaken landscape,
richly fertile but half-cultivated fields, doubtful rel-
iques and vestiges of its ancient history intermixed
with monuments of the Crusader and the half-civil-

ization of the Turk,—these make the traveller's
report of what was fairest in the splendid realm of
Solomon, and the scenes of the ministry of Christ.

But the character of the Hebrew race has given
an interest to this country shared by none other
under heaven. To all the civilized nations of the
earth it is known familiarly as the Holy Land. Its
very local names are the dearest symbols, to multitudes, of sentiments, memories, and hopes that have
become part of their religious nature. Hebron and
Bethlehem, Bethel, Sharon, and Carmel, Mount Zion,
the Sea of Galilee, and the river Jordan, are the
household words of Christian imagery; and "when
David had taken the strong rock-fort of Jebus, he
made of it a city so holy, as that its very name should
be music for ever."

Palestine is in the main a high and hilly region;
although its old name, Chna, or Canaan, is held to
signify "the low,"—i. e. in comparison with the
heights of Syria or Lebanon.* From the "hill-
country of Judæa," it slopes gradually towards
Syria at the north, where it is flanked by the great
mountain-range of Lebanon; and at the east breaks
suddenly down to the thrice-terraced valley, where
the Jordan has graven its rocky gorge, and the deep
gulf where the Dead Sea lies, thirteen hundred feet
below the Mediterranean level. It is a land full of
rugged valleys, glens, and caves, which mark the
localities of sacred legend. The scenes of Mary's
birth, of Gabriel's annunciation, of Christ's nativity,
of his transfiguration, and agony in the garden, are all

* Movers.

shown as so many grottos. The dead were interred
in caves. Sarah's tomb at Mamre, and that of Laz-
arus at Bethany, were hollowed in the rock. A
limestone country (as the valley of Virginia) is
sometimes grooved and channelled by numberless
watercourses under ground, making grotesque and
enormous caverns ; and the natural caves of Canaan, for generations the haunt of half-extermi-
nated tribes, sheltered the prophets of Israel from
the violence of King Ahab, and David from the
angry jealousy of Saul. The "mountains round
about Jerusalem" were from of old the striking
symbol of Divine protection ; their deep glens are
Tophet, the valley of Jehoshaphat, and the bed of
the brook Kedron. Lebanon in the north, and the
mountains of Moab and Edom in the east and south,
not only are great natural landmarks, or barriers,
but, with their majestic scenery and wild or pastoral
traditions, they both make the imagery of Hebrew
psalm, and fill out the visions of Christian fancy.

Then there were other features, of landscape or
climate, that perpetually stimulated and deepened
the religious dread which seems native to the Hebrew mind. The dreary desert-boundary is a more
solemn barrier than the changing sea or the everlasting hills. The earthquake-wave that ran between
the Caucasus and Sicily was often felt in Palestine.*
Swarms of locusts, sudden and terrible, came like
judgments of an angry God : " fire devouring before
them, and flame blasting behind ; the land as the
garden of Eden before them, and behind them a

* Ewald, Vol. I. p. 264.

desolate wilderness." *   Malignant local maladies,
pestilence, and the scalding leprosy of the East, visited and scourged the people, subduing them to the
prophet's vehement appeal, or the burdensome requi-
sition of the priest.   And more than all, local memories and old tradition spoke of stupendous judgments
exercised on a lewd and godless people ; — how the
cities of the hot and fertile plain, which was " as the
garden of the Lord, or like the land of Egypt," for
beauty and richness, were destroyed suddenly by fire
from heaven, its mines of bitumen (or " slime-pits ")
being kindled underneath ; and the bitter water of
the salt lake. flowed over them, wherein no living
thing could dwell, and where, as Josephus tells,
the relics of those old haunts of profligate luxury
might still be seen, by whoever should venture on
that dreadful sea.

" That this was a volcanic region," says Strabo,
" is shown by many proofs.   For they exhibit rocks
near Moasas, rugged and scorched, and clefts in
many places, and a soil like ashes ; and drops of
pitch trickling from smooth rocks, and boiling
streams of vile stench, and dwellings here and
there thrown down : so that one would credit the
tale of the natives, that thirteen cities were once
inhabited there, Sodom, their metropolis, having a
circuit of sixty furlongs ; but by means of earth-
quakes and spoutings forth of flame, and hot springs
of pitchy and sulphurous water, the lake fell on
them, and their very stones took fire ; and of the
cities some were sunk, and from others those who

* Joel ii. 3.

were able fled away. But Eratosthenes says, on the contrary, that, being a lake-country, most of it was ingulfed in the bursting out of water like the sea. Furthermore, in the country of the Gadarenes is a noisome marsh, of which the cattle that drink the water cast their hair and hoofs and horns." *

The Hebrew traditions preserve to us many traces of the aboriginal inhabitants of this land, — relics of buried nations, whose thin ghosts flit across the dimly-lighted stage of the early history. First were *Horites*, the savage tribe indigenous to the soil. Their name signifies mountaineers, or dwellers in caves; for when they had been driven back by the Canaanites, scanty remnants still hung about the caverns and the hills, or inhabited the thousand rocky nests of the Edomite Mount Seir; † and of these wretched outlaws the book of Job may be thought to speak: "They were driven forth from among men, who cried after them as after a thief, to dwell in the cliffs of the valleys, in caves of the earth, and in the rocks; .... wet with the showers of the mountains, and embracing the rock for want of shelter." ‡ There were *Rephaim*, or Giants, fabled by some to be the progeny of a breed so vast that they had outlived the flood, who gave their name to the valley lying westward from Jerusalem. There were *Kadmonites*, "Sons of the East;" and *Philistines*, a relic of the old shepherd race, who had wandered back from Caphtor, or Crete; and *Anakim*, or sons of Anak, said to have roved from Babel, — the terror of the southern

* Lib. XVI. cap. 2. † Ewald. Compare Gen. xxxvi. 20.
‡ Job xxx. 5, 6; xxiv. 8.

border, till slowly driven towards the sea, and finally subdued along with the kindred tribes that gave them shelter. And towards the stony peninsula of Sinai roamed the wild desert tribe of *Amalek* (said in the Arab traditions to have spread northward from Yemen into Syria, where they became a great nation, under mighty kings), who prowled, like the modern Bedouins, upon the southern border of the Promised Land, and long and fiercely disputed its possession with the sons of Israel.

When Abraham, the great forefather of the Hebrew race, came hither in his wandering from the country of the Chaldees, " the Canaanite was already in the land." Their immemorial conquest had decided the name and mastership of Canaan. Their original home, said their tradition, was by the coasts of the Arabian sea,* whence they spread steadily northward and westward towards the Mediterranean. In blood as well as language, in traditional usages and religious rites, they were probably of near kindred with the tribes of Israel, and after the conquest under Joshua they merged their broken fortunes with those of the stronger race ; yet a deep-rooted religious antipathy assigned to them the inexpiable curse pronounced by Noah on his youngest son, and the real connection of the two remains in impenetrable obscurity.

Before the Hebrew invasion, the Canaanites constituted several well-marked petty nationalities. The *Amorites*, or Highlanders, occupied the almost impregnable hills of the south, and (by recent con-

* Herodotus, VII. 89.

quest) the outlying regions beyond Jordan. Here they fought the Hebrews obstinately, under Sihon, king of Heshbon, and Og, king of Bashan, and some of their strongholds were scarce subdued for five centuries. There was peace with them once, under Samuel; and the tribe became tributary to Solomon, among those " whom the children of Israel were not able utterly to destroy." * The *Hittites*,† or Lowlanders, were a milder tribe, that dwelt in valleys, and were generally disposed to peace. While Mamre the Amorite was Abraham's ally in war, to rescue Lot and the king of Sodom, it was from Ephron, of the sons of Heth, that by friendly purchase he had the cave of Machpelah for Sarah's burying-place. Esau's two Canaanitish wives were taken from this tribe, and Uriah the Hittite, the ill-fated husband of Bathsheba, was a brave and faithful officer of David. The *Perizzites* " dwelt by the sea and by the coast of Jordan," the *Hivites* (it is conjectured) in the inland towns; and sundry local clans are mentioned, as *Jebusite, Girgashite, Arkite*, of whose name no account can be given. The natural classing of a rough country, at once seaboard and rural, such as we find it long after in Attica, is thus anticipated in the primeval history of Canaan.

This early race of conquerors had grown into a numerous and comparatively civilized population.‡

---

* 1 Samuel vii. 14; 1 Kings ix. 21.

† *Hittite* (Khatti) is the name for *Syrian* in the Ninevite inscriptions. (Layard.)

‡ The names Kirjath-sepher and Kirjath-sannah (City of the Book, and of the Law) are held to be an indication of ancient Canaanite culture, and even of written codes.

Though they had a strong military equipment, and long held the Israelites at bay with their iron chariots and disciplined skill, yet in the main they preferred the security of peace to the hazards of war. As at Laish, "they dwelt careless, after the manner of the Sidonians, quiet and secure."* Their vices, their superstitions, their cruel human sacrifices, were those of depraved and luxurious, not of barbaric life. The five "cities of the plain" were infamous for luxury and lack of vigour. They had been fourteen years tributary to the leagued kings of Syria when they revolted, and their defeat brought Abraham and his clansmen to the rescue.† When the remnants of this once powerful population were driven back upon the northern portion of the coast, their ancient civilization struck deeper root in the enterprising and seafaring life they were compelled to follow. Sidon, in the antique genealogy, is the eldest son of Canaan.‡ Phœnicia became the mother of rich colonies; the source of arts, commerce, and letters to the Greeks; the head-quarters of naval enterprise, that discovered the silver-mines of Spain and the tin of Cornwall, and circumnavigated Africa about the time of Solon ;§ and when Solomon built the temple at Jerusalem, he must go to Hiram, king of Tyre, and employ the resources of that very culture whose early corrupted germ had been violently transplanted from Judæa and Jericho and the valley of the Jordan.

---

* Judges xviii. 7.   † Genesis, ch. xiv.
‡ Genesis x. 15.   § Herodotus, IV. 42.

The HEBREWS, by their own tradition, had their name from Eber, the sixth in the ascending line before Abraham ; but more probably from the name " emigrant," by which he was first known in Canaan. The great progenitor, or eponyme, of the Shemitic stock, including the Chaldee, Arab, and Phœnician, is Shem, father of the " holy races," and eldest son of Noah. The name signifies " Lofty ;" * as if, from its highland home in the mountains of Armenia, this eldest family looked down upon the sons of Japhet to the north, and of Ham to the south. God should " dwell in the tents of Shem," was the traditionary blessing pronounced by Noah, the second great ancestor of mankind. From Shem, say the Mohammedans, are descended all the holy men and seers : the sons of Japhet are white, but none among them have had the dignity of prophet ; while the curse of Ham, for his insolent demeanour towards his father, has stricken his descendants black.† Thus antipathies of race find their explanation and excuse in holy legend.

The mountainous and temperate region of Armenia seems to have been the cradle of this race. Their traditions make the Garden of Eden, the first earthly Paradise, embrace its two great rivers, the Tigris and Euphrates ; to which their loose geography appended the Indus (or Ganges) and the Nile, as the circle of tradition and migration widened out.‡ When the whole earth had been flooded, and

* Or, perhaps, the Sun.   ‡ Josephus, Antiquities, I. 1. 4.

† Weil, Biblical Legends. See also 2 Esdras vi. 56, and Amos vii. 17.

1 *

the human race extirpated, all but the family of one just man, at the end of the year of desolation the ark rested on its sacred mountain, Ararat. To this day Ararat is the centre and religious home of the people of Armenia; and still, upon its summit, the holy ark is guarded invisibly, say the inhabitants, in a spot which no mortal is suffered to approach. It was among the children of Japhet that "the isles of the Gentiles were divided in their lands, every one after his tongue, after their families, in their nations;"* that is to say, the several countries of Europe. It was from the lawless posterity of Ham that Nimrod went forth, "a mighty hunter before the Lord,"—a violent man and fierce, introduced in the Mohammedan legends as the obstinate perse-cutor of the true faith in Abraham, until the Lord destroyed him by an assault of flies; and from the same cursed brood the builders of Babylon arose, who insolently strove to overtop the Lord's heaven and defy a second flood, until they were smitten with confusion of tongues, and "scattered abroad from thence upon the face of all the earth; and they left off to build the city."† It is with the family of Shem alone that the sacred history has to do.

The genealogy of Shem is a series of geographical names, noting how that family spread itself to the west and south, till it occupied the belt of land be-tween Asia Minor and the highlands of Cabul.‡ These antique genealogies are cast in round or sacred num-

---

* Genesis x. 5.   † Genesis xi. 8.
‡ His five sons are Elam (Persia), Asshur (Assyria), Arphaxad (Ar-menia), Lud (Lydia), and Aram (Syria). Genesis x. 22.   •

bers, to aid the memory, after the fashion of the time when there was no written monument. From Adam to Noah are ten generations, and from Shem to Abraham ten, — a slender thread of historic recollection serving to connect the great epochs of the Creation, the Deluge, and the Hebrew Migration; while the same tradition, magnifying the distant past, seems to have assigned two hundred and fifty years as the limit of man's life in the later period, five hundred before the dispersion of the tribes, and a thousand years for those primeval generations before the flood. Doubtless these barren lists of names were in that ancient day bead-rolls of sacred legends, or muster-rolls of illustrious traditions, of which only wrecks and fragments have come down to us.

The ten generations including Abraham mark the steps of the migration that led the Hebrews to the borders of the "pleasant land," — a migration of some five hundred miles, and including not a single household only, but a people, or at least a clan. Syrian tradition makes Abraham the founder, at any rate the king, of Damascus, — that most ancient of cities, which the Orientals call "a pearl set in the midst of emeralds." The great Hebrew migration, tending southwestwardly from Armenia towards Egypt, paused at that rich and beautiful oasis, that broad garden and forest tract which embosoms "the great and sacred Damascus, surpassing every city," said Julian, twenty-five centuries later, "in the beauty of its temples, the magnitude of its shrines, the timeliness of its seasons, the limpidness of its fountains, the volume of its waters, and the richness of its soil." Its

situation in the great plain on the eastern slope of
Lebanon, with its dense and picturesque garden orchards of all variety of fruit, its clear and generous
streams, and its horizon of distant mountains, is still
the delight of travellers; and among the memorials
of its dateless antiquity, along with the scene of Paul's
conversion, and the Syrian Naaman's Abana and
Pharpar, is the residence of the patriarch Abraham.
The name of his servant, "Eliezer of Damascus," is
a token of his sojourn there; as if, in default of a
lawful heir, this ancient city, his former realm, should
have inherited his wealth of herds, silver, and gold.

According to the tradition of the Arabs, Abraham,
when an infant, had to be hidden (as Moses was) from
the suspicious rage of the tyrant Nimrod, and dwelt
for many months in a dark cave. When he first came
forth, and was journeying towards Damascus, he saw
the glittering firmament at night, and said to the
brightest star (Gad, or Jupiter), "Thou art the Divinity that hast sheltered and watched me in this
cave, and thee will I adore." But presently the moon
arose, and the star grew pale before the splendour of
her beams; and Abraham said, "Thou, and not the
star, art my god." Then the glory of the sun came
forth in the east, and all the living tribes awoke to
hail the sovereign light that ruled the day; and Abraham fell on his face and worshipped, and said, "Thou
art mightier than all, for before thee the moon and
stars hide themselves and flee away; thou art my king
and my god." But the day passed by, and the sun
went down as if weary in his course; and when he
was alone, in darkness and silence, Abraham knew

that the Unseen One who had created them was mightier than all, and that He alone was to be adored.

Then when Abraham was seventy-five years old, "Jehovah said to him, Get thee out of thy country, and from thy kindred, and from thy father's house, into a land that I will show thee : and I will make of thee a great nation, and I will bless thee, and make thy name great, and thou shalt be a blessing : and I will bless them that bless thee, and curse him that curseth thee ; and in thee shall all families of the earth be blessed . . . . . And Abram took Sarai his wife, and Lot his brother's son, and all their substance that they had gathered, and the souls that they had gotten in Haran ; and they went forth to go into the land of Canaan ; and into the land of Canaan they came." *

This pious family legend is all the account we have of that great migration. At Sichem, or Shechem, in the heart of the land, and again at Beth-El (known long after by its old Canaanite name of Luz, or Almond-tree), and again on the high and rich plain of " Mamre, which is Hebron," he pitched his tent and built his altar, " still journeying towards the south." Monuments of stone, landmarks or altars, and ancient trees, served, long generations after, to mark the various resting-places of that migration, the localities of the patriarchal abode. Abraham's grove and altar near the well of Sheba, the " mourning-oak " where Deborah, Rebecca's nurse, was buried, the almond-tree and pile of stones at

* Genesis, chap. xii.

Bethel, the heap of salt which was shown for many ages as the form of Lot's perished wife, were similar monuments, serving to enliven and perpetuate the old household memories, and commemorate that ancient protest against idolatry.

For in Palestine, as in the region of the Euphrates, was the universal sun or star worship of the East. Baal or Bel, the sun-god, whose vast temple, with brazen gates, was the glory of Babylon the great, was the chief deity also of the Canaanites, who adored him with licentious and cruel rites; and the subordinate divinities were the glittering hosts of heaven. "Here, upon the plain of Mamre, nothing was more natural than such worship to men who, living in tents, with the brilliant sky of the East overhead, saw sun and moon daily rise behind the mountains of Moab, and go down towards the sea, to let the dews descend and freshen the grass of the pastures. Here it was that these sun-worshippers found among them the tents of a mighty prince, who did not worship sun or star. Here it was that Abraham fed his flocks, both before and after his visit to Egypt. Here, as he sat under the terebinth-tree in the plain, he could tell neighbour and guest of those wonderful works of Egyptian art, and astonish the shepherds of Mamre with descriptions of the marvels and hints of the mysteries of the pyramids; and with an account of the honours with which he had been treated at Memphis. Here it was that Sarah died; and within view of where we now stood was the field leading up to a hill wherein was a cave in which Abraham wished to bury his dead. There was the hill before us, with the cave in the midst of it, where the patriarch himself was afterwards laid." *

Thus the beautiful hill-country, some twenty miles south of Jerusalem, became the first home of the Hebrew race in the Holy Land, — a region so fertile and populous once that its nestling villages of stone lay in sight of one another for a whole day's journey, and its very local names tell of plenty.† Hebron was their earliest sacred city, and is a town of some importance now ; — perhaps the oldest in the world, for it was built, said the tradition, "seven years before Zoan in Egypt," ‡ one of the oldest capitals of the Delta. It was for seven years the seat of David's royal power : and to this day are shown, in the ancient burial-place, the sepulchres of the three great ancestors of the race, with their wives ; upon the first the pious inscription, "This is the sepulchre of our father Abraham, upon whom be peace ; " and so upon that of Isaac and the rest.

To this hilly southern region belong the earlier incidents of the patriarchal history. Here the peaceable separation took place between Abraham and his nephew, when Lot chose his portion with the luxurious cities of the plain, depriving his descendants (Moab and Ammon) of any hereditary claim to the region that survived their overthrow, and leaving to

* H. Martineau, "Eastern Travel."

† Thus, Beth-lehem, the place of bread; Beth-page, of figs; Bethany, of dates ; and Luz, the Almond-tree ; — all clustered near the Mount of Olives.

‡ Numbers xiii. 22. According to Bunsen, probably built by the Palestinian shepherds (Hycsos), about 2255 B. C. (*Bibelwerk*, Vol. V. p. 111.)

Abraham the highlands and the shore. Here is the scene of his frequent and friendly intercourse with his guardian Deity: and he had visions of a realm so broad, that it should reach "from the river of Egypt unto the great river, the river Euphrates." Later Scripture speaks of him as "a pilgrim and a sojourner," having only the promise of the land for his posterity, after their sorrowful exile of four hundred years in a land that was not their own. But in patriarchal story he challenges respect, as the powerful leader of a formidable force; and his place is high among the chiefs of Canaan. "Thou art a mighty prince among us," said the sons of Heth, when he negotiated with them for a burial-place. "He is a prophet," said Jehovah in a dream to Abimelech, "and shall pray for thee, and thou shalt live." Jewish fancy long after ascribed to him profound knowledge of chemistry, astronomy, and divination, the instructing of the Egyptians in mathematical science, and the invention of written language; and there have not been wanting those who have even identified his name with Brahma, the Hindu incarnation of the Infinite.

Nor is the fame of the mother's beauty inferior to that of the father's dignity. Sarah, "the princess," was of such exceeding loveliness that her honour could be defended only by a miracle. The father of the faithful himself, as two different narrations tell,* deceived the king whose hospitality he shared, by declaring her to be his sister, in fear of dying for her sake. The Arabs say that she was made in the per-

---

* Genesis, chaps. xii. and xx.

fect likeness of Eve, to whom God had given two thirds of all beauty ; while from the remainder a third part was reserved for the patriarch Joseph alone. It is added, that she was taken into Egypt in a chest, like precious merchandise, to be hid from the eye of spoilers ; and when this was opened by the king's order, the whole land was brightened with her effulgence.

From his journey to Egypt Abraham returned, by the king's favour, " very rich in cattle, in silver, and in gold." When the five kings of the plain were beaten by the banded Syrian chieftains, and Lot was carried off captive with them, he armed more than three hundred of his own clan, (represented afterwards as " captains each of a countless force," *) and brought back both prisoners and spoil. As he passed near the Jordan on his return, Melchizedek, " king of Salem " and " priest of the Most High God," (whom Jewish fancy fondly holds to have been Shem himself,) brought forth bread and wine, and blessed him in the name of the mighty EL, " possessor of heaven and earth." † As conqueror and deliverer, his title is thus sanctioned by the most venerable religion of the soil.

It is in his tent at Hebron that he receives, with Oriental hospitality, the mysterious messengers who pass on with their message of doom to the insolent inhabitants of Sodom ; and entreats Jehovah face to face in their behalf, and wins from him the promise that they shall be spared if only ten righteous men are found within the place. Thus in the boldest

---

* Josephus, Wars, V. 9. 4.　　　† Genesis, chap. xiv.

strain of legendary narrative ever framed are combined the pathos of a drama and the piety of antique
faith. The vividest possible picture is presented, both
of Abraham's own free access to the Deity, and of the
awful and unredeemed depravity of the Canaanitish
race. The dread Power of the earthquake-convulsion
and the volcanic fire is a person in the dialogue, and
yields, step by step, to the powerful intercession of
the holy man. The inexorably Just pauses in the
execution of his decree ; and, for Abraham's sake,
will relent on the easiest terms of mercy, — sparing
from destruction all that share his blood. The patriarch intercedes for a people that must finally be
swept away before his descendants, and thus lays by
for them, as it were, a claim on the gratitude of those
tribes, requited only by their obstinate hate ; while,
on the other hand, the race doomed to perish is shown
to be so desperately and unredeemably abandoned,
that the " ten righteous " are nowhere to be found.

The work of vengeance could no longer be delayed.
The volcanic fire burst forth. The earthquake swallowed the cities of the polluted plain, and the bitter
waters flowed over them. " And Abraham gat up
early in the morning, to the place where he had
stood before Jehovah's face ; and he looked towards
Sodom and Gomorrah, and beheld, and lo ! the smoke
of the country went up as the smoke of a furnace."
Lot, by the lead of the two messengers, had fled
" out of the midst of the overthrow," and dwelt with
his daughters still in the country towards the east ;
where he became the father of Moab and Ammon,
the two great tribes of the hill-country southward

from Damascus. The animosity cherished towards them in after years by the tribes of Israel has its justifying pretext in the hateful legend of their birth.

Abraham, meanwhile, had removed from the near vicinity of so frightful a catastrophe, and lived farther to the southwest, near Beer-sheba, — the well consecrated by his league with Abimelech, the local chief. Here Ishmael, born of the Egyptian Hagar, was expelled with his mother from Abraham's tent. By the beautiful tradition prevailing through the East, the young boy's life was saved by an angel discovering to Hagar a spring of water when he was just perishing with thirst. The Arabs call the name of that fountain Zemzem, from the bubbling of its waters, and say it is in Mecca, their holy city ; but the Hebrews call it Beer-lahai-roi, that is, the " Well of the Vision of Life." So Ishmael became a dweller in the desert, with an Egyptian princess for his bride ; and was the father of those wild tribes whose hand has been against every man, and every man's hand against them, until this day.

Still later, after Sarah's death, from another bondwoman, Keturah, were born the fathers of Midian and other tribes, that bordered on and harassed Israel. And thus, in purer or baser degrees of blood, all the outlying populations are traced to the great Hebrew stock, by common descent from Abraham.

In this later residence nearer the great sea, Isaac, " child of the promise," is born, when Abraham is already a hundred years old. And here too is the locality of the touching narrative, which tells how the last and highest revelation came to him, delivering him from the dismal superstition of human sacrifice. This, like the other illustrative legends, is told in a dramatic form, the persons being still the Patriarch and the Divinity. The sacrifice commanded should take place upon Moriah; but a victim is suddenly provided which it would be innocent to slay. The narrative is a favorite one with the family of Shem. The Arabs repeat and enlarge it; telling it of Ishmael instead of Isaac, and adding, that an invisible band of brass guarded the child's throat when the father thrice attempted to cut it with a knife. The New Testament writers quote it, moreover, as the glorious example of obedience. Doubtless it was urged, if not cast in its present form, by the prophets when they strove to wean the people from the rites of Canaanite idolatry. The lesson they would enforce is this, — that the holy family was even thus early emancipated from that darkest and bloodiest superstition of the tribes among whom they dwelt; and the event of such deliverance they recount in this pathetic tradition of a sacrifice commanded, and fulfilled in a gentler form, upon the very spot where their glorious temple and altar should long after stand.

It is the antique type of pastoral life, as conceived in the popular imagination, or made familiar by many generations of household tradition, that we find reflected in this narrative of the patriarchal times. The history of a people is cast in the form of domestic traditions respecting a single family group. Abraham is the mighty and venerable father, feared and honoured by the inhabitants of the land to which he migrates. His character is holy and austere ; his intercourse direct with God. The type given in our simpler history is exaggerated by after reverence ; and the halo with which religious fancy invests this venerable name is reflected upon the shadows of the invisible world. A region of Paradise was called " Abraham's bosom," whither the faithful were borne by angels to repose in bliss. Still another Jewish legend is, that, when the Lord said to Messiah, " Sit thou on my right hand," Abraham was grieved, and said, " My son's son sits on thy right hand, and I on thy left hand." But the Lord replied, " Thy son's son sits indeed on my right hand, and I on thy right hand : " so Abraham was comforted.* In his life, too, we have another series of round or sacred numbers. His age was a hundred years when Isaac was born to him ; and seventy-five years later he died, having dwelt just a century in the Holy Land.

" If few could aspire to be like Abraham, it were to be wished that all might be as Isaac." He was the promised and gentle child, who went willingly as a lamb to the sacrifice. He was the peaceable and prosperous man, who " sowed in the land, and received in the same year an hundred-fold." The joy at his birth is signified in the perpetual play upon his name, which means " laughter." † His life is made, as it were, only a paler reflection of his father's. He sets out to go (like him) into Egypt, to avoid a fam-

* Bertholdt, " De Usu Philonis."
† Genesis xvii. 17 ; xviii. 12 ; xxi. 6, 9 ; xxvi. 8.

ine, but is withheld.   As with his father, neighbouring
herdsmen covet his wealth, and strive for his well;
and he does not "reprove," or demand a treaty, but
yields unresistingly.   Like him, too, he denies his
wife, lest her beauty should bring him into danger.
For him the eldest servant of Abraham's house is
sent to the family home, in the far eastern country
he had left, and brings back Rebekah,—the legendary type of the modestly-consenting bride,—from
tending sheep and watering camels in the pastoral
scenes of that region.   When his eyes grow dim, so
that he cannot see, his gentle and unsuspicious temper yields to the simple deceit practised by his wife
and younger son; and Jacob, instead of Esau, wins
the patriarchal benediction.   And the narrative thereafter leaves him utterly without mention until his
death, at the age of a hundred and eighty years.

One more step of the genealogy narrows it down to
the family of Israel.   Esau, the elder brother, was
the more bold, frank, and generous man; but, of
hasty and scornful temper, he "sold his birthright
for a mess of pottage," and imbittered his mother's
heart by marrying out of the sacred family.   Enraged
at his brother's fraud, he threatened to kill him as
soon as the days should come of mourning for his
father Isaac.   But Jacob fled.   Esau — already more
than half an alien by his wilder tastes and idolatrous
alliances — went "to live among the eagles" in their
rocky nests about Mount Hor; and that wild region
of ravines and crags, lying across the rough valley
that runs from the Dead Sea to the Gulf of Akaba,
became the home of the indomitable race of Edom.

Here Esau, their progenitor, dwelt (according to the genealogy) side by side with the remnants of the Horites that had been driven out from Canaan long before.* Here grew up the astonishing city of Selah, or Petra, bosomed completely in the craggy hills, yet containing elaborate temples, and thousands of habitations hollowed in the crumbling rock. To this wild region belong the names and the magnificent scenery of the Book of Job.† From Esau, in one line of descent, sprang Amalek, signifying the alliance of Edom with that wild desert tribe, or, as some think, their real ancestry. Thus our narrative connects the last of the bordering and hostile races in the common descent; while acknowledging, half reluctantly, the earlier right and nobler temper of that tribe, which, at a later day, Israel was glad to call his " brother Edom." ‡

From this point of separation the history follows only that group of twelve confederate tribes, or clans, known by the collective name of ISRAEL. Jacob, the younger son of Isaac, is the type and progenitor of this race. His double name expresses that character of dualism, or duplicity, which has from the first distinguished them, — in their own traditions, as well as in the respect had of them among other nations.

Jacob is "the Supplanter," — the wrestler, who, when he is thrown, gets his antagonist by the heel,

* Genesis chap. xxxvi.

† Possibly our one monument of the Edomitic branch of the sacred family.

‡ Deuteronomy xxiii. 7.

and by obstinate stratagem wins the day. He is the younger brother, who cheats the elder, dupes his blind father, and outwits his uncle Laban in a running game of shepherd-craft lasting twenty years. His course represents the secular and unheroic side of the patriarchal life. It is a series of struggles, of craft or strength. His toilsome journey, in flight for his life ; his dispute with the shepherds, and athlete strength in removing the stone from the well's mouth ; his bargain with Laban, and long delay in obtaining his loved and promised bride ; the contentions of his wives ; his adroit tricks of herdsmanship, which a Jew would recount with such infinite relish ;[*] his escape from Laban, and the affair of the teraphim, — are all so many passages of that struggle, in which he perpetually comes off victor. Gaining power and wealth during his long residence in the ancient family home, he heads the second great migration into Canaan, — the several tribes being already represented by the sons born to him in Haran.

Israel is the Prince of God, who " as a prince has wrestled mightily with God (in the night visions) and prevailed." His solemn introduction to the promised land is by " two hosts " of angels. The names Mahanaim, or " Hosts," Galeed, the " Heap of Witness," Peniel, the " Face of God," and Succoth, " the Tents,"

> " Where he saw
> The fields pavilioned with his guardians bright,"

recall some of the most beautiful and impressive memories of the patriarchal story. He hears the renewal

---

[*] So Shylock, in " The Merchant of Venice," Act I. Sc. 3.

of the magnificent promise made to Abraham, "Thou shalt spread abroad to the west and to the east, and to the north and to the south, and in thee and in thy seed shall all the families of the earth be blessed." He returns to settle at Shechem, in the heart of the land, and builds an altar at Bethel, to commemorate the glorious and comforting vision that had cheered his exile, of "a ladder set up on the earth, and the top of it reached to heaven; and behold, the angels of God ascending and descending on it!" With his staff he passed over Jordan, and has become two bands. He went out as a solitary wanderer, with a stone for his pillow on the bare heath of Bethel, and now comes back with the state and fortune of an independent prince. His return, as chief of a great migration, is a continual triumph, after the first three days, when he steals secretly away from keeping Laban's cattle. His wily uncle, foiled in his own game of exaction and deceit, follows him up with a great company, but is warned in a dream, before he overtakes him, to have not a word to say to him, "good or bad." Rachel baffles her father's search for the household gods, whose images she has stolen; so that he gets the advantage of the theft without the crime, and bears with him the peculiar blessing of the ancestral hearth. And finally, he is able to build the "heap of witness," as a sign of the treaty he has made with Laban, that neither shall hereafter cross that boundary with a hostile force.

Nay, more. When he hears that Esau, with his numerous troop, is coming to meet him, he is struck with terror, and a sort of contrition; and hastens to

2

offer him a rich present, with all the marks of honour due to him as the first-born. Thus he acknowledges, freely and obsequiously, the birthright won from Esau by fraud and lies, and says, with even slavish homage, "These are to find grace in the sight of my lord: receive my present at my hand, for therefore I have seen thy face, as though I had seen the face of God." But this evident feeling of retribution in the narrative opens the way to still further triumph. Esau not only met him generously and kindly, and "fell on his neck and kissed him," but yielded of his own accord the rich plains of Canaan, which he was strong enough to contest with him by force, and retreated peaceably to his Mount Seir in the wilderness, where he continued the chieftain of the tribe that had their dwelling "in the clefts of the rocks, and in the tops of the ragged rocks."

Coming thus as a prince, and as an acknowledged independent force into the land of his inheritance, Jacob established himself near Shechem, Abraham's first resting-place, some fifty miles farther north than his father's home at Hebron. And when he journeyed, "the terror of God was upon the cities that were round about;" for his sons were strong-handed and crafty men, and bloodily they had avenged themselves upon the town whose chief offered insult to their sister. By the massacre at Shechem, the patriarchal family sets its stamp of reprobation upon the proposed alliance, and the fusion of the races. It is a rehearsal of the scene of the Conquest. The first aggression is duly shown to be on the part of the Canaanites; and the bloody stain can be expiated only by the extirpation of one or the other house. Thus Jacob, as he afterwards recounts, is no peaceable settler, like his fathers, but has "wrested" his possession "out of the hand of the Amorite, with his sword and with his bow." *

It only remained to consecrate his new acquisition to his ancestral faith. The teraphim, or household gods, that Rachel had brought from Padan-Aram, with all the ear-rings that were in the ears of his household, he solemnly buried under the oak at Shechem, and built at Bethel an altar and pillar to "EL, the God of Israel." †

This series of events leaves Jacob in peaceable possession of a secure position and considerable power in Canaan. Whether a family or a people, Israel is now in apparently full enjoyment of his inheritance. But the moral of his wrestling with that mysterious phantom of the night, at Peniel beyond Jordan, was to be manifest in his history, and the history of his race. That conflict had left him lame, and "halting upon his thigh;" yet with the richer heritage of the future, and the title of a prince of God. What man has won from man, by the strength of his hand or the cunning of his brain, he must win again, as it were, from the invisible powers of his life, in conflict with secret pain and grief. Touchingly is this moral told in the later history of Jacob. His sons gave him deep shame, by their quarrels and violent revenge and profligate deeds. Rachel, his best beloved, mother of his two youngest sons, died, and was buried at Bethlehem-

---

* Genesis, chap. xxxiv. and xlviii. 22.   † Ibid., chap. xxxv.

on the way to Hebron. When he had gathered up his heart upon his favourite boy, he both injured the child's open innocence by mischievous partiality, and brought upon him his brothers' jealous hate; so that, when Joseph went to visit them in the field, they "stripped him of his coat, his coat of many colours, that was on him, and they took him and cast him into a pit," to die there, and finally sold him for a slave to a caravan of Midianite traders that were going into Egypt. "And Jacob rent his clothes, and put sackcloth upon his loins, and mourned for his son many days: and all his sons and all his daughters rose up to comfort him; but he refused to be comforted, and he said, For I will go down into the grave unto my son mourning. Thus his father wept for him."

By this most beautiful of all relations of domestic grief, the Hebrew narrative guides the events of Jacob's life upon the broader stage of history, which the race is henceforth to occupy. It was needful for them, as had been already revealed (they said) to Abraham, that they "should first be strangers in a strange land that was not theirs, and should serve them, and they should afflict them four hundred years." As Abraham and Isaac had each by reason of famine gone up (in fact or intention) to the la of Egypt, so the whole race of Israel must go up thither, and for the same cause, before they could return and take the land of Canaan for their lasting possession. Such was the religious necessity, as conceived long after in the Hebrew mind. But there was a deeper historic necessity; since the residence in Egypt was needful for those germs of character and culture which made the Hebrews what they were, and rendered their after evolution possible.

This decisive event in the history, as represented in their Scripture, God brought about in his own way, overruling the hatred and ill-treatment of Joseph's brethren to his own glory and their great advantage. For when, twenty years after the crime was wrought, they went up to Egypt to buy corn for themselves and their families, that they might not die, the discreet and powerful viceroy of that splendid monarchy, before whom they prostrated themselves so humbly, was their own despised and long-lost brother. With infinite skill, Judah, afterwards the proud rival of the family of Joseph on the soil of Palestine, is made to intercede in behalf of the suppliant house. With infinite tenderness Joseph soothes his brothers' self-reproach by showing how Providence has wrought their crime towards him into a blessing upon them all; then satisfies the prompting of his own generous heart, settling them on the rich border-land of Egypt that looks towards Arabia and Palestine, as guardsmen of the frontier, and keepers of Pharaoh's herds.

The traditions say that Jacob had wept himself blind with grief at Joseph's loss; and that, when his brothers knew his safety, they did not venture to bring him the tidings, lest he should die from excess of joy. But Sarah, the young daughter of Asher,* sat at her grandfather's knee, and took a harp, and sang a pleasant chant of Joseph's loss, and his changing fortunes, and his great glory in the realm of

* Her name is preserved in Numbers xxvi. 46.

Egypt; "and Jacob's heart fainted, for he believed it not. And they told him all the words of Joseph, which he said to them; and when he saw the waggons which Joseph had sent to carry him, the spirit of Jacob their father revived; and Israel said, It is enough; Joseph my son is yet alive; I will go and see him before I die."

How fondly the Hebrew narrative dwelt on the magnificent contrast of Joseph's fortunes, and told over the course of innocence and integrity by which, from his humble -condition as a slave, as a prisoner and as keeper of the prison, he had risen to be the great executive officer of the kingdom, and the saviour of a whole people from starvation; through what fiery trials his virtue passed unscathed; how nobly and kindly he had dealt by all he came in contact with; how magnanimous and tender was his demeanour towards his brothers,—there is no need to tell. Joseph becomes the fourth great patriarch of the Hebrew history. Though not the father, he is the deliverer and guardian of the entire race; and, through his two sons, the inheritor of a double portion in the Promised Land. So sacred was his memory, that it was their oath, religiously fulfilled, to carry his bones with them whenever they should return and take possession, and bury them in the ground that Jacob had bought at Shechem, where pious tradition guards his sepulchre until this day.

Such, in brief outline, is the account we have of this most critical event of the Hebrew destinies,—the transferring of Israel and his fortunes to Egypt. It was an event indispensable for their culture, and most significant for their whole later history, — an event wholly essential to the after type of Hebrew nationality, one which saved it from being merged undistinguishably among the petty populations of Canaan.

Egypt then, as Athens and Rome at a later day, was the educator of nations. To her Greece owed its first germs of culture, and its first civilizing colonies. The hierarchy of the narrow Nile valley, with its immensely fertile and comparatively well-ordered domain, and its stupendous temples and public monuments, offered every attraction of wealth, astonishing works, and ancient wisdom. By its riches it tempted conquest; by its secret arts, and the fame of its knowledge, it invited the curious to become its pupils. And, furthermore, it offered now the example of peace and plenty, together with a degree of social order hitherto unknown. For when the famine had put the people utterly into the hands of the king, he easily availed himself of the advantage of his position to bring about that condition of things which regal policy most desires. His forethought, by Joseph's prompting, had already stored by vast granaries while there was plenty; and now the sagacious exile-statesman, to insure the benefits of a strong central power, exacted such conditions of supply, that the entire population became retainers of the king. The whole wealth and effective power of the country were in the monarch's grasp alone, while the people dwelt in cities.*

This great social revolution is ascribed to the

* Genesis xlvii. 20, 21. See Blackstone, Vol. II. p. 51.

energy and foresight of Joseph alone, — a revolution, if it were indeed the work of Hebrew hands,
bitterly felt afterwards by the Hebrew people. The
entire theocratic organization of Egypt, by this account, — at least the social despotism it brought about,
— should be the work of their exile-patriarch.

But here a faint side-light from other sources
strikes across the track of our history. The Hycsos,
or Shepherd dynasty, said Manetho, had subdued the
Egyptian monarchy, and held the land under their
sway for about five hundred years; "burning down
the cities and demolishing the temples of the gods."
That they were a tribe kindred with the Hebrews
has long been thought; and even that they might
be the very children of Israel, but that this would
too completely contradict the only clear account we
have. The Jews, at any rate, have claimed their
kinship and hinted their identity. "The Egyptians,"
says Josephus,* "took many occasions to hate us and
envy us, because our ancestors had had dominion
over their country." Perhaps statements so wholly
at variance as we find with regard to this event
cannot be fully reconciled; yet, assuming that it is
one event they all refer to, the following seems the
simplest and clearest outline of it that we can
trace.

The long dynasty of the Shepherds — a Phœnician
or Palestinian tribe — seems to have some connection with the frequent reference made to Egypt
in the course of the patriarchal history. As nearly
as the chronology can be made out, the conquest of

* Against Apion, ch. 25.

that country by the Shepherds was not far from the assumed time of Abraham's migration; as if both were parts of one great movement of the Asiatic tribes upon the West;* and as if the wealth which Abraham carried away from Egypt were part of the spoils of that invasion.† The alien dynasty must long have found its footing insecure, and would naturally, in the course of time, seek to accommodate itself to the elder theocratic institutions of the land. In this it gladly employed the wise co-operation of the exiled Hebrew chieftain.‡ Embracing such an occasion as that afforded by the famine to strengthen its hold upon the soil and people of Egypt, it would welcome the aid that was offered by the stalwart and formidable forces of his·Shepherd brethren,—already a terror to the Canaanitish tribes, —who were summoned by his influence, and settled in Goshen, as defenders of the frontier against fresh invasion.

In the course of a few generations after the settlement of Israel upon Egyptian soil, the native kings of that country (who had hitherto maintained themselves in the district of Thebes and Upper Egypt) succeeded in expelling the invaders; and " another king arose, who knew not Joseph," commencing the eighteenth dynasty of Manetho. The majority of

---

* See Pococke's " India in Greece."

† This conjecture is fortified by what we learn of Abraham's numerous slaves, especially the Egyptian Hagar.

‡ A monument of Sesortosis I. (B. C. 2755) alluding to a famine, and the statement of Herodotus (II. 409) that Sesostris divided the lands of Egypt, lead Bunsen to place the administration of Joseph at that date, and to make the Egyptian exile endure fourteen centuries.

the alien race were driven out, and became the kindred and bordering tribes of Edom, Moab, and Ammon; while those who remained, constituting the family of Israel, were more and more reduced to the condition of slavery as the native dynasty extended itself farther down upon the territory of the Delta. Still, however, they retained traces of their mountain blood, and the bolder daring of the earlier time. The Egyptian historians, treating them as an unclean and leprous caste, recount their revolt and brief rule under Moses, and their final expulsion into the wilderness towards Syria. And in their own narrative the same qualities of the race are shown, as fitting them for the same great enterprise. After their four centuries of Egyptian service, when the centralizing hierarchy pressed despotically upon their independence, and the quarrel became inexpiable, we find this warrior-tribe, fully armed and equipped, ready to march over the border to the reconquest of their native Canaan.

Whether this, or something like it, was the train of events which we discern so dimly through the beautiful domestic narrative of the Hebrews, we cannot tell with any certainty. It may be only one among the many fruitless conjectures that have been framed, to weave in the thread of sacred legend with the web of secular history. But the suggesting of it, together with the introduction of the Egyptian Pharaohs upon the stage, shows that we have come into a new period. Henceforth, the narrative comes before the light of the world, and its scenes are in the sight of nations. Patriarchal history, which is

but the casting of historical events into the picturesque and dramatic form of family tradition, becomes merged in the broader stream that embraces
the institutions and life of a nation, and events acted
out on the theatre of the world.

A single word as to the sources of the narrative
that has now been presented. As soon as we apply
to this primitive cycle of events the usual principles
of historical criticism, and judge of these traditions
as we do those of other nations, we find ourselves in
possession of most precious, but fragmentary, relics
of that remote and obscure Past. We cannot hope
to read it all into accurate and coherent history.
But if we have only the smallest remnants of the
world's most ancient poetry; if only the faint reflection of that primitive way of life; if only the traditions of the shepherd's tent or the Hebrew watch-
fire, dwelling fondly on the memory of ancestors so
pious and so noble, — even at this estimate, we have,
in the Book of Genesis, the most unique and precious
inheritance of all the remoter past; and our gratitude cannot be too great for the pious care and reverence with which it has been guarded through so
many ages: especially, when it is considered that
here we have the half-hid and mysterious sources of
that stream of purer faith which widened afterwards
into "the river of the water of life," to heal and
bless all nations.

MOSES is the great representative man of the Hebrew people, — by far the greatest man of that race. He is one of the very few men in the history of the world who have moulded from the first the institutions and character of an entire people. Working first upon that unique and peculiar race, from whom we have received our inheritance of religious thought, he has stamped more deeply than all other men of antiquity the mark of his own mind upon the ideas, language, and customs of the modern world. Of all the men of history he is perhaps the clearest example of a Providential Man.

As usual, the traditions of Jew and Mussulman have been busy with this great name. He was so holy a man, they said, that he knew only by their names the passions other men are subject to, having never felt the like himself; and God determined that the age to which he might live should fix the extreme limit of human life. His birth was announced long beforehand by astrologers to the Egyptian king, as the birth of one who should prove the ruin of that monarchy; and it was watched for so cruelly, that seven thousand Hebrew infants were slain, in the hope that he might perish with them. And when the king was won by his daughter's supplication to spare the beautiful infant, and adopt it as his heir, he trampled the offered crown under his feet, overturned the royal throne, and was only saved by miracles from the king's revived and superstitious jealousy. He led an expedition to repulse the armies of Ethiopia, — the suspicious monarch still hoping that he might perish in that campaign; crossed safely a region infested with venomous serpents, by the aid of a battalion of tamed storks; cut the enemy to pieces by his sudden attack; and married the Ethiopian princess, who passionately loved him for his valour and beauty, and betrayed her father's royal city for his sake.*

The Egyptians confounded his name with that of the great patriarch Joseph; saying that, when they were ordered by an oracle to expel all lepers from their country, a vast number of them, headed by "Osarsiph" (afterwards called Moses), fortified the city Rhamses, or Abaris, the old capital of the Shepherd kings, and held it against them by aid of an immense force from Canaan, and ruled the land of Egypt for thirteen years; then, on the return of Pharaoh from his exile, were driven back into the wilderness, and pursued as far as Syria.† The account received among the Greeks and Romans made him to be an Egyptian priest, the leader and founder of the Hebrew people, — a worshipper of one God in silent thought only, or one who denied all deities, and adored only the circuit of the heavens, which

---

* Josephus, Antiquities, I. 6.   † Ibid., Against Apion.

embraces all things.* So deep and broad has the distorted shadow of the great Prophet and Lawgiver fallen across the path of the world's history!

The Hebrew account of his birth is simple and beautiful. In the. lapse of time, the great service rendered to Egypt by the Hebrews was forgotten, and "another king arose, who knew not Joseph." Then the Egyptians said: "The children of Israel are more and mightier than we : let us deal wisely with them, lest they multiply and join our enemies, and fight against us, and so get them up out of the land." The "wise dealing" was to keep down their numbers by stripes and hard work; so they "made their lives bitter with hard bondage in mortar and in brick, and in all manner of service in the field." But in Egypt (as since in Ireland) misery proved no check to numbers; "the more they afflicted them, the more they multiplied and grew;" till the horrid scheme was formed of casting every male child of theirs into the river. But the child of Amram and Jochebed, of the family of Levi, was a goodly child, and by his mother's care was hid safely for three months, — the Arabs say, concealed in an oven by faggots, which the search-officers set on fire several times, each time an angel guarding him from the flame. Then his mother "took for him an ark of bulrushes, and daubed it with slime and with pitch, and put the child therein, and she laid it in the flags by the river's brink." The king's daughter, who came to bathe, sent to fetch the frail basket with the

---

* Strabo, Lib. XVI. c. 2. Tacitus, Hist., V. 4, 5.

crying child; his sister, who stood near, called her own mother for a nurse; and so, providentially rescued, the boy Moses became an adopted son in the royal family, entered the sacred caste of priests, and was "learned in all the wisdom of the Egyptians."

But the instinct of race, or the leading of Providence, was strong enough to overrule his high-caste culture; and when Moses came to be a man, he took his people's part so heartily, that he killed an Egyptian taskmaster whom he saw abusing one of the Hebrews, — having first foreseen (as his Jewish apologist very characteristically says) that neither that man, nor any of his descendants, would ever repent or become a proselyte to all future time.* The deed was noised about, and Moses had to flee into the wilderness for his safety. The tribe of Midian followed a quiet pastoral life in the rugged peninsula of Sinai, between the two arms of the Red Sea. Among them he found a shelter; married a daughter of the head of the tribe; and dwelt in the mountain solitudes for forty years. Then came the vision of the mysterious fire on the sacred hill, the revelation of God to his soul as the One Living and Eternal, and the commission to go back without fear to Egypt, and lead the people of Israel to the conquest of the Promised Land, seeing that "those men were dead that sought his life." Aaron, his elder brother, met him in the Mount of God, and together they went with the divine message to the afflicted people; "and the people believed; and when they heard that Jehovah had vis-

---

* Winer. That "the sword of his lips leaped forth and slew the Egyptian" is the Talmudic version of the narrative.

ited the children of Israel, and that he had looked
upon their affliction, they bowed their heads and worshipped.''

The theocratic despotism of Egypt had at length
brought things to such a pass for this stranger nation
in its borders, that there was only one alternative
before them. If they yielded any longer, they must
forfeit their distinctive character, submit to customs
and institutions alien and hateful to them, and become absorbed in the stagnant level of the lowest
Egyptian caste, — the caste of shepherds, so degraded
by the hierarchy to perpetuate their scornful and
vindictive memory of the dynasty of Shepherd kings.
From the nature of its constitution, and from its
inevitable instincts, such a theocracy is inexorable.
Its divine right (just as we find it now in Rome)
compels the denial of every other right. Its imperative dogmatism, its despotic socialism, must, in the
long run, absorb or suppress every other element of
the state.

While the people were in the helpless, improvi-
dent, disorganized condition of chance settlers in a
rich valley like that of the Nile, — a tempting and
defenceless spoil to every such invader as that barbarous shepherd tribe, — the beginning of such a centralizing power may have had its need and use. The
story of Joseph relates that it was absolutely required,
to save the people from starvation. While the decisive social revolution was going on, and the balance
wavered, and the ruling power craved all aid against
the recent foe and the people's restiveness under new
restraints, the shepherd alliance of Joseph's kindred

was doubtless welcome; and, while it fortified the border, might keep in a good degree its separate nationality, — like the Sclaves and Magyars on the Austrian frontier.

But the terrible, all-absorbing central power encroaches on the boundaries once granted willingly. The tribe, with its instincts of desert and mountain freedom, feels itself caught in the outer eddy of a whirlpool, from which, once in, there is no escape. There is every motive of quiet, comfort, habit, and plenty to submit: but the violent instincts of the blood rebel. The whole force of Egyptian despotism was finally put forth to reduce this stubborn tribe to the degraded level of the shepherd caste, to be the lowest bondmen, and slaves of the soil. Effectual resistance was not to be thought of. Discipline and skill were on one side; on the other, numbers, disorganization, ignorance, and fear. Conquest and dominion on the soil of Egypt were utterly hopeless. There remained, as the only alternative to complete submission, the desperate possibility that by combined resistance, under an able head, they might win their way back to that wilderness-region of Asia, to try again the perilous chances of nomadic life.

Their servitude had not endured long enough to crush their national temper, or spoil the quality of their patriarchal blood. For a long time they had lived as equal allies, perhaps with the pride of an equipped and organized force, on the frontier; and the warm and fertile Nile valley, while it tempered their fierce courage, yet, by multiplying their numbers, gave them a more decided feeling of their

strength. From seventy souls, they had risen in the
four centuries (to trust their reckoning *) to something more than two million. Even supposing, with
some, that this number is ten times too great, or, as
others suggest, that it includes the leagued tribes of
the desert, the Kenites, and possibly some nomadic
Hebrews, who joined them when they had come out
of Egypt, and of whom but few ever went to dwell
in Canaan, — still they made a numerous and formidable force. By the lowest reckoning, they were
some sixty thousand armed men who went up in battle array, and " harnessed, out of the land of Egypt ; "
besides the " mixed multitude " of Egyptian fugitives,
who chose to share their fortunes in the wilderness.†

It was this immense armed emigration that found
its lead in Moses. The elder brother, who represents the people still suffering in Egypt, defers to
the younger, who brings the decisive alliance from
beyond the border. " The man Moses was very
great in the land of Egypt, in the sight of Pharaoh's
servants, and in the sight of the people." Aaron
was but " his spokesman unto the people ; instead of
a mouth to Moses, while he should be to him instead
of God." The consummate leadership of Moses is
even enhanced by his self-distrust, because he had
not the gift of ready speech, or popular arts. The
position he took and held so vigorously until his

* One example of this reckoning is shown in the case of Kohath,
the grandfather of Moses, whose descendants, during the migration,
are set down as 8,600. The number of the first-born (Numbers iii. 43)
makes the Hebrew families average thirty or forty children each.

† Bunsen places the date of the Exodus very confidently at about
B. C. 1314.

death, was "not of his own mind." It was only after a long struggle that he yielded to the summons, and suffered himself to become master of the event. It was only by long experience of command that he found the resources of his own resolute and unconquered will ; or learned to rely on that austere and high conviction developed in the desert solitude out of the early germs of his Egyptian culture. The God of Israel had chosen for his champion the one man in whom the needed qualities met, to inaugurate a new era in the destinies of mankind.

Moses left no successor, no inheritor of his rank and peculiar office. Of the sons of Zipporah we know almost nothing ; and his later alliance with an "Ethiopian" or Arab woman only brought on him the reproaches of his kindred. He lived, as he died, alone. Aaron the Levite could fulfil the ritual, and the priest's routine ; he could use the sacred rod at the bidding of Moses, or fabricate the golden calf at the people's clamour ; and when, disarrayed of his vestments, he died upon Mount Hor, he left a family line of priests, that continued till the day of Christ, and (according to the Jewish idea) must be holding its functions in reserve even now. But Moses, the Prophet, the Lawgiver, the great-hearted and unwearied leader of a turbulent multitude for the "forty years" of their desert-wandering, filled a place which no one after him was able to fill. Ancient priesthoods all descended through the family or tribe ; but there is no primogeniture in the succession of providential men.

Divine wonders, in the Hebrew narrative, precede
and attend that wonderful migration. The people's
just demand was backed by the irresistible power
of God. The prophet's staff became a serpent, and
devoured the rods of the magicians who dared to
vie with him in wonder-working skill. The water
of the sacred river was turned to blood. The land
swarmed with noisome heaps of frogs. Gnats and
gad-flies tormented the Egyptian people. A pestilence assailed their cattle. Their reproach of the
Hebrews as an unclean race was revenged by ulcers
and leprosy, invading even the sacred persons of
their priests. Violent hail from that generally cloud-
less sky, and then great armies of locusts, ravaged
the crops of the rich valley, destroying utterly every
green thing. A " darkness that might be felt " gathered upon the land, lasting three whole days. Still
" Pharaoh's heart was hardened, that he would not
let the people go."

It is a contest between Jehovah, the guardian
Deity of the Hebrews, and Pharaoh their implacable
tyrant ; a declaration of war against the idol-gods of
Egypt ; " a divine drama carried out in human history, — so both to be regarded and prized." At each
stage of it Jehovah makes the tyrant's heart more
stubborn, so as to furnish room for a fresh display of
his irresistible strength. The scourge that smote the
people struck just where it would be most keenly
felt in their religious sensibility ; for of all nations
the Egyptians were most scrupulous in their superstitions. It was the river they honoured as " the
good Osiris," and prayed to yearly for its propitious

overflow, whose waters ran blood and bred innumerable swarms of unclean creatures. It was the sacred bullock, representative of the divine Apis, that perished with the pestilence. The diseases that came on them defiled them for religious rites, as well as tortured their miserable bodies; and their own accounts, even more emphatically than the Hebrew ones, declare their secret dismay before this new religious Terror. But in a religious quarrel, it is more fatal to yield than to suffer. And it was not until the mysterious death-angel had smitten the first-born in every house, " from the first-born of Pharaoh that sat on his throne unto the first-born of the captive that was in the dungeon," that the obstinate king relented. In the mourning and alarm of that dreadful night, the Egyptians not only allowed but hastened the Israelites' flight, and urged propitiatory gifts upon them; for they said in their terror, " We be all dead men." So Jehovah led them out "in battalions; and they spoiled the Egyptians." *

The treacherous king, rallying from that panic terror, followed them with an immense force, — " all the chariots of Egypt, and captains over every one of them." From the direct course toward the desert, that leads to Canaan, Moses turned boldly to the south, so as to be hemmed inevitably between the mountain and the sea. There was only one narrow way of escape; and that would lead right back to the land of bondage. The hosts lay en-

* According to Goethe (*West-östliches Divan*), a massacre like the Sicilian Vespers.

camped close by each other all night, and in the morning the deliverance came. For "Jehovah had caused the sea to go back by a strong east wind all that night ; . . . . . and the children of Israel went in the midst of the sea upon the dry ground ; and the waters were a rampart to them on their right hand and on their left." And when the Egyptians had hastily pursued, and were now in the channel of the waters, "the sea returned to his strength when the morning appeared ; " and the full flood so utterly overwhelmed them, that "there remained not so much as one of them ; . . . . . and Israel saw the Egyptians dead upon the sea-shore." *

That noblest of the Hebrew odes, which celebrates this stupendous deliverance, is related to have been sung by Moses and the whole host of Israel, while Miriam and all the women accompanied them " with timbrels and with dances." It has been called " the song of the Pass-over ; " and may have made a part of the yearly festivities in after ages, which still looked back to this as the most glorious day in all the Hebrew annals.

SONG OF MOSES.†

Sing praises to Jehovah, who hath triumphed gloriously !
The war-horse and his rider hath he cast into the sea !
Jehovah is our strength and song, — his victory proclaim ;
Jehovah is a man of war, — ETERNAL is his name !

---

* The ebb and flow of the tides in the Red Sea, (noticed by Herodotus, II. 11,) reaches a height of six or seven feet.

† Exodus, chap. xv.

The sea hath overwhelmed King Pharaoh's chariots and his host;
The chosen of his captains all are in the Red Sea lost!
Proud Pharaoh's troop is swallowed up! by mighty floods o'er-
    thrown,
Horseman and chariot sank into the bottom like a stone!

Glorious in strength is thy hand, O Jehovah!
    Thy hand, O Jehovah, hath crushed the proud foe!
By thy might overwhelmed are the men that defied thee, —
    Like stubble consumed by thine anger's fierce glow!
  At the blast of thy nostrils' terrible breath,
  Together the sea roaring gathereth!
  The flood-tide mounts in a towering heap;
  The waves are congealed in the heart of the deep!

To the chase! overtake them! the enemy cried:
There is vengeance to satisfy, spoil to divide:
    The sword in my hand shall be red with slaughter!
But Thou with thy storm-wind dost heavily blow;
Thy waves and thy billows in strength overflow;
    They sank like lead in the mighty water!

What other god is like to thee, Jehovah?
    What other god can stand before thy sight?
Alone art Thou, of glorious majesty,
    Fearful in praises, wonderful in might!
Earth swallowed them when thou held'st out thine hand:
    But Thou in mercy leadest forth thine own,
Thy people, — their oppressor overthrown, —
    In strength dost lead them to thy holy land.

  Now shall the nations all the tidings hear;
  Our fathers' foes, — their hearts shall faint with fear;
  And sorrow shall lay hold on Palestine,
  Astonishment on Edom's royal line;
  Trembling shall seize on Moab's men of might;
  The tribes of Canaan melt before our sight.

For fear is come upon them, and alarm,
A mighty dread before thy stretched-out arm.
Still as a stone they sit while we pass by,
The people thou hast ransomed gloriously.

Jehovah! bring thy people in, and plant them
Upon the mount of thine inheritance;
The place which thou hast made for thee to dwell in,
The sanctuary which thy hands have built;
There shall Jehovah reign for evermore!

The entire track of the Israelite wandering is
fringed with mystery and miracle. A pillar of cloud
by day, and of fire by night, led the whole weary
march. When the people were perishing for want of
food, manna, the sweet gum of a desert shrub, fell
like hoar-frost about the camp; or quails, in incredible numbers, afforded them an over-supply of flesh.
Through their forty years' journeying, their very garments and sandals waxed not old. The bitter spring
of Marah was made sweet by the wood of a certain
tree; and when Moses struck the rock in Horeb,
abundant water gushed out to quench their raging
thirst, following the camp (by after tradition) through
all the years of wandering in an unfailing rill. The
marauding tribe of the Amalekites assault them at
Rephidim; but there is no weariness or discomfiture
to the Israelites as long as the sacred rod is held out
in the hand of Moses; and in the hour of victory Jehovah assures him by an oath that he will have war
against Amalek from generation to generation.*

* Thus is assigned the date of that inexpiable hatred borne towards
Amalek by the race of Israel, of which we find scattered hints down to
a late period. The separation between Samuel and Saul is referred to

Then follows the astonishing scene of the announcement of the Law: when "Mount Sinai was altogether on a smoke, because Jehovah came down upon it in fire; and the smoke thereof ascended as the smoke of a furnace; and the whole mount quaked greatly: and when the voice of the trumpet sounded long, and waxed louder and louder, Moses spake, and God answered him by a voice."

The region of Mount Sinai, or Horeb, is one admirably fitted for the purpose Moses had in view, — the discipline of his fugitive multitudes, and the establishing of his institutions and laws. The scenery is of a sort to impress them powerfully, — all the more by its contrast to the Nile valley they had lately left. The rugged desert pathway, the precipitous crags, the torrents of water gushing from the rock, the sudden rains which make the climate of that peninsula so different from the opposite Egyptian shore, the unaccustomed thunder and lightning, and mountain tempests, — these, added to the change suddenly introduced into their whole manner of life, and contrasted in each particular with the stifling oppression and ample diet they had known in Egypt, made their daily existence one of perpetual marvel and excitement. It was in the still fresh experience of this overwhelming change that Moses gathered them on one of the

the anger of the former, because Saul had come to terms with them when already "utterly destroyed." When they had been quelled by repeated inroads, a band of five hundred, in Hezekiah's time, went out to Mount Seir, and "smote the remainder of them that were escaped." And when the Jews would curse the memory of Haman, their persecutor in Queen Esther's time, they said he was of Agag's blood, as tracing his descent from this hated and exterminated tribe.

3   D

broad levels embosomed among the mountain ranges,
where he established the form of their camp-discipline, and dictated the principles of their national
code.

No one could know as well as he the need of giving the people a strong bond of union, and a distinct
stamp of nationality. Their quarrel with the Egyptians was a religious one, in its nature irreconcilable.
From the course they had taken there was no retreat.
The king's treachery in pursuing them had forfeited
whatever claim there might be for the return of the
rich prize they had "borrowed" in their flight; while
the utter destruction of his armament had made them,
instead of fugitive slaves, triumphant foes. Their
complaints of the severe discipline they must submit
to, or the privations of the wilderness, and their hungry looking back to the leeks, onions, and flesh-pots
of Egypt, might spoil them for the future, but could
not bring back the past. Their only help now was
in yielding themselves to be governed by the one
master mind.

Of that prodigious and decisive event of the Hebrew history, which we call the forty years' wandering in the desert, we have but the scantiest fragments
of tradition. By far the larger portion of the narrative that contains them is made up of the detail of
law and ritual, such as it was doubtless fabricated
through long ages of the theocracy. The "Institutions of Moses" present us the ideal system of the
national government and faith as conceived long
after by the ruling Order of the Jewish priesthood:
not a practical and working polity, much less one

enforced during that period of nomadic life. The ideal of the Hebrew life and institutions is projected upon the remote background of an half-historic, half-legendary Past. The name of the great Lawgiver, with the solemn sanctions of the Divine command, is assumed as authority for a system which certainly lay in abeyance for several centuries, and then was only attempted to be carried out by the zeal of priests, with the countenance of pious kings. Moses himself is not much known by name until the time of David, or even later. We can by no means treat the Hebrew history as if the theory of it were ever realized in fact. Some of the most marked features of the Law, as the Sabbatical Year and the Year of Jubilee, were probably never carried out, except partially, after the return from the captivity. Even the sacrifice of victims, so essential in the propitiatory rites of the later Jewish faith, was almost certainly an infrequent thing in the desert life (where flesh-meat was nearly unknown), and was held of small account by several of the prophets, who declared that it was never divinely instituted at all.* It is only when we consider the broader features of the Hebrew nationality, and the radical type of character in the Hebrew institutions, that we can feel confident in determining the idea of the great Lawgiver himself. What is essential to this we are justified in ascribing, at least in germ, to him; whatever goes beyond it is open to the largest and freest criticism, and may be attributed either to prior customs and tribal institutions, or to later developments of

* See Jeremiah vii. 22, 23, and Amos v. 25.

the Hebrew hierarchy.* Considering the circumstances under which he acted, and the practical exigencies of his command, his aim was doubtless far simpler than that usually ascribed to him. His immediate task, at any rate, was this: to take a tribe, once valiant and fierce, but now corrupted by a generation or two of slavery; to restore its courage and self-reliance, and make it a united people, fit to subdue and occupy its traditional heritage in Canaan.

The bond of union, the centre of loyalty and authority for the entire people, should be the worship of their powerful Deliverer from bondage and their nation's God. It was no abstract, infinite, universal Deity they were to honour in their tabernacle service; but " the God of their fathers, the God of Abraham, Isaac, and Jacob," known in that earlier age as " EL, the Mighty," † but now more personally as JEHOVAH. The name is significant both of life and immortality; and in it is broadly indicated the type of the Hebrew faith. This has been called a religion of Life, in contrast to the Egyptian, — a religion of Death. Jehovah is the " God of the spirits of all flesh," in contrast to the worship of idols and the fetichistic adoration of beasts. Among the Egyptians the body was held sacred and embalmed; the Hebrews retained some of their rites of burial, but held in reverence only the spirit, and the blood which was its symbol. The Egyptians had an elaborate ritual, representing the judgments of the future world, which unseen realm was the prominent fact of their theology: Moses kept even the doctrine of immortality

* See hereafter, on " The Law." † Exodus vi. 3.

itself in abeyance, and made both his religion and
its retributions to refer to the present life only.
While "the Egyptians" (says Tacitus) "worship
many animals and wrought images, the Jews acknowledge but one Divinity, and with their mind
alone." * These points of strong contrast are apparent on the surface, and are justly referred to
Moses, who retained the interior vitality, while he
renounced the enslaving superstitions, of the "wisdom" he had learned.

As the lowest caste in the Egyptian theocratic system, the Hebrews had doubtless been excluded from
the religious privileges of their masters.† Now, it
should be their glory to claim an inheritance grander
than every other: they should be "a kingdom of
priests, and an holy nation." It was the sin of those
who composed the Egyptian hierarchy, that, while
they revered in sacred mysteries the One eternal and
unspeakable Divinity, they taught the people only in
the gross symbols of the old nature-religion, and encouraged a grovelling and slavish superstition. Moses
nobly disclaimed every exclusive privilege, or monopoly of divine truth; he would have "all Jehovah's
people to be prophets;" ‡ and, in announcing the
Decalogue as the Hebrew fundamental law, he began
with the grandest declaration of His paramount sovereignty over nature, and the strict forbidding of
worship to any other. This was the central and the
loftiest thought of Moses, — not so much an absolute
Monotheism, as the emancipation of an entire people

* Historiæ, V. 5.   † Lessing.
‡ Numbers xi. 29.

from the sensuous bondage and degrading terrors of
that ancient superstition.

This was the theoretical aim, such as we may conceive it to have been long maturing in the mind of
Moses. The practical task — one of immense and
unforeseen difficulties — was to make it the real centre of the national life, and to change it from a speculative to a working faith. The conditions in which
he found himself dictated the terms. In the style
of the Mosaic legislation, as we may venture to interpret it, we see the nature of those conditions.

The Decalogue was the form of Covenant between
the people and their Divinity, — the primitive type
and nucleus of the entire code. Of its ten brief
precepts, we may reckon five to the right hand for
divine duties,* or Piety, and five to the left for social
duties, or Humanity. The code, in its complete development, is apparently made up of groups of ten
precepts each. Eight such groups have been thought
to be pretty clearly traced; and the entire scheme
was probably meant to make up the complement of
a hundred.†

The custom of Sacrifice was retained from the
practices of ancient tribes, with many forms taken
from the Egyptian ritual. A large number of special
precepts and allusions give vivid expression to the
primitive instincts associated with that immemorial
rite; — a sense of the sacredness of all life; a keen
and trembling sympathy with the natural world; rev-

---

* In which Philo includes reverence to parents.

† See Ewald. Also, the full illustration in Bunsen, *Bibelwerk,*
Vol. V.

erence at the half-human intelligence of the lower
animals, or their inexplicable instincts approaching
to divination; and the mysterious awe felt at the
sight of blood; — qualities traceable throughout the
Hebrew history and literature.* A remarkable vestige of remoter and more inhuman superstitions has
been thought, perhaps unjustly, to lie in the hint,
that the victim of the Passover is a substitute for the
first-born child,† — recalling the mythic offering up
of Isaac. And still another relic of an obscure and
almost vanished superstition is found in the remarkable rite of expiation, in which two goats were
set apart, one "for Jehovah," and the other "for
Azazel," — the demon of the wilderness, whom the
Egyptians in like manner appeased under the name
of Typhon.‡

Festivals, at new and full moon, which led to the
primitive and simple division of time by weeks,§ also
great annual holidays in spring and harvest, belong
to the most remote antiquity of the East. These
were celebrated with all the solemn splendour of the
Hebrew ritual. Thus they became the occasion of
developing the germs of the much-needed feeling and
faith; at the same time that this indulgence of ancient habit was a partial check on the invasion of
alien superstitions, — the Syrian form being invested
with a Hebrew sense, and made (as in the Passover,
Pentecost, and Tabernacles) the consecration of great
national memories.

* See Exodus xxiii. 19; Levit. xvii. 13; Jer. xii. 4; Ezek. xxiv. 7.
† Exodus xiii. 12.
‡ Leviticus, chap. xvi. See Movers, " Die Phönizer," Vol. I.
§ Ewald, " Anhang," p. 356.

We thus discern in the Hebrew institutions traces of strange rites and primeval manners, adopted or inherited from Arabia, Syria, or Egypt. Blending, as they did, such a diversity of elements, they required a corresponding luxury and complexity of ceremonial. What the design of the lawgiver might have withheld, the people's demand enforced. An elaborate ritual, prepared with all the gorgeousness their desert wealth could muster, with shrine and ark of Egyptian pattern, and an altar of incense ever burning, — with symbolic vestments for the priests, and the oracular Urim and Thummim in the breastplate, all closely copied from the practice of the Egyptians,* — satisfied the popular imagination, which craved the stately ceremonial they had left behind. The simple and austere morality of the Decalogue, or the patriarchal worship enlarged to the new proportions of their national life, was not enough for them. The transient fervor of enthusiasm had forsaken them. From his solitude of forty days Moses returned to find them in a noisy and lewd carouse about a "golden calf" that Aaron had moulded in the likeness of the bull Apis which the Egyptians worshipped. Then he broke the two stone tables that contained the simpler law; and then (as we may conceive) he framed, to meet their lower apprehension, whatever of that elaborate ceremonial is justly ascribed to him.†

The primitive system of the Tribe or Clan lies at

* Kitto.

† The form of Decalogue, or "Covenant," given in Exodus, chap. xxxiv., is almost purely ritual. See Newman's Hebrew Monarchy, Chap. IV., and Bunsen, Vol. V.

the base of the social institutions of the Hebrews. It was closely associated with most of the religious rites or symbols of antiquity.* It was recognized throughout by Moses, and was only gradually and imperfectly absorbed in the later institution of the Monarchy. The earlier relics of Hebrew literature (as the Song of Deborah and the Oracle of Jacob) present very vividly the characteristics of the several tribes of Israel. Nothing is more essential to the clear understanding of the history than this distinct and jealous individuality of the petty clans. The family interest is somewhat merged in the nationality of the faith and worship; but it is the turning-point in determining the rights of property. Destined to an agricultural life, with moderate possessions, each man held his estate as tenant of the tribe. The family title was the only inalienable one; every holding must revert at last to the original tenant; and no sale or transfer of land could be effected for a longer period than fifty years.

"Many of the laws given by Moses were instituted partly in compliance to the people's prejudice, and partly in opposition to their superstitions." † The laws of custom which he was forced to allow were those of nomadic and barbarous life, — such as polygamy or arbitrary divorce, the extraordinary ordeals of the husband's jealousy, and the duty of the nearest relative to avenge a homicide.‡ The most apt commentary on a large portion of the Pentateuch is

---

* See Grote's Greece, Vol. III. chap. 10.
† Warburton.
‡ See Michaëlis. Also, Layard's "Babylon and Nineveh," p. 305.

a comparison of the customs still prevailing among the people of the East.

It would not be doing justice to the man (or to the system of which he was founder) to omit the humane and merciful provisions of the code. The seventh day should be a day of rest to labouring man and beast; for, heavily as they had been oppressed, the Hebrews might never inflict on their bondmen as heavy and unrelieved a yoke. The Hebrew servant went free at the end of six years; maiming, or other cruelty, entitled the bondman to his freedom; the fugitive had earned full title to his liberty, and might not be returned to slavery; and among the most sacred duties was that of charity to the poor.* Peace, said the later law, must be first offered before assault should be made upon a town; the fruit-trees of an enemy's country might not be destroyed; it was a crime to mislead the blind or deaf; and even the ox should not be muzzled when treading out the · corn.†

It was one great merit of the old theocracies — Egyptian and Etruscan as well as Hebrew — that they despotically enforced those conditions of the general health which most modern states so perilously neglect. Very many of the Mosaic laws are sanitary regulations, dictated perhaps by the traditions of the Egyptian priesthood (which embodied the best medical knowledge of the time), and adapted to the necessities and exposures of a camp-life in the

---

* Exodus xxi. 2, 26, 27. Deuteronomy xxiii. 15; xxiv. 19, 20.

† Leviticus xix. 14. Deuteronomy xx. 10, 19; xxvii. 18; xxv. 4. But see 2 Kings iii. 19.

desert, or to the conditions of settlement, as conquerors, in a strange land. The distinction of clean
and unclean beasts, the minute regulations concerning leprosy, and other maladies of the race and climate, and many of the ceremonial ordinances (re-
garding, for instance, the rite — both sacrificial and
sanitary — of circumcision, and personal uncleanness) testify to the anxious oversight bestowed on
the conditions of health.* A large portion of these
statutes must be judged simply by the rules of health,
decency, and convenience, as applied to the circumstances of the " wandering." No sanitary police in
modern times, it has been said, and the discipline of
no European army, has equalled in effectiveness and
skill the health regulations of the Hebrew Law.†

Fortified with this discipline, and taking advantage
of the first flush of enterprise and confidence they
would beget, Moses led his people to the southern
border of Canaan. But now their hearts began to
fail them. Unnerved by the peaceable and slavish
life they had led in the hot marsh-lands of the Nile,
they were in no condition to cope with the giant
mountaineers, the sons of Anak, before whom they
were in their sight " as grasshoppers." The land was
very rich and fair, said the spies sent to survey its
quality; and from the valley of Eshcol two men
brought a cluster of grapes between them on a staff,

---

* Some of the ordinances (as the prohibition of camel's flesh) seem
partly designed to prevent association with the Arab tribes. The earlier
law permits the use of locusts, which a life in the desert might require ; the later, unconscious of the reason, omits the law. Leviticus,
chap. xi. Deuteronomy, chap. xiv.

† Michaëlis.

to prove their words. But, withal, so formidable were the tribes of the hill-country which guarded that frontier, that the Israelites absolutely refused to advance another step. A violent mutiny rose in the camp; all confidence in the leadership of Moses was gone; and Jehovah was on the point of giving over the recreant people, but for his passionate intercession.[*]

There was but one course to follow. The leader's mind was too clear not to see it, too calm and strong to flinch from it. Perhaps such another instance of resolute and high-minded patience is not to be found in all history as this: when the old man Moses, already (by our account) more than eighty, turned deliberately back from the Promised Land,—the goal just reached of his hope and expectation, — and adopted the far-seeing policy of adhering to that nomadic life till a whole generation should be trained of sinewy and determined men, inured to the toil, and bred to the hardy valour of the wilderness.

The period which follows is an utter blank; — no date, no incident, to mark the course of events; nothing but the barren register of forty encampments, and the vague tradition of a wandering of forty years.[†]

---

[*] Numbers, chaps. xiii., xiv.

[†] Numbers, chap. xxxiii. Goethe, whom Bohlen follows, (Comm. on Genesis,) denies the existence of this blank; holding that Moses gave back through sheer incapacity, and that the expedition was finally saved by his opportune death at the hands of Joshua and Caleb. That the history of Moses is cast in cycles of the sacred number forty is sufficiently evident; but without being responsible for the figures, we may be justified in accepting a fact which left so deep a mark on the national mind and temper. The earlier allusions to it are Ex. xvi. 35; Num. xiv. 33, xxxii. 13; Josh. v. 6, xiv. 10. It is needless to say, that

A few months' margin on either side of this great chasm contains the scanty record of a few incidents that relieve the bare monotony. Apparently, the head-quarters were established at Kadesh,* not far from the southern boundary of Canaan. Here Miriam died, and here the holy tabernacle rested, while the tribes dispersed for easier subsistence about the rocky region inhabited by allied and kindred people.

The few incidents that are preserved tell of formidable seditions, suppressed by appalling and miraculous punishment; — how Nadab and Abihu, sons of Aaron, who offered " strange fire," were consumed by a flame that leaped on them from the altar; and a sudden chasm in the ground ingulfed the rebellious Korah, Dathan, and Abiram, with their partisans and families; how at three several times a terrible pestilence was only checked by the interposing of the priest; and fiery serpents bit the people so that great numbers of them died, when they " spake against God and against Moses," till the plague was stayed by the brazen figure of a serpent exhibited on a staff.† It is told, too, how the pitiless camp-discipline stoned a man to death who gathered sticks upon the Sabbath, and punished blasphemy in the same summary way, as treason against Jehovah, the nation's king.‡

---

geographical details of such a campaign are wholly conjectural and worthless. As to the capability of the peninsula at this time to support a considerable population, see Ewald, Vol. II. p. 201. Goethe says, " The subsistence of a migratory horde is no mystery; they live by the law of plunder"!

* Numbers xx. 1. The name signifies a sanctuary.

† Leviticus, chap. x. Numbers, chaps. xi., xvi., xxi., xxv.

‡ Numbers, chap. xv. Leviticus, chap. xxiv.

These are but so many illustrations of the rigour of Levitical or theocratic rule. Dissent, and if possible discontent, must be suppressed at any hazard ; just as the common sense of military service is, that mutiny is death. They are preserved, as if to show the stringent handling that moulded this people's infancy, and revenged contumacy, and guarded it from contamination, as well as to assert the inviolable sanctity of the commission which Moses and Aaron held.

Among these scanty memorials, too, are preserved a few fragments of Hebrew song, — relics (as they may well be thought) even of that remote and dim antiquity. Such are the form of benediction : —

> " Jehovah bless and keep thee !
> Jehovah make his face to shine upon thee,
> And shield thee with his grace !
> Jehovah lift his countenance upon thee,
> And give thee peace ! "

the Hebrew battle-song : —

> " Our God, Jehovah, rise !
> Scatter thine enemies !
> Let them that hate thee flee before thy face ! "

and the night-song of the camp : —

> " Return, O Jehovah ! return to dwell
> With the myriad thousands of Israel ! " *

The weary term of desert life was at length over, and the children of Israel were once more marshalled towards the border of their inheritance. Aaron had died upon Mount Hor, in the land of Edom ; † where

---

* Numbers vi. 24 – 26 ; x. 35, 36. † Numbers, chap. xx.

the Arabs revere his sepulchre to this day, and call
the mountain by his name. Even Moses had been
once untrue to the quiet dignity and resolute faith
of his position, when the people " chode with him at
the water of Meribah; " and might not enter the
" promised land," but only behold it from afar.
Passing round to the east of the Dead Sea, far
from the formidable frontier they had approached
before, they came to the rich pasture district where
the Amorite conquest parted the kindred tribes of
Moab and Ammon. This was the scene of the first
decisive victories; and this district (known by the
general name of Gilead) became the earliest Hebrew
settlement and the patrimony of the three pastoral
tribes.

The revived cheer and fiercer spirit of the people
appear in all the incidents of the way. The " Song
of the Well " expresses the exulting joy of the host
at finding itself once more in a land of brooks and
living springs, and the spirit of that league in which
the people and their chief were one : —

> " Sing to the springing well!
> By captains brave the well was made, —
> Princes of Israel:
> Their staff and sceptre were the spade
> That dug the people's well!" *

Sihon, king of the Amorites, and afterwards the
giant Og, king of Bashan, came out to defend their
newly-got conquest; but in obstinate battle were de- .
feated and slain. The following brief battle-song
commemorates with sarcastic triumph the victory

* Numbers xxi. 18.

over Sihon, and insults the helplessness of the gods
of Moab : —

> " Come into Heshbon ! build and prepare
>   The city of Sihon ! But fire blazes there !
> A fire out of Heshbon, a flame lit by Sihon,
> Devours Ar of Moab, and the dwellers by Arnon !

> "Wo to Heshbon ! O people of Chemosh forsaken,
>   Your sons are in flight, and your daughters are taken !
> We have shot them ! and Heshbon is waste far as Dibon,
> And Nophah is desolate hard by Medeba." *

The king of Moab naturally distrusted the good-
will of these formidable allies, who wrested back his
cities from the conqueror to keep them for their own.
The soothsayer Balaam † was called in to foil them
by his incantations : but the very beast he rode re-
proved him in human words ; his curses were turned
to blessings in his mouth, and became a splendid
prophetic ode, declaring the future fortune and
strength of Israel, and the ruin of all the tribes
that should league themselves against him. Of this
prophecy the following passages dwelt long in the
popular imagination, and had a powerful effect to
the last in stimulating the hopeless struggle of the
Jews against their oppressors : —

---

* Numbers xxi. 27 – 30.

† Balaam is the "Archimage " of later Jewish fancy, the type of
hostility to Jehovah, and the perpetual adversary of Moses. His two
sons, Jannes and Jambres, are magicians at Pharaoh's court, where
they predict the birth of the wondrous child, and seek to compass his
destruction ; they are afterwards foiled by him when they try to rival
the wonders of his miraculous staff. Balaam is at length worsted and
flung down to perish by Phinehas, with whom he wages a battle of
enchantments in the air.

Mine eyes shall see it, but not now.   Afar
In Jacob I behold the coming Star.
From Israel a Sceptre shall arise
That heavily shall smite his enemies.
Moab is struck through temple and through crown,
And all the sons of strife are beaten down;
Spoil of their foes shall Seir and Edom be,
While Israel goes forth to victory.
From Jacob cometh one whose conquering hand
Destroys the remnant of the hostile land.*

High was thy place, and haughty was thy neck, —
At last forever fall'n, O Amalek!
Strong was thy dwelling in thy rocky nest,
O Kenité! till by Asshur dispossest, —
Thy sons a prey, thy land a wilderness:
Alas! and who shall live when God doeth this?
Armed ships 'gainst Asshur sail from Cyprus' shore;
Asshur and Eber then shall fall to rise no more!

The baffled king now sought to effect his purpose
by a treacherous league with the desert tribe of
Midian, and by tampering with the allegiance of the
Hebrews. But by this time the vindictive and bloody
temper of conquest was fully roused. The desert
alliance was cut to pieces. Balaam himself was slain
in the rout. The Moabites were compelled to a sullen peace. The tribe of Midian was cut off to a
man, and nothing spared but cattle for spoil, and
the young girls for slaves. The command was given,
that no quarter should be granted, and no mercy
shown to any of the corrupted blood of the Canaanites, — a command impossible to be completely obeyed,

* Numbers xxiv. 17 - 19. Composed, according to Bunsen, in the
time of David; the succeeding verses (20 - 24) some centuries later.

E

however frightful the carnage it set on foot; and probably in itself an afterthought, it has been suggested,* when the nation came to feel the inconvenience and peril of living among a half-subdued and exasperated population. Eager for the coveted prize that lay before them, and well united now in a hope just on the edge of fulfilment, the tribes encamped at the fords of the river Jordan.

Then Moses, in his stern and vigorous old age of a hundred and twenty years, "his eye not dim, nor his natural force abated, . . went up from the plains of Moab to the mountain over against Jericho; and Jehovah showed him all the land of Judah unto the utmost sea, and the south, and the plain of the valley of Jericho, the city of palm-trees; and said, I have caused thee to see it with thine eyes, but thou shalt not go over thither. So Moses the servant of Jehovah died there, in the land of Moab, according to Jehovah's word; and he buried him in a valley in that land; but no man knoweth of his sepulchre unto this day." †

The unfinished task of Moses was carried on by Joshua, whom he had already selected as the most competent leader. With a far narrower range of

---

* Newman. See, hereafter, pages 73, 74.

† Deut. xxxiv. Josephus relates that, "while he was still discoursing, a cloud stood over him, and he disappeared in a certain valley; although he wrote in the holy books that he died, out of fear lest they should venture to say, that because of his extraordinary virtue he went to God." For the divine honour in which Moses was held by the later Jews, and the extraordinary legends respecting his death, see Gfrörer, "Jahrhundert des Heils," Vol. II.

character, Joshua had an equally stern and determined will. His temper and his work were essentially warlike. His task was the vindictive and cruel business of conquest. The Canaanites were a numerous people, and highly civilized for that time. They dwelt in cities, and exercised the peaceable arts of life. Their equipment was of horses, and chariots of iron. They were formidable mainly from their numbers. Their seven nations were each more populous (said later fame) than the twelve tribes of Israel.* The war with them was a war of race and religion ; to be effectual, it must be a war of extermination. The Hebrews must "smite them and utterly destroy them ; make no covenant with them, and show them no mercy, but destroy their altars, and break down their images, and cut down their groves, and burn their graven images with fire." Such were the savage and relentless terms of warfare in that age : such were the conditions on which the Hebrew conquest could be secure, and the national worship unmolested.

It is needless to say, that the frightful task was never thoroughly done. But the records of the conquest, and the laws of procedure enjoined for it, tell well enough the nature of such a struggle. Its justification, if at all, is to be found in the event, where we seek the justification of all great historical facts : certainly not in the motive or temper of the conquerors. Neither the age nor the people was one to feel strong scruples. To the tribes of Israel it was a matter of spoil, and animosity of race. To

* Deuteronomy vii. 2, 7.

their leaders it was a political, and (in the sense of
that day) a religious necessity. Conquest was the
only alternative besides going back to Egyptian
bondage, or else wasting the people's life in the
hazards of the wilderness,—conquest the more complete, the better.

During the years of wandering, the Hebrews had
dwelt among confederate and kindred tribes. The
repulsed forces of the Shepherd dynasty made up
(perhaps) those which they recognized as brother
nations, Edom and Moab. They had kept on friendly
terms with them, and sought their alliance always,
and dealt with them, in the main, with desert courtesy. But these tribes were now jealous of their
growing strength, and encroached on by their presence. And so they were compelled to try their fortune further, even though they had no design of it
when they left the land of Egypt. Like the Franks
in Europe, they were the last of a succession of conquering hordes, and had to pass beyond the rest, to
come at richer and remoter territories, which these
had spared.*

The indigenous tribes of Canaan had already, by
this series of invasions, been crowded into the scanty
region between the Jordan and the sea. This region
was well defended, abounding in " cities fenced with
high walls, gates, and bars, besides unwalled towns
a great many." As the conquest went on, the invaders must spoil where they could not destroy, and
cripple where they could not kill. Their own force
was on foot, with the ruder outfit of swords, pikes,

* This view, and the historical parallel, are suggested by Ewald.

slings, and bows; and in their desperate warfare they could not acquire the training, or wield the more cumbrous armament, of the natives. The horse was a creature they feared and hated, from their Egyptian memories, and from the habits of their nomadic life; and the genuine Israelite never to the last got the better of this fixed antipathy. Their savage practice was to slaughter their prisoners without mercy, hamstring the horses, and destroy the chariots with fire.

They got slow and gradual possession of the land, seizing first the strongholds and forest-clad hills. They marked out the territory with boundaries for the several tribes, and spent five years in reducing it to submission. The proud clans Ephraim and Manasseh claimed a larger share, and complained that they could hold only the highlands, and were kept out of the populous valleys; but Joshua answered scornfully, that if they were strong enough to make the larger claim, they must be strong enough to make it good; and bade them go hew themselves a clearing in the forest (of men?) that was round them. In their northern conquests, it is related, "every man they smote with the edge of the sword, until they had destroyed them, neither left they any to breathe." And so far were they from always asserting a religious motive, or commission, that, at a little later date, a party from the tribe of Dan fell treacherously upon the peaceable town of Laish, far to the north, massacred all the inhabitants, and then "set them up Micah's graven image, all the time that the house of God was in Shiloh." *

* Judges xviii. 31.

But seen with the eyes of a grateful posterity, who could overlook the detail of its horrors in its national and religious benefits, this ferocious conquest, any more than the Exodus out of Egypt, was not without its traditionary marvels and its signal marks of special aid from God. The Jordan, overflowing its banks at harvest-time, had stopped its course, and left its channel dry for the invaders. The strong walls of Jericho had fallen at the people's shout and the blast of the priests' trumpet. Jehovah drove the inhabitants in terror before a swarm of hornets. If they suffered a momentary repulse at Ai, a miracle pointed out the guilty man whose crime had brought on the disaster. When five confederate kings had rallied the forces of the entire south for a last desperate resistance, " the sun stood still on Gibeon, and the moon in the vale of Ajalon," at Joshua's command, and " hasted not to go down for a whole day," till the hosts were put to rout; and even in their flight, a terrific hail-storm destroyed more of them than the Israelites had been able to slay.

The head-quarters were removed, with the advancing conquest, from Gilgal, over against Jericho, to Shiloh, in the heart of the land ; and here the sanctuary was fixed till quieter times should come. The " reproach of Egypt " had been taken off by the renewal, or solemn adoption, of the Egyptian rite of circumcision. The national ordinances of feast-days and ceremonial came, we may suppose, into partial use. And though, from their inferior skill in military art and equipment, the victories of the Hebrews were but slow, and for generations they led a campaign life among the rugged hills, and carried on a warfare of hasty assault or treachery, "like quaking islands in a stormy sea," — though, scattered as they were among hostile and populous communities, they had to come to terms with them, and so lost for a time their unity and strength, — still the central force was slowly organized, under Joshua the commander and Eleazar the priest; and a firm administration of five and twenty years gave every pledge that the grand design of Moses would be accomplished.

With Joshua's death* expires the latest gleam of this heroic age of the Hebrew history. Hitherto, the will and character of Moses had exercised, as it were, a personal control, and had guarded the unity of the chosen people. The last of that generation was now passed away. And here followed the inevitable period of anarchy, disaster, violence, and misrule, which we know as the *period of the Judges.

The Conquest of Canaan, as we have now seen some of its leading incidents and features, was an event such as the historian becomes only too familiar with in the annals of mankind. It is equally unworthy to attempt to justify its frightful atrocities by any maxims of ordinary or extraordinary ethics; or, on the other hand, to make the master-spirit of this movement bear the guilt of them. Placed as he was for the guiding of a people so debased, he demands the allowance that should be made for their passions as he found them, and for the bloody morality of that age. Seen at this distance, and treated with a generous historical criticism, the Hebrew conquest becomes one of the critical events of the world's history ; and its consequences have immensely operated on the human race for good. It is when we come to see the difference between this and a multitude of other conquests, no more rapacious or sanguinary, but utterly powerless for any influence on mankind at large, — as the aggressions of Persia in Asia Minor, and the ravages of Attila or Genghis Khan, — that we discern where the greatness and glory of Moses lie.

To no nation of antiquity are we more profoundly indebted than to the Hebrews. It is not too much to say, that they have fixed in the intellect of the world the type of the most exalted religious thought, and have thrown infinitely clearer light than all other races upon the problem of man's religious destiny. This was the providential mission of that race, wrought out through the twenty centuries of its history. And this most exalted mission, this noblest providential destiny, was confided in its germ to the fidelity of the man Moses, — a fidelity which through his whole long life endured every test. It was he who rescued that chosen people from the lot of vulgar conquerors, and won for them a title to the gratitude, and not the execration, of the world. When the germs of their national character and faith became developed, and Israel was known as a strong and united people, it was his guiding thought, the august memory of his paramount and inspired greatness, that made their noblest heritage in the land to which he led them.

III. THE JUDGES.

FOR a generation or two after the Conquest under Joshua, there was going on "a silent revolution, by the gradual absorption of the Canaanite populations into the name and sympathies of Israel."[*] In other words, that compromise which Moses and Joshua had dreaded, and sought to prevent by a religious war of extermination, did in fact take place. The Hebrew tribes had to a great degree lost their fierce nationality, and yielded to the looser customs and morals of the people among whom they lived. They were no longer "separated from all the people on the face of the earth." They "dwelt among the Canaanites, Hittites, and Amorites, and Perizzites, and Hivites, and Jebusites; and they took their daughters to be their wives, and gave their daughters to their sons, and served their gods."[†]

These coalitions, however plausible or even necessary then, were "generally reprobated by a distant posterity," who ascribed to them all the miseries of the time. From loyal and closely leagued invaders, the Israelites had become scattered and jealous local populations. Humiliated in war, deprived sometimes even of the arts of peace, distrustful of one another,

---

[*] Newman, p. 23.   [†] Judges iii. 5, 6.

4

and with nothing that could be called national spirit, or worship, or faith, or institutions, they underwent a long process of disintegration. Only scanty and doubtful recollections are preserved of the centuries that preceded the organizing of the Hebrew monarchy by Samuel; and these, in the warning words of the chronicler, marked that as the dismal time when "there was no king in Israel, but every man did that which was right in his own eyes."

Unity of the tribe was the only unity that seems at all times to have been recognized. Independent groups or transient alliances were formed, as occasion urged, when neighbourhood of territory required some common right, or exposed to a common danger. Tolerably secure possession of the land, as against the old inhabitants, was almost the only positive gain as yet. This, though purchased at the price often of humiliation and disloyalty, did yet permit some roots of a native Hebrew culture to strike into the soil.

Certainty of dates, and orderly sequence of events, are by no means to be looked for in the annals of such a time. Such chronology as we have is purely artificial and arbitrary. In the later history, we find the period of four hundred and eighty years assumed, as bridging the space between the march from Egypt and the building of the temple.* This is the earliest and simplest scheme. But different estimates of the same period vary as widely as from three hundred and twenty to near seven hundred and fifty years. Taking the first-mentioned, we have in it twelve divisions of forty years each, — the constant unit of time in the

* 1 Kings vi. 11.

Hebrew records. Deducting the times of Moses, Joshua, and David, there remain three hundred and sixty years for that disastrous period which closed with the nearly contemporary deaths of Samuel and of Saul. Then forty years may be assigned to each of the nine heroic names.*

We notice from the very first that *cleavage* in the structure of the Hebrew nationality, which resulted at last in the separation of the two kingdoms. Ephraim and Judah appear as the heads respectively of the families of Rachel and Leah, Jacob's wives.

Ephraim and Manasseh (heirs of the more favoured branch) at once claim pre-eminence on the soil of Canaan. Judah had led the march in the desert wandering, claiming the birthright of the elder race ; but " the sceptre departed from him, and the leader's staff from between his feet," when the sanctuary was fixed at Shiloh. Joseph, the favoured son, assumes the superior rank, and claims his double portion. Joshua, the great hero of the tribe of Ephraim, and thus the direct representative of Joseph, chose his portion at Shiloh. The heart, and impregnable stronghold, and fairest region of the land, belonged to the banded brothers. Only the rashness and arrogance of Ephraim prevented its maintaining a permanent ascendency. The intolerable temper of that tribe, manifested on several occasions, exposed it to the enmity of all the rest, — prefigured in the story of Joseph's treatment

---

* Othniel, Ehud, Shamgar, Deborah (Barak), Gideon, Jephthah, Samson, Eli, Samuel. Besides these, we find room, in broken intervals, for the names of Tola, Jair, Ibzan, Elom, and Abdon.

at his brothers' hands. The men of Ephraim menaced the victorious Gideon, because he had not
summoned them to the first onset against the Midianites; and were only turned aside by his adroit
reply, "Is not the gleaning of the grapes of Ephraim
better than the vintage of Abiezer?" since they had
done great slaughter in the pursuit. Assaulting
Jephthah for the same cause of offended pride, they
brought on that sanguinary feud, in which forty-two
thousand of them were slain at the fords of Jordan,
— known by the test-word Shibboleth; for in their
dialect it was Sibboleth, and " they could not frame
to pronounce it right."

Benjamin, the youngest and favourite in the legend,
lay guarded, as it were, by Joseph's stronger arm.
He occupied a territory small in space, but crowded
with religious and heroic recollections; the sacred
Bethel lying on its northern frontier, and on the
south the fortressed site of Moriah. Of all the
tribes Benjamin was fiercest in war, and trained to
the most skilful handling of sword and sling. These
three make up the family of Rachel.

Judah proudly claimed for his portion Hebron and
the strong hill-country of the Amorites and giants in
the south. Here Caleb, the compeer of Joshua in
desert warfare and the conquest, held his own with a
strong hand; and Othniel his son-in-law, who had
won the hero's daughter Achsah by his capture of a
fortified town, received " the upper springs and the
nether springs " for his portion, and became the first
Judge, or Champion of Israel. " And Jehovah was
with Judah, and he drave out the inhabitants of the

mountain, but could not drive out the inhabitants of the valley, because they had chariots of iron." Simeon (whose force had been crippled by great losses in the perilous marches of the desert*) became a subordinate ally, and was gradually merged in the stronger tribe. So Judah became, from the first, to a good degree independent of the rest, securing peace at times by separate treaties. His name is not once mentioned in the catalogue of the tribes given in the song of Deborah; while the idyllic tale of Ruth seems to show the far greater quiet and security that prevailed in this southern confederacy.

The younger sons of Leah, Issachar and Zebulon, flanked these central portions towards the north; while those of less honourable descent, Naphtali, Dan, and Asher, lay on the remoter borders, where no local recollections pledged them to the national faith. Once, in time of imminent peril, Dan betook himself to his ships, as if for flight; while Asher " continued by the shore, and lingered in his bays." The same recreant temper is stigmatized in the strain of Jacob's prophecy which applies to Issachar.

East of the Jordan was a pasturing country, — the wide plains of Moab and Ammon stretching towards the desert and the Euphrates. This was the land of Gilead. Here dwelt, with uncertain boundaries, the nomadic tribes that would not part with the lawless freedom of the desert, — Reuben, Gad, and half of Manasseh, — who lived in tents long after the time of David. Gilead was peopled, said the

* Of nearly forty thousand men, comparing Numbers i. 23 and xxvi. 14.

western tribes, with their own runaways. There was always danger of their complete estrangement and separation from the rest. Once, hearing that they had built on that side " a great altar to see to," the other tribes were on the point of declaring war to compel their reluctant loyalty; and were only pacified by the assurance that the altar was not for sacrifice, but only as a memorial of the one God of Israel.*

The Oracle or Prophecy ascribed to the dying Jacob may be taken as a Catalogue of the Tribes in their recent settlement. It thus becomes a link, connecting the later history with the patriarchal or legendary memories, and is one of the most important monuments of the earliest period of Hebrew literature. Its vivid portraiture of the tribes, and the equal eminence it assigns to the two great rivals, together with the disguised taunt of its appeal to the "sleeping lion" of Judah, seem to assign it to this portion of the history; at any rate, to an age preceding the monarchy.†

ORACLE OF JACOB.‡

Then Jacob called his sons to him, and thus the old man said:
" Come near me now, and hear what shall befall when I am dead.
Come, sons of Jacob, near me now ; about my death-bed gather,
And hearken to the prophecy of Israel your father.

* See Joshua, chap. xxii.; Judges xii. 4; 2 Kings xiii. 5; 1 Chron. v. 10.

† The contrast of its tone with that of a later period will be seen by comparing it with the " Oracle of Moses " (Deut. chap. xxxiii.), in which the tribal characteristics are mostly faded out; especially with regard to the tribes of Levi and Benjamin.

‡ Genesis xlix. 1 – 28.

" My first-born, Reuben, might of my young prime, —
  How like unstable water is it fled,
Thy excellent dignity and power ! — his crime,
  To stain the honour of his father's bed.

" Next, Simeon and Levi, — brothers they, —
  Sharp were their swords and instruments of death.
My soul went not along their secret way,
  Nor of their plot mine honour reckoneth.
In rage and violence a man they slay :
  As hamstrung oxen fall he perisheth.
Cursed was the strife, — their bloody vengeance cursed :
In Israel they are scattered and dispersed.

" Thy brethren, Judah, shall give honour to thee :
  Thy hand shall smite their neck who do thee wrong.
Thy father's children shall bow down before thee,
  Judah, my son ! thou lion young and strong !
Returning from the spoil, behold him where
He couches, like a lion in his lair, —
A lion fierce, — to rouse him who shall dare ?
From him the sceptre shall not pass away,
  Nor from his hand the staff of dignity,
Till ye to Shiloh come, your place of rest ;
  There shall the gathering of the people be.
Among the clustering grapes his foal he binds,
His ass's colt beside the fruitful vines.
Bathed are his garments in the wine-vat red,
His robes in crimson that the grapes have bled.
His teeth are whiter than new milk, and shine
His eyes with brightness of the ruddy wine.

" The home of Zebulon is by the sea :
  His dwelling near the haven of ships shall be :
  To Zidon he shall stretch his boundary.

" A sturdy Ass and strong is Issachar,
  Between two burdens bending.

He saw that rest was sweet, — the land was fair;
He bowed his stubborn shoulder down to bear, —
   Service and tribute lending.

  " Dan rules — a judge — the tribes of Israel:
   Dan lurks — a serpent — by the wayside wall, —
A coiling snake that bites the horse's heel;
   Rider and horse together backward fall.

   " Gad is a troop: a troop shall make him fly,
  But at the last he troops to victory.

   " Rich is the bread from Asher's fertile field,
  And royal dainties shall his harvests yield.

   " A slender fallow-deer is Naphtali:
  His is the gift of pleasant minstrelsy.

" Joseph, — a fruitful tree beside a spring,
   Whose boughs above the garden wall expand!
By archers hated, hunted, hurt, — yet strong
   Bears he the bow; strong is his arm and hand!
Stayed by the hands of Jacob's Mighty One,
By Israel's Shepherd, and his Corner-Stone,
Thy father's God who ever helpeth thee,
The Almighty who shall bless and prosper thee,
Thine are the blessings from the skies above,
Thine are the blessings from the deeps below,
The blessings of the breast and of the womb!
Thy father's benediction shall prevail
Above the blessings of the eternal mountains,
The glory of the everlasting hills!
Such blessings crown the exile Joseph's head, —
His brow, who lone and far a slave was led!

  " Last, Benjamin — a ravening Wolf — by day
  Devours the spoil; at night divides the prey."

Now these are all the brother tribes, twelve sons of Israel;
And thus their father spake to them; he blessed and spake them
   well.

So the twelve sons of Israel had their settlement in the land, — divided now, and estranged. Each secured as he best could his precarious footing on the soil he had got by the sword and must keep by the sword ; each forfeited more or less of the stern Israel- itish faith, securing the conditions of existence by more or less base terms of compromise. Very dis- united and disloyal were the tribes. Their distracted and humbled condition matched their recreant tem- per. In the days of Shamgar, — who, tradition said, slew six hundred Philistines with an ox-goad, i. e. at the head of a half-armed peasantry, — " there were no highways in Israel, and the travellers walked in by-ways." So deplorable was their position of de- pendence among the hostile populations, that at one time " there was no smith in Israel ; but they went down to the Philistines, to sharpen every man his share, and his coulter, and his axe, and his mattock." The proud tribe of Judah, which had even then withdrawn from the rest in a sullen and separate nationality, degraded itself so far as to deliver up bound the great champion Samson, on the Philis- tine summons, and to plead, as an excuse to its treachery, that they were masters of the land.*

As an example of the temper of the time, and of the sudden animosities that now and then broke out among the tribes, the following is related. In re- venge for a shocking outrage done by a mob at Gibeah, the tribe of Benjamin had been almost wholly cut off by a combined assault, — all but a band of six hundred men, who held out in a sort of

* Judges iii. 31, v. 6, xv. 11 ; 1 Samuel xiii. 19, 20.

4 *   F

garrison. Then the people relented. They were struck with remorse that a tribe should perish; but had taken an oath not to intermarry with them, and the Benjamite women had all been slain. To build up the lost tribe without violating a sacred pledge, their expedient was to massacre the inhabitants of a town that had not joined in their ferocious crusade and their oath, and to take the virgin captives as wives of the Benjamites; then, to make good what was still wanting, they violently dragged off two hundred maidens, who came to join in some religious festival at Shiloh.*

The desperate struggle by which the land was won from its ancient masters was quickly over. Similarity of language and customs, and a nearer kinship of blood (doubtless) than the conquerors would acknowledge, brought the two races into something like amity. After the memorable defeat of the five allied kings in the vale of Ajalon, no powerful native leagues harassed the victorious people. Some, indeed, clung obstinately to their ancient footholds, till exterminated long afterwards by Solomon, with aid from Egypt. Some, after the conquest, fled to Libya; some withdrew to the coasts of Sidon. But in the main, Canaanite and Israelite seem to have coalesced. Distinctions of race were lost in intimate family alliances. Differences of faith were merged in community of rites; and the people of Jehovah were content to "serve Baalim and the groves." Old antipathies of blood were forgotten, in dangers that menaced all alike; and the two populations made

* Judges, chaps. xx., xxi.

common cause against more formidable invaders, who came upon them from abroad.*

Six such invasions are recounted.

1. Cushan Rishathaim, king of Mesopotamia, held the land in subjection for eight years; till Jehovah raised up Othniel, nephew and son-in-law of Caleb, as a deliverer. He drove out the invader, and gave the land rest for forty years.

2. Next, Eglon, king of Moab, oppressed the Israelites for eighteen years; till Ehud the Benjamite, a crafty, vigorous, left-handed man, being sent to carry the tribute, and pretending a secret message to the king, despatched him with a dagger, and proclaimed a rescue.

3. Then, after a respite of eighty years (including Shamgar's championship), they were oppressed for twenty more, under the king of the north country, where the more compact force of the Phœnicians had tamed the valour of the frontier tribes. But the strong-hearted prophetess Deborah roused the people with her patriotic and impassioned appeals. In a great battle at Megiddo, near the brook Kishon (then swollen by the spring-freshets into a headlong torrent), Sisera was discomfited with all his host. His array of nine hundred chariots of iron was broken and dispersed. Sisera himself, fleeing away on foot, sought shelter in the tent of Heber the Kenite; where Jael, Heber's wife, smote him in his sleep with a tent-pin through the brain, and nailed him dead to the ground. The fierce

* "Kings of the provinces," or, as has been suggested, satraps of the new empire of Ninus.

triumphant song of Deborah, — at once the earliest
and finest specimen of the Hebrew ballad, — with its
scorn of the coward tribes that would not come to
the rescue, its exulting boast of the victory, and its
pitiless sarcasm at the anguish of the mothers and
families of the slain, presents by far the most vivid
picture we have of the condition and temper of that
time.

SONG OF DEBORAH.*

There Sisera lay dead, and in his temples was the nail.
So did our God make Israel's hand to prosper and prevail,
Till Jabin, king of Canaan, was defeated utterly.
Then Deborah and Barak sang this song of victory : —

" Now Israel's champions are gone forth. Thank God, the people
    came !
Hear, kings! hear, princes! while I sing Jehovah's mighty name.

" Jehovah! when thou wentest forth from Seir, from Edom's
    plain,
The earth did quake, the skies dropt dew, the clouds poured
    floods of rain ;
The mountains melted from before Jehovah's awful face ;
Yea, Sinai, when the God of Israel visited the place.

" In the days of Shamgar, Anath's son, and Jael, all the highways
Were empty and forsaken, and the wanderers walked in by-ways.
The gatherings of Israel ceased, — for sore the people feared, —
Till I, a mother in the land, I, Deborah, appeared.

" They had chosen them strange gods; war at their gates was
    raging then ;
No spear or shield was seen among their forty thousand men.

* Judges, chap. v.

" To you, O Israel's leaders ! turns my heart, — ye came so free !
Sing praises to Jehovah! sing triumphantly with me !
Sing, ye that ride on asses white, and sit on vestments gay ; *
And ye that walk secure, with none to harm you by the way !

" The voice of herdsmen, watering their cattle by the springs ! †
Where the battle was most hotly fought the shout of victory
    rings !
The people of Jehovah were hard pressed ; but let them tell
The goodness of Jehovah, — his good work for Israel !

" Arouse thee, Deborah ! awake ! sing the triumphal song !
Rise, Barak, son of Abinoam ! lead thy captive trains along !
A remnant fought the mighty ; but our God withstood the
    strong !

" First, Ephraim came, towards Amalek ; ‡ next, Benjamin's
    trained bands ;
Then Machir's § chiefs, and Zebulon's, with truncheons in their
    hands ;
With Deborah followed Issachar, his captains and his men ;
Issachar's footmen, — Barak led them down upon the plain.

" By Reuben's brooks, brave words, grave looks ! why sit among
    your cattle ?
To hear the shepherd's piping ? do ye fear the shout of battle ?
Gad beyond Jordan with his sheep, Dan by his shipping stays ;
Asher keeps snugly by the shore, and lingers in his bays.
But Zebulon will jeopard his life, and so will Naphtali,
Where death is deepest on the field, press forward dauntlessly !

" At Taanach, by Megiddo's stream, the kings of Canaan fought ;
Fiercely they fought, yet found they not the booty that they
    sought.

* The equipage of magistrates in Israel.
† Herder's version.
‡ A mountain in the territory of Ephraim.
§ Manasseh.

From heaven they fought! Stars in their courses fought with
 Sisera !

Old Kishon's flood, — swift Kishon's flood, — it swept his host
 away !

O, then we smote and trampled down proud Canaan's men of
 might,

And loud and fleet the horse-hoofs beat that sped their captain's
 flight !

" Curse ye Meroz, said God's angel then; ay, curse the coward
 clan

That came not to Jehovah's aid, that sent not spear nor man !

" But Jael, Heber's wife, above all women blessed be !

Of all the tribes that dwell in tents, no woman such as she !

He asked to drink: with brimming bowl the creamy milk she
 gave ;

Her left hand held the spike, — her right the heavy hammer
 drave !

The hammer smote proud Sisera through the brain and through
 the head:

At her feet he bowed, he fell, he lay; at her feet he dropt down
 dead !   .

" From her window cries his mother, — where the lattice half
 conceals, —

' Why tarry my son's chariots? why delay his chariot-wheels ? '

' Must they not then,' her ladies say, ' find and divide the prey ?

Each man his captive maid or two; rich robes for Sisera, —

A prize of bright embroidered robes, fine wrought, with curious
 toil, —

Richly embroidered, scarlet robes, the glory of the spoil ? '

" So perish all thine enemies, Jehovah ! but may those

Who honour thee be like the sun when forth in strength he
 goes ! "

So fell King Jabin's host that day. Our God from all our fears
Delivered us, and Israel had rest for forty years.

4. But a far more terrible assault was made by the predatory nations of the east and south. The Midianites were a tribe long known in the desert-country, " half traders, half marauders, like the Carthaginians." It was a band of them that had carried Joseph as a slave to Egypt; and among the later acts of Moses had been a desperate conflict with them, in which the bloody orders were, not to leave a male creature of them alive. They were a tribe not powerful in numbers, but formidable for alacrity and cunning. They had the skill to put themselves at the head of immense marauding parties of the roving populations of the desert; and then their visitation was like that of a pestilence, or the terrible scourge of locusts. For seven years the country was desolated by such an invasion. " The Midianites came up, and the Amalekites, and the children of the East, and encamped against them, and destroyed the increase of the land, as far as [the seacoast at] Gaza; and left no sustenance for Israel, neither sheep, nor ox, nor ass; for they came up with their cattle and their tents, like locust-swarms for multitude; for both they and their camels were without number; and they entered into the land to destroy it." If they gave such respite that the wretched inhabitants ventured to crawl out of " the dens of the mountains and caves and strongholds" where they hid themselves, and sow their fields, presently a fresh horde, with camels and horses, trampled through the land again, and devoured or trod to pieces the rising crop.

Then Jehovah took pity at the cries of the distressed and impoverished people, and called Gideon, of the tribe of Manasseh, to the rescue. He was Jehovah's champion in a double sense : for, first, by a bold act of religious zeal, he destroyed the grove and altar of Baal, at Ophrah ; and then, at the head of three hundred trusty men, surprised the Midianite camp, and put their countless forces to rout. It was while he " threshed wheat by the wine-press, to hide it from the Midianites," and brooded on the heroic memories of his people, and their present humiliation, that " Jehovah's messenger " came to him, and he received his commission as deliverer of Israel. His tempered and steadfast courage, unmoved by the elation or despondency of those about him, is strikingly symbolized by the " sign " given him, — that his fleece remained dry when a thick dew lay on all the ground, and was wringing wet when all the field around was dry. In four hard-fought battles he so utterly cut to pieces that Midianite alliance that it never afterwards menaced the Hebrew territory. His rich spoil of " golden ear-rings, ornaments and collars, and purple raiment that was on the kings of Midian, and chains that were on their camels' necks," he made into a sacred ephod, or breastplate, which at once attracted the eager superstition of the tribes. They would have made him king, but he said, " Not I or my son, but Jehovah, shall rule over you ; " and accepted only their spontaneous obedience as judge, — by far the greatest of that line before Samuel.

Of his sons, the worst of all, the base-born Abimelech, prevailed so far on the general gratitude to his father's memory as to slay sixty-nine of his seventy brothers, and to make a premature and tyrannous dis-

play of royalty; but this was speedily overthrown.
Jotham's fable of the trees in council to choose a
king, and the absurd pretensions of a bramble-bush
when fruit and forest-tree had declined the dignity,
is the most notable relic of that abortive monarchy.
The victories of Gideon had given rest to the land
for another term of forty years.

5. Next, the eastern tribes beyond the Jordan suffered for many years by the invasion of the Ammonites, from the northeast country near Damascus.
Ammon, in the patriarchal genealogy, is the son of
Lot, and younger brother of Moab, — that is to say,
a feebler tribe, or one unknown to Israel till a later
day. The nomade tribes of Gad and Reuben doubtless encroached on the undefined territory of Ammon; and the source of quarrel, as would seem from
the curious parley before battle, was traced back to
the time when Moses drove off the Amorites and
seized the land. "Ye have forsaken me and served
other gods," said Jehovah to the Israelites, when they
cried for mercy, "and I will deliver you no more.
Go, cry to the gods ye have chosen: let them deliver
you in the time of your distress." But he relented
when they confessed their sin; "his soul was grieved
for the misery of Israel;" and while they encamped
in Mizpeh a new champion appeared.

Jephthah the Gileadite had been an outlaw and a
refugee; but his townsmen were glad to claim his
prowess when their turn of misery came, and to take
a strict oath of fidelity to him as their chief. Then
"the spirit of Jehovah came upon Jephthah, and he
drove back the invaders with a very great slaughter,

and smote twenty of their cities." And as he returned, his daughter, his only child, came out to
meet him with timbrels and dances, singing with her
companions his song of victory, after the manner
of the time. But he had made the horrid vow, to
sacrifice as a burnt offering whoever should first
" come forth out of the doors of his house to meet
him when he should return in peace," — trusting,
doubtless, that it would be the cheaper ransom of a
clansman or a slave. To his jealous divinity he
durst not deny the offering, but " did with her according to his vow." Exulting still that at least her
death had purchased her father's victory, the brave
girl accepted her fate ; only bewailing, that, maiden
as she was, none should live after her to share his
name and lineage.*

6. More formidable and obstinate than all the rest
was the hostility which Israel now encountered from
the Philistines. These (to trust a plausible hypothesis) were of an eastern race that had migrated
in former times from Canaan to Crete, where they
learned the Hellenic or Pelasgic arts and manners
of the time, and lost something of their native customs. They were an uncircumcised people, like the
Greeks ; and worshipped not Baal, or the Sun, but
Dagon, or the Sea, — as in allusion to their double
migration.† But the tie of blood was strong. The

---

* The language of the narrative, borne out by all we know of the
time and people, affords no pretext for withholding the darkest interpretation of this act, in spite of the natural anxiety of critics to make
out a better case for the Gileadite chieftain. Compare Sophocles, *Antigone*, 814 – 816, 916 – 920. Euripides, *Hecuba*, 416.

† As likely, perhaps, as any interpretation of the myth, that their

memory of the Jordan was preserved in the name of a Cretan river ; * and, when occasion summoned, they came back to the coasts of Canaan, — perhaps (to judge from some obscure hints in our narrative †) to the rescue of the Avims when hard pressed by the Israelite conquest, — like the Saxons, subjugating and ruling those they came to serve. Grecian legend ‡ said that Minos, son of Zeus and Europa, had expelled from Crete a barbarous tribe which took refuge in Asia, — probably a portion of the old Shepherd race, — and these may have been identical with the Philistines. They occupied the sea-coast with their five strong cities, — Gaza, Ashdod, Askalon, Gath, and Ekron. Their trade gave them enterprise and knowledge of foreign arts; and, as the best known of all the Canaanite inhabitants to other maritime nations, they gave the name of Palestine to the entire region.§

As a seafaring and trading nation, their policy was peace. Some of the Hebrews, and especially the tribe of Judah, were not sorry to take advantage of their superior skill in the arts, even at the cost of subjugation and tribute. But either the ferocity of the earlier conquest had created an inexpiable feud, or else the Philistines followed up the design

---

tutelar goddess had changed herself to a fish. Their name has been interpreted as signifying "wanderer." See Movers, "Die Phönizer," Vol. I. Some ancient relation with Egypt is indicated in Genesis x. 14.

* ἧχι Κύδωνες ἔναιον, Ἰαρδάνου ἀμφὶ ῥέεθρα. Odyss. III. 292.

† Compare Deuteronomy ii. 23 ; Joshua xiii. 3.

‡ Herodotus, I. 173.

§ Pococke ("India in Greece") says that the true name is Pali-stan, or Shepherd-land, and is of Sanscrit derivation.

of crowding steadily on the Hebrews, so as to win back the whole territory in their turn. The region they now occupied was already claimed by Simeon and Dan ; and conflicting titles admitted no lasting peace. Until the realm was settled by the strong and skilful hand of David, the annals record only the various fortunes of one long campaign. And even then, the Cherethites and Pelethites of his body-guard recalled in these designations the name of the island from which their fathers came, and the title of their independent nationality.*

The memories of this long warfare are among the most heroic of the Hebrew History. It was the Philistines of whom Shamgar slew six hundred with no more formidable weapon than an ox-goad. They were among the enemies who harassed the land before the Ammonite victories of the Gileadite Jephthah. Before the ark of Jehovah, their fish-idol, Dagon, had twice fallen in unwilling homage, and was maimed and broken on the threshold of his own temple. By a great victory over them, Samuel revived the expiring nationality of Israel. And, in a later time, their giant champion, Goliath of Gath, fell by the sling and smooth stone wielded by a smooth-faced shepherd-boy.

But the great hero of the Hebrew people in their struggle against the Philistines was Samson, of the tribe of Dan. Marvels were told of his birth and his prodigies of strength. An angel had announced his coming ; and, for a sign to confirm their faith, his parents' sacrifice flamed of itself upon the rock,

* See Winer, art. " Crethi."

and the angel ascended to heaven in the flame. He
was bound, from his childhood, by the Nazarite vow
not to drink wine or suffer the hair of his head to be
cut. Going down to Timnah, to his bridal, he rent
with his hands, unarmed, a lion that roared at him
on his way; and to pay the forfeit of his wager, that
the bridal guests should not answer his riddle, he
slew thirty men of Askalon, and brought their garments to their countrymen. When his bride was
given to another man, he revenged himself by send-
ing three hundred jackals, with firebrands at their
tails, into the enemy's standing corn. When the
men of Judah had basely given him up, bound "with
two new cords," rather than break peace with "the
masters of their land," and in their deriding triumph
" the Philistines shouted against him, — the Spirit of
Jehovah came mightily upon him, and the cords that
were upon his arms became as flax that was burnt
with fire, and his bands loosed from off his hands;
and he found a new jaw-bone of an ass, and put
forth his hand, and took it, and slew a thousand men
therewith!" Being shut up at night in the town
of Gaza, he burst through the city gates, "and went
away with them, bar and all, and put them upon his
shoulders, and carried them to the top of an hill
that looks towards Hebron." And when at last he
had weakly surrendered his secret to the traitress
Delilah, and was shorn of his locks and blinded, and
made to grind in the prison-house, — a task for a
woman-slave, — and taken to make sport on a feast-
day for the Philistines by the exhibition of his returning strength, with one bitter prayer " to be revenged

on them for his two eyes," he bowed himself upon the pillars of the house where they were assembled, and crushed the whole multitude of two thousand beneath its ruins. " So the dead which he slew at his death were more than they which he slew in his life."

These are the last of the heroic recollections of that long period of the Judges. With fond exaggeration they are thus dwelt upon and magnified, as a relief to the deep humiliation of almost perpetual defeat. Samson was the hero of the people. The tales of his prodigious strength are set off with the jesting humour and ready wit that befit a man of the people. His dissolute morals, that put him again and again in his enemies' power, were such as the popular temper easily forgives; while the rude valour, and the levity that turned these chances to their mischief, were a grateful retaliation for their success. In the favourite style of popular tales of prowess, one man is pitched against a nation or an army; and as in a later generation the entire host is said to tremble and flee before Goliath, to magnify the youthful intrepidity of David, so (they were eager to tell) the whole Philistine people were kept in terror by the single arm of Samson. He was backed by no Israelite force. He had no authority with the people at large. He was an adventurer and an outlaw,—scarce known beyond his tribe of Dan, and surrendered to Philistine vengeance by the treachery of his countrymen who chose to remain at peace. In his strange history, standing thus as he did alone and unrelieved, we have the clearest illustration of the

disorganized condition into which Israel was now
fallen, — a condition scarcely known to us, except
from the revolting incidents that disfigure the close
of the Book of Judges.

But during these centuries of humiliation, and the
dissolution of the bond of ancient loyalty, a spirit
had nevertheless been growing up, destined, under
able guidance, to work the regeneration of the Hebrew people. The Prophetic gift — which, as understood among the Hebrews, is a blending of religious
and poetic fervour with the power of addressing effectively the popular mind — has been justly regarded
as a distinguishing characteristic of this race. If not
in its elements, religious, intellectual, or moral, at
least in its quality, and its preponderating influence
on the social destinies of the nation, it is here without a parallel in history. How deep is the religious
colouring of all Hebrew thought — whether historic,
poetic, martial, or meditative — there is no need of
insisting here. In these times that gift did not lie
waste. Save the few scraps and fragments of popular
song which may be plausibly referred to the time of
the Conquest, the earliest passages of Hebrew literature bear the clear impress of this age. A later generation was hardly likely to reproduce the vivid feeling of the Song of Deborah, or to retain the sharp
characterizing of the tribes in the Oracle of Jacob.
The first fragmentary outlines of the patriarchal history, and the national Passover Ode which bears the
name of Moses, are likewise, with some show of probability, conceived as belonging to this period. If so,
the popular mind was far from being stagnant during

those long passages of time which to the history are an utter blank.

Then there were other traits, or popular habits, which aided in preparing for the larger development of Hebrew life that was in store. Popular music, of a rude yet stirring and effective character, was practised on all festive or state occasions. The timbrel and dance and enthusiastic song were part of the most ancient inheritance of the race. And it was a generous trait, distinguishing this from most Oriental nations, that women claimed a share, freely yielded them, in all matters of public interest; and were often the controlling or saving power in great emergencies of the state. Miriam and Deborah, the daughter of Jephthah and the mother of Samuel, are instances which show how freely and heartily the influence of women entered, as one of the motive powers of the Hebrew commonwealth; * and how the freedom of their position was often met with a respect and delicacy too infrequent in the life of ancient nations. As has been aptly said,† the written history of this period is the narrative of its diseases. The unwritten history, as we can here and there construct it, is by no means without its marks of vigorous health. At first glance, we see only barbarism and misrule everywhere; but presently traces appear of a genuine popular culture, native to the blood and rooted in the soil.

---

* The "wise woman" (2 Sam. xx. 16), who pledges herself to Joab for the surrender of Maachah, is probably an example of this elder Hebrew spirit, lingering in that remote border-district, when a centralizing monarchy had altered the habits of the more southern region.

† Kitto.

Misfortune and defeat, to judge from our meagre chronicle, were always an effectual summons to the people's conscience. Recreant and superstitious they might be; but they never lost the conviction that Jehovah was their nation's God, — a conviction truly inestimable, when the later prophetic spirit could assume it as the groundwork of a still loftier appeal. The fault was, that with servile and cruel superstition they sought to propitiate the gods of other nations too. When these failed them, as was evident in a season of defeat, they came back with ready zeal to the service of their own. The cause of the Hebrew faith, in such an age, was alike the cause of religion, morals, and humanity.* That Jehovah was regarded as a *jealous* God, — using the strong term that denotes the temper in which an Oriental husband guards and avenges the honour of his wife, — had at least this good effect, that it was a standing appeal to the nation's loyalty, or sense of duty. How the image was carried out is familiar through the writings of the later prophets.† And though, to their mind, he was far from being the Infinite God of Philosophy, or the Spiritual Father of Christianity, yet the ethical conditions of the purer and loftier conception were already found, in the Hebrews' faith towards Jehovah, the God of their Fathers, who ever was and is the same.

The revival of religious loyalty, after the deep depression of the national character, had already begun to manifest itself in the growing consequence of the priesthood. The germ of what we call the Mosaic

---

* Newman.   † Especially Hosea.

5   G

Institutions was striking root and taking shape.
Companies of priests became proprietors of towns
and districts, — as we see in the example of Nob,
— carrying out to some extent the theory of the
forty-eight Levitical cities : and there were sacred
places of authentic and solemn worship, especially
where the " ark of God " was, in Shiloh.

Eli, at once Judge and High Priest, represents
this period. Of his long magistracy — " he had
judged Israel forty years " — we know only the
sorrowful and shameful close. In his youth he may
have been a stout champion against the public enemy, — since by some stroke of successful valour the
authority of that position was generally won ; but in
his old age it is only as the official guardian of the
sanctuary that we know him, while his profligate
sons abuse their delegated power, and tamper pro-
fanely with the sacred things. The abused and
decrepit administration came to a tragical end.
Being worsted in battle with the Philistines, Hophni
and Phinehas brought the holy ark, the most sacred
deposit in the sanctuary, to the Hebrew camp ; trusting either to its magical efficacy, or else to the superstitious feeling it might stimulate on both sides.
The Philistines rallied from their first terror. The
battle was speedily decided. The ark was taken ;
Hophni and Phinehas were slain ; and their wretched
father, at the news, fell back from his seat and died.

The sanctuary at Shiloh had been captured and
destroyed, it would seem, as one of the results of
this disaster ; and for twenty years we hear of
nothing but the people's deeper humiliation. It

was relieved in part by the restoring of the ark to Hebrew soil; for in an hour of religious terror the Philistines had sent it back with peace-offerings. A sacred deposit (according to the ancient feeling) must work either good or harm. They believed in its mysterious powers, most likely, full as much as the Hebrews. A troublesome epidemic, and a plague of field-mice were ascribed to the captured ark. Nay, when it was restored, seventy men of Beth-shemesh, it was said, — our account even gives it with the enormous addition of fifty thousand, — were struck dead in that one village for looking into it.*

But in these twenty years "the child Samuel" had grown to manhood. Upon him all the hopes of the people gradually came to be gathered. His mother's affectionate and watchful piety had devoted his life from infancy to the temple-service. And that early consecration, made only the more intense by the dissolute example of Eli's sons, was now ripened to the stern spirit of self-consecration which fitted him for the great work of the regeneration of Israel. With the reluctance of a noble and clear mind, that measures its strength against the magnitude of an almost hopeless task, yet with a resolute will, that never wavered or relaxed in what it had once under-taken, he accepted the commission which Providence as it were compelled upon him, — to be the Deliverer of his people in a far larger sense than they were ready to conceive.

For, as Moses was the founder, Samuel was the

* 1 Samuel vi. 19.

restorer of the Hebrew character and institutions.
His is next in the line of sacred and illustrious names.
He is second to Moses alone in that austere dignity
which after ages associate with his memory; and is
represented to be as nearly as possible his equal in
the decisive acts which show his authority and power.
Fond tradition related him to have been the watched
and guarded favorite of heaven from a child; brought
up in the temple-service; charged in the night-visions
with the terrible message of doom to the guilty
family of Eli.   When "the word of Jehovah was
precious, and there was no open vision," the prophetic spirit fell on Samuel. "Jehovah was with him,
and did let none of his words fall to the ground;
and all Israel, from Dan even unto Beersheba, knew
that he was established to be a prophet of Jehovah."

He now called a gathering of the people at Mizpeh,
near his native Ramah, and "judged them there."
When the Philistines mustered a great host, to crush
(as they had so often done before) this germ of rising
nationality, "Jehovah thundered with a great thunder upon them, and discomfited them, and they were
smitten before Israel;" and Samuel set up a stone
for a trophy, "and called its name Eben-ezer, saying,
Hitherto hath Jehovah helped us."

This timely victory — the first for many years,
and by far the most important in its consequences
since the days of Joshua — at once confirmed the
authority of Samuel as chief of Israel. Loyal tradition even magnified his services, by adding, that
"the Philistines came no more into the coast of
Israel; and the hand of Jehovah was against them

all the days of Samuel,"—a statement sufficiently contradicted by their garrisons, which we find shortly after almost as far eastward as the Jordan. But his personal supremacy was not questioned; and though for near twenty years contemporary with the king whom the people compelled him to appoint, "Samuel judged Israel all the days of his life."

It is not so much in the acts as in the effects of his administration that we perceive the extraordinary vigour and power of the man. He breathed into the soul of the Israelite people the forgotten hope of being really masters of their own soil. He revived in them the conception of Hebrew institutions on the basis of national independence. He inspired that hopeful and resolute intrepidity which was for them the condition of developing their own life and of fulfilling their providential mission as a people. So that what was said falsely of him as history was spoken truly as prophecy; for, in result if not in immediate act, he did found and secure the free commonwealth of Israel.

Necessarily, from the genius of the Hebrew mind and institutions, and of an age when no other than a theocratic civilization could be so much as thought of, the basis he sought for the national life was a religious basis. He seems to have entertained the magnificent but impracticable conception, that the real, acknowledged sovereign of Israel should be the invisible Divinity and Protector, whose arm had guarded the nation in so many perils, whose spirit had from the first commissioned and inspired its faithful men; and that the actual ruler should be

only as it were a Regent, or Viceroy, of this unseen
Sovereign. How greatly he was disappointed, when
not only the people craved, but the exigencies of the
time and his own sons' recreancy demanded, a human
king to lead in battle and wield the executive force
of the state, the after history shows. The almost
fierce severity of the treatment he exercised in his
old age toward Saul (as related in the two accounts
of his alienation from him) is best explained from
this failure of his loftiest ideal, and the forced surrender of his cherished hope.

One inestimable and lasting service Samuel rendered to the Hebrew people, by which he has won
the gratitude of all the world. He, more than any
other man, was the father of the long line of Hebrew
prophets. The office of Moses, indeed, in the reverent view of a late posterity, finally resolved itself into
that of a prophet, — a conception so strikingly presented in the book of Deuteronomy ; but his true
work was too complicated and peculiar to admit so
definite a title. The prophetic mantle had fallen on
Miriam and on Deborah, to the enduring glory of
Hebrew womanhood ; and special messengers, charged
with special warnings, appear here and there on the
page of the scanty annals. But under Samuel prophecy first became (so to speak) a Hebrew institution
and a fixed fact. Not hereditary, like the priesthood,
or of man's appointment, as any magistrate's function, it depended essentially on a divine call, and on
the moral aptitude of a man's soul. Institutions
could only guide, train, instruct, and put to actual
service, the spirit which came by its own laws, free

as the unfettered wind. The " Schools of the Prophets," with their music strangely fascinating, and their
sacred discipline, their gathering and concentrating
of the fresh religious zeal there might be in the body
of the people, were of Samuel's foundation. This
institution of prophecy, — the fountain-head of the
world's noblest poetry, and in after times the bold
protest against tyranny, the altar-fire of the nation's
faith, the sacred hearth and shrine of a hope whose
destined fulfilment was in one who should be the
world's spiritual Sovereign, and the Prince of Peace,
— is the magnificent legacy bequeathed to Humanity
by the great restorer of the Hebrew faith.

But while labouring thus effectively, and with so
large a hope, for the remote future, the mind of Samuel was perplexed by present and pressing anxieties.
The office of Judge had no self-sustaining dignity.
Its multitude of cares could not be shared among
subordinates. Such power as it had could never be
a delegated power. It rested solely on a man's personal influence, and on the generally felt conviction
of his Divine commission or his personal superiority.
Its truest basis, as well as its noblest representative,
it had in Samuel; and the failure, with all his commanding qualities, served to show that the office was
no longer suited to the public need. The theocracy
had been a fact with Moses; with Samuel it was
only a reminiscence and a hope; as with the later
prophets a splendid dream.

It was a heavy grief for the heroic and faithful
Judge, when the conviction compelled itself upon
him, that one more radical change must be made in

the government of the state; that the invisible King with human regents was not such a sovereign as the state demanded; that the grand hope and noblest ambition of his life had, as it were, failed. But the notorious incompetency of his own sons (to whom he intrusted the administration of the southern border), the loud complaints of the people, which he was wholly unable to control, and, above all, another invasion pressing from the Ammonites on the northeast, opened his eyes at length to the unwelcome truth. The vision of a theocratic Republic had proved delusive. The name and traditionary prestige of royalty must be bestowed on the most competent man; or else the very first object of his concern — the independence of the state itself — was forfeited.

However clear and imperative the necessity, Samuel did not accept it without a struggle. The painful vacillation of his mind is curiously reflected in the varying statements of the narrative. By one account, he vehemently reproached the people with disloyalty to Jehovah, warning them at much length of the bitter fruits of despotism; and would grant their petition only at the express command of God, who took that method of chastising them for their guilt. By another account, he saw the need at once, selected a candidate with every mark of confidence and good-will, and inaugurated the new dynasty with elated hope, and was only driven into opposition by the long-proved unworthiness of Saul.*

Whatever may have been Samuel's sincere reluc-

* 1 Samuel, chaps. viii., x.

tance or apprehension, the people's urgency and the impending peril of the state at length prevailed. Saul, the son of Kish, a Benjamite, was anointed king. The reasons of policy which influenced the choice were these: The tribe of Benjamin was small, but valiant. Its territory lay near the seat of Samuel's regency, and abounded in sacred localities. A choice from this tribe avoided the resentment that might be felt at the sullen isolation of Judah, or the intolerable arrogance of Ephraim, as well as their more formidable jealousy of each other. These reasons were fully justified by the feud which, a century later, alienated the ten tribes from the house of David; though the personal ascendency of the two great kings had long reconciled the nation at large to the hated supremacy of Judah.

In many personal qualities, too, Saul amply vindicated Samuel's choice. A stately and commanding presence, and prompt vigour in action, were enough to win at once the popular admiration. His politic magnanimity put a stop to the proposal, started upon his first victory, to take vengeance on such as chose to sneer at their rustic prince. His domestic character was far more exemplary than that of any other of the earlier kings: but one wife of his is mentioned, and one of inferior rank, whom he may have taken after her death, — a striking contrast to the loose polygamy of David and his successors. The personal attachment towards him was in some quarters so strong that the men of Gilead risked their lives to give him honorable burial; and more than half the nation clung obstinately to the fortunes

of his son till repelled by his own hopeless incapacity.

At first, too, Saul seems to have heartily co-operated
with the religious party. He built altars to Jehovah, and was once even among the company of the
prophets. It was only at a later date that the fatal
and implacable feud broke out which cost the realm
so many sorrows, and himself his crown and his life,
— a feud which bred the characteristic suspicion that
Jehovah had selected him on purpose to punish the
people for their infidelity in demanding a king, and
had repented of it afterwards.*

For the future, Samuel must be, not the nominal
head, but only the chief adviser, in public affairs.
His presence was a reminiscence of the departed or
imagined Theocracy which never had been and never
could be fully realized. He was the representative
or embodiment of the spiritual power, which, with
boundaries as yet unsettled by any just theory, or
implied in the prescriptions of experience, sought
such terms with the temporal power, and exerted
such independent jurisdiction, as from the nature
of the case it could.

Saul's personal prowess and promptness of enterprise were manifest in the exigency that first called
him to the actual leadership. The Ammonite chief
Nahash had summoned the beleaguered town of Ja-
besh Gilead to surrender, — menacing its people, that
even as his slaves he would only accept them after
blinding them of the right eye, so as to unfit them
for war ; and scornfully gave them leave to get what-

* See 1 Samuel, chap. xii. ; xiv. 35 ; xv. 35.

ever aid they could from the distracted and helpless
state of Israel. The tidings came to Saul as he was
with a yoke of oxen in the field. At the word, " he
took the oxen and hewed them in pieces, and sent
them throughout all the coasts of Israel by the hands
of his messengers, saying, Whosoever cometh not
forth after Saul and after Samuel, so shall it be done
to his oxen." With his suddenly mustered force he
gained so complete a victory, that " not two of the
enemy were left together." He relieved the distressed city; and with the welcome of popular enthusiasm was solemnly crowned king in the ancient
sacred town of Gilgal.

As a permanent means of national defence, Saul
organized, within two years, the nucleus of a standing army, — a small regular force of three thousand
men. For " there was sore war against the Philistines all the days of Saul; and when Saul saw any
strong man, or any valiant man, he took him unto
him." Then began that career of romantic adventure, of brilliant partial success or ignoble failure,
of popular terror or exultation, which made memorable the early valour of Jonathan and the chivalrous
exploits of David. The Philistine garrisons, far in
the interior of the country, struck such dismay that
the people retreated once more to the mountain re-
cesses; and " did hide themselves in caves and in
thickets and in rocks and in high places and in
pits; and some of the Hebrews went over Jordan
to the land of Gad and Gilead. As for Saul, he
was yet in Gilgal, and all the people followed him
trembling." The presence of a foreign ruler is

doubtless a sorer thing in a war for independence
when he comes as an armed enemy, than when there
is peaceable tax-paying and non-resistance. But independence was the very thing Saul had been chosen
to secure, and the people must not complain of the
needful severity of the terms.

Change of habit and intoxication of power, coming
so suddenly upon a grown-up man of rustic training, might well unsettle a larger intellect and more
balanced character than Saul's. Vigorous and able
in the stress of war, he seems to have been quite
unfit for civil administration. Samuel, as became
but too apparent, had been unfortunate, or else at
fault, in selecting a man whose narrowness of mind
made him at once unfit for any large responsibility,
and jealous of superior ability in others. A breach
began, and was fast widening, between the incompetent king and the adviser to whom he had been attached at first by every motive of gratitude and
respect. Saul became moody and suspicious. His
jealous, brooding temper was subject to fits of mor-
bid melancholy, amounting at times to madness.
"The spirit of Jehovah was departed from Saul,
and an evil spirit from Jehovah troubled him."
How David, "the sweet singer of Israel," soothed
him with harp and song; and how Saul at first loved
him as a son, and made him his man-at-arms, and
then was jealous of his prowess, and sought to kill
him unless prevented by Jonathan's vigilant love,
and twice repented, with fitful nobleness of spirit,
when he found David had spared his life, is told
in that most varied and romantic narrative of Scrip-

ture biography which bears the name of Samuel.
The few scattered incidents of the king's career are
only interspersed among the personal adventures of
him who was the true representative man of the time,
and the real founder of the Hebrew monarchy.

For several years the aged prophet and the wrong-
headed king had kept such uncertain alliance as
they might. Samuel retained to the last his strong
personal ascendency. In the course of time he had
withdrawn his confidence from Saul; and at length,
it is related, he carried his resentment to the open
act of nominating an antagonist king to seize his
place under the auspices of the priesthood. A deed
so fatal as this to the peace and integrity of the kingdom was not at any rate publicly committed; though
Samuel, by the symbolic act of consecration, may
have declared how fondly his hope for Israel rested
on the minstrel-boy, — probably his own pupil in the
school of sacred minstrelsy, — the youngest son of
Jesse. The later undisguised antagonism of king
and prophet is referred by one account to a sacrifice which Saul offered when Samuel came not at
the appointed time; and by another to his sparing
the spoil of the Amalekites and their king Agag,
whom Samuel thereupon "hewed in pieces before
the face of Jehovah;" for it was a sacred war, a war
of extermination, and in it there must be no booty.*
Whatever the cause, it had now led to open rupture.

The quarrel involved not Samuel alone, but the
entire class he represented. The king's capricious
and insane temper exaggerated every favour shown

---

* 1 Samuel, chaps. xiii., xv.

to his fancied rival into treason against himself.
His own son Jonathan he had nearly slain at a banquet for saying a word in behalf of his banished
friend. He armed himself against the popular feeling by a foreign body-guard. Annoyed at the influence of the priesthood, he sought to make head
against them by encouraging alien rites of worship.
The Gibeonites, or menials of the sanctuary,— a tribe
spared by Joshua in a treaty they had fraudulently
got, and thereafter made " hewers of wood and
drawers of water " for the conquerors, — became the
victims of his cruelty. When he learned that David
had received food and shelter at the priests' city of
Nob, he sent Doeg the Edomite, captain of his guard,
to do a deed no Hebrew would lift his hand to, and
massacred the whole company of priests, amounting
to eighty-five, together, it is added, with every living
creature in the place. This last act, more than any
other, cut him off from the affection of a people only
too ready to overlook his faults, who could not but
regard him with horror now. The crime was strictly
expiated in his own fall, and in the ruin of his
house.

To these outbreaks of frantic passion Samuel
opposed only his grave remonstrance, and, at last,
the total withholding of his confidence. " The only
weapon he used was to keep aloof from Saul." Awed
by his austere and composed superiority, Saul never
once attacked him ; or, if he had designs against
his life, when Samuel went with David to dwell at
Naioth, yet as soon as he came near, his resolution
forsook him ; he caught the contagion of the sacred

ground he trespassed on; and lay down in a prophetic raving all day and all night, "naked," or stripped of his royal robes; so that again the saying went abroad, "Is Saul also among the prophets?"

When Samuel resigned the regency he had borne so worthily, and saw the dominion intrusted to the hands of Saul, he had made an emphatic appeal to the people; who with one voice bore witness to his integrity in office, and the unswerving fidelity of his administration. The proud consciousness of it in his own mind was matched by the grateful sense of it in the popular veneration. Through a long life he had been true to his single purpose of securing the integrity of the national institutions, and the regeneration of the Hebrew faith. And now that the nation was so violently distracted by the feud between the powers he was not able to reconcile, — now that the government and religion of the people were in collision, and the man whom his prophetic eye saw to be most fit for the occasion was a fugitive and outlaw, and the obstinate enemy was taking advantage of distraction and weakness to complete the ruin of the state, — his own work might seem all undone, unless the people's loyalty to him were a pledge of some better future.

It was at the darkest period of this unhappy quarrel, just before the very crisis of the desperate struggle for independence, that the old man died, — leaving Saul, restless and wretched, to be preyed on by remorse and brooding jealousies; leaving the kingdom distracted for the time by civil feud, and the transient outlawry and recreancy of its noblest son, the man of genius and the man of destiny.

Once more Samuel appears upon the stage ;— not now as the Prophet, stern and faithful in a degenerate age, or as the trusted Counsellor and Judge ; but as the avenging Phantom that warns the wretched king of his impending defeat and death,— a fitting announcement of the gloomy close that awaited the forfeited honour of the royal station.   The awful shade of the Prophet whose free choice had made him the offer of the noblest destiny, whose counsel he had scorned, whose hostility he had defied, whose aid he had foolishly thought to despise and reject, all for pure incompetency to bear the great trust of royalty, appals him at the eve of battle, and utters the dreadful warning, never to be recalled : " Jehovah hath rent the kingdom out of thine hand ; and to-morrow thou and thy sons shall be with me ! " It was the phantom of a despised and affronted Majesty, " as gods ascending out of the earth." "And Saul fell straightway on the earth, and was sore afraid because of the words of Samuel ; and there was no strength in him."

The next day the battle was joined.   And when Israel was smitten, and fled before the Philistines on Mount Gilboa, Saul, being " sore wounded of the archers," died there by his own hand.

IV. DAVID.

AT the time of the fatal battle on Mount Gilboa,
David was thirty years old; and for the next
forty years the history of the Hebrew people is the
history of his reign and life. By force of circumstances and force of character he had already reached
a position which made him the inevitable and welcome successor of the fallen king. His early bravery
and discretion had won him the hearts of all the
people. His youth was signalized by feats of romantic gallantry, told in popular song and story. Almost
from boyhood up he had been the one acknowledged
champion of Israel; and on no other could the parties
of priest and people unite so well.

Whatever was wanting of ancient claim was more
than made up by recent services. For years of a
marauding life, at the head of a lawless and adventurous troop, he had been the guardian of the frontier
against the desert hordes from the south. To his own
free companions he had endeared himself by a bold,
frank, and generous demeanour; and their violent
and rude temper was thoroughly subdued to his native superiority of mind, and his well-timed policy.
Possessing in the highest degree the personal qualities
of a leader of men, he never, from first to last, lost

the warm and enthusiastic regard of his immediate
followers. When Bethlehem, his native town, was
once beleaguered, and he happened to express a
_longing for a draught of water from the spring
he used to drink of there, three of his men broke
through the enemies' force, and at the hazard of
their lives brought it to him : but David would not
drink " the blood of the men that went in jeopardy
of their lives," and poured it out as a libation to
Jehovah. This is but a single example of the generous rivalry of that camp-life, and of the devoted
allegiance of his troop. The same spirit with which
he had inspired them was shown, too, in the entreaty
made to him once and again in his later life, to avoid
personal exposure in battle : he should not " quench
the light of Israel ; " his life was worth, his warriors
said, " ten thousand of such as we."

To the captivating personal qualities of a military
chief he added a sagacious policy, which showed yet
more plainly his superiority to the rude men about
him. He enforced on his troop an equitable division
of the spoil taken from the Amalekites ; and established the rule that the guards of the camp should
have an equal share with those who went to the
battle, — instead of the disorderly scramble, in which
might is the only right. His own share he sent in
gifts to the leading men of the towns of Judah, reminding them of his present power and past services;
and when the news came of Saul's defeat and death,
he had only to go up to Hebron, where he was at
once inaugurated king. His policy towards the Philistines was of a more questionable sort, and had

nearly committed him fatally to an act of treason. From this, however, he was saved by a happy accident; and kept the strength of his position as their ally, without paying down the ruinous price they claimed.

Then he was not only a man of action: he was a man of thought and emotion, — in both, a type of the better tendencies of the Hebrew mind. His early culture had been full as much in the school of arts as in the school of arms. He had doubtless shared the religious training of Samuel, which included all the mental accomplishments known to the time. In the first report to Saul of "the son of Jesse the Bethlehemite," he is told of as one "skilled in playing, and a mighty valiant man, prudent in affairs, and of beautiful person, and Jehovah is with him." By temperament he shared profoundly in the popular religious impressions and beliefs. His songs and odes, composed on occasions of victory or defeat, of penitence or gratitude, in the fields where he kept his flocks, or in caves where he lay hid from an insane and violent king, or on some high festival of public joy, have touched religiously more hearts than perhaps any other human compositions, and are to this day the model of the devotional poetry of the world. Both early culture and later circumstances had brought him into a hearty good understanding with the religious party of the nation, or the priesthood. Saul had long broken with them, and had deeply exasperated them. From the time of his brutal massacre of the priests at Nob, the outlaw David, to whom Abiathar had fled, taking with him the high-priest's prestige and the patrimonial right, had been the recognized champion of that party. He had previously gained to his cause the sanction of a holy man, the prophet Gad, — a personal friend, perhaps, — whose counsel carried with it something of a Divine sanction ; but with Abiathar he possessed the sacred oracle of Urim, and the avowed adhesion of the representatives of the nation's faith. Their opposition had been fatal to the reign and life of Saul ; their steady and unwavering support secured to David not only his security from first to last, but his almost unchallenged place in history.

Though long an outlaw and fugitive, and for near a year and a half an exile in the enemies' service, David was not without his strong claims on the nation's respect and gratitude. In his boyhood, the prophetic eye of Samuel had selected him as the one fit to bear the charge of the rule of Jehovah's people. His symbolic anointing, if it did not make him openly suspected to the king, must (if any were privy to it) have turned on him the eyes of a loyal and enthusiastic party, who deplored Saul's widening defection from the national faith ; while at the same time it must have done much to elevate and fix the temper of his own thought, and to give him that secret religious assurance and trust in the living Providence which was so strongly characteristic of him. The popular mind, too, dwelt fondly on the almost fabulous exploits that had first brought him into public favour. While a shepherd-boy, tending flocks at Bethlehem, he had killed a lion and a bear that came

to take a lamb out of the fold. When the giant
Goliath of Gath, whose height was six cubits and a
span, and whose spear was like a weaver's beam,
had for forty days defied the armies of Israel, and
no man was found bold enough to meet him, David,
armed only with a sling and five smooth stones from
the brook, smote him on the forehead with a sudden
well-aimed blow that brought him to the ground,
slew him with his own sword, and so put all the
Philistine host to flight. Jonathan, Saul's eldest
son, loved him " as his own soul," with all the
warmth of a kindred and generous spirit : each had
distinguished himself by romantic feats of valour, and
with equal frankness each recognized a brother and
true friend. Saul, from the first, with a kingly eye
as yet undarkened by jealousy, saw his high qualities, and did them honour : made him first his armour-
bearer and captain of a thousand men ; then gave
him his daughter for a bride, and the next place in
station after his own cousin Abner, chief commander
of the forces. And the people could not but remember the time when, as each hostile inroad came, David
was the man to meet it ; how he " behaved himself
wisely " in every commission the king intrusted to
him, and " was accepted in the sight of all the people ; " and how when " the women came out of all
the cities of Israel, singing and dancing, to meet
King Saul, with tabrets, with joy, and with instruments of music, they answered one another as they
played, and said : —

> " Saul hath slain his thousands,
> But David his ten thousands."

Such was the youth which had introduced this new hero upon the stage, — a youth soon imbittered by the king's distrust and insane jealousy. Twice, when "the evil spirit from Jehovah troubled him," and David played to soothe him, as was his wont, he had hurled his javelin at him unprovoked ; and David knew that his life was not safe in the king's hands. He had escaped one snare, by returning successful from the perilous exploit that was to win his bride, or more likely forfeit his life ; and when Michal loved him, and all the people loved him, Saul "was yet the more afraid of him, and became his enemy continually." Jonathan's generous intercession reconciled his father to him for a time ; then only a hasty flight by night, and Michal's stratagem (who feigned that he was sick, and deceived the messengers by showing a wooden image in his bed), saved him from seizure and death. Again Jonathan endeavoured to bring about a reconciliation, which his father's sudden rage convinced him was impossible ; and he met him by appointment in a harvest-field, to take farewell, and bid him fly for his life. He saw his friend's noble qualities, and the doom that must inevitably come upon his father's house ; and, in the tenderest appeal to his gratitude and honour, urged him to remember their friendship, and deal kindly by his own family who would come hereafter into his charge. So they took a sacred oath of mutual fidelity, "and kissed one another, and wept one with another," till Jonathan, who saw that time must not be lost, bade him go in peace, and he arose and departed. They saw each other only once again,

when Jonathan came out into the wilderness to warn
him of new designs against his life. Then, parting
forever, they once more solemnly renewed their
pledge, — a pledge but coldly fulfilled in David's
tardy and suspicious hospitalities towards Mephibo-
sheth, Jonathan's lame son.

The period which followed was a critical and eventful one for David's fortunes. Amidst the dangers
and privations he was exposed to, his force of mind
became developed, and his true destiny was found,
along with the self-reliance he now learned to prac-
tise. A dark and fatal deed, of which he was the
unwilling cause, touched him keenly with remorse.
When in his loneliness he had applied for counsel
and supplies to the priest Abimelech, who fed his
fainting troop with "shew-bread" from the sacred
table, he had feigned the king's commission; and the
old man was thus deceived into an act of hospitality
which provoked the jealous king to the massacre of
himself and his whole company. Thus driven from
the realm by the calamity his presence seemed to
carry with it, David thought to take refuge with the
Philistine king. Insecure here as elsewhere, he returned to Judah, and roughly fortified himself in
the cave of Adullam. Here "every one that was in
distress, and every one that was in debt, and every
one that was discontented, gathered themselves to
him; and he became captain over them; and there
were with him about four hundred men," — a number
that shortly grew to six hundred.

With this outlaw troop, devoted to his service, he
did not revolt against Saul, or do mischief to the

country. A deeper or else a more generous policy
dictated another course. He assumed the position
of defender of the region against hostile inroads, and
became a self-appointed guard of the frontier. Formidable as of old was his name as foe of the Philistines, while he relieved a beleaguered town or dispersed their forces in the field. The supplies he
needed would be freely rendered by the people, who
found his protection so much more effective than
that of the crippled monarchy; and, from one instance, — that of Nabal, whose wife he afterwards
married, — we know that if these had been refused,
neither he nor his freebooters would have scrupled
to take them with a strong hand, and pay for them
in blood. Towards Saul he cherished, according to
the narrative, even a romantic loyalty. While in
imminent hazard of his life, betrayed by the people
of the city he had rescued, or the district in which
he lodged; once saved only by the sudden tidings of
a Philistine invasion to the north, and finally fleeing
in utter desperation to the enemy, — an account twice
told, with different incidents, relates how he spared
the king's life when completely in his power, and so
worked on his better feeling as to make him desist
from his persecution, and swear again the faith he
had treacherously broken.

Very abruptly, upon this last reconciliation, we
find him despairing of his life, and taking refuge
with Achish, king of Gath. As the captain of a
large company of bold and well-trained men, and
as the object of Saul's unappeasable resentment, he
presented claims quite different from those of the

solitary exile who had fled from their hospitality years before. Their Philistine policy was to disable the Hebrew power by dividing and distracting it. As head of a formidable party at home, he might be turned to great account in their scheme of conquest. Accordingly, he made his terms as something of an independent power. The border town or stronghold of Ziklag was put into his hands, — a petty principality of his own, from which he afterwards treated so independently about the kingdom of Judah. He would not fight his countrymen directly in his border skirmishes, and spared them carefully in all his expeditions, — hoodwinking by his adroitness (says our narrative) the king's credulous confidence. But such good service he rendered to his new allies, by beating back the marauders of the wilderness, that he came at length to be regarded with a trust almost unlimited.

The approaching decisive battle of Gilboa, in which Saul and his sons were slain, must have put David to the most terrible alternative. Evasion and ambiguity would no longer serve his turn. Hitherto he was scrupulously neutral, and might be reckoned the friend of either party. Now he must make up his mind whether to meet his sovereign and friend and countrymen in open fight, and so forfeit every higher aim and better hope he might have cherished, or else betray the confidence placed in him by his new allies, who would certainly show no mercy to a deserter on the eve of battle. . Either case would have rendered his name justly infamous, and his further ambition hopeless. For-

6

tunately for him, he was spared the decision. The
jealousy of the Philistine chiefs was roused. They
suspected his good faith. "How should he reconcile
himself to his master?" said they; "should it not
be with the blood of these men?" So they compelled him to withdraw, though against his plausible
and skilful protest, and with the amplest assurance
of the king's entire confidence. The battle was
fought. The forces of Israel were dispersed and
overthrown. The Philistines held undisputed mastery of the middle country. And David, who had
returned just in time to recapture his men's families
and treasures from an Amalekite horde, was peaceably
established as king of the south country, at Hebron.

For, in the mean time, his force was continually
increased by men who thronged to him from every
quarter of the land, "until it was a great host like
the host of God." They were men formidable for
strength and daring, and armed to the teeth; as the
later chronicler describes them, "men of might and
men of war, fit for the battle, that could handle
shield and buckler, whose faces were like the faces
of lions, and swift as roes upon the mountains, —
one of the least of them a match for a hundred, and
one of the greatest for a thousand." * A gathering
host of such a stamp left no doubt in what direction
lay the destiny of Israel.

As king, the military force of David had still for its
base and nucleus the same regiment of six hundred
"mighty men" that had gathered about him in the
wilderness. From first to last, they were the strong-

* 1 Chronicles xii. 8.

hold of his power, and the soul of every great
achievement of his reign. Their leaders were men
distinguished each by some marvellous feat of personal prowess, such as making stand against whole
armies, slaying entire battalions, or coping unarmed
with a giant in panoply, or a lion in a pit. By a
strict gradation of rank, they were marshalled under
thirty officers, above whom were two ranks of three
each, — "mighty men of valour." Joab, son of David's sister, held the almost undisputed station of
"leader of the host," — a wily, fierce, unscrupulous,
and relentless man, dangerous to keep in power, yet
more dangerous to deprive of it. Twice, by a base
and treacherous assassination, he rid himself of a
troublesome rival, — killing Abner in revenge for
his brother Asahel, and Amasa out of pure jealousy.
Brutal and remorseless as he was, however, he was
a man whom David could not spare ; and after three
several attempts to supersede him, he kept his position until Solomon's guardsmen slew him at the
very altar. He was one of the first and boldest
of those who had joined David in his flight ; and
was indisputable chief of that formidable body
which secured him the throne, and made his armies
practically invincible. The *Cherethites* and *Pelethites* were an alien corps, — both body-guard and ex-
ecutioners, like the Roman lictors ; the last resource
of royal power and the first instrument of despotism.

For the present, the great interest of David was
peace. He must gain time for his power to become
firmly knit and independently strong. At Hebron,
accordingly, he remained something more than seven

years. His six hundred men with their families he quartered upon the towns of Judah, and probably paid tribute to the Philistines, who were not sorry to see Judah thus made a separate dependent province. He interfered neither with the pretensions of Saul's family — represented now by the weak boy Ishbosheth — nor with the slow expulsion of the Philistines from their late conquest, which was effected probably in the course of the ensuing five years by the able generalship of Abner.

One fiercely contested battle, preceded by a singular combat of twelve champions on each side, of whom all were slain, measured the strength of the two parties now in possession of the Hebrew realm; and for two years more, "David waxed stronger and stronger, and the house of Saul waxed weaker and weaker," till Abner began to feel that David's hand alone was equal to the rule of the disorganized state. Ishbosheth suspected his coolness, and charged him with seeking the power for himself, — implied in his marrying Saul's concubine, Rizpah. Upon this Abner, the only able man on that side, promptly made terms with David, and pledged himself to bring him the allegiance of all Israel: and this he would have done, reserving honourable terms, doubtless, for the son of Saul, but Joab called him back on his way, and stabbed him with his own hand, — an act of revenge for the death of Asahel, whom Abner had slain by a sudden back-thrust of his spear, when close pressed in flight. Ishbosheth was presently after murdered in his bed; and, nothing standing in David's way, he was at once received unchallenged, as the sovereign of all Israel.

The first acts of David's reign were parts of a consistent and determined policy, to fortify and extend his independent power. This must be done by conquest first, at home, of the remnants of old tribes that still held out against the Hebrews; and next abroad, by absorbing or suppressing, at any hazard, the outlying races that might menace the frontier. This policy was to prepare the way for converting the Hebrew realm itself into a strong, compact, and well-ordered state, on the familiar model of an Oriental autocracy. The germs of it were fully developed under the long reign of Solomon; it was checked only by the revolt of the ten tribes, and the final division of the kingdom.

The Jebusite settlement, or encampment, about Mount Moriah had maintained till now a scanty fragment of the old Canaanitish power. The place was so strong by nature that its defenders told David, in defiance, that their lame and blind could hold it out against him. But Joab, dauntless as unscrupulous, seized their stronghold on the neighbouring hill of Zion, and the garrison was speedily reduced. This cluster of hills David chose for his capital, naming it Jerusalem, the " heritage of Peace." It was on the border of his own tribe, Judah, belonging almost equally to the territory of Benjamin, — as nearly central, therefore, as any place not too far from the actual seat of his power. The high and rocky hill of Zion, well watered by springs from surrounding heights, lies toward the southwest, flanked by the rugged vales of Hinnom and Jehoshaphat, and separated by a deep ravine

from Moriah on the east and the gentler slopes of
Millo at the north. The whole site covers no more
than a square mile. The portion known as the
"city of David," the original stronghold of Zion,
was strongly entrenched as the citadel of the realm.
The smooth slopes of Millo became the populous
quarter, while the broad summit of Moriah lay open
till the next reign.

That nothing might be wanting to the honours of
the new capital, it was made the head-quarters of the
national religion. The ark had remained at Kirjath-
jearim ever since its recovery from the Philistines in
Samuel's time; and one of the first of David's public
acts, delayed three months by the evil omen of Uz-
zah's death, was now to bring it, with songs and a
great procession, in triumph to the capital; himself,
in a Levite's garb, leaping and dancing at the head.
It was placed in a new tabernacle on Mount Zion,
until there should be means and time to build a
temple corresponding in magnificence with the new
position the nation had now assumed. The order of
Levites was now for the first time established, or else
reinstated with far more splendour than ever before.
The religious orders were allied or incorporated with
the monarchy, which thus secured the support of the
religious feeling of the people; while the two high-
priests required by this policy (one belonging to the
old rural sanctuary) would not easily combine to
form a power dangerous to the king's supremacy.

These were the earlier steps of that vigorous centralizing policy characteristic of the reign of David
and his successor. Very naturally, they roused the

jealousy of neighbouring powers. The Philistines were alarmed for their security, and at once commenced a new invasion. David first beat them thoroughly in the vale of Rephaim, the Giants' Valley, near Jerusalem; then, by counsel of an oracle, stole a march upon them when the rising night-wind stirred " the tops of the mulberry-trees," and drove them back within their ancient boundaries; then, on a third attack, he " smote them, and subdued them, and took from them the Bridle-Arm," * — that is, hampered them by seizing the strong posts which curbed the frontier, — so that they troubled him no more till close on the termination of his reign. The most formidable peril to the nation's independence was thus timely overcome.

The three wars which followed — with Moab, Ammon, and Edom — were further steps of the same steady and perhaps necessary policy. Each was a painful illustration of the ferocious temper in which these border feuds were waged.

The case of Moab seems especially cruel and wantonly vindictive. It was the home of David's ancestry, the native land of Ruth, his father's grandmother; and at the darkest hour of his peril from the animosity of Saul, he had placed the family of Jesse there for security. What the pretext or provocation was we do not know. The story of the war is told in a single sentence. " He smote Moab, and measured them with a line, casting them down to the ground (as helpless prisoners of war); with two lines he measured to put to death, and with one full

* Metheg Ammah.

line to keep alive." The sole object of this savage massacre was apparently to destroy the nation's force so thoroughly that he might find no resistance in that quarter to any future scheme of conquest or defence. Effectually as this policy was carried out, there is no room to doubt that it was wholly successful so far as his own reign only was concerned ; but we learn from the prophets how dearly the debt of blood was paid in the border hostilities that harassed the later monarchy.

The turn of Edom came next, — Edom, that dwelt in the rocky and almost inaccessible ravines skirting the Arabian desert. The Edomites, perhaps in retaliation for Saul's invasion of them, had joined in a concerted attack, by which the outlying tribes of the east and south hoped to crush the rising supremacy of Israel. They were beaten in a sanguinary battle in the Salt Valley, south of the Dead Sea, El Arabah ; and Joab, following them up to their rocky fastnesses, quartered himself there for six months, exterminating every male creature he could find. They were driven from their old capital, Selah, or Petra, farther back into the wilderness, utterly broken and disabled, so that for fifty years they could gather no effective force ; but they bloodily avenged themselves long after, and maintained a feud with Israel that lasted for several centuries.*

But the great and eventful conflict of David's reign was with the allied forces of the east and north. The

* Psalm xviii. is thought to be the song of triumph at the meeting of David, victorious in the east, with Joab, returning from this expedition in the south.

Ammonites were already jealous and alarmed; the fate of Moab hurried them into a rash defiance of the conqueror. David had sent courteous messages to the young chief, Hanun, whose father was just dead. But Hanun suspected treachery in his bold and wily neighbour. The envoys he treated as spies. By way of aggravated insult, he " shaved off one half of their beards, and cut off their garments in the middle, and sent them away; " then mustered the forces of his Syrian alliance, and made war at once. David, bidding the degraded messengers " tarry at Jericho till their beards were grown," was not slow to avenge the affront, — to Eastern notions the most unpardonable that could be offered. The war lasted three years. The numerous cavalry from the great plains of Syria was broken and foiled in the rough region beyond Jordan. The obstinate courage and thorough training of David's men made good any lack of numbers. As the result of the struggle, both Damascus and the whole country as far as the Euphrates became tributary to Israel. The Ammonites, deprived of their allies, had no hope but in holding out to the utmost in the strongly built town of Rammah. Here Joab besieged them; and here Uriah the Hittite perished by the base treachery of David, who had ordered that brave and loyal officer to be deserted in the front post of danger. In a year or more the town was effectually reduced; and the politic Joab sent to David to come and claim for himself the honours of its capture. So David, his hands stained with his still fresh guilt in the affair of Uriah, came and took the place, and

6 *

I

inflicted a far more cruel vengeance than even the massacres of Moab and Edom. He "brought forth the people that were therein, and put them under saws and harrows of iron," — that is, tortured them in various ways, — and some he smothered in heated ovens ("brick-kilns"); "and thus did he to all the cities of the children of Ammon."*

David was now near the middle of his reign, and at the summit of his power. Under the influence of unbridled passion, and gratified ambition, and pampered lust of sway, had ripened the seeds of all that was base and cruel in his nature. How he backed the passions of the blood by infamous treachery towards a loyal and unsuspecting companion-in-arms had been shown in that most guilty act of his life, the affair of Bathsheba and Uriah. The same capricious and despotic indulgence led to the other fast-coming calamities of his life. Departing from the simpler example Saul had set, he had followed from the first one of the worst practices of Eastern despotism, — a multiplicity of wives. Polygamy was a custom which the Hebrew institutions did not approve, and which the patriarchal history warned against, — the more mischievous, perhaps, because tolerated against the protest of the general sense. Saul's daughter Michal had been given to another man; but David had reclaimed her at once on coming to the throne, so as to unite the claims of both royal

---

* The Assyrian monuments leave no doubt as to what was the ordinary treatment of a captured town in this early age. Compare Judges viii. 16; Proverbs xx. 26; Amos i. 3. Psalm xxi. is held to be the ode written to commemorate this frightful act of vengeance.

houses,—taking her forcibly from a husband who loved her and long followed her weeping when she was torn from him; then letting her live in solitude and neglect. At Hebron there were already six wives in his seraglio, and at Jerusalem at least ten,—each with her wasteful separate household, liable to shameful exhibitions of jealousy and strife, and stimulating still more highly the despotic appetite for change. It was this that brought on him the fatal act of the abduction of Bathsheba, with its train of evil consequences, and its maiming of his moral strength. Remorse as deep and penitence as sincere as that he unquestionably felt might restore in part the inward harmony and the spiritual force he had lost; but it could not restore the dignity of his position, or the confidence he had forfeited, or the domestic peace he had invaded. The coarse and unscrupulous Joab, whom he had made partner and confidant of his guilt, would be never backward in using the advantage it gave him over a master who could not shake him off,—a bitter cross to the nobler nature of the king.* Still more, while the vicious custom was retained, the same root of bitterness would put forth similar shoots.

In such a state of things as now existed in his establishment, violent jealousies break out, and hatred, among the children of different mothers. By Oriental custom, the brother, even more than the father, is the defender of his sister's honour. Among the twenty or more children of David's household it is

* How deeply David must have felt this thraldom is apparent from the language of Psalm ci.

not surprising that we find instances of fraternal feud ending in blood. Absalom avenged his sister Tamar by the murder of his half-brother Amnon; then fled to his mother's country towards Assyria, where he remained three years. By Joab's crafty intercession he was at length recalled; but, though David's private indignation was appeased, some penalty must be suffered for public justice' sake, and for two years longer Absalom was not permitted to see the king's face. When at length he was restored to his former place, and became the acknowledged heir of the crown, he had brooded so long over his disgrace, that his one settled purpose was revenge, and he used his new advantage to stir up a desperate conspiracy.

In the simple fashion of Oriental monarchy, then as now, the sovereign must listen to many complaints, and, in a multitude of cases, render justice in his own person. This exposes him to all the rancour of private disappointment, and complaints of favouritism. In David's case, it laid him open to the further jealousy always ready to break out against his own tribe of Judah. Absalom took advantage of the disaffection he saw gathering from this source. When any came for justice, he would not so much as receive the ordinary respect paid to a king's son; but gave an equal greeting, regretted the king's inefficiency and the law's delay, and said, " O that I were made judge, that any man which hath any suit or cause might come to me, and I would do him justice." And " when any man came to do him obeisance, he put forth his hand and took him and kissed him. So

Absalom stole the hearts of the men of Israel." A natural indulgence towards the proud beauty and hasty passions of his youth grew easily into an impatient wish to see him in his father's seat. David, partially fond and weakly indulgent towards Absalom, — now his eldest son, and of royal blood too on his mother's side, — suspected nothing. When Absalom on a feast-day* gave the signal for revolt in Hebron, things took so sudden a turn, that by noon he was master of Jerusalem ; and in the same evening, his father, a sorrowful exile, with a few trusty friends and the right arm of his power, his guard of mighty men, took such hasty flight, that "by the morning light there lacked not one of them that was not gone over Jordan." Absalom's purpose was now to follow him up, and crush him before his force could rally. This was the "wise counsel" of Ahithophel. It was foiled by Hushai, a confidential adviser of the king's, who took the discreet step of volunteering his service, and humoured Absalom's idle temper by framing plausible reasons of delay.

For some three months the young prince now wantoned in the exercise of his ill-got power. But, thanks to Hushai, David had gained all he required, — time. His name and cause were daily gathering strength. The priestly party in Jerusalem acted as his spies, and extemporized a hazardous but very effective way of communication. Supplies came in from the loyal east-country, which he had delivered from the border feuds with Ammon, and where he

---

* After a delay of "forty years," says the narrative, returning quaintly upon the old style of chronology.

now staked his fortunes. When the army of the conspiracy invested his stronghold at Mahanaim, it was
already too late. A bloody battle was fought in the
"woods of Ephraim." Twenty thousand of the Israelites are said to have been slain, and many more
perished miserably in forest and fen. Absalom him-.
self, caught from his mule by his luxuriant hair, and
swinging helpless from the branches of an oak tree,
was thrust through the heart by Joab's own hand.
Anything less prompt and summary than this, he
argued, would have been ineffectual to stay the guilt
of a son's rebellion, or make the future safe. But it
was against David's express command; and all the
sovereign's sternness was lost in the father's tenderness, as he broke into the passionate lamentation, "O
my son Absalom! my son, my son Absalom! Would
God I had died for thee, O Absalom, my son, my
son!"

Like a beaten army the force slunk back into the
city, and the king's grief was fast becoming their
discontent; when Joab roughly chided him, and
brought him to himself, threatening a worse rebellion
before night than that just crushed. How divided
and sensitive the popular temper was, was shown just
after, when the old jealousy against Judah broke out
afresh in the north, and again the rough promptness
of Joab was needful to check the new conspiracy in
the bud.

Hitherto the nation had felt the advantage, rather
than any heavy pressure, of the strong consolidated
force of monarchy. It was free from fear of enemies
abroad, and delivered from the violence of feuds at

home. The eventful and decisive wars into which
the commencement of David's reign was plunged,
give the impression that it was a period of military
action chiefly, and perhaps of military despotism.
But, on the contrary, as compared with previous times,
and even with whole centuries of modern history, it
was rather a period of peace. Of the thirty-three
years of his sovereignty, not more than ten were
probably taken up in warfare; at least twenty were
years of greater security and quiet than had ever
been known in Israel. The arts of peace throve even
more than the fame of war. Conquest for its own
sake David did not attempt: it was against the genius
of the Hebrew people, and against their standing jealousy of a military despotism, or indeed of any form
of centralization. Tyre and Sidon, which lay on his
northern seaboard, the conqueror of Syria spared; nor
was there any interruption of the friendly relation in
which they stood towards the Hebrew state. Perhaps
the absorption of the Canaanite populations had been
brought about by a compromise which respected their
old title to such domains as they still possessed; and
this may account for the Jebusite garrison at Jerusalem, and the enrolling of Hittites, Cherethites, and
Pelethites in David's force, as well as for the politic
sparing of Phœnicia: or, again, the public interest
was better served by trade than conquest, and Tyre
was too good a market to lose. At any rate, commerce, and a large increase of wealth and gain in the
arts of peace, especially in agriculture, were quite as
important features of this reign as either services of
religion or feats of arms, — features of which the con-

sequence was seen more fully in the time of Solomon. Immense access of riches and population, the natural growth of untaxed peace, had given quite a new material basis to the Hebrew empire.

For the sake of knowing his own strength more accurately, or with some design of further conquests, or (still more likely) with a view to greater consolidation, and an organized despotism similar to that of Egypt, David now sent Joab to take a census of the tribes. Whatever his design, it was broken short in the beginning. The popular instinct, even under the freest form of government, is restive and suspicious when private affairs are made matter of close inspection to public agents, — a feeling curiously reflected in the Mosaic law,* that a piece of silver should be paid, on such an occasion, as the ransom of each man's life, to propitiate, apparently, the dread of an ignorant superstition. In David's case, the law was perhaps not known, — at any rate, not regarded ; so that the popular feeling had full sway. Joab, as spokesman of this feeling, remonstrated in vain. He wished the people might be a hundred times as many, but protested, along with all the captains of the host, against what they thought the mad project of the king. The census was taken, notwithstanding, and with results amply to gratify the royal pride.

But at that, and much later ages,† fantastic and unreal causes were assigned to any great calamity.

---

* Exodus xxx. 12.

† Thns cholera, famine, and the Russian war were all three confidently traced to the guilt which the British nation had incurred by the "Maynooth grant" in 1845.

A pestilence or famine was no strange thing in that climate; but the religious terror of its coming must be met by assigning a religious and not a physical cause. A little while before, at such a visitation, instead of referring it to any recent guilt of the present dynasty, an oracle had said,* that it was "for Saul's bloody house, because he had slaughtered the Gibeonites;" and, on the strength of this, David had appeased their kinsmen's sullen revenge by giving them seven innocent boys to hang, which they mercilessly did, —seven of the sons and grandsons of Saul: The lonely watch of the bereaved Rizpah, protecting (like Antigone) the dear remains from desecration, sheds a single gleam of humanity across the tragical gloom.

The same cruel superstition, shared this time by the king himself, saw in a similar infliction the chastisement of his fault in numbering the people. The "seventy thousand" who perished were thought to be vicarious sufferers for his guilt. The calamity was so far relieved, that no inhuman expiation was enjoined this time, as before; and it was so far a mercy that it probably checked the too rapid advance the state was making towards a pure and compact despotism. The event dwelt so profoundly in the popular mind, that the first thought of the census was referred to God's own prompting, who sought an occasion to punish the sins of the people; and afterwards to Satan, the nation's adversary. It was further said, that a prophet warned David to make his choice of the three calamities of war, famine, and

* 2 Samuel, chap. xxi.

pestilence, and that his piety chose the last; and, finally, that the angel of Death was seen to stand on Mount Moriah, on the spot where the brazen altar of the temple afterwards stood, and for fifty shekels of silver (which the later account magnifies into six hundred of gold) David bought the piece of ground from the Jebusite king Araunah, and built an altar there.*

This census of the tribes is King David's last recorded public act. It is significant of the fixed purpose he had held, only deferred by the troubles of his reign, to provide for the more perfect organization of a priesthood, and the splendour of a temple ritual. As expiation of his faults, or as the free-will offering of his piety, he had made large preparations for the work so magnificently executed by his successor. Ever since the establishing of the high place of worship with the sacred ark at Jerusalem, he had worked steadily to that end. We have still the weary chronicle of names, which the hierarchy gratefully preserved, in memory of his pious labours. But it was now too late for him to engage in any further enterprise on a large scale. Exhausted by the fatigues and exposures of his arduous life, he had reached already at seventy a decrepit and comfortless old age. His failing energy was yet enough to baffle Adonijah's hasty ambition, and establish the boy Solomon as his successor,—already a singular stretch of arbitrary power for the free state of Israel, to which he had been called by the popular voice, and had taken oath as a constitutional king,—and then he died; leaving to Solomon, as his last bequest, a few

* 2 Samuel, chap. xxiv.; and 1 Chronicles, chap. xxi.

instructions of his implacable policy, and a brief hymn to set forth the pattern of kingly virtue.*

There are few characters in history which perplex the moral judgment more than that of David. To the grateful thought of an after age he was the model prince of the Hebrew monarchy, the type of the Messiah, or ideal Prince, who should hereafter fulfil the nation's hope, and be sovereign of the world. The religious mind of Christendom has represented him as the "man after God's own heart;" the royal Psalmist, or inspired and prophetic Bard; the peculiar champion and favourite of Jehovah; the man who could fearlessly and truly say, "My transgression is forgiven, and my sin is covered over." It has even been believed that God's covenant, made with Abraham, Isaac, and Jacob, was explicitly renewed with him and his posterity; and that the future Sovereign of the world must by a divine guaranty be one of lineal descent from him. All these views, again, are reflected in the various utterances of the Hebrew mind, in various passages of Scripture. His faults and crimes have been forgotten, in the vague splendour that illuminates his princely name. This is due in part to the gratitude of the priesthood towards its royal patron. It was a necessary policy with him, even if it had not been a cause so much after his own heart, to reconcile that body to the monarchy, especially after its wide estrangement from Saul. Whatever the service was, it was amply recompensed in the eulogies of the religious historians, and in a quality of fame such as scarce belongs to any other.

* 2 Samuel xxiii. 2 – 5; 1 Kings ii. 2 – 9.

Facts were willingly forgotten, or studiously suppressed, to make history an echo of grateful fancy. The writer of the Chronicles passes by in silence what the Book of Samuel records and reprobates as crime; enlarging to weariness, instead, on the services he rendered to the priestly body. So that, almost as far back as our records date, the true character of the man is in danger of being covered up in undiscriminating eulogy.

Almost in direct contrast to this is the judgment we should be apt to form from the bare detail of his acts. On the page of history names of the darkest reproach would be set against him, — names hardly to be effaced by any service he could be shown to have rendered. It is something more than charity, it is fanatical partisanship, which could overlook the gross and horrid charges of treachery, licentiousness, and murder. The man so idealized in the fond apprehension of the religious world, shows his splendid qualities on a dark background of passion, weakness, and guilt. And it is not an easy task to reconcile the two contending views, or to persuade ourselves that we are rendering account of the same man. Yet, unquestionably, each is in its measure right; and extravagant eulogy is no more false than unqualified condemnation.

The crimes of David are sternly and sufficiently told in the plain story of his life. They need no exaggeration, no rhetorical exhibition, to set them forth. And what was regarded as no crime then, — his remorseless policy of extermination, the savage tortures he wreaked on defenceless prisoners, the piratical freedom with which he enforced an outlaw's claim for food and shelter, — are such as shock our moral sense too much to let us err easily on the side of lenity. A grave historical judgment will be quite as apt to wrong him in one way, as the blindly national judgment of his people wrongs the simple truth in another way.

In the very fact of the exalting and idealizing view that has commonly been held of him, we see the strongest proof that he was eminently a man for his own time and people. No other could have rendered, then and there, the service rendered by him. It is not so much by the detail of a man's acts, as by the mark he makes in human history, that we know his real greatness, and the quality of his soul. David has unquestionably exalted and not debased our apprehension of the standard of human character. His lasting influence upon the world has not been for evil, but very greatly for good. Here is his real vindication. His faults, his crimes, black and base as they were, have been honestly told by one who was bold enough to censure, yet in the main strongly moved to honour. A man who looks his own worst fault in the face, and gathers up the whole energy of his soul in the struggle against it, may be pitiable or execrable in his fall, but he is heroic in his recovery. And it was so with him. The parable of the ewe-lamb, and Nathan's honest *Thou art the man*, startled him at once from his passionate and infatuated dream, revealed to him the very bottom of his corrupted heart, and put him upon a course of penitence how deep and sincere, a struggle how agonizing and prolonged, none doubt who have ever known him through the medium of his own confessions in the Psalms.*

To say nothing of the plea that his vices and criminal exercises of power were only such as were common to his age and station, as Oriental despot, while his virtues and repentance were his own, — a plea to be used with caution as vindicating a superior nature, that should disdain to employ or allow it, — a single thought shows David's high and true position in Hebrew history. Compare his reign as it was, — with all its calamities and faults' a reign that has dwelt so gratefully in the popular memory to this day, — with the troubled time that went before, and with what it would have been had its fortunes been intrusted to the best and ablest of the men by whom he was surrounded. We know not one in whom some quality of ferocity or weakness would not have been fatal. Still less can we think of one who, with the powers requisite to the mere task of sustaining his position, combined that higher quality of intellect and religious fervour which made David so truly the representative of the best traits of that race and age. In him first the nation of Israel found its name and place as a nation vindicated : in him alone — the warrior, minstrel, ruler, counsellor, man of the people, and even (on occasion) priest or prophet — the fulfilment of its just desire, and the embodiment at once of its noblest and most various tendency.

At the heart and centre of his spiritual nature there is a degree of tenderness, generosity, and re-

* See especially Psalms xxxii. and li.

ligious trust, which have always, in the last resort, after every deduction of stern and even unfriendly criticism, compelled those who truly understood him to sum up their judgment in terms of admiration and honour. His life, in its long and varied course, is an expression of the want, the struggle, the hope, the passion, the lawlessness, the aspiration, of his age. On the page of history we see him, from first to last, the type and embodiment of his people's character; and we can almost forget the man in this spectacle of the working out of a nation's life. But another and more enduring record he has left of himself, wherein his personality is never lost, and can never be forgotten. Here, the man David becomes a living element in the world's life of religious thought. It was real occasions that bred those psalms of his, — their true expression ; — so true to the type of thought and the nature of the occasion, that more than all other compositions they reflect our own deepest and highest moods, and meet the precise condition of our spiritual nature. This other life of himself he has given to the world, — running in a plane so far higher than that eventful course already traced, yet touching it and made one with it at each crisis of his destiny. The song that echoed in a lonely cave, or rang in the shout of a joyous multitude, or consoled a father's weary exile in the rebellion of a son, registers to the world a spiritual fact, and becomes the precise utterance, the cherished record, of every religious mind touched by a kindred experience. From the attitude of apologists we rise unconsciously to the mood of earnest and grateful admiration. We remember the human features only in this nobler transfigured likeness. The vexed and passionate life of the petty sovereign of Israel is forgotten; and as a monarch in the realm of emotion and thought, as a living power in the world of mind, we render grateful and willing honour to the religious genius and the exalted destiny of David.

V. SOLOMON.

THE reign of Solomon, lasting for another sacred period of forty years, crowned and completed the brief splendour of the Hebrew monarchy. It was the culmination of the people's opulence, power, enterprise, and intellectual activity, — the fullest maturity which the national existence ever reached. Preceded as it was by the dissension and sorrows of David's time, and followed by the distractions of an enfeebled and divided realm, it became to later memory the golden noon of the prosperity of Israel. The report of Solomon's wealth was fabulous, and his name a synonyme of wisdom and magnificence. He knew, said the traditions of the East, the secrets of the invisible world, and familiar spirits brought him the hidden treasures of the earth, gold and gems and pearls. To this day, in Jewish and Arab fancy, he is the Prince of Magicians; and Solomon's name and seal are the most potent spell to control dæmonic agencies, or compel the genii to their task.

It was while almost a boy, in the flush and confidence of boyhood, that he assumed the charge left him by his dying father. It was David's partiality, and Bathsheba's jealous vigilance, that foiled the rival palace intrigues, and made Solomon heir of the royal power. With far other qualifications than those which had identified his father's fortunes with the destiny of the Hebrew people, he entered upon a task that must try most severely his wisdom and ability. Without the depth of personal experience, the fervid passion tempered by wary policy, the profound popular sympathies, the fine religious sensibility, the instinct and the habit of command, which were the outfit of "the heroic and royal psalmist," and without the spontaneous welcome and approval of the people, which recognized in David both a providential and a constitutional sovereign,—a boy,* brought up within the palace-walls, selected by a mother's fondness and a father's arbitrary choice, obliged to put down by the bloody policy of a jealous despotism the rivals of his power, though his brothers in blood,—he made but an inauspicious entrance upon a course fruitful of so much mingled good and evil to his realm. Deep was his need of that guiding wisdom, which was his first and only prayer, when "at Gibeon, in a dream by night," Jehovah appeared before him, and he besought "an understanding heart to judge the people, to discern between good and bad ; for who (said he) is able to judge this thy so great a people ? '

The first recorded acts of Solomon's reign illustrate the wide departure already made from the customs of a people by instinct free and tenacious of their liberty, and the rapid advance that was

* Only twelve years old at his accession, according to the Jewish tradition.

making towards an irresponsible absolutism. They illustrate, too, that precocious sagacity and remorseless policy often nursed in those brought up in the habit and anticipation of authority. A delicate prince of the harem, he had already seen his elder brother Adonijah put down in his favour at his father's dictate, and his life only conditionally spared; and when the elder still hoped to supplant the younger, and cautiously solicited through Bathsheba to be allowed to marry the beautiful Abishag, and with her to take the late king's household, Solomon detected the lurking conspiracy, and had him despatched at once. An Oriental monarchy suffers " no brother near the throne." Joab, who was charged with sharing the conspiracy, was slain at the altar in expiation of his many crimes. Abiathar, the high-priest, was banished, as in fulfilment of the traditionary curse on Eli's family, that they should become beggars, and the meanest underlings of the priests. Nor was a pretext long wanting to make way with Shimei, a man of Saul's family, who had mocked David in his misfortunes, and been guarded since with the jealous eye of despotism. These acts were the familiar policy of irresponsible sovereignty, and are related quietly, as things of course. A more pleasing instance of the young king's sagacity is told, in the case of the two women, mothers of a dead and living child. He offered to divide the living child between the two, when the agony of the real mother at once revealed to him on which side the true claim lay.

Inexorable promptness of state policy, and sagacity

in dispensing justice, thus confirmed whatever was wanting in Solomon's title. The royal power was effectually settled upon him, and during his long life the sceptre never once wavered in his grasp. The kingdom came to his hands, on the whole, strong, flourishing, united, and loyal. He felt his strength and the advantage of his position. His clear native intellect taught him that inactivity was weakness, and that he must build upon the foundation his father had laid. The genius of the people was averse to conquest. The frontier was already larger than could be well maintained. Independent Canaanitish tribes were still existing, that might easily league themselves with the formidable tributaries Damascus and Idumæa. These seem to have taken advantage of the first unsettled years of his reign, for a combined revolt.* Some of them compromised their hostility on easy terms, so as to keep a good share of independence. Others held walled towns on the Philistine frontier, defying from their ramparts the field-force of the Hebrews. Only after the alliance with Egypt were they compelled to a surrender by the skill of the Egyptians and their engines of assault. The towns were made the dowry of Pharaoh's daughter, and the inhabitants reduced to slavery. Thus, like the kings of Egypt and Assyria, Solomon had a numerous class of slaves, as the raw material of his public works.†

The policy of the kingdom was clearly peace. In-

---

* The Second Psalm is considered to be an ode of defiance, written at this emergency.

† 1 Kings ix. 16, 21.

ternal resources were to be developed, and former
conquests to be turned to practical account. At the
same time, political unity must be consolidated, and
the splendour of the monarchy enhanced, by such
great national works as should make Jerusalem the
rival or equal of neighbouring capitals; while the
state religion should be organized in an Establishment, with temple and ritual to befit its claim of
pre-eminence over the religion of every other people.
These several points define what was the aim, and in
some regards the brilliant success, of the reign of
Solomon.

For the first time, therefore, under this splendid
and imposing rule, the Hebrew nation found itself
abreast of the enterprise of the day, and in active
competition for a lucrative commerce. Solomon's
discreet policy secured the alliance of the two border monarchies, Egypt and Phœnicia. His father's
prowess had given him control of the Syrian desert
and the ports of the Red Sea, Elath and Ezion-
geber.

Egypt had before been jealous of the growing
monarchy of the Hebrews. David's chieftains had
signalized themselves by personal encounter with
Egyptian champions; and Hadad, the Edomite prince
who fled from Joab's massacre, had found welcome, and a queen's sister in marriage, at Memphis.
But now the course of policy was changed. Pharaoh — the last monarch of a dynasty perhaps already weakened and broken — was glad to recognize
the firm sovereignty of Jerusalem as a fixed fact.
His daughter became Solomon's queen, and highest

in station of his many wives. The military skill of
Egypt was now brought in to extinguish the petty
independencies it had once aided to harass the Israelite border; and its friendly temper was of profitable account in the growing commerce of the Red
Sea.

The narrow strip of seaboard called Phœnicia was
the last remnant of the once proud dynasty of the
Canaanites, — the inheritor of its arts, its civilization, and its cruel religious rites. The seat of Phœnician power was already transferred to the almost
impregnable island of Tyre, where it stood five years
at bay against Shalmanezer, and long after defied
the forces of Alexander in a siege of seven months.
What it had lost on land it had more than made up
by sea. The rich commerce of Tarshish (Tartessus,
or Spain), and a monopoly of trade among the Grecian isles, poured the wealth of the Western world
into the splendid ports of Tyre and Sidon; while the
empire of Carthage retained, centuries later, the inhuman rites of Canaan, and obstinately disputed with
Rome the mastery of the world. David had withheld his hand from making good the patriarchal
claim to this portion of the Promised Land; and
Solomon was too sagacious and worldly wise to overlook the superior advantage of commerce over conquest. A league was easily entered into, and to all
appearance faithfully kept. For trade, there should
be no interference with the Phœnician monopoly of
the Mediterranean; for public works, ample assist-
ance might be had from the superior Tyrian skill.
The expanding commercial enterprise of the He-

brews found its way along the Red Sea to Sheba, or
Yemen, the fertile southern shore of Arabia, the native land of rare spices and pearls.   Their traffickers
gathered gold and ivory, sandal-wood (for musical
instruments and ornamental work), and rare animals,
" apes and peacocks," from the African or Indian
coast, while their Tyrian allies opened to them the
market of the Levant; and that first Ionic Confederacy of Greece, at its stately festival in Delos, burned
perhaps the incense brought in Solomon's merchant-
ships : —

> " Sabæan odours from the spicy shore ,
> Of Arabie the blest."

The extensive and profitable commerce of which
Palestine thus became the centre laid the foundation of the immense wealth of Solomon's realm, and
bore out the lavish expenditure of his public edifices.
His ambition, largely gratified here, outran his pru-
dence in other quarters; and the uncertain traffic
across the desert — for which he established the
princely station of Tadmor or Palmyra, and maintained other costly and vexatious outposts — may have
led to those exactions which imbittered the people,
and ultimately broke up the integrity of the kingdom.

Of Solomon's public works, by far the most gorgeous, and the one most familiarly associated with his
name, as well as most important in the religious history of the Jews, was the Temple on Mount Moriah.
This steep and rugged elevation, half a mile to the
northeast of Zion, had been left outside the original
city of David, though one of the little cluster of hills
making the well-defined site of Jerusalem.   Neither

was it a spot of any special traditionary sanctity ; for ancient worship sought "high places," and David's place of prayer had been the loftier summit of Olivet, hard by. The altar erected on Moriah when the pestilence was stayed was the first consecration of the ground afterwards so holy : it was a later tradition, probably, that identified it as the spot where Abraham prepared to sacrifice his son. The new religious consecration made it a fit centre of the national worship and faith. Nothing could so strengthen the monarch in his capital as the founding of a permanent loyal priesthood, a splendid central sanctuary, and a gorgeous temple ritual; while local jealousies or the rival claims of priestly families would be merged in a single establishment, that should defy all rivalry. One family of chief-priests had, at the king's edict, gone into banishment and disgrace. The remaining one should be the nucleus of an Order to represent by authority the religion of the nation, and conduct its stately ritual.

The gathered treasures and pious gifts of David, as well as the fast increasing revenue of the kingdom, were lavishly spent upon this favourite scheme of combined piety, policy, and pride. The rough summit of the hill was levelled with immense toil, and widened by terraces and vast embankments. From the deep valley of Jehoshaphat, where runs the narrow stream of Kedron, a wall was built, four hundred and fifty feet in height, of enormous blocks of limestone mortised into the solid rock, — some single stones being more than thirty feet in length. While the rest of the edifice is utterly destroyed, not a vestige even remaining of the two Jewish temples, or of the Christian church that afterwards occupied its site, portions of the enormous rock-embankment, rivalling the great works of Egypt or the Cyclopic architecture of the early Greeks, still flank the sacred hill.

The Temple itself was built after the pattern of the old tabernacle, — i. e. on the square model of a tent, — the curtains being replaced by solid walls of stone. In size it was but a small chapel, thirty feet wide and something more than a hundred long. The "oracle," shrine, or most sacred place, — where in Pagan temples was the image of the Divinity, and perhaps the city treasury, — was a cube of thirty feet, divided from the rest by doors elaborately carved, and a richly embroidered "veil" of blue, crimson, and scarlet drapery. Its walls were wainscotted with cedar and overlaid with gold. As the special dwelling-place of Jehovah, it was a place of splendour and mystery, impenetrably dark, and to be trodden by no human foot, save when once a year the high-priest touched the "mercy-seat" with the blood of the victim slain for ransom of the people's sin. In this most secret and holy habitation was nothing but the "Ark of Jehovah," a small gilded chest of Egyptian pattern, fabricated (it was said) as far back as the wandering in the desert, and containing the inestimable relic of the stone tables of the Law, graven by Jehovah's own hand. Tradition had added to these Aaron's flowering rod and a golden vase of manna ; but when the ark was opened in Solomon's time, only the two stone tables were found in it. The lid of the chest was of solid gold, and was the "mercy-seat," or

7

Jehovah's own resting-place, where he dwelt "between the cherubim." These were winged figures of uncertain form,* whose outstretched wings met above its centre, and touched the opposite walls of the shrine. An apartment twice as long, containing the table of shew-bread, the incense-altar, and the sacred candlesticks, and a narrow porch,† completed what is properly known as the Temple, — a structure small in dimensions, but most lavishly decorated with carved and gilded wood, and furnished with costly and sumptuous furniture for every office of the Hebrew worship. This was Jehovah's house, into which none but his priests might enter.

The levelled space around it was enclosed by walls and porches, the widest court of all being about a furlong square. Of its details no accurate notion can be had from the accounts preserved to us. It is enough to say, that apartments were reserved for a large number of attendants on the temple-service ; and that ample provision was made for sacrifices, or other public ceremonials, on the largest scale. The great brazen altar was thirty feet square and fifteen feet high. Its fire was kept always burning, and every facility was furnished for the despatch of the enormous number of victims sometimes slaughtered. In some of the many apartments were kept relics of the ancient tabernacle. Spacious courts were provided for the people, for women, and for

---

* They were probably similar to the winged bulls, or eagle-headed figures, found in Assyria and Egypt.

† Which the later account (2 Chron. iii. 4) converts into a tower near two hundred feet in height.

strangers. In the porches was ample space for walks, for conversation, and for teachers of wisdom with their classes. All was suitably adorned with colonnades, or single columns, with carved work, brazen utensils, prodigious vases of water, and sculptured forms of beasts. In short, while the temple proper was a building of moderate size and no architectural pretensions, remarkable chiefly for its rich Oriental symbolism, the marvellous wealth of its materials, and the sanctity of its relics, the entire structure, like a fort or castle, was as it were a city by itself, — a populous and busy little town, sacred by religious associations, and gorgeous with the perpetual pomp and splendour of the ritual.

For seven years and a half it was in building, under such skilful hands, that, it is said, every stone was carved and matched beforehand to fit its place, and not the blow of a hammer had to be struck in the whole long labour. When it was completed, a grand festival of fourteen days was proclaimed, to follow one of the yearly national feasts. The ark was carried in pomp from the city of David, and laid in its permanent resting-place in the shrine, beneath the outspread wings of the cherubim; — the last of its history, for when or how it perished was never told.* " Two and twenty thousand oxen, and an hundred and twenty thousand sheep," were

---

* Josiah is said (2 Chron. xxxv. 3) to have restored it to the shrine, whence it was taken by Manasseh; and a tradition is recorded (2 Maccabees ii. 5, 7) that Jeremiah, after the destruction of the temple, hid it in a cave on Mount Moriah, where it will be found at the final restoration of the chosen people.

slain as " the sacrifice of peace-offerings," — that is, for food as well as worship, — while the great brazen altar was too little for the slaughter, and all the court was " hallowed " with the sacred blood. For this occasion, or in memory of it, was composed the noble prayer of Dedication ascribed to Solomon ; and it is further added, that when the prayer was spoken a flame from heaven consumed the sacrifice, and Jehovah himself, in visible glory, entered the sacred place, so that the priests could not go in by reason of the intolerable splendour.

The debt of the Hebrew monarchy to the national religion and priesthood was now munificently paid. The holy orders were put upon such a footing that their existence was henceforth identified with that of the nation itself; and a religious centre was established, to be forever the object of the people's most tenacious loyalty and faith. In every possible way — by song, by imposing ceremonial, by solemn reading of the Law, by gathering to the sacred festivals — the temple at Jerusalem came to be associated with the enthusiastic and affectionate reverence of the Jewish mind. Long after the nation of Israel had passed away, when its very name became a reproach and its people a curse, the traditionary glories of its temple lived in the religious imagination of Christendom, and formed the first link in that chain of association which made Jerusalem the holiest of cities, and the type of the invisible glories of the kingdom of heaven.

On the footing of this magnificent establishment the Priesthood acquired new dignity, and the ritual was modelled upon a corresponding scale. It is to this period of the history, therefore, that we must ascribe the more full development of the Levitical institutions which make the chief burden of the Hebrew code. What had been gradually moulded out of old tribal customs, or adopted from the practice of neighbouring religions and sustained by the spontaneous reverence of the people, became now an Institution, fixed and upheld by public authority. The sacred order that waited on the sanctuary made a sort of Ecclesiastical Court, or tribunal to define the rules and conditions of all matters pertaining to religion. The Book of " Leviticus " contains the substance, or the earlier form, of the code of ecclesiastical law, and along with it a few traditionary relics and customs of the earliest time.* A foundation was laid for that prodigious aftergrowth of tradition, which, through Talmud, Cabbala, and the doctrine of Scribes and Pharisees, so overlaid and spoiled the native quality of the Hebrew faith. The form was more and more separated from the spirit. The pompous ceremonial became an enormous scheme of symbolism to the more reflective, a vain and superstitious show to those who looked at it outwardly, a narrow and enslaving formalism to those who would win merit by obedience, a fruitful source of scepticism to the critical temper of a later age. The hearty reverence of the most religious portion of the people could never be thoroughly identified with the

* This book contains no historical matter, properly speaking ; only in two or three instances a narrative form is given to some ritual enactment.

elaborate ritual or the requisitions of the priestly order. The more gorgeous the public show, the more removed from the simplicity of faith that worshipped in secret, and from the vivid, earnest, religious sense which kindles the souls of men as fire out of heaven. The founding of Solomon's Temple and the perfecting of its ritual became the first symptom of a separation of the form from the life. His reign discloses the first marked tokens of the prophetic as opposed to the priestly order. The germ was sown, and had already taken root, of that antagonism which displayed itself so fiercely in the time of Christ.

The entire system of Solomon's public works was carried out in the same spirit that founded his state-religion. All were for the enlarging and adorning of the royal city, for the confirming or ostentatious exhibiting of the royal authority. The labour of thirteen years was spent in the construction of separate palaces for himself and the queen, ostensibly to do honour to the dignity of his Egyptian bride; or, if a religious motive must be assigned, in order that she, pagan by birth and faith, might not dwell in the sacred city which David built. The king's house was greatly superior in extent, and only inferior in costly display, to the temple itself. A colonnade, with steps and galleries cut in the solid rock, was made to connect the two, that by a royal way Solomon might pass to the sanctuary to perform those priestly services which in old time made part of the office of a king.

Nothing could exceed the sumptuous splendour of the royal establishment, as shown in the details which have been preserved. All the vessels of the palace were of pure gold. As for silver, it was "nothing accounted of in the days of Solomon." A most costly equipage of horses and chariots was quartered in the several cities, or kept in attendance at the capital. Water was brought at great expense, for fountains to adorn the city, or for the uses of the temples, from sources so remote as the high grounds of Bethlehem; and, whether by nature or art, the lofty and rugged eminences of the capital were so faithfully supplied, that, in all the distress of the sieges it underwent, the torture of drought was never felt. The pool of Siloam, the healing intermittent spring of Bethesda, and an abundant fountain in the temple-court, supplied from the adjacent heights, were among the most conspicuous advantages of this now stately capital. Where the deep valley skirting the hills of Zion and Moriah spreads and slopes more gently towards the east, a royal garden, or, in the Oriental tongue, a paradise, was laid out in keeping with the luxury of the sumptuous court.*

To crown the whole, as the most brilliant exhibition of the royal magnificence, he had a seraglio of a thousand women, seven hundred of them being of eminent birth, princes' daughters, as they are called, retained, perhaps, as honourable hostages, and as signs of his wide-spread peaceable alliances.

Nor was the personal fame of the sovereign any way unworthy of these surroundings. It is his true and undisputed glory to have contributed as largely to the forming of his people's mind and taste, as his

* See Ecclesiastes ii. 4 - 9.

father had done to their character and national
strength. His wisdom seemed to the popular reverence to justify the Divine promise, " I have given
thee a wise and understanding heart, so that there
was none like thee before thee, neither after thee
shall any arise like unto thee ; " and it is added,
" God gave Solomon wisdom and understanding exceeding much, and largeness of heart, even as the
sand that is on the sea-shore ; and Solomon's wisdom
excelled the wisdom of all children of the east country, and all the wisdom of Egypt ; for he was wiser
than all men, and his fame was in all nations round
about. And he spake three thousand proverbs, and
his songs were a thousand and five. And he spake
of trees, from the cedar-tree that is in Lebanon even
unto the hyssop that 'springeth out of the wall : he
spake also of beasts, and of fowl, and of creeping
things, and of fishes. And there came of all people
to hear the wisdom of Solomon, from all kings of
the earth which had heard of his wisdom." *

The fond and exaggerating style of this report tes-
tifies to the powerful impression left by the new and
elaborate culture of the reign of Solomon, and it is
justified on the whole by what appears of the impulse
which he personally gave to the intellectual progress
of his time. Proverbial· philosophy and the rudiments of natural history — both of moderate rank in
the scale of intellectual achievement — are the departments characteristically assigned to him. The
friendly contests of wisdom, in which tradition reports him to have surpassed the king of Tyre and the

* 1 Kings iv. 29 – 34.

queen of Sheba, consisted in the pleasant play of wit, the guessing of riddles, and the neat and sagacious detecting of devices made to baffle his ingenuity.* The pointed turns of expression, the happy antithesis, the rounding of a sententious phrase, so as to give the effect of wit, are qualities in which such an age delights, and are plentifully shown in the specimens of his proverbs which have come down to us, reminding one of the style of intellectual play at the court of Charlemagne. A higher degree of cultivation and a more various stimulus of the intellect distinguished this golden age of the Hebrew history ; but for the more strongly defined and characteristic qualities of the national mind we must go to an earlier or later period, — to the odes of Deborah and David, the fervid religious poetry and eloquence of Isaiah.

The same cosmopolitan temper which initiated the commercial enterprise, and made both the "wisdom" and magnificence of Solomon's reign, set him most widely apart from the general type of Hebrew character. If it was shown in splendid works that rivalled Egyptian grandeur and Tyrian wealth, in a temple and ritual of unsurpassed gorgeousness, in the luxury and culture of a period of peace, it was shown, too, in acts which sundered him widely from the spirit of his people, cut short his dynasty, and divided the realm. Religion and liberty are the two main sources of a nation's collective life. Both were held to with a tenacious and jealous fondness, through all periods of their history, by the people of

* Of these the most noted was his distinguishing a garland of real from one of artificial flowers, by admitting a swarm of honey-bees.

Israel. Both were alike invaded by the encroaching centralism and the cosmopolite spirit of the king. The close of his reign exhibits the humiliating weakness of his decline from the national liberties and faith, and the popular disaffection resulting from his arbitrary exercise of power.

"For it came to pass," says the simple style of the narrative, "that when Solomon was old, his wives turned away his heart after other gods." It was politic in him doubtless, or so he thought, to indulge the religious customs of his foreign women of the harem; and to some it has appeared as if it were only a prudent toleration, like that which is the rule of policy in an intelligent modern state. But religious culture was not large or deep enough then, and could not be for many ages, to establish toleration on enlightened principle. The superstitions of alien tribes were not only of a gross and revolting, but of an aggressive sort. Some of them were licentious, and some of them were cruel; most, probably, both. If openly practised, they would certainly corrupt the popular morals, degrade the general apprehension respecting worship, and result in practical disloyalty to the spirit of the Hebrew institutions. Thus they were a direct invasion of the national character and faith; and, in this most decisive way, virtual treason against the state. The more wonder that they should have been due to the very man who so emphatically warned the Hebrew youth against the devices of "the strange woman which flattereth with her tongue."

That Solomon himself took that backward step in

religious culture, and became a worshipper of idols, is not positively said. That he shared in the bloody and horrid rites so revolting to his people's better sense seems hardly credible. At any rate, that popular sense made him responsible for the corruption which presently appeared in the national character and faith; and it was told of him, that he "went after Ashtoreth, the goddess of the Sidonians, and after Milcom [Moloch], the abomination of the Ammonites, and built an high place for Chemosh, the abomination of Moab, in the hill that was before Jerusalem." It was seen how false was that worldly policy of his which would purchase foreign favour at the price of his own people's fidelity; still more, how fatal was that despotic and alien custom of polygamy, so abhorrent to the best sense of the Hebrew mind, though the constant sign and type of Oriental magnificence. His numerous alliances, purchased at such a price, might gain a few years of deceitful peace, but were laying by the seeds of mischief for his successors. The priesthood might be loyal, for that was a royal institution and dependency;* but the prophetic spirit, which was but the intense expression and representative of the popular religious spirit, was roused to a resentful and settled hostility.

And the grandeur of his public works entailed its heavy cost. For twenty years together he had employed vast companies of men † in the cedar-forests and quarries of Lebanon, to procure timber and lime-

---

* See 2 Chron. viii. 15.

† In all one hundred and fifty thousand, with three thousand six hundred overseers, according to 2 Chron. v. 13 – 18.

stone, which were sent round in floats to Joppa; and had subsidized the king of Tyre to furnish skilful artisans. The supply of food for all these labourers was a separate and very heavy tax.* Costly and unprofitable enterprises of desert traffic were a drain upon his treasury, to say nothing of the burdensome charge of outposts and garrisons in unfriendly districts. These outlays were a severe strain upon the financial strength of a little state like Israel. We must reckon, besides, the enormous and wasteful establishment of royal houses and gardens, the maintaining of great troops of idle hands, the state equipage of horses and chariots,† and the lavish magnificence of the temple-worship. All had to be paid for by the taxing of a scattered and agricultural people, only beginning to be a commercial one. Successful trade might replenish the royal coffers, or a lucky stroke of policy or conquest might defer the threatening crisis of an invasion; but there was a steady drain upon the energies and resources of the state.

The expedients which Solomon devised to defer the evil day only aggravated the mischiefs of his mistaken policy. Not retrenchment, but heavier taxation, is the usual method a government takes in dealing with

---

* Compare Herodotus, II. 125.

† These were brought at great cost from Egypt (1 Kings x. 29), and were among the standing articles of trade, to supply the neighbouring regions. "The feelings of the pious," says Newman, "boded no good to Israel from this new force; and when, in the next reign, Egypt proved to be a victorious enemy, and the cavalry a useless arm of defence, it probably became a fixed traditional principle with the prophetical body, that this proud force was outlandish, heathenish, and unbelieving."

like embarrassments. A corps of tax-gatherers and purveyors, changed every month and set over every district of the land, exacted food for his establishment and revenue for his wasted treasury. Following the same centralizing policy which abolished the ancient Provinces of France, he merged the twelve tribes of Israel in twelve Departments, managed by as many administrators of finance.* Two of his own sons-in-law were in this ungracious but lucrative office; and this no doubt helped to widen the breach between the nation at large and the house of David. And for one other expedient, more humiliating and base than all the rest, he yielded up to Hiram, on consideration of a large advance of money, including perhaps payment of arrears, a border district, comprising twenty villages.† This vile act of arbitrary power shows the degrading straits to which the brilliant monarchy of Solomon was now reduced. How the popular feeling resented the trade and sale is shown in the story which went abroad, that the ancient name of *Cabul*, or worthless, expressed the disgust of Hiram when he came to view his bargain ; and the later account ‡ would even have it, that Solomon not only outwitted his ingenious ally, but quietly reannexed the province, proceeded to build up the villages, and " caused the children of Israel to dwell there."

The two strongest points of the national character, or prejudice, were thus wantonly affronted. A large portion of the people were thoroughly alienated from

---

* See 1 Kings, chap. iv.   ‡ 2 Chronicles viii. 2.
† 1 Kings ix. 10 – 14.

the reigning family. The lustre of David's name, and the early glories of Solomon, kept back any outbreak for a season; but symptoms were menacing even during his lifetime. What was worst of all, the intense religious feeling of the people was alarmed. Now for the first time appear prophets of eminent name whose influence was thrown against the kingly power, leagued as that was with the priesthood. Saul had defied the entire religious party among the people, and prophet and priest combined had broken his power and transferred it to a worthier hand. Now that class of men known as prophets shared the popular resentment. A large party were apparently disposed to try once more the dangerous experiment of undermining the people's loyalty, and bringing about another change of administration. A change must soon come, at any rate; and the more zealous were disposed to hasten it, even at the hazard of a revolution.

Jeroboam was a young man of marked energy and activity, one of the directors of the public works at Jerusalem. Solomon noted his valuable qualities, and promoted him to be governor of the central district, where the disaffection was greatest, — Ephraim resenting the loss of tribal privilege, and nursing the ancient feud against the rival house of Judah. As he went to assume his new charge, the prophet Ahijah seized the occasion to prompt the young man to open revolt. He snatched his mantle, tore it in twelve pieces, and gave him ten, — signifying that, of the parted kingdom, ten tribes would be pledged to follow him. Such an open act roused Solomon's suspicion; and, to avoid a premature struggle, Jeroboam fled to Egypt. Shishak (or Sheshonk) was king there now, of a new dynasty, and unfriendly to the monarchy of Jerusalem. With him Jeroboam remained in security, abiding his time.

At the first news of the old king's death, which happened shortly after, he hastened back to his native village to be ready for coming events. The time was now ripe for revolution. It was only precipitated by the blind obstinacy and folly of Rehoboam. No popular congress or diet made a regular part of the government; only at rare occasions were the people able to give voice, shape, and force to their collective will. They had borne their burden the more patiently, waiting for the Convention that should ratify the claim of the new king. They met at Shechem, the venerable patriarchal home of Israel, and here demanded a redress of grievances. Jeroboam was their spokesman. The bitter insolence of Rehoboam's answer has become proverbial: "My little finger shall be thicker than my father's loins; my father made your yoke heavy, and I will add to your yoke; my father chastised you with whips, but I will chastise you with scorpions." Then was heard once more the terrible war-cry that had rung in David's ear at the dissension of the tribes after Absalom's death: "What portion have we in David? neither have we inheritance in the son of Jesse. To your tents, O Israel! Now, David, guard well thy own house!"

And so, by a steady and intelligible train of causes, the short-lived monarchy of Israel was sundered. Henceforth, the unity of the Hebrew race is only ideal, — the sharing in one glorious memory and one undying hope. The larger fragment of the nation endured a troubled existence for rather more than two hundred and fifty years, till it was swallowed up by the grasping Assyrian realm, and the "ten lost tribes" disappeared forever from human history. The little kingdom of Judah, adhering to the capital, and cherishing the ritual and culture identified with its past era of prosperity and glory, preserved the line of historical descent unbroken. It continued an independent state for about four centuries; during which it gave birth to the later sublime embodiments of Hebrew thought and faith. With invincible tenacity, even after their conquest and captivity, the Jews kept their title to the Holy Land till a thousand years after the division; and to this very day their sons are looking patiently for the restoring of the kingdom of Israel in far more than its ancient glory.

The popular mind, though it could not trace the causes, felt the necessity, that led to this trying and fatal event. "This thing is from Jehovah," they said; and yielding easily to the counsel of Shemaiah, they forebore to contend against one another, and went home with a heavy heart, to live as a divided and alienated people.

From the course things had taken, this unhappy division was clearly a necessity, — as they reverently called it, a divine necessity. The fault of Solomon was, that he had not sagacity to foresee or wisdom to provide against it. The elements were wanting in him of a robust and manly character, of an educated will. His intellectual eminence was only that which comes from carrying out, in larger development and more elaborate culture, the elements of thought common to all average minds. His knowledge was extensive, his range of observation great; but, save in the plain ethics of every-day life, he never ascended above a low or medium plane of thought. There was no vigour of the higher faculty in him, no practical statesmanship, no moral earnestness, no intellectual grasp. In the main tendency of his mind he only drifted with the common tide, and his wisdom was all the more admired that it was wisdom which all could comprehend. In a position eminently demanding the exercise of the loftier and more generous faculties, he showed only a mean and ordinary soul.

It would seem to have required no consummate and superhuman wisdom to meet the problem of his time more worthily, — at least to avoid his fatal error. He had mental activity, but on a low plane; political talent, but rather of a subtile than comprehensive sort; ambition of splendour and national greatness, but no large popular sympathies. His was a short-sighted policy, a wilful, petulant, despotic rule. Unless he had the deliberate intention to absorb and crush the liberties of his people in one inexorable, absolute, central rule, and so was a traitor to the genius and destinies of the nation, and only failed for want of power in a design as profligate as it was able, — unless we save his intellect at the expense of his character, or his subtle policy at the

expense of both,— we must regard him as weak and
incapable at bottom, a man unfit for his station or
his trust.

In so judging him, we should only take from his
name its false glitter, and rate Solomon among ordinary men. It is only that he had not that rare
strength of will, that inspired loftiness of motive,
which would break through the network of circumstance. It is only that he did not reach the moral
elevation, where his naturally active and fertile mind
might work by the guiding of that God whom his fathers knew better than he. It is not to condemn him
personally to say that that critical time found not
its providential man in him. A Solon would have
been glorious precisely where Solomon was most
weak. He did not govern, but yielded to the baser
tendencies of his age. He followed to the uttermost
the path that happened to be open to him. He
developed fully the style of culture that humoured
the temper of the time. He magnified the glory
of the kingdom at the expense of its liberty and
quiet. His rule was fast tending to an unmitigated
and oppressive absolutism; and the nation was only
saved from that at the cost of its unity, its outward
vigour, and ultimately its existence.

VI. THE KINGS.

THE entire duration of the Hebrew monarchy was not far from five hundred years.* Of this period a century is occupied with the reign of the first three kings, down to the division of the kingdom. The remainder consists of three unequal periods: *first*, of rather more than a century (B. C. 985 – 883), to the bloody revolution of Jehu, which shattered both the royal houses, and led to a complete reconstruction of the monarchy; *second*, of a hundred and sixty-four years (B. C. 883 – 719), to the destruction of Samaria and the dispersion of the ten tribes; *third*, of about a hundred and thirty years (B. C. 719–586), to the capture of Jerusalem and the carrying away into Babylon. The first of these periods is marked by hostilities between Israel and Judah, merged finally in their alliance against Damascus; the second, by the struggles against Syria, followed by the conquering advance of the Assyrians; the third by violent religious contentions in the state of Judah, until it was finally overthrown by the Chaldæan conquest. The extinction of Hebrew nationality is just ten years later than the great constitutional reform of

* This is the reckoning of Ewald, from which Newman deducts thirty years, placing Solomon's death in 955.

Solon,—the first well marked and important event of the political history of Greece (B. C. 596).

I. The revolt of the ten tribes was a protest of the old Hebrew spirit against the system of religious and political centralization, which was already carried to such a length by Solomon. The blow was struck at the instigation of the prophets, representatives of the popular instinct of local freedom and religious independence. On the one hand, a deep-rooted jealousy had grown up against the increasing power and despotic temper of the monarchy, which in so many respects shocked the habits and moral feeling of the people ; and, on the other hand, the organized priesthood of Jerusalem roused the antipathy of those in whom the fire of the antique faith burned most vehemently. The people had been wonted from of old to the free worship of Jehovah on hill-tops and in the open air. Reasons of permanence, security, and uniformity might be urged in favour of the temple ritual, and the splendid establishment of the capital ; but it was hard to forego the immemorial rights and tribal privileges of the rural sanctuaries ; and even in Judah it was not till the great reformation achieved by Hezekiah that the "high places" were removed, and the worship of the brazen serpent was abolished.* Appealing to this confirmed popular sentiment, Jeroboam established at once two district sanctuaries, at Dan and Bethel, with symbolic images of Egyptian device, which the prophets called in derision his golden calves ; and when this irregular local worship had degenerated, and allied itself

* 2 Kings xviii. 4.

with corrupt foreign superstitions, his title was known
as by a proverb among the more religious of the
nation, as "the son of Nebat, who made Israel to
sin."

The protest against the centralizing and despotic
policy of the monarchy seemed at first likely to be
completely successful. It enlisted the popular sentiment, for it promised a return to the spirit of the
elder Hebrew institutions, — the "good old times"
of the Lawgiver and Judges. The deep-seated local
feeling and jealous independence by which the race
had been so strongly marked from the first seemed
in this revolt to fortify itself anew. The first patriarchal home in Canaan, the seat of Samuel's prophetic and of Saul's regal power, the abode of Joshua,
the great conqueror, and of Gideon, the champion
of the nation's independence, and the track of the
mythic migration under Jacob, the Prince of God, —
all were included in the region that now threw off the
hated supremacy of Judah. And so it claimed the
proud patriarchal name of ISRAEL, — changed (sometimes in scorn, sometimes in tenderness) to Ephraim,
when the frontier tribes were pressed by invaders,
and not much more than that citadel of power remained. It held sway over most of the conquests
that made up the empire of David and Solomon, —
except the great tributary, Damascus, which had
revolted successfully even in Solomon's time. The
upper Philistine coast, the country east of Jordan, as
far south as Moab and the Dead Sea, even Bethel and
Jericho, that bordered so closely on the capital, were
kept in the hands of this more powerful division.

And for many years it seemed no hopeless ambition to recover the strongholds of Judah, and extend the proud name of Israel over the whole territory claimed as the heritage of the race.

Meanwhile the smaller kingdom held itself on the defensive. The struggle to retain its hold upon the revolted district was at once given up as hopeless, and JUDAH began to gather slowly the elements of its isolated strength. Its first rallying force was seen in the thronging back to Jerusalem of the levitical body,* including, doubtless, a large portion of the more serious-minded and better-cultured of the nation, who were thoroughly disgusted with the lawless and retrograde temper shown in "the provinces." And then were seen the immense advantages of a firm and compacted organization. Jerusalem had already become the peculiar home of national memories and worship. The house of David had in its favour the habitual loyalty of near a century of successful and imposing rule. By far the greatest part of the intellectual culture, as well as religious prestige, was gathered about the court and capital. Here was a firm centre and a vigorous root of the national vitality. The region itself is one less tempting to the cupidity of an invader. While, accordingly, the larger kingdom was almost from the first distracted by the most violent feuds; while three royal houses were cut off in the second generation, and of the longest enduring every individual perished by a violent death; while the religious party, headed by Elijah and Elisha, was in almost

* 2 Chronicles xi. 14.

perpetual contention with the kings, and was at length bloodily extinguished,—in Judah, on the other hand, the sanctuary became the rallying-point of loyalty and faith; those institutions were matured whose powerful influence still outlives the downfall of the nation; the larger part of the Hebrew Scriptures were composed, constituting so marked an element in the literature of the world; and the Hebrew religious culture culminated in the splendid series of the Prophets.

It was not long before the causes that resulted in so striking a contrast were seen to be at work. The religious party that had instigated the revolt flattered itself, doubtless, with the prospect of being paramount in the new state; but it quickly appeared that it could never be anything more than a party, and generally one in opposition to the royal power. The fortune of the kingdom showed a return to "what was worst in the policy of Saul, with no delivering David." An able man like Jeroboam, whose notions of state policy and state religion were got from his experiences under Solomon and at the Egyptian court, was not likely to put himself in the hands of what he would regard as a fanatical sect, however indebted to it for the first germ of his power. It was an unscrupulous secular ambition that guided him, not any serious design of restoring the fond ideal of a theocracy. He shared the passion for royal splendour that had built the edifices of Jerusalem and Memphis, and for that despotic absolutism which was the only type he knew of monarchy. For reasons of policy, he transferred his capital first to

Peniel, beyond the Jordan, and then to Tirzah, whose beauty became proverbial as a rival to Jerusalem.* Ahab's ivory palace at Jezreel and the splendid hill-town of Samaria were later monuments of that taste for regal magnificence which was manifest from the very beginning of the Israelite monarchy.

An aggressive and military policy, too, marked the first years of the sundered state. An angry jealousy prevailed between Israel and Judah, so that the story of two or three of the early reigns is of continual war between them.† Shishak, king of Egypt, as ally of Jeroboam, menaced Jerusalem with a formidable invasion, and carried away, for spoil or tribute, "all" the magnificent gold furnishing of both temple and palace, which had to be replaced by brass. Baasha — who got the power by the massacre of all Jeroboam's family two years after his death — followed still more vigorously this hostile policy. He seized the frontier town of Ramah, and made it a military post to harass the traders or travellers of Judah, till Asa, the grandson of Rehoboam, took the richest remaining treasures of the temple and capital to muster the Syrian forces from Damascus, — seducing them from their alliance with Baasha, — and so forced him to quit the fortress, which was instantly demolished. Thus the first three reigns on either side exhibit the two kingdoms as bitter and jealous rivals, willing even to employ alien forces for each other's ruin. This desperate and fatal course

---

* See Canticles vi. 4.

† Jeroboam is said (2 Chronicles xiii. 17) to have been defeated with the loss of 500,000 in a single battle.

was not discontinued till Asa's son, Jehoshaphat, saw how much more the Syrian power was to be dreaded; and then, too late, by his disastrous league with Ahab, he endeavoured to make good the irretrievable error of the past.

The secular and vindictive temper shown by the monarchs of the northern kingdom could not but bring bitter disappointment and exasperation to the party that had prompted the revolution. It is related [*] how a prophet was divinely sent from Judah, with a message of doom to the apostate house of Jeroboam, — a doom frightfully accomplished in Baasha's massacre of every one who shared his blood; a message of such fearful moment, that the returning prophet was torn in pieces by a lion for staying so much as to taste of food. And Ahijah, the first counseller of the great revolt, bitterly deploring in old age and blindness the recreancy of the man he had selected as champion of the ancient faith, denounced a similar fatal message, when the wife of Jeroboam came to consult him concerning the sickness of her child. The religious party in Israel was becoming deeply alienated from the sovereign power; and a struggle was impending, in which that party, after displaying every extremity of heroism in endurance, and of even fierce and desperate resource in retaliation, was finally absorbed or suppressed, and Israel was left, to all intents and purposes, a heathen kingdom till its fall.

The crisis of this religious struggle was brought on by the tyrannical and persecuting temper of the third

* 1 Kings, chap. xiii.

reigning family, that of Omri. The son of Baasha
was killed at a drunken revel by Zimri, a court
officer, who, after a week's play at despotism, burned
the palace in despair over his own head. After a
few years' struggle with Tibni, (who perhaps held the
territory east of Jordan,) Omri had become both
avenger and successor of the fallen house. The
Philistines had been troublesome on one side, and
the realm distracted on the other by civil feuds ; and
to fortify himself, he renewed the old alliance with
the king of Tyre, and took Jezebel, the spirited and
beautiful Phœnician princess, as wife to his son
Ahab.

Ahab was a weak-minded, kind-tempered, well-
meaning man, ruled completely by the vindictive and
imperious temper of his wife. She made it her business to defy, insult, and if possible suppress the national religious spirit of the people. Her father Eth-
baal had been a priest, which may partly account
for the fervours of her religious rage. To what
length she carried her persecution we do not know,
nor what especial provocation may have induced it ;
only, that out of what was meant as an entire massacre of the body of prophets, Obadiah, a court
officer, hid a hundred, at the hazard of his life, in two
caves ; and that when Elijah fled to Sinai, he thought
himself the only survivor of the slaughter. In rivalry
of the great sanctuary of the Hebrew worship, she
built a gorgeous temple to the sun-god Baal, and had
it attended by four hundred and fifty priests. It was
apparently to insult and override in every way the
popular feeling she despised, that she violated the

sacred common law of the realm; causing Naboth, whose vineyard Ahab would annex to the royal gardens, to be stoned on a got-up charge of treason, and so confiscating the coveted estate.

Only one man was bold enough to confront steadily this storm of tyranny, — a man whose real influence and power are imperfectly represented in the splendid series of acts ascribed to him. The remarkable episode in the meagre annals of the kingdom which constitutes the personal history of Elijah and his successor affords the most valuable picture of the manners and popular feeling of the period. It is almost the only glimpse we have of the body of men known as the " prophets " of the northern kingdom; and, however perplexing in its details, it must be accepted as their historical legacy. It presents a combination, almost unique, of miraculous acts and bold personal adventure; and the period it describes may well be called the heroic age of Hebrew prophecy.

Elijah is the principal person of this religious epic, — a man who, for the boldness and splendour of his acts, his agency in restoring the worship of Jehovah, and the mystery of his final disappearance, has been placed even on the same high eminence with Moses, unapproachable by any other. In a time of drought and famine, which he predicts, ravens feed him by a solitary brook. When that dries up, he is supported by the unspent meal of a poor widow of Zarephath, whose dead child he brings to life. Demanding an interview with the king, and a public controversy with the priests of Baal, he convicts them by the

stupendous miracle of the kindling of the sacrifice
on Mount Carmel ; and the false priests are slaughtered by the popular vengeance, in retaliation for the
massacre' of Jehovah's people.   While the rain-storm
is gathering which puts a period to the long distress,
he runs before the king's chariot all the way to the
capital ; then, at the threats of Jezebel, we find him
as suddenly beyond the southern frontier of Judah.
Strengthened by miraculous food, he fasts forty days
in the bleak peninsula of Sinai ; and then comes that
noble scene, in which God reveals himself, not in the
rushing wind, or earthquake, or fire, but in the "still
small voice."   He is sought after Ahab's death by
his son Ahaziah, who was crushed fatally by a fall
from the palace window, that his prophetic skill may
tell the chances of life and death ; and twice a company of fifty men, with their commander, perish by
fire out of heaven, to insure his inviolability.   Finally, when the season of his labour is over, he is
taken up in a fiery chariot, in full sight of Elisha,
upon whom his mantle falls as his successor.*

The acts ascribed to Elisha are a series somewhat
similar, as if a certain parallelism had been observed
in them.   The chief difference is, that they denote a
career less wild and lonely, but of far greater political
importance, and greater variety of human interest.
Several of Elisha's miracles are wrought in the service of a community or school of younger prophets.
He has a permanent home in the dwelling of the

* The only allusion to him in Chronicles is the mention of a letter
sent to the king of Judah, after the supposed time of his ascension.
(2 Chron. xxi. 12.)

wealthy Shunamite. He accompanies the army of
Judah in an attack upon the Moabites, and miraculously obtains water in the parched soil of the desert
for the distressed camp. Twice his foresight was the
means of saving Israel from the Syrians, and it was
by his agency their armies were alarmed from the
siege of Samaria. For fifty years he was held in
singular honour by nearly every king who reigned
in Israel. On his death-bed Jehoash hailed him "the
chariot and horseman of Israel," in testimony of his
powerful championship; and long after his death his
bones restored to life a dead body that chanced to be
placed in contact with them. The esteem in which
he was held reached as far as Damascus, where we
find him, on a friendly visit, predicting the king's
decease and the coming calamities of his country;
and among his miracles is recorded the healing of
Naaman, a Syrian officer, of his leprosy.

But the political agency of Elisha was most decisive
in this, — that he brought about that bloody revolution in which Jehu extinguished the idolatrous family of Omri, and closed the first period of the Israelite
monarchy.

The reign of Ahab had been weak and ineffectual.
State power being utterly divorced from popular
faith or feeling, the kingdom appears to have been
in a perpetual decline. The close of the first century
of the monarchy was marked by defeat and shame.
Damascus, whose power had been courted by each
of the kingdoms in their short-sighted rivalry, was
beginning now to overshadow both. Samaria itself
had been beleaguered and reduced to the last straits

by famine; and two women wrangled about the
keeping of a horrid agreement, to kill and share the
bodies of their babes for food. The territory east of
Jordan was hard pressed by Syria. To defend it,
Jehoshaphat, whose wise and vigorous rule had restored the prosperity of Judah,* formed a close alliance with Ahab; and to screen him from personal
danger had in the last and fatal battle put on his
armour, while Ahab was apparalled as a private
soldier. But Micaiah's bold prophecy of disaster,
spoken in a gathering of four hundred prophets who
all predicted that the alliance would be triumphant,†
proved true. Ahab was killed by a chance arrow-
shot, and his body borne away by the retreating
force. His elder son Ahaziah died of his fall (before
alluded to), and Jehoram was badly wounded in the
same disastrous war in which his father perished.
Then Elisha, despairing of the kingdom unless some
desperate blow were struck against the apostate and
ill-fated house, sent by a swift messenger and anointed Jehu, who was now commander of the army, com-
missioning him to take vengeance on those that had
dealt so cruelly with the faithful.

Jehu was a hasty, crafty, unscrupulous man; one
not to hesitate in fulfilling such a commission, even
to the horror of those who had given it to his hands,
—if, indeed, the exasperated temper of the persecuted party would shrink at any degree of vengeance.
He struck his blow without delay. By swift relays
of horses he drove to the palace at Jezreel, met

---

* See 2 Chron., chap. xvii.
† See the remarkable narrative in 1 Kings, chap. xxii.

Jehoram in Naboth's vineyard, struck him with a
javelin through the back as he turned to fly; then
gratuitously slew the king of Judah, Ahaziah, grandson of Jehoshaphat, who happened to be with him.
He next ordered Jezebel to be flung out of the palace-
window, and trampled her under his horses' feet; then
directed the massacre of seventy of Ahab's kindred,
and of forty-two who were coming unsuspiciously
from Judah; and ended by enticing a great crowd
of Baal-worshippers to the temple, under pretence of
solemn sacrifice, and slaughtering them all. This
frightful series of massacres stifled for the present
the alien worship, and introduced a new period of
seeming, though transient, vigour. But the nation
could not easily recover from the guilt and terror
of such a season; and "in those days," says the an-
nalist, "Jehovah began to cut Israel short." Hazael
of Damascus, whose murder-purchased rule Elisha is
related to have foretold to him, fulfilled the prediction of cruelly ravaging the land. The people in
their distress were driven from their old pastoral
courses, and no longer "dwelt in tents as before-
time;" while their military equipment was beaten
to pieces and made "like the dust by threshing."
From Israel were wrested Gilead and Bashan, or
almost all that lay eastward of the Jordan; and
Hazael was only bought off from Jerusalem by gifts.
It was not till half a century later that Samaria recovered for a while the external security it had lost.

II. Thus the civil and religious forces of the northern kingdom had nearly annihilated each other in
their long struggle. Its crisis, just related, reacted

on the sister realm, in a revolution, almost as violent, but far less disastrous in its results. Athaliah, the daughter of Jezebel and queen-mother at Jerusalem, revenged herself on the party of Jehovah — treating them as authors of the massacre in which her kindred had perished — by putting to death the whole royal family, and establishing a dynasty of Baal-worshippers, which lasted six years. But in a series of politic and able reigns, especially those of Asa and his son Jehoshaphat,* the priesthood had become greatly confirmed in its power, and was prepared to make its own terms with royalty.† Jehoiada, in the name of the child Joash, who had been secreted and saved from the massacre by an adroit and bold conspiracy, restored the house of David.

For about twenty years there was now a peaceful regency of priests. It was no season to attempt any hazardous stroke of policy, or to challenge the strength of parties that might be hostile to the ruling power. Peace must be had at any cost. The position and temper of the priestly regency would secure it at home; and in such a season of weakness it was purchased abroad by large gifts, to stay the threatened incursion of the Syrians. The young king, under his foster-father's guidance, went easily and willingly along in the lines of the priestly policy. It was not till after Jehoiada's death, and he began to doubt the

---

* See in Chronicles the extraordinary expansions of the simple narrative of the Kings as to these two reigns. (2 Chron. chaps. xv.–xvii.) Asa routs an Ethiopian force of a million men and three hundred chariots, while Jehoshaphat keeps a standing army of 1,260,000.

† The mention of the Sabbath now first occurs in the historical books. (2 Kings xi. 5, 7.)

priests' good faith in appropriating the pious contributions for the repairs of the temple, that he showed any disposition to take the reins of government himself. This led to another feud of royalty and priesthood; to accusations of the king's apostasy; and even to the charge * that his own cousin Zechariah perished by his order, "between the temple and the altar." Joash himself at last fell a victim to the disaffection growing out of these party strifes, being assassinated by his own servants. The twenty years' rash and unfortunate reign of Amaziah † followed before the kingdom regained its full prosperity and strength under Uzziah.

Meanwhile, the work of religious and intellectual cultivation had found a favouring impulse in the regency of priests. To that period is generally referred the beginning of written prophecy, — a product of the Hebrew mind widely different from the extemporized political or religious agencies known by that name in the earlier age of Israel. A severe plague of locusts had ravaged the land in a series of devastations, coinciding with the menaces or injuries which Judah was enduring from neighbouring powers. This called forth the brief but noble composition of Joel, which announces the moral of that scourge in a powerful appeal to the popular conscience, — the demand of sacrificial penance, the lofty promise of the outpouring of God's spirit for the final deliverance of Judah, and the grateful assurance of revenge.

* 2 Chron. xxiv. 20–22.

† In which three thousand *cities of Judah* are said (2 Chron. xxv. 14) to have been smitten by the Israelites.

Tyre, which had kidnapped their children for sale in Greece,* should be enslaved to Judah; while Egypt and Edom should become a desolation.

From this time forth, the changing fortunes of the time are most faithfully reflected in the prophetical writings. Uzziah's long reign, of more than fifty years, was in the main a season of prosperity and peace. The frontier was secured at the south, and the fortifications of the capital were kept in good repair. And, while the more religious of the people bewailed the avarice and corruption that came in with the arts of peace, and seemed to flood the land with the vices of the old Canaanites,† they yet improved the leisure given, for culture and the practice of written composition. The eventful time that followed found its utterance in Amos, Hosea, Isaiah, and Micah. While ominous clouds hung in the horizon, still higher and higher rose the strain of prophecy; and Isaiah's triumphant predictions of a Messiah ‡ were uttered when the king of Israel had allied himself with a foreign invader for the ruin of Judah, when the most formidable power the world had yet known was lowering in the far northeast, and "the king's heart and the heart of his people were moved, as trees of the forest are moved with the wind." §

In the eighty years that had elapsed since Elisha's death, great changes had come upon the northern king-

---

* Compare Odyssey, XV. 414.   † See Isaiah, ch. iii. – v.

‡ Isaiah, ch. vii. – ix.

§ Ibid., vii. 2. Compare Ewald, Die Propheten des Alten Bundes, Vol. I. p. 294.

dom. The long and vigorous reign of Jeroboam II.
had secured a good degree of external security and
strength, and had even restored for a time the old
boundaries of Israel. But causes of dissolution were
at work within. Amos, the " herdsman of Tekoah,"
a petty town of Judah, had given himself to earnest
missionary service in the north; and he powerfully
depicts the military oppression, the wantonness of
wealth, the riots, lewdness, and idolatry that accompanied the external prosperity and splendour of
Jeroboam's rule. Hosea, the only remaining native
prophet of the north, — whose passionate yet tender
objurgations were mostly made during the convulsions that followed Jeroboam's death, — was persecuted by his own countrymen, and driven into Judah,
where he wrote out his ministrations at his leisure.
Thus the prophetic body, once so numerous there,
and identified with so much of fanaticism and violence in their earlier projects to recover the kingdom
from apostasy, had utterly died out; and was not,
as in Judah, replaced by that body of men of calmer
temper and more cultivated mind whom we in general understand by that name. There remained
nothing to give permanence to the religious ideas,
or a higher tone to the personal and home life of the
people. It was an age of deep moral corruption, as
well as of violence and crime. A series of assassi-
nations following the death of Jeroboam disabled
the monarchy from keeping any hold on the popular
loyalty, or adhering to any clear line of policy. The
terrible Assyrian invasion, long menaced by the
prophets, and only deferred a little by the bribe with

which Menahem bought a longer lease of his brutal despotism, came in the reign of Pekah, and swept away the northern and eastern portions of Israel, — "Zebulon, Naphtali, the parts beyond Jordan, and Galilee of the Gentiles," — and by a cruel and forced migration drove the inhabitants to live in the strange country beyond the Euphrates.* At length Hoshea, the last who reigned in Samaria, slew Pekah for his dastardy, and strove for seven years to retrieve the failing fortunes of the kingdom.

The Assyrians were a formidable nation from the north, flushed with recent conquest, and sweeping on terrifically with the barbarous hordes of Scythians and Kurds, or Chaldæans, in their train. The passion of dominion was carrying them towards Egypt, that land so tempting for its ancient fame and wealth to every conqueror, from Sennacherib to Napoleon. Syria, Phœnicia, and the several tribes of Palestine lay in the track of that terrible march. Resistless as destiny, it seemed as if it were only a question of time, when one by one they should be crushed and overpassed.

Ahaz, king of Judah, after an invasion from Pekah, leagued with Rezin of Damascus,† and while still menaced by Edom and the Philistines, had taken

---

* The prophet Nahum was born of one of the families of this captivity. He witnesses and describes, a century later, the gathering ruin of Nineveh under the invasion of the Medes.

† For a vivid description of the circumstances leading to this invasion, see Newman's "Hebrew Monarchy," 2d edit., pages 228 – 230. The alliance of Pekah and Rezin stripped Judah of its commercial outposts on the Red Sea, and might have resulted in the fall of the kingdom, but that Ahaz (whose "crime was that at the age of twenty

the desperate step of inviting this formidable power with bribes to the attack of his allied neighbours, Syria and Israel. Tiglath-pileser had captured Damascus, accordingly, and then swept into his net the outlying districts of Israel; so that Pekah (as was just mentioned) found himself a vassal and tributary, and was slain by Hoshea, who resolved on a policy of bold resistance. He masked this policy for a time by the tribute he still continued to pay the Assyrians, meanwhile negotiating terms of alliance with Egypt.

But internal commotions in this latter country rendered the Egyptian alliance "a broken reed, which if a man lean on, it should pierce his hand." A struggle there between the military and priestly caste made it impossible for Sethon to render any real service. The correspondence was detected. The threatened nations were preparing for a combined resistance. Hoshea was instantly seized, and sent as prisoner to Nineveh, and Shalmanezer laid siege to Samaria.

The downfall of the kingdom was now at hand. Its internal disorganization was such that its national life could not have endured long in vigour at any rate. Crippled by its recent losses, it had little to depend upon except the main strength of its fortifi-

he could not withstand the combined force of Damascus, Israel, Philistia, Edom, and perhaps Moab") sent to offer his allegiance to the Assyrian monarch, who presently swept away the Syrian force, captured Damascus, and reduced Samaria to the condition of vassalage. The Chronicler adds (2 Chr. xxviii. 6, 8) to the disasters of Pekah's invasion the slaughter of 120,000 in a day, and the capture of near twice as many prisoners, who are restored without ransom at the intercession of the prophet Oded.

cations, the unskilfulness of its besiegers, and the resolution of despair. For three years Samaria continued to hold its assailants at bay. The conflict was watched with anxiety and terror by the neighbouring population of Judah. Some of the most pathetic and earnest of the prophetic odes* cluster about this critical point of the Hebrew fortunes; and the epitomist departs from his usual meagre brevity,† as he mournfully sums up the reasons of that downfall in the nation's corrupted life and departure from its faith. Samaria fell, and the kingdom of Israel was blotted out. Its people were taken to fill the vast spaces of the half-built Assyrian capital, or else were distributed among the subject districts.‡ The ten tribes were utterly extinguished, and had no longer a name or place in human history. The rich territory of Samaria and Galilee lay half wild until its scattered colonists were in terror from the increase of wild beasts upon them, and sought to be instructed in the worship of Jehovah, as the local god, who might be able to protect them.§ A few missionary priests were sent to dwell among them, and the mongrel religion that grew up was the heresy of the Samaritans, — most hateful of all misbeliefs to the Jew, who prided himself on the strict purity of his creed. A scanty remnant of the sect still forms a little community in Palestine.

* Isaiah, chaps. xxviii.–xxxii.
† 2 Kings, chap. xvii. The book purports to be only an abstract, or compend, from more copious annals. The conqueror of Samaria was Sargon. (See Rawlinson's Herodotus.)
‡ A policy of mercy, as following the frightful barbarities of the siege. See Layard.
§ 1 Kings xvii. 26.

It was fortunate for Judah, at this period, that the weak and idolatrous reign of Ahaz — who had bartered for the Assyrian alliance both the treasures of the temple and the independence of the state * — was followed by that of Hezekiah, perhaps the noblest and best of all the Hebrew kings, whose trusted counsellor was Isaiah, the noblest and best of all the Hebrew prophets. For once, the secular and spiritual forces of the kingdom were brought into complete harmony; and the result was a firm attitude and ultimate security amidst the most formidable impending dangers. It was early in Hezekiah's reign that the northern kingdom was submerged in the flood of Assyrian invasion; and to most it seemed inevitable † that the same fate must follow for Jerusalem. But the spirit of the great prophet remained undaunted. His timely counsel averted each base expedient, and fortified the sometimes wavering resolution of the king. In the wanton invasion from Pekah and Rezin, he had foretold the triumphant advent of Judah's new sovereign, the " prince of peace." ‡ He had warned Damascus of her fall, and bidden Philistia not to exult in the desolation that seemed impending over Judah.§ It was his counsel or vehement appeal that defeated the proposed treaty

---

* By means of which, indeed, says Newman, he husbanded the resources which afterwards proved effectual in the crisis then impending.

† Even, apparently, to the prophet Micah (iii. 12), who speaks as a country villager (i. 10 - 15) of the events which Isaiah witnessed from the capital.

‡ Isaiah, chaps. vii. - ix. See, also, Zechariah, chaps. ix. - xi., which are referred to this period.

§ Isaiah xvii. 14.

with Assyria, and deposed the king's minister, Shebna,
who was too ready to yield the claim of tribute; and
so committed the state to its final attitude of resistance.*   He even boldly rebuked the favourite policy
of seeking aid from Egypt, — chariots and horsemen
in exchange for subsidies of men and money to fight
for the common deliverance.†   When Tyre maintained alone the desperate battle of her independence, and for five years delayed the stroke that
menaced the little state of Judah, his clear eye saw
the causes of ruin at work within, and he seemed
even with a sort of triumph to anticipate the period of her downfall, predicting that this trader-
city, splendid but corrupt, "whose merchants were
princes, and her traffickers the honourable of the
earth," would utterly perish before the terrible invader.‡   But this doom was to be deferred for yet
many centuries.   While the rest of Phœnicia was
overrun, Tyre held out bravely in her island-fortress;
her little squadron of twelve battle-ships vanquished
the hostile fleet of sixty; § and Sennacherib, who succeeded to the baffled Shalmanezer, hastened to the
easier conquests of the south.

The Hebrew king had not failed to improve the
opportunity of delay.   The fortifications of Jerusalem were freshly repaired and manned.   The policy
of the Egyptian alliance was held in reserve, if not
positively acted on.‖   An Ethiopian embassy, from

* Isaiah, chap. xxii.   † Ibid., chap. xxxi.
‡ Ibid., chap. xxiii.
§ Grote's Greece, Chap. XVIII.; Josephus, IX. 14, 2.
‖ 2 Kings xviii. 21.

the far highlands of Africa, came to negotiate in Jerusalem for mutual defence against a power that seemed to aim at the conquest of the world.* The firm and powerful league thus secured among the menaced nations, the successful defence of Tyre, and, possibly, the threatened revolt of Babylon, all combined to check what had seemed the resistless invasion of Sennacherib. While he was engaged in securing the conquest of the hill-country and the sea-board, the terror of the capital (excited probably by the dreadful barbarities exercised on Lachish †) had gone so far that Hezekiah sent him propitiatory gifts, and would have become his vassal but for his treacherous attack and the insolent terms he offered, which drove the nation upon a last desperate defence.

But the storm of invasion passed away as mysteriously and suddenly as it had been formidable in its gathering. Sennacherib was turned aside from Judah by the rumour of an Ethiopian host said to be gathering in his rear. To oppose his attack, the Egyptians had only a suddenly mustered force of artisans, over whom the Assyrian records claim a signal victory. But an invisible power, which both Hebrew and Egyptian represent as a special interpo-

---

* See 2 Kings xix. 9 and Isaiah, chap. xviii., in which the prophet bids the messengers return and announce the impending ruin of the Assyrians. Ethiopia was the power that now ruled in Upper Egypt. (Newman, p. 263.)

† Which are represented in detail in the sculptured works of Nineveh. (See Layard's "Babylon and Nineveh," p. 149.) The inscriptions coincide with the Hebrew narrative, as to the exact number of golden talents of Hezekiah's tribute. For Isaiah's message of defiance, on hearing of these enormities, see chap. xxxiii.

9 .   M

sition of the Divine Protector, baffled the conquering
host. According to the narrative of the latter, the
Assyrian army, after crossing the desert, was encountered on the Egyptian border by a multitude of field-
mice, which gnawed their shield-thongs, quiver-bands,
and bowstrings, and so rendered the whole equipment
worthless.* As the Hebrew account proceeds, the
forces of Sennacherib were advancing upon Jerusalem, and the city lay in a hush of terrified expectation,
when the angel of Jehovah, in the form of a deadly
pestilence, destroyed in a single night a hundred
and eighty-five thousand men. The discomfited
king hastened back to his capital, where he presently
encountered the revolt of the warlike Medes, the open
hostility of Babylon, and the impending dissolution
of his empire. He perished by assassination at the
hands of his own sons ; but not before the victories
and splendours of his reign had converted the wide
district-city of Nineveh into a capital of unparalleled
magnificence.

The sudden deliverance exalted to the highest pitch
both the glory and the confidence of Judah. The
fame of Hezekiah, the first of monarchs who had
turned back the fury of Assyrian conquest, spread as
far as to the revolted satrap of Babylon, and messengers from Merodach-Baladan came to solicit the alliance of Jerusalem,—a policy which Isaiah prudently
discouraged. A later composition of the great proph-
et† expresses his confidence that the tumults and
commotions now prevailing in Egypt ‡ might be Je-

---

* Herodotus, II. 141.   † Isaiah, chap. xix.
‡ See Herodotus, II. 141, 147, 151.

hovah's method of winning that ancient kingdom from idolatry, so that a reign of peace might come, and hate might cease, and alliance and harmony prevail between Egypt, Assyria, and Judah. Songs of victory and prophetic odes of this period,* still further express the temper of a fond and exulting confidence, which was the reaction from long dismay. Trust in the inviolability of Zion's sacred hill, sufficiently defended by the arm of its invisible Champion and Deliverer, and by

> "Siloa's fount that flowed
> Hard by the oracle of God,"

became a point of religious faith, which it were almost traitorous to doubt, — a fatal confidence it proved, leading to rash contempt of real dangers, and bitterly rebuked, a century later, in the overthrow of the holy city and the pillage of the temple by Nebuchadnezzar. But for the present there was no such drawback to the nation's exalted and kindling hope ; and Hezekiah recovered from what seemed a fatal sickness, taken as some have thought by the contagion of that great pestilence, to live fifteen years longer, as in answer to his pathetic prayer, and finally to close his life in glory and peace.

III. The closing century of the Hebrew monarchy is almost equally divided between two violent — and, in their later consequences, fatal — revolutions affecting the political interests along with the religion of the kingdom.

Manasseh was but a boy of twelve when he came to the inheritance of his father's crown. There were

* Psalms xlvi., xlviii., lxv., lxxv., lxxvi.

now apparently no men of eminence, of the party most faithful to the national institutions, to claim a controlling influence in his counsels. Isaiah had probably died during the latter portion of Hezekiah's reign.* The young king fell under the control of the men who had brought on the disgraces of the rule of Ahaz. Comparisons began to be drawn to the disadvantage of the Jewish state, in point of opulence and refinement, between that and neighbouring regions. The Hebrew faith had not emancipated itself from the limited and exclusive sense which had once been a matter of necessity. The more generous temper of Isaiah or Micah was by no means reflected in the general religious mind. What we call liberality and tolerance was most likely unfitted to the temper of the nation, and unsuited to the condition of the time. Exclusiveness may have been the price which even the best were too glad to pay for zeal. At any rate, no common ground seems to have been found for the two parties in Judah to occupy together. The supremacy, even the security, of one could be purchased only by the ruin of the other.

It may be, too, that some actually existing religious wants and longings were imperfectly met by the Hebrew faith, at least in the popular understanding of it. Mosaism stood always in an attitude either of aggression or defence before the religions of the world. Being essentially an antagonistic and not a reconciling faith, it was very likely to reject elements of culture which should have been freely sought.

---

* The tradition that he was sawn asunder in Manasseh's persecution has neither proof nor probability.

By its rejection of Christianity, long after, it condemned itself to stand forever in the light of history as a truncated religion. Its own intellectual manhood it never reached. Something its intrinsic character seems always to have lacked for its own harmony and fulness; and when this could not be supplied from a higher intellectual or moral type, it would naturally be sought elsewhere.

We find indications of this fact in the people's obstinate attachment from of old to the relics of Canaanite superstition,* and in the craving now exhibited for foreign mysteries and rites. In imitation of Babylonish or Syrian custom, Ahaz had introduced chariots and horses of the sun-god, and built a " sundial," or watch-tower, to observe the courses of the stars. Manasseh now followed still further this policy of his grandfather. Star-worship was again assiduously cultivated. The horrid rites of Moloch were performed afresh by making the king's own children " pass through the fire " in honour of that grim idol; and the vale of Hinnom, with its ghastly mound for sacrifice,† became the polluted place which it ever after remained in the imagination of the Jew. Altar and ark were taken from the temple. In retaliation for Hezekiah's vigorous reform, the first example was set in Judah of making the foreign religion an exclusive, inexorable, persecuting faith. As if to

---

* See 1 Kings, chap. xvii.

† This is one probable signification of the name " Tophet," which has been variously held to denote the place of *loathing, burning, burial,* or of the *drum,* which instrument, it is said, was used to drown the victims' cries. See Gesenius ; also Ghillany, " Die Menschenöpfer der alten Hebräer."

provide against future disasters, foreign divinities
were assiduously sought; for it was one of the superstitions of antiquity, that so the gods of other nations
might be propitiated, and the power of their wor-
shippers reduced. And, as a final defiance of the
prejudices of his countrymen, the king's son was
called by the Egyptian name Amoun, as if he were
devoted from his birth to that divinity of the realm
of sand.

The religious spirit of the people was utterly de-
pressed. No one was found to wear the mantle that
had•been borne so worthily by an Elijah or an Isaiah.
That nobler generation of prophets had passed away.
Those who now bore the name were " dumb dogs that
would not bark;" and if Ezekiel * charges the prophets of his time with magic rites, it is because they too
shared in the demoralization of this unhappy period,
and had learned to distrust the efficiency of the genuine Hebrew faith. Those who were so bold as to
resist the invading superstitions were mercilessly put
down, until " Jerusalem was filled with blood from
one end to the other;" and a large number, despairing of life or peace otherwise, took refuge in Egypt,
among those who had fled thither in terror of the
Assyrian invasion.

The long reign of Manasseh, the longest in the
Hebrew annals, thus witnessed the violent persecution of the ancient faith of Israel, and the expatria-
tion of those who should have been the centre of the
nation's strength. The price thus paid seems for a
long time to have secured the outward tranquillity

---

* Chap. xiii. 17.

which was partly its motive. Judah was for this whole half-century unmolested by foreign enemies. Nothing is told in the earlier narrative of any other events than those touching the religious affairs of the kingdom; and the later account, that Manasseh was carried captive to Babylon, where he repented and afterwards made public atonement of his wrong, reads like a moral apologue, or a veil to disguise the unbroken tranquillity of so impious a reign.*

But the retribution attending the king's criminal policy fell heavily upon the nation after his death. His cruelties were speedily avenged in the assassination of his son. He had deeply affronted the most sacred sentiments and recollections of his people; and he was long after † regarded as the real author of the nation's downfall. The popular conscience, though silenced for a time, would be heard at length. A revolution had been long preparing in men's thoughts; which, in the reign of Josiah, immediately succeeding, was carried out in the stern policy of retaliation.

Perhaps it is at this period that we are to date the beginning of the influence, afterwards so decisive and profound, of Egyptian culture upon the Hebrew mind. A long residence in Egypt had given to a body of intelligent, religious, and faithful men leisure for recasting the memories and old records of their nation, after the model formed by the style of thought illustrated in the prophets. The early history was in

---

* 2 Chronicles xxxiii. 11 – 17. The account makes him to be taken to Babylon by the Assyrians, now in the later stage of their decline; while his reign is directly followed (as in Kings) by the idolatries of Amon. Ewald, however, accepts Manasseh's captivity as a fact.

† See Jeremiah xv. 4.

some measure re-written in this spirit, and made to preach the lessons of the day. Debarred from the favourite forms of the prophetic appeal and occasional ode, the Hebrew writers of the time carried the thought and style of prophecy far back into the legendary past. The eventful history of the nation was read in the kindling light of that religious and providential significance with which early faith and later memory fondly clothed it. Especially the book of Deuteronomy, the " later law," was very probably composed about this time, — from some indications in Egypt itself; * and a foundation was laid, in the earnest, solemn, and impressive character of that most remarkable of the prophetic books, for what was afterwards carried out in practice as the " Deuteronomical Reform." †

The volume of the Law, thus completed and recast, found its way to Jerusalem, and made the most profound impression on the young King Josiah, to whom it was presented by the priest. It formed at once the rallying-point of reviving loyalty, and a channel for the returning tide of patriotic faith. From this

---

* See Deuteronomy xxiii. 7; xxviii. 68.

† This view is suggested by Ewald, and coincides with the analogies which have long been observed between some details of the Hebrew ritual, as recounted in Deuteronomy, — especially the formula of blessing and cursing, — with similar forms in the Egyptian liturgy. It is adopted here, not on critical grounds chiefly, but in order to present a fair, connected view of this portion of the admirable narrative of Ewald. By the aid of a doubtful chronology, the reform here spoken of has been connected with the reform of the "nature-religion" in India by Buddha, in Persia by Zoroaster, and in Greece by Xenophanes and others. (See Mackay's "Progress of the Intellect," Vol. II. p. 438.)

time forth, with more or less of variation, the Pentateuch, which was previously unknown, at least as a
whole, to king or people, became the central object
of Jewish veneration, and began to be preserved with
religious care. Its stern admonitions against apostasy, reflecting the temper roused in that bitter time
of persecution, were observed in Josiah's zealous
abolition of all traces of alien worship ; while the
humane and gentle spirit of the later law, embodying the sorrows and sympathies of exile, was carried
out in his merciful and popular rule.

The reform begun under royal auspices was heartily responded to by the people. A brief period followed of prosperity and glory. Only the deep wounds
inflicted by these successive and too violent changes,
together with fresh perils from abroad, prevented a
complete regeneration of the Hebrew state. The religious spirit could scarce avoid being affected by the
precision, formalism, and pedantic dogmatism which
would result from the reverence now encouraged towards sacred books and institutions. A tyrannous
and violent apostasy had brought on a violent recoil.
There was something, indeed, spasmodic in the entire
conduct of the reform, as its details are hinted in
our brief chronicle ; and the incessant complaints of
Jeremiah and Ezekiel show how little the general
character of the people was penetrated by the spiritual doctrine so rigorously enforced.

Meanwhile, the gathering forces of rival empires
threatened new calamities from the northeast. The
conquering progress of the Medes, before whom the
splendid capital of the Assyrians already tottered to

its fall,* was checked by a sudden irruption of one
of those Scythian or Tartar hordes from Central Asia,
causing the same consternation among the more civilized nations as was felt in Europe at the invasion
of the Huns. They came as far as Palestine, where
the frightful desolation of their inroad, as of wild
beasts rather than men, is told in all images of horror
by the prophets; † and, under the obscure name of
Magog, they have furnished the Scripture imagery
for the terrors of the latter day. But an undisci-
plined barbarian horde spreads and loses itself, like
water in the sand, or else is drafted into the service
of some more civilized power. The Scythians were
thought to have been struck with "womanish disease," or nervelessness, in vengeance for their rob-
bery of a Syrian temple of Astarte; their chieftains
were massacred by the Medes at a banquet where
they had been received as guests; and, being enrolled
in the Assyrian forces during their last defence, theirs
is perhaps one of the unknown tongues of the Ninevite inscriptions. The brief tempest spent itself; and
within thirty years the great powers were ready to
begin their game anew.‡

The fortunes of Judah now hastened rapidly to a
crisis. Josiah may have relied on some favouring
oracle,§ declaring him the invincible champion of

---

* See the spirited description of Nahum, who writes as an eyewit-
ness of their invasion. Compare Herodotus, I. 102.

† See Zephaniah; Jeremiah, chap. iv.–vi.; Psalm lix.

‡ Herodotus, I. 103–106.

§ Huldah had foretold (2 Kings xxii. 20) that he should be "gathered to his grave in peace," without witnessing the calamities that
would follow.

the true faith. He may have conceived the rash ambition to recover the boundaries as he had restored
the institutions of David's kingdom. With his slender force he undertook to resist the king of Egypt,
who hastened to anticipate the advance of the Medes
in Syria. In vain Necho represented that his design
was altogether friendly to Judah, and that he was
engaged in keeping off a common enemy. His policy in occupying the seaports of Palestine roused the
suspicious jealousy of Josiah, who had already begun
to exercise a sort of protectorate over the whole extent of Canaan, feebly occupied by the scanty Samaritan population. He encountered Necho near the
Galilean seaboard ; and the plain of Megiddo, which
had witnessed, seven centuries before, the vindication
of Hebrew independence in Deborah's splendid triumph, witnessed now its downfall in the defeat and
death of Josiah, the last worthy inheritor of David's
crown and lineage.

"Weep ye not for the dead," said Jeremiah,
chiding the passionate lamentation of the people,
"neither mourn for him ; but weep bitterly for him
that goeth away, for he shall return no more, nor
see his native land."* The death of Josiah was
only the commencement of that train of calamities
which within twenty years destroyed forever the
monarchy of Judah. His son was detained as prisoner or hostage in Egypt, and Jehoiakim ruled ten
years or more as a vassal of the conqueror. When
Nineveh was taken by the Medes, the star of Babylon
was in the ascendant; and the young chief Nebuchad-

* Jeremiah xxii. 10.

nezzar, leagued with the Medes to destroy the only rival power, discomfited the Egyptian force at Carchemish, and succeeded to its domination over Judah.

In vain Jehoiakim maintained a brief struggle against the Chaldæan power. The weakness of Judah made it a prey to the new spoiler, while old enmities of neighbouring tribes now broke out afresh.* The king died amidst the terror of the impending overthrow, and his son surrendered himself, without a blow, to be taken with ten thousand captives to Babylon. The ill-fated Zedekiah, brother of Jehoiakim, was put upon the throne as a subject-prince, or tool, to serve the pleasure of the Chaldæan despot.

The calamities of the time † again drove many to seek refuge in Egypt; and there seemed even a hope that an alliance with that country might enable Judah to throw off the yoke of Babylon. But the power of Apries, now king there, had been wrecked in a hazardous campaign in Libya, and his strongest vassal, Amasis, slew him shortly after in a revolt.‡ The late king's imprisonment in Babylon, whither he was summoned at the first suspicion of his faith, warned Zedekiah what he had to expect from any recreancy. He swore allegiance anew, and was suffered a few years longer to hold the tottering throne.

But the stimulus constantly afforded by the sor-

---

* Ammon and Moab now appear again (2 Kings xxiv. 2) as enemies; while the fierce vengeance of Edom makes the theme of the brief prophecy of Obadiah. See also Psalm cxxxvii. 7.

† Habakkuk about this season teaches for the first time the profound lesson of *trust* without *hope*.

‡ See Herodotus, II. 161 – 169.

rowful and impatient exiles of the Euphrates, together with the fanatic confidence of a party among the people, the memory of their signal deliverance from Sennacherib, and their fond trust that the ramparts of Zion were impregnable to any heathen force, compelled, as it were, the final hopeless and ruinous revolt. In the uneasy and highly roused temper of the time there were not wanting those who confidently foretold a splendid triumph,* and the immediate coming of the Messiah, or the nation's ideal and victorious king. † So frantic was the assurance of some, that, during a short respite of the siege that followed, they reduced again to bondage certain slaves or captives, whom they had emancipated so as to serve in the desperate defence. ‡

The prophets of clearer vision, as Jeremiah and Habakkuk, saw the condition of affairs too well to hold out any treacherous hope. If anything were wanting to verify their cheerless words, it was found in the civil feud which not even the siege could bring to terms. Zedekiah had staked everything on the cast of this revolt, and played the game out as a desperate man, upheld by a fanatic party of religionists, who conceived it infamous to yield a point of sacred ground, or to harbour a doubt of Jehovah's invincible protection. On the other hand, whatever chance there might have been at least of a longer struggle, if not of eventual triumph, was foiled by the continual despairing protest of Jeremiah. At one time he seems to have stood

---

* See Jeremiah, chap. xxix.   † See Zechariah, chap. xii., xiv.
‡ Jeremiah, chap. xxxiv.

quite alone in his predictions of evil, and was openly
charged with traitorous plottings with the enemy.*
His defence was, that Micah, in the former siege, had
uttered similar predictions; and the shelter of that
name was sufficient for his acquittal. Apparently,
he held defeat or surrender to be only a necessary
prelude to greater security and peace, and that the
king's resistance was the real hostility against the
land; for, to show his confidence in better times
that should follow, he made and publicly registered
the purchase of a field in his native village.† His
sincerity was evident enough, and the sanctity of his
character was a shelter from any act of gross violence. But the party in power charged him with
being the evil genius that tied their hands, demoral-
ized their discipline, and held them from using their
real strength. The king, embarrassed by an influence so wholly out of his control, kept him for some
time confined in an open house-court, or private
jail; then, on a charge of traitorous practices,
threw him into a dungeon, where, in damp and
noisomeness, he was in peril of his life; ‡ then,
in compassion, or in deference to those who revered
the sincere though despairing prophet, restored him
once more to liberty. And so the siege wore on for
about two years.

At length " famine prevailed in the city, and there
was no bread for the people of the land. The city
was broken up, and all the men of war fled away by
night." The king was captured near Jericho, and

---

* Jeremiah, chap. xxxvii. 13.   † Ibid., chap. xxxii.
‡ Ibid., chap. xxxviii.

led before the conqueror. His children were slain before his face, his own eyes were put out, and in this horrible plight he was taken to the prison of Babylon. The fortifications of Jerusalem were broken down. Palace and temple were burned with fire. The gathered treasures of the kings and the sacred vessels of the sanctuary were taken to grace the carousal of the Babylonish conqueror. The slender remnant of the population were either carried into captivity "by the waters of Babylon," or fled to Egypt (whither Jeremiah went unwillingly to pass the remainder of his days*), or else were suffered, under a native governor, to till the desolate fields of Judah. A few helpless struggles against the pressure of that heavy hand, a few stern measures of vengeance or suppression, and the fair land of Canaan, which had been " as Eden or as the garden of Jehovah," the Land of Promise, which for so many centuries had been and was yet to be the centre of Hebrew affection, and the home of Hebrew faith, was in the desolate condition portrayed in the pathetic Lamentations of Jeremiah : —

" How doth the city sit solitary, that was full of people !
How is she become as a widow !
She that was great among the nations, princess among the provinces,
How is she become tributary !
Judah goeth into exile, affliction, and slavery :
Her dwelling is abroad among the nations :
She findeth no repose ! "

* Here he uttered his protest against the national idolatry, strove to revive or keep up the Hebrew spirit of his countrymen, and foretold an approaching conquest (unknown to history) of that land by Nebuchadnezzar.

VII. THE LAW.

IT is among the manners of primeval and patriarchal life that we must seek the germ of those institutions which have given the Hebrews their marked place in history. Many elements of their religion had root in the common soil of Oriental culture. Their customs were the later and developed form of tribal habits, which we faintly trace by their relics in Hebrew song or legend, and by their affinities in the customs of kindred tribes. Whatever influence was brought to bear upon them by the shaping hand of Moses, or by a later and purer monotheism, or by the civil policy of the kings, we must assume for their understanding that background of popular feeling which so slowly yielded before the characteristic faith of Judaism, and that sensuous or bloody superstition embodied in the rites of Syrian worship.

Of the primitive and rude fetichism that seems to belong to the infancy of every people, but faint and as it were second-hand traces are to be discerned in the Hebrew writings. At the earliest period which we can see with any clearness, it had already nearly passed the transition state of star-worship,* and was

* See page 12, for the legend indicating this transition ; also Deuteronomy iv. 19.

supplanted by a pretty well defined polytheism, the
influence of which is strongly marked on the earlier
customs, and on much of the religious language,
of the Hebrews. Each tribe or nation had its several divinity.* The "jealous God" of Israel found
a rival in Baal of the Canaanites, Dagon of the Philistines, Chemosh of Moab, Molech of Ammon, in
Ashera the lewd or Ashteroth the bloody goddess
of the Syrians. To the popular fancy these were
real deities : and down to a late period, spite of the
stern legislation of Moses, and the reproaches of the
prophets, who called them devils, these "gods of the
nations" received the people's obstinate homage.

The strongly marked features of race, climate, and
scenery must all serve in some measure as a guide, in
estimating that common character which ran through
these varieties of Shemitic worship. The group of
tribes, or petty nations, inhabiting the regions of
Syria were kindred not only in blood but in faith.
Their mind was cast in a common mould. Their rites
and institutions were modelled after a common type.
Their fancy was kindled and trained by the same
great natural objects,—sea, desert or mountain, land
and sky. The fascinating, yet often terrible mythology of the East, so imperfectly known to us through
the allusions in Scripture story, or by the later
accounts of the Greeks, is most easily interpreted to
our imagination by the subtile connection which traces

---

* The Alexandrian commentators found this doctrine expressly
taught in Deut. xxxiii. 8, translating the latter clause, "according to
the number of his angels," — the number being held to be seventy-
two, — whom Philo identifies with the "dæmons" of the Greeks.

its symbols and analogies in the soil, the seasons, and the sky of Syria.

EL "the Mighty"* is the name of the mysterious Nature-Deity, and leads the mythic cycle. The vast and vague conception would require nothing less than the universe for its embodiment. But religious fancy seeks a definite symbol, or visible manifestation of the Infinite. This, to the Oriental mind, is found in the sun, which was adored by those ancient tribes under the title Bel or Baal. As "Lord of the hosts of heaven," he was worshipped alike on the "high places" of Canaan and on the plains of Shinar, the moon and the five visible planets being his attendants. The "Queen of heaven," the great light that ruled the night, was the celestial symbol of Ashera † and of Astarte, by which names the Syrians denoted the female element in the universal life. The royal Jupiter, called "Gad," or the fortunate, was the starry symbol corresponding to Baal, or the sun ; and Venus, the fair morning and evening star, would in like manner represent the female companion deity. The planet Mercury may have been most nearly identified with the Earth-god, represented variously by the Greeks as Dionysus or Pan ; as Mars, called also Azazel or Typhon, was with the demon-breath of blasting and pestilential heat. Last of all the heavenly host, the pale and baleful Saturn embraced in his circuit the paths of all the rest, brooding like a gloomy Destiny upon the verge of the outer dark-

---

* See Exodus vi. 3.

† This name is ignorantly rendered "groves" (after the LXX.) throughout the Old Testament. See 2 Kings xxi. 7.

ness.* This became the especial symbol of the mysterious El, — that dark universal power, whom the
Canaanites called by the title IAO, the "Living," a
name allied with the Hebrew Jehovah, and also,
ISRA-EL.†

We have thus, in the imperfectly known mythology
of the East, tolerably clear traces of a circle of at
least seven divine Powers, having each its recognized
heavenly symbol. As the primitive adoration of the
stars or emblems is merged in that of local deities, so
a mythological Person is associated with each of the
celestial bodies thought to have a peculiar influence
on human destinies. The early wide-spread division
of time into weeks, after the well-marked courses of
the moon, assigned to each of these powers its own
day. The week began with the festival of the Sun,
and closed with that of the universal power, whose
heavenly sign was the outmost of the planets, —
known in Italy as Saturn, to the Greeks as all-pro-
ducing, all-devouring Time, in Palestine as Chiun
or Remphan,‡ and later, by the name Sabbatha,
or Rest. This sevenfold division of time became
the basis of the religious or festal periods, both
in Egypt and among all the Oriental tribes, — traces
of it being found also in the customs of Greece and
Rome, and even among the barbarous races of
America.

---

* "Because of the seven heavenly bodies by which mortals are controlled, the star of Saturn is borne in the loftiest orbit and in excelling
might; and, in general, the power and the courses of the celestials are
determined by the number seven." — Tacitus, Hist., V. 4.

† Or, El the Prince. (Compare Gen. xxxii. 28.) Hence, according
to some, the designation "people of Israel."

‡ Amos v. 26 ; Acts vii. 43.

The attributes of the several powers in this mythic hierarchy were gradually blended in the conception of one universal Deity, known to the Hebrews under the plural name ELOHIM.* But each nation would doubtless merge the features of the one Nature-God in those of its own special deity. Hence both the attributes themselves and their celestial symbols are almost indifferently ascribed to each, and the details of the Syrian mythology become inextricably confused.

The names above recited indicate that cycle of Syrian superstitions by which the Hebrews were from the first surrounded, and towards which, even to the last, they were obstinately prone. Its essence has been called " a pantheistic nature-worship, or adoration of the elements, sharply distinguished from the monotheistic religion of Mosaism." † This was in time resolved into the elements symbolized by those " powers of the air." The distinction was at first drawn only between the male and female divine or elemental principles, but was wrought out by degrees into the elaborate mythology which so debauched the Hebrew manners and fascinated the popular mind. Its crude and vague character is strongly contrasted with the pronounced theogony of the Greeks.

Of the several divinities, Bel (or Apollo) and Ashera (Cybele, or Aphrodite), as well as Thammuz

* Variously rendered in the Old Testament by *God*, *gods*, and *angels*.
† See Movers, "Die Phönizer," Vol. I. But Comte says that pantheism is only "a scientific reconstruction of fetichism," which was in fact the real primitive and rude faith.

(perhaps identical with the Earth-god, or Dionysus),
were worshipped especially with licentious rites; all,
no doubt, with human sacrifices. Of the bloody and
horrible character of the Syrian superstition there is
abundant proof in the Hebrew writings, as well as
in what is recounted respecting Tyre and Carthage
by the Greeks.* As Bel, or Baal, represents the quick-
ening splendours of the sun, so Moloch — a word having the same radical signification of lord or king —
represents in that mythology his malignant and destructive rays, or the devouring force of flame.
Nothing more seized and held the imagination of the
shuddering worshipper than the exulting and eager
fury of the flame, as it "leaped forth from the altar"
to devour the sacrifice. This quality is frightfully
signified in the elaborate and horrid idols of that
.grim worship: sometimes a brazen automaton, which,
being heated glowing hot, sprang out to snatch from
the crowd its victim, with whom it plunged back to
the blazing pile ; sometimes a statue, whose outstretched arms threw the offered child into a fire
burning at its feet; sometimes a hollow figure, within
whose scorching bosom the first-born infant was cast
to perish, while wild cries and the beating of drums
drowned the voice alike of mother and babe. This
is the worship dwelt on with such emphasis and
images of horror by the prophets, in their appeals in

---

* See especially, as to the character of this worship and the im-
plication of the Hebrews in it, 2 Kings xxi. 3 - 9; xxiii. 4 - 14; Psalm
cvi. 38 - 40; Ezekiel xx. 24 - 31; Amos v. 26. The last reference
seems to connect the worship of Moloch with that of the planet
Saturn.

behalf of a purer faith. The frantic orgies of Cybele ("Dea Syria"), and of Thammuz, or Adonis, whose worship seems to have had reference especially to the sun of early spring, belong to our more familiar recollections of these religions of the East; and, together with the horrors of human sacrifice, subsisted far into the era of Christianity. The vindictive Power symbolized by "the red planet Mars" had his dwelling amid the fierce glare of the desert. He was named by the Egyptians Typhon, the Destroyer, who consumed the propitious overflows of Osiris, or the Nile; and by the Hebrews, Azazel, the rival of Jehovah, to whom the yearly goat was sent for expiation into the wilderness.*

Two sacred annual seasons were set apart for the high solemnities of this elemental worship: one in the opening spring, and one in the autumn, or season of vintage. Both were kept in the splendours of the full moon, and brought together, for a seven-days' festival, the population of tribes and villages. The darker and more jealous powers were invoked under the impulse of that anxious and superstitious dread with which men anticipated the possible disasters of the new year; and their propitiation could be bought

---

* Mars was the Star of Edom ("the Red"), which is also identified with Azazel, — the same malign power known afterwards as Sammael, or Satan. (Eisenmenger, "Entdecktes Judenthum," Vol. I. pp. 645, 649, 823; Vol. II. p. 155.) The Egyptian epithet of Typhon was *Ros*, or red. (Kenrick's Egypt, Vol. II. p. 157.) It is to the ignorance or fancy of the Alexandrians that we are indebted for the transforming of this into the ritual conception of the "scape-goat." Mr. Gliddon, in the "Types of Mankind," makes the name signify *lord of death*, in contrast to Jehovah, the *lord of life*.

only by the costly offering of blood. The later season brought the joyful festivities of the vintage, or harvest-home. Thank-offerings abounded; the exuberant and teeming forces of nature were celebrated with riotous holiday; and the occasion was the characteristic Syrian one of mingled blood and lust. These, with other traces of antique custom, — as the erection of " Bethels " ($Ba\iota\tau\acute{\upsilon}\lambda\iota a$), said to have been frequent among the Canaanites, the consecration of " high places " and groves, the " teraphim," or sacred images (which have been connected with the Egyptian rites of Serapis), and sundry rites otherwise unexplained, observed with respect to sacrifice, — are in part alluded to in the vehement censures of the prophets, in part sanctioned and adopted in the Hebrew ritual code.

The characteristic rite of Sacrifice seems to belong to the very earliest records of mankind. The story of Cain and Abel already indicates the transition from the simpler offering of food to the more sacred rites of blood. Its first intention was to offer to the Divinity a chosen portion of every gift with which he satisfies human wants. The Altar was originally a table, on which food was left to be consumed or reabsorbed by the elemental forces of earth and air; or, as popular credulity believed, to be literally eaten by the gods. Hence it should be prepared in the most savoury way, and every sacrifice must be seasoned with salt.* The table of shew-bread is a relic of this simplest form of offering.

The active and living force of flame became the

---

* Leviticus ii. 13.

obvious representative of the sun, or of the vital energy of nature. The altar from a table became a hearth; and the sacred fire was kindled to devour or consume the sacrifice. The more precious the offering, the more acceptable. If fruits were used, they must be first-fruits; if grain, wheat; if other possessions, the fairest of their kind. What had no human ownership (as wild fruits or game) could make no part of the pious gift. The natural awe with which men first behold the flow of blood was deepened by the persuasion that it was the peculiar seat of life, or the life itself; and when the more costly gift of domestic animals was brought, the blood that gushed upon the ground, and the fire that consumed the flesh, became the essential features of the rite.

The victim of sacrifice must be an animal " without spot or blemish," — the nearer to the affections of human kind the better. Ascending in the scale of preciousness or dignity, the religious feeling craved nothing less than the sacrifice of one's child, — the eldest or only child. The custom of offering the first-born was deeply rooted in the antiquity of the race. So tenaciously was it held, that it is cited expressly as the type of the paschal lamb; it furnishes a parallel to the religious thought of a writer so late as Micah, and an illustration to those who spoke to the Jewish mind of the sacrifice of Christ.* A detailed examination shows the worships of ancient paganism as literally reeking with human blood.†

---

* Exodus xiii. 13; Micah vi. 6; Hebrews ix. 14.

† See Magee on the Atonement; also, Ghillany, " Die Menschenöpfer der alten Hebräer," where the investigation is quite sufficiently

Superstitious frenzy or fanaticism, with its cold cruelty, demanded it in streams. The earliest care of a humane lawgiver, backed by priestly policy, was to provide a substitute. The several forms of ascetic penance, the ancient tribal rite of circumcision common to both Syria and Africa, and, still later, the offering of a vicarious victim, or the payment of a stipulated price, were the terms on which this horrible flow of human blood was stayed.

Such were the elements of Syrian culture or superstition, which must be assumed as a sort of groundwork in the understanding of many features in the Hebrew institutions. They made, as it were, an outlying circle of ideas and habits, from which the national mind was never completely guarded or divorced. How far they were modified by the sojourn in Egypt, it is impossible to say; or how far, within the sacred family, they were already outgrown in the patriarchal age. This at least we see, that the loftier intelligence of Moses himself, combined with the purer and diviner truth imparted to him during his desert life, and interpreted by the Levitical priesthood long after, was brought to bear on them, as the religious material

carried out. In Rome human sacrifices were abolished by a decree of the Senate, B. C. 93. "But in many expiatory and lustral rites, the shedding of a drop of blood was retained as a type of the ancient usage, with which it has frequently been confounded." (Merivale, Fall of the Roman Republic, p. 119.) For the custom of burying a human victim "alive under every important structure, as a propitiatory sacrifice," — of which an example is given in 1 Kings xvi. 34, in the case of the rebuilder of Jericho, who "laid the foundation thereof in Abiram his first-born, and set up the gate thereof in his youngest son Serug," — see Sophocles's Glossary of Later Greek, p. 613.

already existing in the popular mind. Either the
tenacity with which that shepherd race clung to its
ancient memories, or the revival of old instincts and
associations by the contact of friendly tribes during
the desert wandering, or the alliances and compromise that succeeded the unfinished slaughter of the
Canaanites, made a thousand points of contact between Hebrew faith and alien customs; and the
antique Syrian superstition furnishes the warp upon
which the nobler people wove the pattern of its religious history.

It is not merely in remote antiquity, but down to
the most recent period preceding the Captivity, that
the rites and customs just described were familiar
and influential among the Hebrews. We find the
earlier traces of them in the story of Isaac, the narrative of Jephthah's daughter, and the religious slaughter of Agag at the hands of Samuel, with others
which an over-curious criticism has found or fancied.
We find frequent mention of the rites of Baal, Moloch, and Astarte in the annals of the kings, and in
the undiscriminating censures of the prophets. Even
at Jerusalem, the head-quarters of the priesthood,
there was a "vale of Tophet," where Ahaz and Manasseh made their children "pass through the fire to
Moloch." And nothing seems more clearly shown in
the history than that the milder Hebrew institutions,
as we know them, contended at a disadvantage, and
but very slowly did away what was worst of native
and local superstition.

The narrative of the Conquest represents the race
as just emerging from a nomadic state, the period of

the " Wandering," and gaining by force of arms half-possession of a comparatively fertile, populous, and civilized district. It is at this period that the history of the nation, properly speaking, may be said to begin. Its numbers, to judge from all we know, could hardly at any time before the monarchy have exceeded half a million, and in the earlier period must have been much less.* Apparently they carried with them the modes of life characteristic of their nomadic state. At the time of Deborah, we hear of no fixed habitations, only of tents and sheepfolds, though many of the conquerors would no doubt occupy the deserted villages of the Canaanites; and in the eastern districts this was the way of life until the devastations of Hazael, two centuries after the time of David.† The people were so destitute of the arts of industry, that to repair their tools they must go to the Philistine workshops. They had no equipment to compete with the chariots and armour of the Canaanites. Saul and his son are even said to have been the only Hebrews armed with sword or spear; and Shamgar's sole weapon was an " oxgoad."‡ The horse was never fairly naturalized in Israel, though part of the equipage of David's and Solomon's royalty. As among some Eastern tribes at the present day, bullocks or cows were used for

---

* Perhaps the prodigious numbers we find in Exodus, as well as Chronicles, may be ascribed to the vastly greater scale of population which the Jews found in Babylon. They contrast curiously with the slender census of the new colony of Judæa, recording contemporary fact.

† See Joshua xxii. 6; Judges v. 24, xx. 8; 2 Kings xiii. 5.

‡ 1 Samuel xiii. 18–23; Judges iii. 31.

draught. In travelling, or on state occasions, the
ass or mule was characteristic of the Hebrews till a
late day, and became a symbol of the peaceful reign
of the Messiah.* As a token of the thinly settled
and distracted condition of the country, even in the
time of the monarchy, wild beasts seem to have been
very numerous. Single encounter with a lion was a
frequent test of Hebrew championship, as shown
in the stories of Samson, David, and Benaiah; the
boys who mocked Elisha were torn by bears; and
the new settlers of Samaria, after the Ninevite conquest, found that most fertile district of Palestine so
overrun by wild beasts as to be almost uninhabitable.
It is not till the latter part of David's reign that we
find any trace of the wealth attributed to the patriarchs, the Canaanites, and even to the emigrant
horde in the desert. Remnants of the conquered
populations still made, apparently, the majority of
the inhabitants of Palestine. The stronghold of
the Jebusites was first subdued by Joab, and the
Hebrew nationality had not undisputed dominion till
the time of Solomon. So that, through the earlier
portion of their history, the tribes of Israel exhibit
the condition of a sparse nomadic population, dwelling almost at random among a wealthier, more numerous, and more cultivated people, which they had
only half subdued.

This condition of things easily explains the confusion we find between Hebrew faith and alien superstitions, as well as the late development of the true
Hebrew culture. It is only as they existed in their

* Zechariah ix. 9.

maturity that we can well understand the Mosaic institutions; only by an effort of imagination that we can discern their effect on the mind and temper of the earlier time.* In their completed form, they yet retained distinctness enough of primitive feature to let us trace their parentage or alliances. While they were interpreted to accord with a higher circle of ideas, and spiritualized in the long ages of the nation's life, their Jewish expounders often show unconscious traces of those immemorial rites and superstitions from which they were so slowly and painfully divorced; and the Hebrew Scriptures abound in the same disguised and lurking evidence.

But with the first distinct assertion of Hebrew nationality we find indications of the spirit which, working through the prophets, so powerfully affected the nation's mind for good. The earliest relics of Hebrew song or story, dating at least as high as the age of the Judges, accord well enough with the deep · reverence and exalted conception associated always with that people's thought of God. The Song of Deborah, or the Oracle of Jacob, contains no trace of the hideous and bloody superstition of the Canaanites. As surely as it was an expression of the mind of that early age, so surely it compels us to think of Israel as already well advanced beyond the neighbouring idolatries, or the gross formalism of Egypt. Elevation of the religious thought, culture of the religious affection, and development of the religious life are vindicated, as from the first the peculiar

* See page 51.

office of this people in history. The circumstances which led to the ascendency of the priesthood under Eli, and the systematic prophetic culture instituted by Samuel, have been before noticed.* We have now to consider what was characteristic in the Hebrew institutions as found in their mature form, probably in the more flourishing period of the Monarchy.

The essential features of the religious and civil polity have already been so far indicated as was necessary to a clear understanding of the foregoing history.† To aid in interpreting the Jewish Scriptures, as well as in tracing the influence of this people upon after forms of religious thought, we have to consider, further, a few details of the Civil Code, the Ritual, and the Religious Year, or cycle of national Religious Festivals.

I. CIVIL CODE. This includes the rights of Person, Property, and Family; and the charge of public Health.

As the basis of personal right, the Law assumes the inviolability of human life. This it sanctions by the mysterious sacredness of blood (Gen. ix. 6; Num. xxxv. 33), by the claim of brotherhood (Lev. xix. 17), and by the solemn penalties of the code (Lev. xxiv. 17). The old instincts or customs of the Tribe demanded that the nearest relative of a slain man should hunt down the murderer, and exact life for life. This is an imperative point of honour among a rude and primitive people, let the cause of death be accident, quarrel, or wilful mur-

* See pages 95 – 98, 102.   † See pages 50 – 59.

der;* and so a single chance death might breed a blood-stain which generations would not wash out. The "avenger of blood" had his recognized commission among the Hebrews (Num. xxxv. 19; Deut. xix. 12), restricted only by appointing "cities of refuge," where the involuntary offender might be safe. As by the old law of Athens, what caused a man's death was accursed, whether man or beast. No money compensation could be given. (Num. xxxv. 31, 33.) The vicious ox must die; his owner, too, if the creature was of vicious habit. (Ex. xxi. 28, 29.) A fatal accident left the stain of blood on the house where it befell. (Deut. xxii. 8.) Only the sacred limits of the city of refuge could shelter the involuntary homicide (Num. xxxv. 26); and a remarkable ceremony is detailed by which the magistrates of a city, washing their hands over a heifer beheaded in a desolate ravine, should clear themselves of the guilt of murder done there, if the author of it could not be found. (Deut. xxi. 1–8.) In a similar spirit, the elder law granted "breach for breach, eye for eye, tooth for tooth." (Lev. xxiv. 30; Ex. xxi. 23–25.) It was the humanity of a later code that commuted the penalty afterwards for a fine.

The penalty of death is assumed in a primitive code as the one sanction of violated law, — as it was in Athens under Draco, and as it is said to be now in Japan. Slighter penalties are in theory a substitute or commutation. Among the Hebrews, this commutation for lesser offences might be disfranchisement,

---

* Genesis ix. 5. See Layard's "Babylon and Nineveh," p. 305.

fine, or a sin-offering. Scourging was rarely inflicted, as against the dignity of a freeman; and in any case might not exceed forty stripes (Deut. xxv. 3), "lest thy brother should seem vile unto thee." Imprisonment seems to have been unknown until the latter portion of the monarchy.

The original right of property lay not in the individual, but in the family, — the natural assignment of what was got by conquest. The family derived its title from the tribe or state; this, again, directly from Jehovah. The family estate was in theory inalienable, and must revert to the original holder, or his descendants, at least as often as once in fifty years. If forfeited by debt or suretyship in the mean time, it was still subject to the right of redemption. (Num. xxvii. 8.) The eldest son had a double share of the inheritance (Deut. xxi. 17); and along with it, doubtless, the duty of maintaining the orphans and widows of the household. Still further to secure the same end, a daughter could marry only in her own tribe (Num. xxxvi. 8); and, dying childless, she left her inheritance to her brother. No interest money might be taken from a Hebrew (Ex. xxii. 25; Deut. xxiii. 19); and no absolute purchase of land could be made, except a homestead in a walled town (Lev. xxv. 29, 30). These regulations, it is needless to say, underwent some change when the bulk of property was no longer in land, but in the trades and estates of cities.

Restricted as was the claim of personal property, within these limits it was absolute. Stolen goods

must be restored double, — in some cases, four or
five fold. (Ex. xxii. 1-4.) The penalty of kidnap-
ping was death. (Ex. xxi. 16.) The indorser shared
the liability of him he was surety for. (Prov.
xxii. 26, 27.) The debtor was at the mercy of his
creditor, and probably became his slave (2 Kings
iv. 1; Prov. xxii. 7), according to the barbarous
custom, or common law, of antiquity. So, too, captives spared in war. (Josh. ix. 21.) Slaves purchased from among neighbouring tribes (Lev. xxv.
44-46) became "bondmen forever," and a "property inheritance to children."

Among the Hebrews themselves slavery was greatly
lightened. Religious fellowship and privilege were
still recognized (Deut. xvi. 10, 11); the mutilated
slave went free (Ex. xxi. 27); if a fugitive, he
might not be rendered back (Deut. xxiii. 15); he
had the right of purchasing his ransom, and the
certainty of being free after six years of service
(Ex. xxi. 2). Thus, retaining many of the harsh
features of ancient law, the Hebrew code did very
much to mitigate the bondman's bitter lot. It re-
calls the time when the whole people was captive
in a strange land; and makes the hardship of the
past a plea for humanity in the future. (Lev. xxv.
43; Deut. xv. 15, 22, xviii. 22, xxvi. 5.)

The right of the Family, as the sacred centre of
the life of the state, was guarded with peculiar care.
Its prototype was found in the scrupulous severity
of patriarchal rule. Honour to the aged was sedulously enjoined. (Ex. xix. 32.) The wife's honour
(Lev. xx. 10) and the child's obedience (Deut.

10* o

xxi. 18) were enforced by the same sharp penalty of death. Widows and orphans were a sacred charge to the community. (Ex. xxii. 22.) A man might nullify his wife's religious vow (Num. xxx. 8), or sell his children into bondage (Ex. xxi. 7). The spirit of the Hebrew law restrained the license of polygamy and divorce (Ex. xxi. 10; Deut xxii. 19, xxiv. 11), though yielding, in this as in other matters, to a sovereign's wilfulness or policy, or the sanction of earlier customs.

Of these was the custom of "levirate marriage," by which (as among several Eastern nations) a childless widow might demand of her husband's brother to marry her, and so keep unbroken the family inheritance. If he refused, she drew off his sandal and spat "to his face," as a ceremony of contempt (Deut. xxv. 5 – 10), and his refusal became a standing reproach upon his house. The remarkable ordeal of "jealousy" (Num. v. 12 – 31), and the forbidding of impure rites (Lev. xvii. 7, xx. 2 – 5), are evidence of both the spirit and the circumstances of the Hebrew family code. Its general effect, however we may interpret it in detail, was to assign to the women of Israel a far nobler influence and higher social rank than we find them holding among most other Asiatic peoples.

Lastly, the civil code assumed a religious sanction in guarding the paramount public interest of Health. Food, popular customs, and the diseases of the climate, were all put under regulations that made part of the religion itself. What was unwholesome was stigmatized as "unclean," as well as certain customs of desert or city life, from which the state of Israel was to be strictly kept apart. Fruit of the first three years' bearing was called "uncircumcised," and might not be eaten; that of the fourth year was to be made a religious offering. (Lev. xix. 23 – 25.) The brutish and loathsome habits that belong to nomadic hordes were well guarded against by the simple, intelligible precept, to eat no greasy, bloody, "dead," or mangled flesh (Lev. vii. 23; xi. 32; xxii. 8); and to take as food such creatures only as "part the hoof and chew the cud," together with a restricted list of birds and fishes. No vegetable diet was condemned as unclean, — a sufficient indication that the motive of the law was sanitary, not superstitious.

From the same motive, a dead body could not be touched without incurring seven days' "uncleanness" and the grateful ritual of a bath, lest perhaps there should be danger of contagion.* Mutilation of every sort was prohibited, as well as any mixture of breed in plant or animal (Lev. xix. 19); and an obscure kindred feeling forbade dam and young to be killed on the same day (Lev. xxii. 28), or a kid to be "seethed in its mother's milk." (Ex. xxxiv. 26.) The first symptom of the enervating and destructive diseases of a hot climate was met by the same vigilant precaution. (Lev. chap. xv.) Especially leprosy — that frightful plague by which (to trust the tenor of tradition) the Jews in Egypt had been almost universally cursed, and which was only

---

* See the law respecting the "water of separation." (Num. xix. 1 – 22.)

partially worn away by the stern regimen of Moses
— was watched with a certain terror by the Hebrew
sanitary code. (Lev. chap. xiii.) Its first ominous,
angry swelling was carefully noted by the priests; its
course was duly reported to them at certain intervals; and, when beyond their pharmacy, its victim
was pitilessly banished from all human intercourse.*
Cruelty to him was the only security to the rest.

II. RITUAL. The Hebrew state was a theocracy.
Its civil law was merged in ecclesiastical or ritual
law, which gave it character and sanction. From
infancy through life every person was subject to its
vigilant guardianship. The ritual, accordingly, in
its broader sense, comprehended a large part of the
civil law, particularly that which had in charge the
public health. It appointed seasons and forms of
prayer, and a thousand details of ceremonial. It
prescribed the rank of the priesthood, and the rules
of expiatory sacrifice, or fine, — such as the "ransom" for the census. (Ex. xxxviii. 12.) By
far the greater portion of it becomes a matter of
mere antiquarian curiosity. What is most characteristic in it, and essential to a right interpreting of
Hebrew thought and custom, is that which concerns
the rites of Circumcision and Sacrifice.

The rite of Circumcision — common to most of
the Syrian and several African tribes † — was of the

* See too the law respecting "leprosy," or unwholesome mould, in
the walls of a house. (Lev. xiv. 34.)

† Among the Phœnicians it was a rite of consecration to Saturn.
(Movers, in Winer.) It was regarded in later ages as a sacrifice to
Satan of that which is his peculiar share in the human body. (Eisen-
menger, Vol. I. p. 673.)

nature of a bloody sacrifice (Ex. iv. 24 – 26), expiatory, and, in its first sense, a substitute for the
infant's life. It was performed at the age of eight
days, and was the initiation into the religious community. Hence it became a mark of exclusive privilege and sanctity, and it is always alluded to as the
particular badge of the "chosen people." Its sanitary
use in that climate is well understood, and was doubtless had in view by those who engrafted it upon the
customs of the race. In later time it came to be .
regarded as a special sacrifice to the evil spirit, and
a special consecration to Jehovah; and it formed the
test question of the divorce between Judaism and
Christianity.

The rite of Sacrifice was administered with many
forms borrowed from Egyptian or Syrian usage, or
from immemorial custom; but was invested with a
significance and an elaborate detail of ceremonial
quite peculiar to the Hebrews. Its simplest form
and meaning were recalled by the Table, which stood
at the side of the sanctuary towards the north (Ex.
xxvi. 35), where the peculiar habitation of the Deity
was of old supposed to be. Upon it were piled twelve
loaves of "shew-bread," strewn with incense (Lev.
xxiv. 5), — his perpetual food, — which were ex-
changed each week, the old loaves being eaten by the
priests. In distinction from more costly gifts, flour
and oil were even in later time called the "meat-
offering," or gift of food.* Libations of wine or
water are a further example of the same general
meaning.

* Leviticus ii. 1. See Palfrey's Lectures, Vol. I. p. 245.

The Altar, originally of earth or stone, unprofaned by any tool (Ex. xx. 24, 25), was the hearth-stone and sacred centre of the religion. Its holy fire was the especial symbol of the living presence of the Deity. The fire must be always burning (Lev. vi. 13); and no day or night should pass without the customary offering, for thanksgiving or expiation. Fire and Blood were the two emblems inseparable from the more solemn forms of service, — fire as the symbol of Divinity, and blood as the seat of life. Blood could not be lawfully touched or used as food. (Lev. vii. 27.) No pious man would stain himself with that which was the peculiar share of the Lord of life. It was " blood that made atonement for the soul " (Lev. xvii. 11), according to the maxim, " life for life." If not sprinkled on the altar, by the requirement of the ritual, it must be shed on the ground " like water." (Deut. xii. 16.)

In the earlier time, it was not lawful to taste of any food of which a part should not have been offered in sacrifice. The first sheaf of harvest, and a particular portion of each slain beast, must be brought to the altar as a " wave-offering " or " heave-offering ; " and, unless burnt, as in some particular cases (Ex. xxix. 25), became the perquisite of the priest. (Lev. ii. 12 ; Num. xviii. 8.) In the dark religious terror roused by the sense of guilt or sudden calamity, or strange natural events, no gift seemed too costly to allay the Divine wrath. The most elaborate ceremonial of the sin-offering did but provide satisfaction for that craving instinct so deeply implanted in the religious constitution of that primitive age, which sought to be

ppeased even by the hideous sacrifice of children on
he altar of heathen deities.

The general name " burnt-offering " denotes the
original and essential rite, which consisted in the
utter renunciation to the Deity of some object valu-
ble and dear to man. This was at all times inseparable from the Hebrew ceremonial. It was the daily
night and morning service of the sanctuary; and accompanied or made part of every other form of offer-
ng. The daily victim (Ex. xxix. 39) was a lamb;
on the Sabbath two lambs. Rams and goats were
lain for special services; and the noblest offering
if all was a bullock, — which with the Hebrews, as
among various other nations, was made the repre-
entative of certain attributes of the Deity, as we see
n the imagery of the prophets. Game and the like,
not being property, could not be brought for sacrifice,
only these domestic creatures; and the habit of sympathy with them among a pastoral people must be
aken into the account in estimating their fitness to
epresent man's penitence and supplication. The
only birds esteemed fit for sacrifice were doves or
pigeons (Lev. v. 7); in a single instance a sparrow
Lev. xiv. 14). The only relic of the rite among the
modern Jews is the slaying of a cock or hen.

The animal in all cases was duly inspected, to as-
ertain if it were sound and fit; then slain on the
north side of the altar, the priest's hands being first
aid upon its head, as a solemn form of expiation or
" atonement." (Lev. i. 3, 4, 11; xxii. 20.) The blood
was caught in a sacred dish and sprinkled on the
ltar-stones, — the most essential feature of the rite.

The flesh was divided in a particular way and burned; reserving " the wave-breast and heave-shoulder," together with the hide (Lev. vii. 8, 34), as the perquisite of the priest. In rare cases the victim was totally consumed by fire, and became the "whole burnt-offering." While the ceremony proceeded, those who partook in the service " compassed the altar " in sacred procession, with a chant or hymn. Incense was employed to mitigate the " sweet savour " of the burning flesh, and came by such use to have a sacredness of its own, so that it might not be prepared for private use. (Ex. xxx. 37.) If wheat was burned instead of flesh, a certain proportion of olive-oil (Num. xv. 1) was essential to its value as a symbol or substitute for the more costly gift.

The " peace-offering " was the first and simplest form of the stated sacrifice, being either the fulfilment of a vow, or a service of gratitude for the divine favour. (Lev. iii. 1; vii. 12.) In its original sense it was a banquet, of which man partook as a guest of his divinity. It demanded a less scrupulous inspection of the victim, and permitted the use of leavened bread. It was not a required act, but purely voluntary. (Lev. xix. 5.) When private altars made part of each family establishment, it is likely that every animal slain for food was " offered " at the altar, the head of the household acting as priest. (Lev. xvii. 3, 4.) Thus Saul, as the head of the people, built a hasty altar of stones, lest his famished troops should do violence to the ancient sanctity. (1 Sam. xiv. 33 – 35.) In later times, when the ritual belonged exclusively to the temple at Jerusalem, the thank-offering became an occasional thing, and often a banquet to the poor, like the costly pomp of sacrifice exhibited by Solomon and Josiah. It could be partaken only by those legally pure ; and what the multitude of guests did not consume was destroyed within three days by fire. (Lev. vii. 18, 21.)

The sin and trespass-offerings made the second marked feature of the ritual. It has been called the "night-side" of the ceremonial, — a mournful and solitary rite, — a single victim being slain, with sad formalities, to restore the broken harmony between man and God.

The "sin-offering" (Lev., chap. iv., v.) was the expiation of that whole sum of offences which a man or a people has committed ignorantly; or, in some cases, of ritual impurity. (Lev. xii. 6.) Its origin was in that vague feeling of guilt which refers all natural calamity to human fault, — a feeling constitutionally strong and perpetually worked on among the Hebrews, and leading to most costly and solemn acts of propitiation. By the usual form, — the laying on of hands, — the sin to be atoned for was first laid upon the creature's head, which thenceforth became "most holy," or wholly devoted to Jehovah. A special provision required that in certain cases a part should be eaten by the priest (Lev. vi. 28 ; x. 16) ; otherwise, the blood only was sprinkled for expiation or poured in a pool about the altar, and the body burned whole in some place outside the consecrated ground. For priest or people a bullock must be slain ; for a ruler, a male kid ; for a private offender,

a female kid or lamb ; but the poor might offer " two
turtle-doves or two young pigeons ; " and for the very
poor a measure of fine flour without oil or incense
was the substitute.

The " trespass-offering " was for special known
offences, or for ritual impurity. (Lev. v. 6, 17.)
Besides the legal penalty, or restitution (Lev. vi. 4),
this ritual was necessary to expiate the religious
guilt of the offence. It was purely private and personal in its character. Its end was to restore to the
Hebrew the spiritual privilege he had forfeited by
crime ; and the victim corresponds to the less costly
form of sin-offering. These two constituted the chief
resource of that ritual discipline, which was so sedulously employed in the training of the Hebrew conscience.

III. FESTIVALS. The institution of the Sabbath,
or weekly holiday, has already been noticed as a feature in the primitive Syrian worship, — the seventh
day of the week being especially consecrated to the
worship of the universal Deity. Adopting the custom, the Hebrew law engrafted on it its own more
spiritual uses. In its first sense, it was simply a day
of rest. Its sanction refers to the repose of God after
the six days' work of creation (Ex. xx. 11) or of
Israel, after Egyptian bondage. (Deut. v. 15.) This
feature of it is reproduced and enforced by the humane provision of the law. It is fortified with the
most stringent enactments ; its violation chastised by
the penalty of death. (Num. xv. 32 – 36.) The day
was especially Jehovah's day ; its profanation was
sacrilege or rebellion. Being assigned also for spe-

cial rites of expiation, in connection with the greater festivals, it speedily gathered holy associations of its own.   It became a season not of idleness or holiday merely, but of religious instruction and reminiscences.   The services of the sanctuary were made more solemn by a stated "whole burnt-offering," and twice the complement of the daily sacrifice.   Its sanctity was even enhanced by the lapse of time. The later Jews would perish rather than profane the Sabbath by self-defence in a siege ; and a peculiar Sabbath ritual is not only the most burdensome of their modern observances, but the neglect of it made one of their first reproaches against the spirit and method of the ministry of Jesus.

The seventh-day festival is the simplest element of the Hebrew religious year, and fixes the type of its festal cycle.   Besides the week of seven days, there was the great week, or "week of weeks," consisting of fifty days, and intervening (for example) between the Passover and Pentecost.   This again would nearly divide the year by seven, the lunar twelvemonth consisting of a little more than seven sabbath months. This theoretic partition of the sacred year probably had its influence in assigning the seasons of great national festivals.

Each seventh year was, likewise, a season of rest and religious instruction.*   It was called the Sabbath-year, or "year of release."   The land should lie fallow : even fruit or grapes might not be gathered, — a severe lesson of thrift and foresight, if ever

* Leviticus xxv. 2 – 7, 18 – 22.   These latter verses should intervene before v. 8.

actually enforced.* What grew without human culture, or from the chance scattering of the last harvest, was left free to be consumed by man or beast; — a special provision of charity for the poor. (Ex. xxiii. 11.) The soil of Palestine, sterile in comparison with the rich valley of the Nile, may have seemed to the conquerors to have needed these periods of rest, — an imperfect anticipation of more scientific husbandry. But among the perils, invasions, and revolutions of the realm, it is hard to find room for the realizing of this scrupulous economy ; and it has been greatly suspected to be only one of the ideal features of the theocracy, not observed before the Captivity, but only by the more rigid Judaism of a later day. Its existence, then, is noticed by Josephus, Tacitus, and others ; but in the sacred writings the sabbath-year is spoken of as equivalent to a season of ravage (Lev. xxvi. 34) ; as if the seventy years' desolation should make up for the neglected observance of the times of rest, for the whole duration of the monarchy.

Seven of these periods, or great years, brought round the cycle of the half-century. (Lev. xxv. 8 – 17, 23 – 54.) The year of Jubilee was announced by solemn proclamations of the priests, as the season of the restoration of all things, and a time of religious joy. The theory of the commonwealth supposed every family estate to revert then to its first possessor. Debts were extinguished, and the slave for

---

* A great annoyance in later times to the Roman tax-gatherers, who were compelled to respect what they styled the pious laziness of the Jews. (Josephus, Antiq., XIV. 10, 6. Tacitus, Hist., V. 4.)

debt was again free. The extremes of riches and poverty, so far as they exist at all among a people of so simple manners as the early race of Israel, were reduced to comparative equality. It was in its theory as equitable a solution as the genius of the legislator could devise to the deepest social problem. If it failed in practice, — which the declarations of the prophets make but too apparent, — it was because the conditions suited to the rude economy of a clan are outgrown in the complicated relations of a wealthy and commercial state. The institution of the Jubilee, whether ever realized or not after the model prescribed in the Levitical code, stands as a monument of the far-seeing policy and humane intention of those who laid the foundation of the Hebrew commonwealth.

The type found in the primitive institution of the Sabbath is thus carried out in each larger division of time, and marks the recurring seasons of religious holiday. The great annual feast-days seem to have been distributed with an obscurer reference to the same model. They include seven yearly seasons of sacred commemoration ; * not observing, however, the intervals of the great week, or month of fifty days. No celebration took place in the winter. The year was divided into two equal parts; and the sacred seasons were grouped about the ancient observance of the spring and autumn festivals.

---

* These, according to Philo, are : 1. Passover ; 2. First-Fruits ; 3. Unleavened Bread ; 4. Pentecost ; 5. Trumpets ; 6. Atonement ; 7. Tabernacles. To complete the decade, he adds the daily, Sabbath, and new-moon solemnities.

Of the seven special occasions thus provided for in the theory of the ritual, only five require distinct notice.

The religious year began just after the spring equinox, — the season when the Syrian festival celebrated the new birth of the returning sun. On the fourteenth of the month,* or eve of the first full moon, a lamb was slain for sacrifice by every household, and eaten as in haste, with unleavened bread and bitter herbs. It was a rite of expiation, and of preparation for the coming solemnities; and its memories were the more solemn, that they recalled the deliverance of the people when in silence and haste they fled from Egyptian bondage.

This was the feast of Passover. The blood of the slain lamb was sprinkled on the door-posts, — or afterwards on the altar, — the usual ceremony of expiation. It was then roasted whole, supported on two pomegranate stakes, one passing through the breast, and forming with the other the figure of a cross.† It was a mournful and silent meal, partaken only by men. The lamb was the substitute, or "ransom," of the first-born child; ‡ as if this were in ear-

---

* Leviticus xxiii. 5. Originally the tenth (Exodus xii. 3), leaving before the succeeding festival an interval of half a ten-day week, of which traces have been fancied in the earliest time (Genesis xxiv. 55).

† Which adds to the significance of the allusion in 1 Corinthians v. 7. See Justin, *Trypho*, p. 117.

‡ See Exodus (xii. 13, 23 ; xiii. 2, 15 ; xxii. 29), which connects it with the death of the Egyptian first-born. These and other allusions have suggested the opinion that the Passover is the relic of a more ancient rite, in which a child was slain, and its flesh tasted in the cruel sacrament, — a rite which popular credulity has perpetually charged

lier time a forfeit to the dark Power whose favour for
the year the old superstition sought thus bloodily to
propitiate.

The name Passover belongs strictly to the preliminary rite, but is often applied to the seven days'
"feast of unleavened bread" that followed. The
solemn act of propitiation having been performed,
and all impurities of fermented matter and the like
having been removed, the ensuing festival heralded
the new life of the opening year. Some early ears
of the new wheat-harvest were brought as a "wave-
offering" before the altar (Lev. xxiii. 10); these
kept in mind the original sense of the feast, which required a banquet of first-fruits. They were pounded,
parched, and made into unleavened bread.* Until
the harvest had been thus religiously partaken, it was
not lawful for it to be used at all.† The seven days
made one of the grand religious celebrations of the
whole people. All were supposed to share in its
solemnities; and even those who dwelt as far away
as Babylon or Rome might be represented in the
sanctuary by their annual gift.

The Pentecost was the "feast of first-fruits," or
the thanksgiving for the completed harvest. It was
also religiously associated with the giving of the Law,
as the Passover with the escape from Egypt. It was

upon the Jews at the season of Easter. (See Eisenmenger.) The
blood of criminals put to death at this season was firmly believed to
possess an expiatory value.

* Originally a sign of haste (Exodus xii. 39), — as Tacitus will have
it, because the Jews were hurrying away as thieves.

† A dispensation is said to have been allowed to the hot valley of
Jericho, where the harvest is some two weeks earlier.

a sequel to the earlier festival. It followed at an
interval of seven weeks, and made the third and
closing season of spring holiday. The wheat-harvest
had all been gathered in the interval; and that the
poorest might share in the joy of the festivity, it was
humanely provided that the grain should be loosely
gathered, and a liberal gleaning left. (Lev. xix. 9;
xxiii. 22.) Tithes of the harvest, with their accom-
paniment of oil and leavened cakes (a sign that the
harvest was now free for unlimited use), made the
popular contribution for the support of the priestly
body, — a support augmented by fines and the per-
quisites of sacrifice.

The still more imposing series of autumn festivals
was introduced by the day of annual Atonement, —
the tenth of the seventh month, and the great Sabbath of the year. (Lev. chap. xvi.) It was preceded
by a "holy convocation," or the "day of blowing of
trumpets" (Lev. xxiii. 24; Num. xxix. 1); and
was the day of solemn expiation for the sins of priest
and people, that, cleared from the stain of guilt,
they might be free to join in the approaching festivities. For a week previous (Lev. viii. 33) the high-
priest dwelt almost in solitude, undergoing perpetual
acts of penance, lest any ritual impurity should unfit
him for his office. The day, which commenced at
sunset, was kept strictly as a fast, and a season of
mournful solemnities. At midnight the service
of the priest began, with formal cleansings . prescribed by the ritual code. The great sacrifice of
Atonement marked the most solemn moment of the
Jewish calendar. It was the crisis of the religious

year, the culminating act of the ceremonial. On
this day, and no other, the veil of the inner sanctuary was put aside, and the high-priest stood face to
face before Jehovah. Bearing a vessel of incense
which he dropped upon a censer of live coals from
the great altar, darkening the shrine with its dense
smoke, he brought first the blood of a bullock slain
as a sin-offering for himself, which he sprinkled seven
times upon the ark. Then followed the remarkable
rite of expiation for the people. Two goats, alike in
age, colour, and size, were led before the sanctuary;
and one was assigned by lot "to Jehovah," the
other "to Azazel," the malign power of the wilderness. The first was slain as a sin-offering, in the
usual form, and the blood sprinkled in like manner
on the mercy-seat * and sanctuary floor, where it
mingled with that of the bullock previously slain;
and all that remained was poured out upon the great
brazen altar. Thus the shrine, the sanctuary, and
the altar were successively purified. Upon the head
of the other goat, by a solemn form of imprecation,
were then laid the offences of the people that might
expose them to the hostile power ;† and he was then

* See the interesting exposition of this rite given by Mr. Martineau,
in Lect. VI. of the " Liverpool Lectures," p. 58.

† Such seems the more obvious meaning of this portion of the rite,
which has, however, been very variously interpreted. A similar custom
is related of some Asiatic islanders, who " send a model canoe, cursed
and laden with the sins of the people, far away on the ocean ;" also
of certain tribes that make a horse the bearer of their ritual burden.
As the doctrine of evil spirits made no part of the earlier Hebrew
creed, it has been suggested that Azazel was " only a liturgical idea."
Perhaps the name is easiest understood as suggesting something like
the Greek notion of the infernal deities.

driven away to the supposed haunt of demons in the wilderness. Lastly, the animals already slain for sacrifice were totally consumed with fire.

This most solemn and remarkable act of the Hebrew ritual ushered in, at five days' interval, the last and greatest of the national holidays,— the feast of Tabernacles. If the fast and sacrifice of Atonement were the most mournful, the feast that followed was the occasion of the most unbounded and even riotous joy.* It was at the autumnal equinox, — the close of the year's labours. It celebrated the ripeness of the vintage, the gathering in of all the fruits, the full and luxuriant bounty of the God that ruled the year. For eight days the people dwelt in booths (Lev. xxiii. 40), or huts woven of green boughs and decked with festoons of rich foliage, recalling, by a double allusion, the old Syrian festivities of harvest-home and the memories of a camp-life in the wilderness. The dignity and splendour of this festival were augmented by time. At first it was held of less

---

* The following is Plutarch's description of this festival, interesting to us as a Jewish custom seen with the eyes of a Greek : " The greatest and most sumptuous festival of the Jews is in time and manner like that of Dionysus. For during the so-called fast at the flush of vintage, they spread tables with a variety of fruit, and set them under booths woven mostly of vine and ivy, calling the earlier part of the feast, *Tabernacles.* A few days later they observe another festival, which, without doubt and obviously, is that of the so-called Bacchus. This celebration is a bearing of bowls and festoons, during which they carry wreathed staffs (*thyrsi*) into the temple. What they do there we know not ; most likely it is a Bacchic feast ; for, in calling upon their God, they use little horns, as the Greeks at the Dionysiacs. Others advance playing on the harp ; these they call *Levites,* deriving this name either from the title *Lysius,* or more likely from *Evius.*" (Quoted by Winer.)

account than some of the other holidays. From the
Conquest to the Captivity it iş even said (Neh. viii.
17) to have been never once observed. But in
course of time it came to be more magnificent than
all. The week was a season of continual sacrifice
and festivity. Besides thank-offerings brought by
private hands, and other prescribed acts of devotion,
including the sacrifice of two rams and fourteen
lambs each day, seventy bullocks were slain, commencing with thirteen on the first day and diminish-
ing to seven on the last. Water drawn from sacred
springs was poured out with bowls of wine, in glad
libations. A grand illumination with the candela-
bras of the temple, lighting up (it was said) the
entire city, a religious procession with flutes and
songs, and a popular dance by moonlight, closed the
holy week. As the last of the sacred seasons, and
the termination of the festal year, nothing was omit-
ted that could make the ceremonial splendid and
imposing. And on each returning seventh or Sabbath-year, this was the appointed time for the public
reading of the Law (Deut. xxxi. 10, 11) and the
reviving of the august memories of the nation's
early history.

Thus the three great feasts of Passover, Pentecost,
and Tabernacles, with the day of annual fasting and
Atonement, made the marked features of the year,
and the most characteristic events of the religious
life among the Hebrews. It will have been seen how
they cluster about the ancient seasons of Syrian festivity; and how, if on the one hand they recall the
incidents of that period which shaped the first ele-

ments of the national existence, on the other hand
their significance shades away, and becomes blended
with memories of an earlier worship. The groundwork of Canaanitish custom was assumed, and turned
to the new demands of Hebrew faith, precisely as
the popular festivities of Italy, the Saturnalia and the
Etruscan ceremonial, were adopted into the ritual of
Christian Rome. The real aim of those who framed
the Levitical institutions is seen in this, — that they
sanctioned nothing of those primeval rites so identified with the people's oldest reverence and affections,
without moulding it to serve a higher purpose, and
attaching to it a secondary meaning, derived from
what was essential in the true faith of Israel.

The precise era of the transformation thus effected
it would be impossible to tell with any certainty.
Constant tradition, together with the earliest literary
monuments, attributes it to Moses. But a system of
law is not made in a day. A religious, any more
than a political, constitution cannot be fabricated out-
right, and wrought perforce into the thought and
life of an entire people. To engraft new fruit even
on an old stock, to attach a higher order of ideas
to an hereditary ritual, is a task of ages. How
early was this task accomplished among the Hebrews? Their history, down to the captivity, shows
us almost the whole population adhering obstinately
to traditions and usages which were relics of an ancient superstition, blindly prone even to the most
revolting and abhorrent rites of an idolatrous faith;
while, on the other hand, its religious teachers are
acting generally in the spirit of a purer creed, con-

tending at odds against a fanaticism they seek to
bring within bounds, sedulously cherishing a sentiment of national unity as opposed to the petty hostilities of the clan, and fortifying it by reverence to
the nation's God, as opposed to the alien deities of
tribes more barbarous than their own.* Iu the
course of ages that revolution was brought about,
of such infinite moment to the religious destinies of
mankind. Judæa alone, when the " fulness of time "
was come, was fitted to utter the Word which had
power to bring new life to a corrupt and sceptical
age. Its people, who would not share the grander
faith of the future, have continued the standing
miracle of history by their loyal adherence to the
religion of the past.

The agents of this revolution were the long line
of the prophetical men of Hebrew history, beginning with Moses and ending not till after the Captivity. Its instrument was the gradual building up of
those institutions whose main features have now been
traced. Without entering into questions of purely
literary criticism, we may regard these institutions as
having their root in primitive local rites and sacred
customs of the tribe, allied we know not how nearly
with similar rites and customs among surrounding
nations; then gradually gathered, classified, revised,
recast, after the central spirit or idea of a higher
form of faith, and so wrought up into a code of ec-

---

* See Ex. xxiii. 24, 33; Lev. xx. 2. The later law (see Deut.
vii. 2 – 5; xii. 2, 3, 29 – 31; xvi. 21) seems even more conscious of
invading Syrian superstitions, indicating probably a maturer development of the Mosaic faith.

clesiastic or levitical law, such as we find in the present Hebrew Scriptures, expanding indefinitely from
the type which an unchallenged tradition assigned to
Moses.

To a process such as this the existence and the
gradually increasing power of the Priesthood were
essential. In the patriarchal state its functions
were exercised by the head of the household, and the
chief priest was the chieftain of the clan. The sacred
office descended with the birthright to the eldest son ;
and the result would be a multitude of local rites
utterly divorced from one another, and a hopeless dispersion of the people among adjacent tribes. How
near the people of Israel were to incurring this fatality, the history has shown. After six centuries of
struggle, it ingulfed five sixths of them.

But in the construction of their nationality, under
Moses or his successors, the needful counterpoise, or
centralizing power, was secured by appointing one
sacred tribe, the Levites, as the delegated officials of
the people in all religious offices. (Num. iii. 12;
viii. 15.) At what time this change was introduced
it is impossible to tell. It seems easiest to connect it
with the establishment of the sanctuary at Jerusalem,
under the auspices of the Monarchy.* In memory
of the elder custom, the first-born son in every household, down to this day, purchases his exemption from
the service of the altar by a nominal sum of head-

---

* See pp. 126, 156. No reference is made to the Levitical body in
the books of Kings; and only a single doubtful notice (1 Samuel vi.
15) appears from the time of the Conquest to the later records of the
Monarchy. Samuel, the model priest, was of the tribe of Ephraim.

money (Num. iii. 47), paid when he receives the rite
of circumcision and his name. The males of the
tribe of Levi, not otherwise disqualified, were bound
to the service of the sanctuary from twenty-five to
fifty, the flower of their life. Being set apart, and
attached by an equal alliance to every portion of the
people, they were in theory exempt from civil duties,
and shared no portion of the conquered territory.
Their townships were assigned by lot or free gift.
(Num. xxxv. 2.) Their support must be from tithes
(Lev. xxvii. 30) and voluntary offerings at the altar.
A poor and vagabond priesthood it must have been
mostly in the earlier time,* if the complete theory of
it was then conceived at all, and until the splendid
era of the national life, when it shared the glory of
the monarchy that gave it dignity and strength. Subsequent to the Captivity, during the struggles and
short-lived independence of the little state of Judæa,
it attracted to itself all the functions of government,
and remained still powerful in its narrowing sphere
down to the final conquest by the Romans.

The ritual which was developed under the growing
power of the priesthood gradually formed a cluster
of religious associations about the spots of peculiar
sacredness. Ancient rites of high places, and family
altars, so frequent in the early periods of the history,
were superseded by degrees, as the centralizing policy of monarchy and hierarchy became established.
The Sanctuary, which had been removed from Shiloh
to Nob, Gibeon, or elsewhere, as danger or policy

* See the story of the Levite, in Judges, chap. xvii. and xviii. He
was "of the family of Judah."

might require, was finally transferred to Jerusalem,
and transformed into the magnificent temple of Solomon. Here the ceremonies of the religion acquired a
splendour wholly unmatched by anything in the past.
The Levitical establishment became part of the pomp
of royalty,— however uncertain its fortunes, exposed
to the shifting inclinations of the kings. The Levitical law, adopting the still remaining features of early
custom which it was impotent to overthrow, easily
adjusted them to the new scale of magnitude and
the new order of ideas. Reverence for the temple
and for the holy city was fortified by all that could
be engrafted or retained of the antique symbolism,
inherited as it were along with the patriarchal blood.
The elaborate ceremonial, with its crowd of petty
services, and its numberless cases of casuistry, legal
adjudication, and sanitary police, furnished abundant
occupation for the throng of priests, with their chiefs
and menials. The policy was right in its inception;
and doubtless it saved to the world the very existence
of the Hebrew nationality and name. Nor were the
prestige and privilege of the priest too great, if we
consider him as commissioned to sustain the interest
of the higher type of faith, and as the guardian of the
nation's religious centre. For that, he needed all
the authority, power, and dignity reflected from the
throne.

But the history has already shown that this great
advantage was not got without its heavy price. The
popular affection and faith, nourished on hill-top or
in grove, or within the charmed circle of local rites,
would not bear transplanting. By its change of

place the antique ritual suffered the loss of its identity. The old Hebrew spirit was averse alike to the
religious innovations and the despotic centralizing
of the monarchy. The division of the kingdom has
been exhibited (see page 172) as the protest of the
more ancient elements in the life of Israel against
the policy that invaded them. The lingering superstitions of the country, the relics of Syrian or Canaanitish devotion, the horrid rites even of Baal,
Moloch, and Ashtoreth, must seem to many the more
genuine inheritance of the elder time.* While Le-
vitic ritual flourished in the royal sanctuary, and
began to gather its own circle of tradition and to
gain a reflected sanctity, the corruptions of the old
idolatry became more rife than ever in the provinces.
The whole people, said the better religious teachers,
was given over to them. The priests were corrupt,
the prophets resorted to omens, magic, oracles, and
spells,† while the jealousy of the northern kingdom
against Judah was fostered by the policy of its kings.
The Hebrew religion was essentially and at first a genuine protest against the grossness of surrounding idolatry. In its better days, and while served by its better
men, it fulfilled this purpose well. But it retained
all along innumerable features that allied it with the
superstitions it could not wholly overcome ; and now
that the ritual was fully matured, and brought to its
consummate form in the temple at Jerusalem, these
led, on the one hand, to a slavish formalism that

* An opinion defended by Ghillany, and boldly assumed in Mackay's
"Progress of the Intellect."

† See Jeremiah v. 31 ; xxxii. 32 – 35.

11 *

made its meanest act symbolic of something in the
spiritual realm of God; and, on the other hand, to
that recreancy and degeneracy which finally scattered
ten twelfths of the people into blank oblivion, and
sank their nationality forever.

The danger of such an institution was, of overload-
ing the religion with the multiplicity of forms; of di-
vorcing itself from the antique simplicity and popular
temper of the true Hebrew mind; of smothering the
life in what was projected as its safeguard and defence; of giving birth to a new order of superstitions, as alien from the true faith committed to it as
those it was meant to suppress; or of compromising
unworthily with those customs, whose forms it retained, while professing to invest them with a new
significance.

It would have been against the experience of all
history, if these dangers had been constantly averted.
The Hebrew priesthood became, like other priesthoods, formalistic, domineering, and corrupt.* It
oppressed the people with the growing enormity of
tithes, forced donations, multiplied fines and burdensome penance.† It lost the popular heart. The
splendours of the capital and the seclusion of sacred
courts estranged it from the true temper of the national faith. Its integrity wavered with the changing and despotic policy of the kings. And it required the severe winnowing of a long captivity, the
sorrows of exile, and the close community of feeling
in a little colony after their restoration to the sacred

---

* See Jeremiah i. 18; ii. 8; v. 31.   † See Ezekiel xxxiv. 2 – 4.

hills of Judah, to unite priest and people upon the strict model of the later Judaism. •

Meanwhile, we must recognize an influence gradually developed from within, which strove perpetually to recall the primitive spirit and intent of the Hebrew faith. There existed in Israel, from the earliest time, a class of bolder and more earnest men, standing more independently each by his own conviction and form of thought. These men were now closely allied with the priesthood; now they protested vehemently against its faults. Their appeal was to the popular heart and imagination, for encouragement or reproach. They were now favoured and now persecuted by the kings. They were the orators, the poets, the preachers of the declining state of Israel. They were the honourable succession of the Hebrew Prophets.

VIII. THE PROPHETS.

AS the Hebrew institutions were the mature and regenerated form of rites and customs dating far back in the immemorial antiquity of the race, so in the Prophets was manifested the characteristic religious genius of that race. This genius it was which worked perpetually on the material found in the national mind or inherited in its traditions. It powerfully tempered the Hebrew spirit and character. It gave its distinctive colouring to political events and institutions. It confirmed the native tendency and guided the best culture of the popular mind. It reflected the nation's life and fortunes in a literature of high and peculiar order, and so became its especial representative to later ages. Finally, — which most concerns our present purpose, — it was the influence which moulded the nation's mind and morals from within; the first or spontaneous element in its religious progress; and so the needful preparation for the after stages of that evolution which made this people the harbinger of spiritual life to the entire family of mankind.

In our historic theories, indeed, we may regard every extinct nationality as a growth never quite completed; as the germ of a larger life not yet developed; as prophetic of what only a distant future can bring to fulfilment. But the Hebrews are nearly if not quite alone in consciously accepting this as their appointed destiny. Their gifted men were powerfully aware of a mission connecting them with the future yet more vitally than with the past, and constructed their forms of religious thought or national development in the vast spaces of an endless Hereafter. This it is which distinguishes that race from every other, and makes the religious value of its history inexhaustible.

Such was the peculiar place, and one eminent service, of the prophetical office among the Hebrews. But, in interpreting the phrase to the modern mind, we have to free it of its accidental modern associations, especially those which identify it with a particular department of the Hebrew literature. Prophecy, in the original sense of it, was " not a literature, but an act." It included in its larger meaning all that we understand by the term " spiritual power," as distinguished from the temporal power of the state, and (though more loosely) from the ecclesiastical power of the priesthood. In other words, it implied all the religious, moral, and intellectual agencies brought to bear vitally on the popular mind and conscience, — all, of course, limited by the standard of culture in a rude age, and shaped by the peculiar religious temperament of an Oriental people. It might be, and it often was, administered by a priest in full orders ; but in its essence it was altogether distinct. The priest had to do with the ritual and the stated services. He was, so to speak, the nation's delegate to the throne of its invisible Sovereign; his office was, to propitiate his offended majesty, and supplicate his royal favour. The Prophet — the " Seer," or man of vision, as he was called at first [*]— was the delegate of Jehovah to his people. He was emphatically a man of action and popular address. His sphere of activity was abroad among the people. His influence was one of the determining forces in each critical exigency of the state. In the civil and political life of the nation, as well as in the courses of its religious thought, his position is at once indis pensable and unique.

· The authority and prestige of such an office were sustained by a numerous well-recognized body. The class of men called prophets are reckoned not by soli tary individuals, but by companies, and even by hun dreds.[†] Especially as the ritual establishment ac quires coherency and shape, they appear more and more distinctly in the exercise of their peculiar func tion. Samuel, in his restoring or recasting of the national polity, gathered them in groups and estab lished schools for their special training. Young men of forward and active genius would throng together in them to learn the art of minstrelsy and the use of speech and writing, together with such mechanical or medical skill as the age could furnish. David's faith ful companion in exile and counsellor in the decline of his strength, the prophet Gad, gives a probable ex ample of the associations of this early culture. The prophetic schools were a noble conception of the last and greatest of the Judges, remarkable for that

---

[*] 1 Sam. ix. 9.   [†] Ibid. x. 10, xix. 20; 1 Kings xviii. 4, xxii. 6.

age, and invaluable in the after history of the nation. They furnished the rallying-point of intellect and religious zeal. The sacred traditions and early records of the race must probably have perished but for this germ of a national University. The arts which require most patient and elaborate method in their learning would scarcely have existed without such aid. The very forms and fragments of written history which have been preserved to us are doubtless in great part what after compilers borrowed from "the book of Samuel the seer, and the book of Nathan the prophet, and the book of Gad the seer," or from the later annals of Iddo and Shemaiah.* So that, for whatever made the Hebrews great as a people, or gave their history instruction and avail for after times, they were mainly indebted to that guardianship which Samuel and his successors exercised over the frail and early germs of their mental life.

Those who are at all acquainted with the religious history of the East will be at no loss to account for the profound influence at all times exercised upon the popular mind by this body of enthusiastic, earnest, and comparatively well-cultured men. Courses of a powerful and headlong fanaticism are familiar events in that history. Religious extravagance and frenzy are familiar facts in the mental physiology of Eastern races. The religious terror that gave its crushing weight to Oriental theocracy was easily roused by any

---

* 1 Chronicles xxix. 29 ; 2 Chronicles ix. 29. The books of Kings and Chronicles probably afford us a fair comparison between the mental qualities of the prophets and the priesthood.

vision, omen, or appeal, whether coming in the course
of natural events or in the word of an inspired man.
What might not be easily reconciled to a cooler temperament or a different way of life becomes natural
and familiar when transferred to the soil of the East:
where to the wild Arab the lonely desert is still populous with phantoms, and its drear silence haunted
with misleading demon-voices.* The dry and elec-
tric air may have its subtile influence, or the fierce
glare of the sun, or the mysterious affinities of race,
affecting the temperament of brain and nerve. What
we know is, that facts rare and abnormal in Western
climates or among Western races, are offered daily to
the incredulity of Eastern travellers; and by whatever name we call them, they must greatly affect
our judgment of visions and wonders recounted
among such a people, — still more of their popular
effect.

The same quality that makes one man a seer or
enthusiast will, in feebler degree, make a multitude
susceptible of the most powerful impression from his
words. To the Orientals the Franks have always
seemed cold and irreligious. Among themselves the
race of prophets and visionaries, and the answering
floods of popular fanaticism, never cease. The sudden triumphs of Islam are to be accounted for by no
device of imposture or lunacy, but by laws profoundly
written in the human constitution and working out
under the influences of an Eastern clime. A roving
Christian preacher at this day will rouse to passionate terror the whole population of a Moslem town by

* See De Quincey's Essay on "Modern Superstitions."

his prognostics of disaster;* and the counterpart of Hagar's vision, or Elijah's comforting voices in the desert, is repeated now in the tales of the Bedouin camp and the warnings of the hushed march of the caravan. Profoundly susceptible, like all Eastern races, of that whole class of influences which border on the mysterious and supernatural, the Hebrew people offered just the requisite field for the expansion and development of the prophetic gift. United as it was with a peculiar culture, and that intense and singular pertinacity of character and habit belonging to the race, it could not fail to become the culminating fact of their mental history.

The peculiar constitution of the state itself was based on a conviction that made part of the very life of Hebrew thought, — a conviction which must powerfully co-operate with the quality just spoken of, to give energy and effect to the function of prophecy. The "people of Jehovah" were instructed to ascribe to their Divinity both the direct founding of their institutions and every powerful influence that affected their destiny. Everything inexplicable and unseen must necessarily be referred to him, — the more certainly the more nearly it bore upon their own fortunes. Even such fatal events as the great pestilence of David's reign, the revolt of the tribes, and the massacres committed by Jehu, are ascribed to his express interposition and forethought; and the four hundred prophets who gave Ahab his false hopes of victory were really inspired by "a lying spirit" from Jehovah, as declared in Micaiah's eloquent story

* See Layard's "Babylon and Nineveh," p. 632.

Q

of his vision.* Of course, a man powerfully in earnest must derive his conviction from the same source. A rapt visionary, a poetical declaimer, a victorious champion, a skilled artificer, a sagacious and confident declarer of the future, a successful practiser of healing, or one who should exercise the now more familiar yet inexplicable power of finding hidden water-springs, or controlling mesmerically the bodily condition of others to hurt or heal, would even more certainly be regarded as deriving his gift from the particular favour of the unseen Sovereign.

Here, in the popular feeling and belief, was an ally by which the class of men known as prophets would be most powerfully aided, — all the more because the feeling and conviction were their own. The gift of bodily temperament or mental genius, of which they were conscious, they were expressly taught to regard as the commission or favour of Jehovah. A man of profound feeling, like Jeremiah, might shrink in trembling and tears from the pressure of the awful burden ; but it must be borne nevertheless, for the commission it implied could never once be doubted, — a commission that must crush every scruple, over-rule every thought of policy, and still every throb of fear. A barbarian chieftain, like Jephthah, or one of the incorrigible levity of Samson, might be forti-fied by believing in his own divine legation, though it should not save him from the worst superstition or the grossest vice ; while to one of resolute purpose, like Samuel, or of ardent and confident conviction, like Isaiah, the same belief would be the inspiration

* 1 Kings xxii. 19 - 23.

of the purest moral heroism. However shaded or stained, there is not the smallest reason to doubt that the belief was real. It made part of the temperament of the race and the creed of the religion. It was shared alike by prophet and king, by priest and people. This consideration is absolutely essential, if we would estimate correctly a single one of the many perplexing phenomena which the history of prophecy presents. Whatever else they were, they were not acts of shrewd jugglery or vulgar imposture; but, in the main, the acts of very confident and earnest men, who were instructed to believe thoroughly that what they did or thought was inspired directly by their nation's God. Both in their own and the popular belief, they were in the strictest sense ambassadors or representatives, to speak before the nation messages from the invisible and dread majesty of its King.

A single word is further necessary to state the true relation of Prophecy to the political power of the realm. It seems to have been clearly recognized and deferred to as a co-ordinate power with the monarchy, and as of at least equal authority. The theocratic constitution of the Hebrews acknowledged one full as much as the other. Each was a legitimate working force. Each was essential to the existence and the true development of the state. If they ever came into open collision, which they were too apt to do, certainly the divine element was not held more guilty of criminal ambition than the human. Nay, the Hebrew mind would probably regard it as rightfully paramount on the whole, however ill-judged at times we may regard its opposition; and what would be punished as treason or usurpation in a modern state offered no violence to that vague and simple polity. The high-handed control of Samuel over the royalty he had ordained; the political revolutions set on foot by Elisha; the practical statesmanship of Isaiah, who at a moment of extreme peril displaced Hezekiah's chief minister of state and inaugurated a most hazardous change of policy; the baffling remonstrance of Jeremiah against the last desperate defence of the capital, — have all been censured from the point of view of modern custom;* but the power that controlled the event in each of these instances was unquestionably felt to be a legitimate power in the state, however opposed to a "parliamentary regime," or the rude Erastianism of a democracy.

Doubtless it was perplexing to lay down rules to govern the fluctuating and unstable equilibrium of the two powers, spiritual and temporal; impossible often to secure the needful independence of the executive in the task of public defence against the sudden assault of a divine fury or an irresponsible enthusiasm. What form of government is without its own particular weak point? Yet, whatever the risk, it was one which the genius of the Hebrew state made inevitable, one which its lawgivers deliberately assumed. The national existence itself might be put at hazard, as in Saul's feud with the religious party, by the conflicts of policy that set prophet and king at variance; but no limit was suffered to be put to the "liberty of prophesying." Jeremiah's proclamations.

* See Newman's "Hebrew Monarchy."

of disaster.might unnerve the city's defenders in the
very crisis of a siege ; but he pleads the precedent of
Micah, and cannot be forbidden. Shebna might protest in behalf of a prudent policy, but Isaiah's eloquent and indignant boldness gets the victory. At
most, some uncertain test was offered to distinguish
true from false ; but, provided the profession of loyalty to Jehovah was unequivocal, nothing but tyrannical violence and usurpation could bridle the enthusiast, or even silence the impostor. The Hebrew
constitutional law abode courageously by the maxims
of a primitive devoutness, and the express edict of
the state * sanctioned that reverence towards the man
of God which made part of the popular religion.

Among the multitude whether of graduates from
the prophetic seminary or of solitary and self-taught
men, the qualities of wisdom, devotion, and even
mental honesty, were far from universal. In the
Scripture record, "false prophets" appear nearly as
often as the true ; and some of the most striking
scenes of the prophetic history are those of conflict
waged against them. The distinction is in many
cases quite independent of false worships and alien
superstitions. It is drawn among those who claim,
with equal apparent sincerity, the sanction and inspiration of Jehovah.† Nay, so far is it from always
implying a false pretension, that of Zedekiah and his
four hundred (just referred to) it is expressly said
that "Jehovah put a lying spirit in their mouth."
The distinction is not only very embarrassing to the
critic now, but it was at least equally so to the law-

* Deuteronomy xviii. 18, 19.   † Ibid. xviii. 22.

makers of the Hebrews themselves. Infinitely dis-
tressing in its perplexity, in the religious terrors and
counter-terrors that grew from it, it must have been
to the people, — perhaps in apprehension of some disaster, perhaps under the scourge of some affliction.
It is probably to be fully comprehended only by a
better understanding than we possess of the conditions of religious progress among the Hebrews, and
the steps by which a new order of ideas crowded out
the old. The state of Israel, doubtless, offers no ex-
ception to the "natural history of enthusiasm," or
the laws of growth observed in heresies. What we
read of as false prophets then would be reckoned
now as factious sectaries, or dissenters from the
stricter creed, — if our modern standard could measure the dim proportions of such ancient heresy.
Emphatic and repeated warnings are given to " be-
ware of false prophets;" but at a time when the
rancour of recent revolution made a test of falsity
especially desirable, the law is fluctuating and uncertain. At one time, prophecy takes the sense of prediction, and is to be proved by the event. At
another, neither miracle nor true prediction is a
sufficient test, but only fidelity to the law already
established, and to the exclusive worship of Jehovah.* In the later period of the monarchy the collision of the true and false became very frequent, as
testified by Jeremiah and Ezekiel, — a natural consequence of revolutions within the state, and of an irregular progress of religious thought stimulated from
abroad. But so few are our monuments and so

* See Deuteronomy xviii. 22; xiii. 2, 3.

imperfect our knowledge of the time, that we cannot draw the line of heresy with much more certainty than has now been done. We can only add, that the true faith of Israel may be assumed as that which history has preserved and ratified ; and that those prophets whose acts and words have survived to us, have at least their nation's verdict that they are its authentic spokesmen.

Neither can the entire amount and drift of their influence upon their countrymen be determined with much greater confidence than has already been implied in the description of their office. Some have compared them to the mendicant or preaching friars of the Roman Church, as messengers and agents of the hierarchy among the people. Some have imagined them as forming a sort of "opposition clubs" in the Hebrew state. Such conjectures, though they may do a little to pique the imagination, are quite as likely to lead it astray from the fact. The clearest picture we have of the prophets' way of life is found in the remarkable episode in the history of the Kings which details the acts of Elijah and Elisha. Here they appear as the instructors and familiar companions of the people. They dwell either in strange solitudes, like the first, or, like Elisha, in industrial communities, fathers of the monastic life. From these retreats they go forth, or send out their trusty messengers, to the special service which the time demands. They are bold to rebuke tyranny, stanch champions of the faith of Israel, tender in their sympathy with a people under oppression, stern and unflinching when the time comes

to avenge upon a guilty dynasty the arrears of accu-
mulated wrong. They are skilful in the treatment
of maladies with simple remedies, whether by human
or superhuman means ; practised observers both of
natural phenomena and political events ; adepts, apparently, in the rude handicraft and simple science
of the day. Knowledge and skill beyond the ordinary reach of men are ascribed to supernatural aid,
and recounted in tales of wonder. To predict a
change of sky and to foil a hostile policy are among
the examples related of prophetic skill. The notion
of Divine agency conveyed in the narration is often
untempered and harsh. The prophet becomes a
messenger of God's vengeance as well as of his
mercy. The healing of a leper or the. blasting of
a company of men by Divine fire, the restoring of
a dead child to its mother or the tearing of more
than forty by bears out of a wood when Elisha
" turned and cursed them " for their childish mockery, are told with equal unconcern, as parts of the
same marvellous. tale, superseding all human judgment of equity or cruelty. But of far more value
than any such narratives as these is the picture which
is suggested of the prophet's way of life in that early
time, — the real tenderness and confidence of his
intercourse with the people, — the mingling of his
personal agency in the great events of war or state
policy which were acting out around him. It is a
picture of one portion of the old Hebrew life, without which our knowledge of that people would be
quite otherwise incomplete than it is. And it leaves
us little to ask, except those questions, forever vain,

touching the exact degree of religious development then reached, and the real nature of the controversies which we discern so dimly among the obscure movements of the earlier Hebrew thought.

From the manner of instruction employed, we may infer the untaught simplicity of the minds the prophets addressed, as well as something of their own style of genius. The language of symbols — sometimes ingenious and suggestive, sometimes grotesque and quaint — is the favourite language of popular address. The touching simplicity of Nathan's parable of the ewe-lamb is an example standing nearly by itself, wherein the imagery is more delicate and pure, and the peculiar style of Hebrew religious teaching is shown in its most pleasing form. The prophetic imagery, or symbolic language, detailed in act or speech, is generally of a ruder and coarser sort. Zedekiah binds iron horns to his forehead and butts with them to signify that Ahab shall push victoriously against the Syrians. Hosea takes for his wife a woman of notorious ill life, to illustrate the infidelity of Israel in its nuptial relation to Jehovah. Isaiah walks openly for three years "naked and barefoot," or in the squalid garb of a captive, to picture the coming servitude of the Egyptians. A characteristic part of Jeremiah's ministry consists in a variety of symbolic acts which might easily seem trivial in the telling, though doubtless effective and serious enough in the acting; and in his predicting of subjugation he loads his shoulders with a yoke, which the bolder Hananiah breaks, to reverse the omen, or emblematic sense.

12

From pictorial or symbolic acts the prophetic style easily ascended into language of the same characteristic quality. The vast and vague magnificence of the Hebrew imagery is the most marked feature in that literature and the familiar representative to us of the national genius; by the consent of critics, it has become our conventional standard of the sublime. Nothing in the writings of any age, excepting what has been directly inspired from that source, surpasses the grandeur of the images in which the Hebrew prophets discourse of the state and sovereignty of Jehovah, or menace the doom of a profligate tyranny. The stern and obscure brevity of their style, condensing the images of a pictorial fancy, has given the writers of this people a hold upon the imagination of later ages such that they must always be the grand examples of this one element in the literature of the world. Nothing, indeed, gives us so high a notion of the general quality of the Hebrew mind, as the fact that these nobler passages of language, whether prophetic ode or vision or religious appeal, were portions of real and living address, — employed to move the popular conscience to a definite end, or to shape the actual policy of the state.

Enough has appeared, from time to time, in the course of the foregoing narrative, to enable us easily to generalize the history of the prophetical office, by casting it into three well-marked periods. The first is the period of unwritten prophecy, lasting down to the age of Elisha, and its general features have already been sufficiently described. The third, or latest period, including such compositions as appeared during the Captivity, or later, belongs to another place. There remains the second, or the earlier period of written prophecy, commencing about the middle of the ninth century before Christ, and terminating with the fall of Jerusalem. This period begins with Joel and ends with Jeremiah, covering a space of about two hundred and fifty years.

It was during this time, or the latter half of the monarchy, that these chief monuments of the Hebrew mind were wrought; and probably, along with them, a large proportion of the remaining Scripture was either for the first time written, or at least cast in its present shape. So that this is the most prolific and active period of the national genius, and that which most fully exhibits to us the intellectual character of that people. The changing fortunes of the state would stimulate all men to whatever mental activity they were capable of, while perpetual encounter with other nations would bring out in strong relief the peculiar qualities of thought that characterize the race. Thus another ground of interest is suggested in this discussion; since the period under review will give us a point of departure by which we may measure the mental advance made afterwards, under a different set of influences.

Those occasions in the history which brought forward, one after another, the series of the prophets, have been already briefly noticed, and need not be repeated here. The questions remaining to be considered are, what is the style of religious thought to be discerned in them; and especially what is their true interpretation with respect to the religious life, hopes, and progress of humanity ? *

The first obvious thing that occurs to us, as we glance along the line of honoured names, is that the series culminates near midway, in the glorious hopes and visions, the firm attitude of religious confidence, the exultation arising from an unlooked-for deliverance, and the generous and wise temper of an enlarged charity, associated with the name and public ministry of Isaiah. The eldest of the company are harsh and brief, bitter in their denouncing, vindic-

---

* The following brief outline, or recapitulation, is condensed from Ewald, "Die Propheten des Alten Bundes." The dates are only approximate : —

B. C. 830. JOEL, in the reign of Amaziah, bewails a plague of locusts, and censures the neglect of sacrifice. Atonement being made, he predicts the divine favour to Judah, conquest and slavery to Edom, Tyre, and Egypt.

B. C. 800. AMOS, a missionary in the northern kingdom, details the splendour and prosperity of the reign of Jeroboam II., together with its oppression, riots, licentiousness, and idolatry. The Assyrian power threatened.

B. C. 770. HOSEA, the last prophet of the northern kingdom, speaks of the idolatry, etc. at the close of Jeroboam's reign, and the convulsions succeeding ; factions, seeking foreign aid. He suffers persecution and exile.

B. C. 750 – 700. ISAIAH : his visions and consecration (ch. vi.) ; early Assyrian conquests (ii. 2 – v. 25 ; ix. 8 – x. 4 ; v. 26 – 30) ; their further advance (xvii. 1 – 11) ; invasion by Pekah and Rezin (vii. 1 – ix. 7) ; warning to Philistines (xiv. 28 – 32) ; to Moab (ch. xv., xvi.) ; to Dumah and Arabian tribes (xxi. 11 – 17) ; to Damascus (ch. xxiii.) ; imminent invasion of Assyrians (i. 2 – 31, — the remonstrance was effectual, in Hezekiah's reforms) ; base treaty with them ; charges against Shebna (xxii. 1 – 25) ; proposed Egyptian alliance (ch. xxviii. – xxxii. and xx.) ; promised deliverance from Assyria (x. 5 – xii. 6) ; message to Ethiopians (xvii. 12 – xviii. 7 ; xiv. 24 – 27) ; defiance of Sennacherib (ch. xxxiii. ; xxxviii. 22 – 35) ; national judgments, resulting in restoration of the true faith ; alliance and harmony of Egypt, Assyria, and Judah (ch. xix.).

tive in their threatening. The later have more of despondency than hope, express rather complaint than confidence : so that we feel, for Jeremiah especially, rather sympathy in the sorrow of his burden than gladness and honour for his bearing of it. We cannot nicely discriminate the temper of the different stages, where all is at once so strongly national and so intensely personal. Yet, with the culminating of this period of the nation's life in the reign of Hezekiah, we feel that the richest harvest of Hebrew thought is gathered ; that what went before was of

B. C. 750. UNKNOWN (Zech. ix. 1 – xi. 17 ; xiii. 7 – 9), parallel with Isaiah, ch. ix., but referring to the northern kingdom.

B. C. 720. MICAH : parallel with Isaiah ch. x. – xii., etc. (see p. 191) ; false prophets and unfaithful statesmen ; decay of faith ; destruction of city and temple apprehended.

B. C. 650. NAHUM, an exile in Assyria : threatened destruction of Nineveh and Thebes by Medes.

B. C. 630. ZEPHANIAH: terror at inroad of Scythians ; deliverance can come only after judgment.

B. C. 600. HABAKKUK : invasion of Scythians and Chaldees, after Josiah ; no allusion to old offences, but the new lesson of trust in hopeless calamity.

B. C. 588. UNKNOWN (Zech. xii. 1 – xiii. 6 ; ch. xiv., written just before the destruction of Jerusalem) : a dweller in the country; he confides in the deliverance of the city, while Jeremiah desponds.

B. C. 585. OBADIAH (after the fall of Jerusalem) : the malignant vengeance of Edom, to be revenged by Arab marauders.

B. C. 620 – 580. JEREMIAH : personal incidents, appeals, predictions, etc., giving a full picture of the siege and fall of Jerusalem ; struggles with persecutions ; confuting of delusive predictions of triumph.

B. C. 590 – 570. EZEKIEL (one of the earlier exiles ; "rather a writer than a prophet ") : visions of the restored Theocracy.

UNKNOWN (Isaiah, ch. xl.–lxvi. the great prophet of the captivity, living probably in Egypt ; by Bunsen considered to be Baruch, the scribe of Jeremiah) : general and exalted predictions of restoration, the higher destiny of Israel, and the Messiah.

crude unripeness, that what is later will be the more
spare and solitary gleaning. The declining light is
often more gentle and soft, but it has not the fresh
glory of the day.

In estimating these works as literary compositions,
we have to remember that they are only relics and
specimens of what was probably a large mass of
similar address, written or unwritten. It was not
till the later period that prophecy became a literature
by main intention. Such compositions as those of
Ezekiel, or the magnificent chapters appended to the
book of Isaiah, may have been the production of
more cultivated minds, wrought out in solitary study.
But the earlier prophets spoke or acted as the occasion moved, and to an instant practical end, of warning, rebuke, or cheer. The writing down of their
message was an afterthought, and was left till the
imminency of the occasion had passed by. Indeed,
by the peculiar genius of the Hebrew tongue much
is wrought up in the impassioned style of prediction
or appeal, which a more cultured dialect would have
discriminated in the colder tone of history, — being
written or recast years perhaps after it was delivered, and when the contingency foretold was already
past.* It was in the retreat from persecution, or in
the loneliness of exile, that Amos and Hosea composed their elaborate pictures of the declining state
of Israel, embodying the symbols and appeals they
had employed in their active ministry ; and Isaiah's
noble ode of defiance was unquestionably written
down after the tumult and terror of the invasion had

* See Isaiah xxx. 8; Jeremiah xxxvi. 2.

passed away. So that the writing is in some regards an uncertain reflection of the speech, while the speech suggests the type and affords the criterion by which to judge the more elaborate writing. Much of the abrupt and lively manner is retained; the symbolic acts are detailed in all their freshness; while, in the fashion of the popular speaker, fragments of address are interspersed, suggested by the occasion, or directed to a particular class of hearers.* Not only the fitness of the language or order of ideas must be measured by the needs of the occasion, but the thought itself is often disguised in a symbol of doubtful interpretation. It is only with considerable freedom of criticism, and with the allowance of a wide margin of uncertainty, that we can trace at all the course of positive opinion hinted in the prophets; still less can we ascertain the real condition of the popular belief. Besides the general character of the Hebrew literature and institutions, already described, a few more striking passages of imagery, or veins of religious thought, are all we have to mark the advance of mind in that age, and ascertain its amount of preparation for a later and higher culture.

In our estimate of the mind of this period, we must take into account, furthermore, such compositions as the Book of Job and many of the Psalms; which not only, as seems likely, belong here in point of time, but are genuine prophetical writings as much as any, if we adopt the only consistent interpretation of this phrase. Aided by these, our estimate of the

---

* As, for example, to women. See Amos iv. 1 - 3; Isaiah iii. 16 - iv. 1, xxxii. 9 - 12.

truth and spirituality of religious ideas among the
Hebrews will be very greatly enhanced. We may
except to many a special image or point of view ; but
religious writings that have survived so many revolutions of human thought, and still hold their place in
the general reverence and affection, must in some
essential regards be alike beyond our censure or our
praise.

The religious significance of such writings lies
not so much in clearness of outline or distinctness
of intellectual view as in the tone and elevation of
thought.   It would be idle to go to them for instruction on particular points of faith, save as instruction
may be hinted in their often spontaneous and fervid
utterance of a spiritual fact.   To construct a theological scheme, even to require consistency of religious
opinion, could not possibly have entered into the
mind of that day.   The faith which the prophets
demanded was a moral quality.   It was loyalty to
Israel's God ; fidelity in the line of service which the
conscience of that time could apprehend.   The spiritual attributes of the Almighty were never presented
with any consistency or clearness ; neither the precise relation in which outward acts of faith stood to
the Divine ordinance and will.   Sovereign power,
bare and absolute, made the basis of the popular
conception of Jehovah's rule, modified only by such
special favours as he bestowed on his chosen people.
" I form the light and create darkness, I make peace
and create evil," is the language the prophets ascribe
to him ; and the sublime passages of the Book of Job
crush the mind under the awful sense of his irresisti-

ble and unquestioned sovereignty, before its calmer lesson is given, of trust in his equal recompense.

Again, the prophets, as moved by an intenser and clearer moral sense, stood often in the attitude of protestants and reformers, as regarded the priesthood or the ritual ; but not always, or in any such sense as to represent an opposition party, or even to indicate any decided advance in that direction. Their language or their attitude was determined partly by the temper of the time they had to meet, partly by the conduct of the priesthood and the overgrowth or decay of ritual observances. Instead of heaping weight in a single scale, they seem rather to have laboured to keep that degree of equilibrium of form and spirit which to the Hebrew conscience would best represent the normal condition of things. The extravagances of religious independence were no more to be admitted than the deadening oppression of a corrupt formalism. Joel — of a priest's family, and perhaps a priest himself — calls for a sacrificial atonement to avert the visiting scourge; while, with Amos, God will accept no sacrifice, but demands that " judgment run down as waters, and righteousness as a mighty stream." Isaiah and Micah, in the golden age of prophecy, vindicate the moral as far above the ritual meaning of the code, and Jeremiah denies that sacrifices were ever the Divine command ; * while Ezekiel, at a later day, exhibits the most elaborate and painful formalism of all, along with the severest invective against past abuses. If there is such a thing as unity of purpose among the whole number of the prophets, it is

* Isaiah, ch. i. ; Micah vi. 8 ; Jeremiah vii. 22.

at any rate concealed under that diversity of circumstance which gave shape and colour to their appeal.

As to the invisible world, the prophetic visions only reproduce the familiar images of regal state, enhanced by the splendours of such symbolism as we find wrought out in the imposing works of Egypt and Assyria,* where winged figures are emblematic of God's swift decree, and the human countenance of the seraph denotes that wisdom which men but faintly apprehend. The hierarchy of the heavenly hosts, with the characteristic names of the archangels, belong to the fancies of a mythology not yet learned. An angel, in the earlier Hebrew belief, was but an envoy of Jehovah, sent on some special errand; the " thrones, dominions, and powers of heavenly places," so vividly presented in the poetic imagery of a later age, made part of that more gorgeous and positive creed adopted during the long sojourn in the East.

The shadowy realm of the Departed, the abode of gloom and dreariness, which is the only relief to the blank oblivion that follows death, is of a piece with the untaught and fanciful mythology which prevailed among every ancient people, till its dark shade was illumined by the dawning light of immortality. Job hints, with pathetic patience, his trust in a living Redeemer, who shall vindicate him from the heavy reproach of guilt, and so take away the sting of his calamity; but the clear and positive anticipation of a life to come made no part of the Hebrew faith. At best, its dismal imagery could make the apparition

* See especially Isaiah, ch. vi.; Ezekiel, ch. i.; Hab., ch. iii.

of Samuel a real terror to the conscience of the
shuddering king, or give force and vividness to the
gloomy sublimity of Isaiah's image of the powers of
the under-world moved to meet the oppressor at his
coming, or startle us with the story of a dead man
restored to life at the touch of the sacred relics of a
prophet. The apprehension of a future state was
distinct enough to haunt the imagination and clothe
itself in forms of a religious fancy, but not to suggest any profound lessons of retribution, or minister
comfort in anguish, or furnish the key to a ritual
symbolism, or vindicate the mystery of a half-hidden
Providence. It required the teaching of another
order of events, and the contact of another system
of belief, to develop in the Hebrew mind the latent
faith in the Unseen, and so complete the circle of its
religious thought.

As an intellectual system, nothing could be more
simple and undefined than the theology assumed by
the Hebrew prophets, beyond the few points that
have now been named. As such, they did not much
to develop or extend it. Their real office was in
part as its preservers, bringing the mind of the
people continually back upon the faith and loyalty
which were from of old their noblest attribute ; and
in part as its reformers, testifying in the name of
Jehovah against many forms of abuse, and by the
very honesty of their purpose insensibly enhancing
their own and the popular sense of right. When
their task was done, and the career of their nation
closed, the animosity or narrowness due to the pressure of their time would gradually subside ; so that

their true legacy to after ages would be the residue
of higher thought, and single-hearted zeal which it
was their mission to associate forever with the name
and worship of Jehovah.

Barred by the narrowness of their creed from the
vast and illimitable spaces of a heavenly Future, and
alike from the vision of a reign of humanity upon
earth, their faith in the providence of God, as manifest
in Israel, concentrated itself in a boundless and be-
nignant hope for their own chosen people.   Early in
the prophetic history, and especially when the gloom
of the present prospect required the strong contrast of
a positive glory in the future, we find the dawn of the
"Messianic prophecy."*   There seems almost a wilful
positiveness and grandeur in the confident assertions
of triumph made so often under the very pressure of
impending ruin.   That it was a real and sustaining
faith, that, in spite of a thousand defeats and centuries of disappointment, it remains so to this day, is
the singular glory of the Hebrew race, — like one ray
of Divine light resting upon it through the dark and
dreadful humiliation it has sustained.   If its original
meaning were never to be verified, yet the hidden and
unintended meaning, which gave an unflagging courage, which revived the perishing germ of nationality,
which nourished a sacred zeal by lingering and precious memories, and prepared the world's welcome
for the "Father of an everlasting age and Prince of
Peace," was a divine prophecy of truth given and
heard unawares.   The words it was spoken in may
seem to us the natural utterance of the occasion,

* See Joel ii. 28, iii. 17; Isaiah vii. 14, ix. 1 – 7, ch. xi.

working on the profound and passionate conviction of a Hebrew mind ; but their sense to the imagination and heart will always be what the genius of triumphant melody has made it,* — the homage of Humanity to its Spiritual Sovereign, the inspired longing and promise of a Divine Redeemer.

The more definite forms of Messianic prophecy, the beautiful lyrical amplifications of the earlier hope (found especially in the closing chapters of Isaiah), belong to the subsequent age. They bear the spiritual quality, and expand in the purity of anticipation, triumphant or tender, which were wrought out in a period of larger culture and less violent vicissitude. The declarations of the elder prophets are brief, occasional, and vague. They abound not so much in clearness of statement, making them distinct to the reason, as in clusters of imagery, making them vivid to the imagination. Their garb is not that of definite prediction, but of vague anticipation and poetic rhapsody.

And, still further to denote their character, they occur miscellaneously among the appeals to conscience or the declaiming on political events, without any hint that they are of broader scope than that connection would seem to indicate.† They come in incidentally, to round out the circle of the prophet's familiar thought, rather than dwell minutely or fondly on the visions of a remote future. In short, like other modes of prophetic doctrine or appeal, they take the precise form and pressure of the time.

* In the "Wonderful Chorus" of Handel's *Messiah*.
† See Isaiah, chaps. vii. - ix.

They are held out as encouragement in particular emergencies, or as assurance against particular disasters. They are a vindication of the permanency of the Hebrew faith, and the faithfulness of Jehovah, who will not suffer his people to perish. They seize some passing event, or domestic incident, or symbolic personal name, as a "sign," omen, or hint to the imagination, that the national hope is not doomed to fail. Its triumph is generally heralded, as if it should come with the vanishing of the immediate danger; * and it is not till those of clearest foresight despaired of the city's defence against the king of Babylon that its fulfilment is deferred for a period of seventy years, — till the land should have expiated the guilt of its five centuries' neglect of its seasons of religious rest.†

Such is the general character of what are known as the Messianic prophecies of the Old Testament, — including in that phrase not only such as hint at a coming Sovereign and everlasting reign of peace, but all which foretell the nation's deliverance and triumph amidst impending danger. That these predictions should gradually shape themselves towards the announcement of a restored monarchy, in renovated and purer form, after the fondly imagined type of David's reign, was inevitable under the conditions of Hebrew thought. That they should include the

---

* See Isaiah x. 24 – 27, in connection with chap. xi.

† 2 Chronicles xxxvi. 21. The real duration of the Captivity was about fifty years; and the disappointment of the prophetic hope (which looked successively to Cyrus and Zerubbabel) seems to have suggested the interpretation of "seventy weeks," or five centuries. See Isaiah xlv. 1; Haggai ii. 23; Daniel ix. 24.

firm and universal dominion of the national institutions,* was part of the prophet's loyalty to the
only form he could imagine of the true religion,
and was required by the homage he paid his nation's
God. It is needless to repeat the imagery, sometimes splendid, sometimes tender, in which the indomitable hope was variously portrayed. It is not
the particular form of. declaration, but the mental
quality so perpetually active and so characteristic
of the race, that gives its chief value to this portion of
the Hebrew literature, together with the answering
quality in the popular mind, which so fondly echoed
the words, and cherished the hope, and expanded
into large proportion each detail of the imagery, and
so, out of what had grown to be a gorgeous dream,
created the magnificent type of mankind's conception of its Redeemer.

This one element, refined and almost purely spiritual, has survived to us, out of the vast influence
wielded upon their own generation by "the goodly
fellowship of the Prophets." How mingled and
various was that influence, how tempered by passion,
delusion, and narrowness of view among some who
bore the name, how affected by superstition, obstinacy, craft, hate, or fear, among those who, with a
vague awe, received it, how misinterpreted by the
fiery zeal or ignorant prejudice of after times, has
been sufficiently shown. A single word suffices to restore us to the right point of view, which regards the
history as a whole, and seeks its significance for the
later evolution of human thought. The divine or

* Isaiah ii. 2; Micah iv. 1.

providential aspect of that history is reflected precisely here, — in the highest reach of thought and purest moral aspiration attained by the foremost men of the race. While so much of the nation's life is utterly forgotten, or grown unintelligible and obsolete, — while most of its records have perished, and its very name is but dimly and apologetically inscribed in the registers of. the ancient world, — while the race that bore it, after centuries of ignominious persecution at the hands of generations that disowned their great debt, is even now struggling for some equal recognition of its religious and civil right, — these bravest and loftiest words, spoken by its true representative men, make even now a spell to stir men's thought, and a living power in the permanent literature of the world. For, through their often meagre brevity and dense obscurity and wearisome perplexity, still shines the light which guided the desert-march of Israel ; still sounds that "voice crying in the wilderness," which from distant ages yet heralds to our heart the latest and purest hope of Humanity.

IX. THE CAPTIVITY.

THE two and a half centuries succeeding the fall of Jerusalem cover the entire brilliant period of Grecian history, from Solon to Alexander. They begin just before those first conquests of Persian power that threatened an Oriental despotism to domineer over the destinies of Europe : their close finds the little Jewish state, after twenty years of buffeting in the game of ambition between Syria and Egypt, annexed as an appendage to the empire of Ptolemy, the Macedonian master of the South.

To the fortunes of Israel this period was a critical one, though not eventful. The political unity of the nation was utterly broken. There remained only its sacred memories, its ritual, and its religious polity. The royal theocracy of Solomon and Hezekiah becomes a regency of priests. The brief annals of the time, almost blank of historical recital, present us only the broken, yet zealous efforts to restore the perished state, the petty feuds of a covenanting sect, and the gradual strengthening of the priestly power. It is the era of Jewish Puritanism. It begins in the longing and sorrow of exile ; it continues with the sad and slender fortunes of a pilgrim colony. It begins with the blazing out of the brightest flame of Prophecy; it ends with its pale and expiring light. The ancient ritual is adopted under new pledges as the basis of a narrower zeal and a more exclusive polity. The form of old faith is guarded more jealously than ever, while its creative spirit becomes extinct: and the canon of Hebrew Scripture is closed — like a casket that should keep untouched the treasure held in trust for another age — just as the Grecian mind and arms become dominant in the East.

When Jerusalem was taken, the national life and hope of Israel had all but utterly perished. Of the inhabitants of Judah, some clung as they could about the wasted fields and dismantled towns; some lived miserably, by sufferance of the hostile garrison, among the highlands near Jerusalem; some were scattered through Arabia, or among the colonies and islands of the west, as far probably as Carthage or even Spain; and some, more fortunate, found friendly shelter in Egypt, where germs of a more ideal faith, and trust in a destiny yet in store for Israel, began presently to grow afresh. The bulk of the population — of whom Jeremiah reckons up only forty-six hundred;* in all, perhaps, about as many thousand — were taken to fill the void spaces of a capital so vast, that, when half of it was afterwards in the hands of an enemy, the rumour of attack was in some districts still unheard.

It was the humane policy of the great Eastern monarchies,† not to treat their captives as slaves or sell them into foreign bondage, but to make them useful colonists, — if possible, contented subjects.

* Chap. lii. 28 – 30.
† See Grote's History of Greece, Chap. XLII.

The Jews along the Euphrates were thus left with
no small amount of personal liberty. They had their
own local rulers, their religious chiefs, and the free
practice of their forms of faith. They embarked in
various forms of enterprise and trade. They had
property in houses, lands, and slaves.* Numbers
of them at a later day attained considerable local
importance; some even, as Daniel and Mordecai,
came to the highest dignities at court. The inevitable hardship of exile was made keener, doubtless,
at first, by the insolent and dissolute idolatry of the
great capital of heathendom, and by something like
religious persecution when the heart was too full of
a loyal grief to furnish mirth for a pagan revel.
"I have given Jacob to the curse and Israel to reproaches," Jehovah is made to say; "they that rule
over them make them to howl, and my name is continually blasphemed." "The visage of my people is
blacker than a coal; they are not known in the
streets; the slain with the sword are better than
those that perish with hunger, for these pine away,
stricken through for want of the fruits of the land."
And hanging their harps upon the willows, by the
rivers of Babylon, the captives "wept when they re-
membered Zion." † But even in this regard there
came to be freedom, at least indulgence. Ezekiel
could tell his visions unmolested among "the captives by the river of Chebar;" messages of counsel
or rebuke were sent from Egypt or Palestine, by the
aged Jeremiah, to his fellow-exiles across the Syrian

---

* See the accounts respecting Mordecai, Tobit, etc.

† See Isaiah xliii. 28, lii. 5; Lamentations iv. 8, 9; Psalm cxxxvii.

desert; and the "great unnamed" Prophet of the Captivity could cheer them at a distance with his glowing promises of a divine Champion, and a coming spiritual reign of Israel. Thus the national hope had not perished. The destiny of the race was not wholly accomplished. The divine instinct which looks to the future was not lost. The "remnant" which elder prophecy * said should return, and build up again from the desolation it foresaw, was ready to answer, unembarrassed, the first summons to the holy land.

In the mean time, relations peaceable and friendly grew up between the exiles and the conquerors. Chaldæan forms of speech invaded the purity of the old Hebrew tongue, and Chaldæan names were adopted in Hebrew homes. Local attachments were formed as older memories faded out. The half-century of forced banishment brought many to adopt a foreign land from choice. The purest Hebrew blood was naturalized in Babylon. The pining exiles became first contented subjects, then prosperous and willing colonists. Their characteristic thrift did not desert them; and no pious scruple deterred them from a profitable tenure on the plain of Shinar. "This captivity is long," Jeremiah had forewarned them, "build ye houses and dwell in them; plant gardens and eat the fruit of them." With the majority the new tie was stronger than the old. The Babylonian Jews continued a flourishing community long after the later state of Judah was crushed by the merciless revenge of Rome. Their long existence as

* Isaiah x. 20, etc.

a distinct body, their independent schools of learning, their wealth and consequence, as shown in the style of their tradition, and the repute had of them in Oriental story, all attest the tenacious hold which the transplanted stock had laid upon the soil.*

It was with jealous alarm that the more pious and patriotic saw the course of this denationalizing. The most vehement expostulations of Jeremiah are directed against the threatening apostasy. " My people, go ye out of the midst of her," he exclaims, after denouncing woe and ruin against the city, " and deliver ye every man his soul from the fierce anger of Jehovah. Go away ; stand not still ; remember Jehovah afar off, and let Jerusalem come into your mind!" The pride and splendour of Babylon became a symbol of everything that is hostile and hateful to Jehovah, — an evil eminence which " that great city " holds in the visions of the Apocalypse, and in the polemic metaphors of this very day.

The greater jealousy and dread were felt, because here was the centre of Oriental civilization, with its intellectual pride, its insolent and cruel despotism, its gorgeous idol-worship, its effeminate and infamous luxury. The conquest of Jerusalem had taken place in the middle of the long reign of Nebuchadnezzar, the most famous and splendid of the Chaldæan monarchs. His ambition was to adorn and fortify, by the most lavish outlay, his enormous capital : in curious testimony of it, every brick of its ruin bears the

* For the titles and dignity of the Son of David, " Prince of the Captivity " in Bagdad, in the twelfth century, see the Travels of R. Benjamin of Tudela. (Bohn's " Early Travels in Palestine.")

stamp of his name.* One wonted to the compact
and picturesque scenery of Judah, with its irregular,
close-built towns, and the pastoral landscape, home
of pious and venerable story, would be not so much
astonished as lost and appalled among the vast splendours of " Babylon the great," — a city connected by
tradition with the lewd violence of primeval giants,
and Nimrod's bold impiety, and the rebellious blasphemy of Babel.

A district fifteen miles square, rich with gardens,
orchards, palaces, and the low, scattered dwellings of
an Asiatic population, was enclosed in a prodigious
wall of sixty miles in circuit and three hundred feet
high. Such was the scale of grandeur of this proud
Oriental capital. The great " gates of brass and bars
of iron " that defied an enemy's approach ; the gorgeous temple of the Sun, a furlong high ; the terraced
or " hanging " gardens of more than three acres, —
orchard and forest being lifted on stupendous arches
to the height of the city-wall itself, to please the
homesick fancy of a highland queen ; the system of
drainage, such that it was said the whole water of
the Euphrates could be drawn off into an artificial
lake, and fatally exposing the city to the night-strata-
gem of Cyrus ; the fortifications of corresponding
magnitude that defended a region far greater than
all Palestine, — works of fabulous and terrifying vastness to an unaccustomed eye, as if wrought by demons and not by men, — all were part of that insolent pomp of idolatry which had challenged and destroyed the poor district-worship of Jehovah. Partly

* See Layard.

with terror and hate, partly with an heroic trust in
the Arm they believed to be àlmighty, the faithful
now answered back the challenge of their conqueror;
and the bolder prophetic spirit triumphed already in
the sure prospect of his overthrow.

This passionate and vindictive hope grew more
vivid as the time of deliverance drew near. "These
nations shall serve the king of Babylon seventy
years," said Jeremiah,* — and when these were accomplished, that is, before the close of the second
generation, — the captivity should be at an end.
Fifty years had not yet passed, when the great Conqueror Cyrus, with his freshly organized military
monarchy of leagued Medes and Persians, advanced
from the north upon the plain of the Euphrates. In
him the Jews were eager to find their promised
deliverer. Already, in the prophecies of the later
Isaiah,† Jehovah addresses him as "his shepherd,"
and "his Messiah, — whose hand he has upheld to
subdue the nations."

Besides, the Persians brought from their clear, cool
mountain-region a simplicity of manners, and a purer
type of worship, that might easily make them seem
the natural allies of Israel in the great conflict with
idolatry. An austere and imaginative temperament
had — at least among the better interpreters of their
doctrine — turned the gross nature-religion common
to the East from the worship of the Sun or fire, to
adoration of the pure elemental Light, which the recent reform of Zoroaster ‡ had closely assimilated to

---

* Ch. xxv. 11 ,12.   † Ch. xlv. 1.
‡ According to the most probable chronology.

the simple monotheism of the Hebrews. The Dualism of the Parsic creed, the struggle it announced between the eternal powers of Good and Evil, would not be unwelcome to them now, as figuring the type of contest to which their religion had committed them. Ormuzd and Ahriman were but the more vague Oriental symbol of the God and Adversary of their people. At any rate, this, with other doctrines of Persian origin, is found strongly colouring the style of later Hebrew thought; and, however undefined, may have had its effect now in making the new invaders seem to be expressly commissioned by Jehovah.

The war of religion, therefore, which the Persians waged, more or less concealed under the war of policy or conquest,* was one which would call out the strong partisanship of the Jews. In the confident tone of prediction, and in the suddenness of the reward, one might even infer a serviceable secret league between the conqueror and the expectant exiles within the gates. The Scripture narrative † summons the great Daniel to the royal banquet, to announce the doom which that very night would befall the sacrilegious and dissolute king. And within a year after his victory, Cyrus issues the decree

* See extracts from the "Behistun Inscription," in Rawlinson's Herodotus, Vol. II.

† Daniel, chap. v. The manner in which Daniel is mentioned by Ezekiel (xiv. 14), who wrote from thirty-five to fifty-eight years before this event, has suggested the opinion that he was one of the earlier captives of Nineveh; the "Book of Daniel" (written three centuries later) naturally placing him in the more famous epoch. Ewald, "Die Propheten," Vol. II.

acknowledging the sovereignty of the One God who gave him victory, redeeming the captivity of the Jews, and authorizing their return to Palestine.*

Henceforth the fortunes of the Hebrew race are narrowed down to those of the single colony of Judah, with its outlying branches in Babylon and Egypt; and the title " Jews " becomes appropriate, instead of that which more broadly designates the nation or the race. Here, too, we begin to trace the marked effects on the national life and thought both of their experience of exile and of the wider intercourse henceforth open to them with the mind of other nations. The predominating influence was by turns Persian, Greek, and Roman. And the matter of chief interest in the later history is to follow the course of the successive influences, whereby the original type of Hebrew faith is so moulded and transformed, and so blended with other elements of the world's culture, that its germ of truth should finally ripen in a faith limitless and universal, and become the religion of the civilized world.

The Captivity of Babylon had lasted a little more than fifty years.† We cannot tell the story of it in its events, for of these there are none, but only in its effects. One effect has been seen already, in weaning away the affections and interests of many from the

---

* B. C. 536. See the decree in its Jewish dress, Ezra i. 2 – 4.

† To complete the prophetic seventy, some suppose an earlier transportation in the time of Jehoiakim, together with the hostages mentioned in Daniel, ch. i.; some, that Jeremiah dates from the time of his own announcement at the first rise of the Chaldæan power; and some, that the period closes with the dedication of the second temple. But most narrators proceed without noticing the flaw in the chronology.

land of their fathers, and naturalizing them in the
East. It did not alienate their affections or pervert
their faith as to their inherited religion. On the contrary, they seem to have kept a loyal regard towards
Jerusalem, and to have prided themselves on the assiduous zeal of their piety, and the superior purity
of their blood.* But they had no share in the adventurous faith and pious enterprise of the Jewish Puri-
tans. .Their home was in another land. It was not
for them to undergo again the privations and pains
of exile. Their good-will and charity might attend
the pilgrims ; and from their condition of comfort or
command near the Persian throne, they might be of
generous and timely service, as mediating between
their countrymen and their monarch. But the half-
century had made a gulf that broadly sundered them
from the fortunes and sympathies of the West. Its
first effect was seen, accordingly, in drawing this new
line of separation, and making of Judah a divided
people.

Nor were its effects less marked on those who
accepted the royal offer, and who represent henceforth the state and destinies of Israel. As it introduced a new line of demarcation, so it blotted out
the old ones. Hereafter, we know no distinctions
of the tribe. The register of the returning Jews
classes them only by families. The fiction of the
twelve original tribes was still kept up in sundry

---

* Signified in the statement cited from the Talmud, that Ezra took
with him to Jerusalem all those of doubtful parentage, "so that the
Jews left in Babylon should be pure like flour." "Whosoever dwells
in Babylon," it is added, "is as though he dwelt in the land of Israel,
and is reputed as clean." (Lightfoot.)

vague traditions and in many a religious allusion ; but the reality of it was irrecoverably lost. The fortunes of the ten northern tribes have never been followed with the least approach to certainty. Jewish legend transplants them far eastward, towards central Asia ; where their identity is miraculously guarded, and where a vast and splendid kingdom, never visited by the traveller or to be seen by Gentile eye, preserves the chosen race (" an immense multitude not to be reckoned by numbers ") for their august coming destiny.* Modern fancy has traced their likeness in the character or customs of many a race, — the Affghans, the Persian Nestorians, and the Algonquins of North America. Looking merely to the likelihood of fact, one remnant of them may have mingled in Palestine among the mixed breeds that made up the Samaritan population ; and another, if it escaped fusion with other races during its long exile, may have joined the returning Jews, and so the blood of every tribe should flow in the veins of each. Except in family genealogies, or in the sacred line of priests, nothing is known, since the first capture of Jerusalem, of those tribal divisions, or characteristic traits, so marked throughout the earlier history. Even the long feud of Ephraim and Judah survived only in the religious antipathy between Samaritans and Jews.

The ancient aristocracy represented in the honours of the Tribe being lost, there remained only the " caste aristocracy " of the religious orders. The

---

* 2 Esdras xiii. 40 – 46. See also Eisenmenger, " Entdecktes Judenthum," concerning the fabulous empire of " Presther John."

Priesthood now appears, far more prominently than ever before, as a privileged and powerful class. It includes, or by degrees absorbs, all the power and dignity of the state. This was the consequence, in part, of circumstances none could control; in part, of the separation that took place in Babylon. Doubtless it was a heavy disappointment, both to the prophets and to the religious leaders generally, that so small a share of the people followed their lead to Palestine.* Including many families of doubtful descent, together with household servants, hirelings or slaves, the whole migration was less than fifty thousand. As a general thing, the more important and able of the population remained behind,—that part, too, which claimed purer degrees of blood. Besides sincere enthusiasts, the most valuable portion of such a colony, the migration must have gathered in its ranks the poor, the ignorant, the adventurous,—an untrained and motley mass. Their single common object was a religious one; their one bond of union, loyalty to their religious chiefs. Thus every circumstance favoured the exclusive ascendency of the priests. As every way the ablest and most intelligent, they were also the fit and rightful leaders. Besides, it was a matter of importance not to excite the jealousy of the royal power at Babylon. An ambitious secular chief or a turn of political agitation might have blasted the enterprise at a breath. No thought of possible independence must be suggested; no fear that the new settlement might ever be turned into a hostile gar-

---

* See Jeremiah l. 4, 19; Ezekiel xxxvii. 11, 12.

rison. The quarrel with the Samaritans once nearly defeated the entire object by rousing such a suspicion. To avoid it, a religious enterprise must be the only front it should present; the only power to rule it should be a spiritual power. The regency of Priests was both the natural and the effectual resort, to check any budding jealousy and secure the germ of the infant colony from perishing.

This immediate and decided ascendency of the priestly class aided to form several strongly marked features of the later Jewish character. The Ritual became a thing of exaggerated and exclusive consequence. So far as the local government was concerned, it was in fact almost the entire law. The Sacred Books were regarded with new and superstitious veneration. This is the era of proselytism, of elaborate compilation, of assiduous comment, of canon-making. An anxious and minute erudition, or implicit deference to the closed canon of any book, always marks the decay of intellectual life. The age of Prophecy expired when the age of Creeds began. In place of the free, glad loyalty with which the Divine Sovereign of Israel is named in tales and ballads or religious songs of the elder time, we find presently the scrupulous superstition which held it profane to utter aloud the name Jehovah, and disguised it even in writing.* In place of the national faith, the spontaneous creative spirit that dictated psalm or

---

* In Hebrew, by vowel-points corresponding not with the true name itself, but with another word signifying "Lord;" which was substituted for it in reading, and is its usual representative in Greek and English. The probable pronunciation, *Yahveh*, was preserved by the Samaritans. (Theodoret, quoted in Sophocles's Glossary, *s. v.* 'Ιαβέ.)

prophecy, we find the careful dividing of sections and numbering of words and letters in Holy Writ. The outline of the grand old theocracy is painfully preserved; its meaning trimmed to the proportions of a feebler time and people, — instead of a free desert horde, or ambitious independent monarchy, a poor scant colony under the rule of priests. It was, indeed, a shadow of the old Hebrew institutions that remained, — a type of the new condition of things, showing what part had been fulfilled, and what was yet wanting to the nation's destiny.

Some features of law or ritual were extended, and urged with scrupulous strictness, as those relating to holy time, — the fanatical observance of the Sabbath, and the realizing or revival of the sabbatical year. And while the Levitical law was thus strictly kept, the encroachments of Grecian culture on one hand, and on the other the great growth of Oriental tradition or laborious comment, give us presently germs of the contending sects of later Jewish times. In the style of additions now made to the sacred books (such as the "Chronicles" and the later Prophets) we see the marked change in the type of Hebrew mind that resulted from the exclusive ascendency of the holy order. The priestly rule, in many essential regards, met both the fact and the want of the time. But by an inevitable fatality it prepared the way, through the steps just hinted at, for that bigoted formalism, that truculent and unlovely fanaticism, so marked in the later Jewish character.

In the social condition and temper of the people we trace yet another influence of the Captivity.

Twice within two generations their hold upon the
soil of their birth had been wrenched away; and,
in the interval between, they were exiles in a land
strange to their ancient ways. So the great change
was wrought, which, from patient husbandmen on a
scanty soil, made them traders, ready at any hazard
for adventure, trade, and gain. The Jewish stock,
too, was now very widely spread. It had three main
branches, — the colonies in Babylon, Palestine, and
Egypt, — and among these some way of constant communication would be found. And so there came
about that singular blending of traits, which made
the most bigoted provincial in the realm of faith at
the same time the most thorough cosmopolite in the
world of trade. The chance and broken settlements
in Judæa, and the unsettled condition of that age of
conquest, must have further helped to form this feature of Jewish character, so exaggerated in later
times by a thousand years of persecution, dispersion,
and reproach.

Still another result of the Captivity remains to be
more distinctly noted, — its effect on religious doctrines and ideas. Close contact with the Chaldee
and Persian theocracies had very considerably enlarged the circle of Hebrew speculation. The Zoro-
astrian doctrine of immortality, in the form of
bodily resurrection from the realms of death, begins
to be current in the dominant Jewish sect, and becomes, a little later, a received article in the popular
creed, the root of many an extravagant fable that
decked the dream of an earthly paradise.* To this

* See Eisenmenger.

was added a gorgeous and fanciful mythology of the
invisible world. The general notion and hierarchy
of the Angels is derived mainly from the Persian,
names of Hebrew origin being assigned to the seven
" Amschaspands " that surround the Throne of
Light; * while the particular forms of fancy, vividly
drawn in the visions of Ezekiel and Zechariah, reproduce the well-known symbols found in the buried
palaces of Nineveh.

We find henceforth no trace of the old proneness to
idolatry, the sensual Syrian fancy being utterly taken
captive by the dreamy vastness of Oriental fable. Jehovah is no longer the local deity of Palestine, or the
"jealous God" of a petty clan; but is more and more
invested with the attributes of a spiritual and universal
God.† His enemies or rivals are no longer the divinities of surrounding tribes, but the types of natural
or moral evil symbolized in the Zòroastrian creed.
The doctrine of the celestial hierarchy, and rebellious
angels, with their influence on human destiny, prepares the way for the later fables of the Talmud, and
the "endless genealogies" of Gnosticism. A profounder, at least a more grave and earnest, philosophy of Good and Evil sprang from commerce with

---

* R. Simeon ben Lachish says : " The names of the angels came up
in the hand of Israel out of Babylon. For before it was said, *Then flew
one of the Seraphim unto me; Before him stood the Seraphim.* (Isaiah vi.)
But afterwards, *The man Gabriel; Michael your prince.* (Daniel ix. 21;
x. 21.)" Lightfoot on Luke i. 26.

† In the book of Nehemiah the word "God" is almost invariably
used instead of the proper name "Jehovah," — a symptom of foreign
influence found also in many of the later Psalms, among which may
be reckoned the 103d and 139th.

this Oriental style of thought. Satan now appears,[*] after the likeness of the Persian Ahriman, as the foe of good, and the especial Adversary of Jehovah's people. And the conception of a fearful retribution of guilt after death, even if earlier rudiments of it may be traced, at least begins now to have a distinct effect to shape the doctrines of the Jewish creed.

We find, too, a breadth and pliancy of speculation, a cosmopolitan temper in thinking, a yielding to foreign invasion in the realm of abstract ideas, characteristic of the later Jewish mind, curiously contrasted with its former bare simplicity, and curiously blended with its precise and rigid formalism in matters of faith. The very narrowness of their previous culture, and their superstitious deference to the letter of the Law, seem rather paradoxically to have made the Jews all the more open to these importations of opinion. Every analogy they found or fancied between their Scripture and the sacred traditions of Chaldee or Persian, — as afterwards with the philosophy of the Greeks, — they would lay hold on as a divine sanction to the doctrine that claimed a speculative assent. And a later age is astonished to find not only the speculations of Plato traced to a Hebrew source, but Moses himself made the prince of philosophers, and a subtile creed of metaphysics prefigured in the naive legends of the book of Genesis.[†] This trait of mind was first brought into activity and relief during the time of the Babylonish Captivity.

The colony that accepted the grant of a settlement

[*] I Chronicles xxi. 1.
[†] See below, " The Alexandrians."

13 *

among the ruined villages and forts of Judah put itself under the lead of Zerubbabel the governor * and Joshua the priest. Zerubbabel had been a favourite at the Persian court for his accomplishments and wit.† He now showed himself a stanch Israelite in affectionate and patient loyalty, — a man of resolute and enterprising temper, such as the forlorn pilgrimage demanded. He was the deputy and representative of the royal authority in the new and dependent state. Joshua, the high-priest, brought in his hands the symbols of the spiritual power, and by his presence gave it the sanction of ancient institutions and a national worship. The whole colony amounted to near fifty thousand.‡ A single and sacred aim swallowed up whatever there might be of difference in opinion or incongruity of material. The enterprise was a religious one. Those who shared it were of the straitest sect of Jews, Covenanters in their creed, and exiles for their faith. The temper of the rising province was that of a narrow, intense, and bigoted nationality, tenacious of ancient custom, and rigidly exclusive of alien blood, chafing no doubt at the protectorate the time compelled, and impatiently looking for the triumphant sovereignty which ancient seers foretold.

Nor were circumstances wanting to exasperate, and bind all the closer the new sectarian national-

---

* Called also Sheshbazzar. His title under the Persian commission was "Tirshatha," or governor. (Ezra i. 8, ii. 63 ; Nehemiah viii. 9.)

† See the narrative in Esdras, chaps. iii., iv.

‡ Ezra ii. 64, 65. In exact numbers, 49,697, of whom 7,337 were servants, including " two hundred singing men and singing women."

ity. The Holy Land — since half a century trampled
and defiled by hostile feet — offered her slender hospitality to the new migration. The mixed race of
Samaritans had long held the better parts of it; and
during the long disorder the tribe of Edom, still hostile and resentful, had spread towards the north, seizing many a possession in Judah or along the banks of
Jordan. A miserable remnant of the former inhabitants clung round the ruin of the sacred city, where
the garrison that was left behind to keep down any
tumult or rebellion continued long after to mark the
presence and domination of a foreign power on the
very heights of Moriah.

The new temple, the first great undertaking of the
colony, was a work of cost and hazard, beset by the
straits of poverty, and the jealous ill-will of those who
resented this new occupation of their territory. It
may have been a wise precaution of Zerubbabel
against an encroachment that would have demoral-
ized the only motive he could trust to build on, when
he rejected the suspicious aid of the Samaritans, but
it had nearly nipped the enterprise in its germ.
The foundations of the temple had been already laid,
amidst religious festivities, the tears of a burdened
and grateful memory, and the shouts of patriotic joy,
when a deputation came from Samaria claiming kinship in faith, and proposing alliance in the religious
work. This was promptly and disdainfully refused;
and "then the people of the land weakened the
hands of the people of Judah, and troubled them
in building." They found it no hard matter to de-
fame the new colony with the wayward and suspi-

cious despotism of Cambyses, and a royal order forbade the rebuilding of the "bad and rebellious city." Then came the confusion of Cambyses' Egyptian conquest, the disasters suffered by the colony during his march, and the plots that followed his death, when the Chaldæans (now degenerated from a great military power to a caste of "Magi") made their desperate attempt to retrieve their fortunes by installing the false Smerdis as king in Babylon. During all these troubles there could be no hope in resuming the unfinished work; "so it ceased unto the second year of Darius, king of Persia."

This politic and sagacious sovereign was not slow to discover the error of blasting the still loyal colony by an ill-timed jealousy. The early years of his reign were spent in quelling the insurrections of the provinces, and constructing the admirable system of finance and police by which he built together the disjointed fragments of his empire.* The Jewish settlers, encouraged by the return of peace, and the exhortations of their prophets Haggai and Zechariah, were already moving afresh in their enterprise. When accused by Samaritan informers as building "a citadel rather than a temple," it was easy to refer to their charter given by the great Cyrus; which Darius ratified at once, adding munificent gifts, with orders to his satrap to encourage and defend them. Already they had gathered something of stability and comfort about the settlement. They "dwelt in their ceiled houses," and their defences were enough to give

---

* In the popular Persian phrase, Cyrus was a father; Cambyses, a master; Darius, a truckster, or "merchant-king." Herodotus, III. 89.

colour to the invidious charges of their neighbours. And in about twenty years from the time of their first-migration the great task was done, the seventy years of desolation were accomplished, and "the children of the Captivity kept the dedication of this house with joy." (B. C. 516.)

For more than half a century, until the time of Ezra, there is absolutely no record of the Jewish state; * and we find only two or three fragments from the history of the next hundred and fifty years. The wise policy of Darius was followed by his successors, who indeed were too deeply involved in the great ambitions and disasters of the monarchy to heed a petty outlying province. That policy yielded to the Jews a qualified independence, and trusted their strong local partisanship to guard the exposed frontier of Judah. The sympathy of their numerous kinspeople in Babylon was a sufficient pledge of their fidelity to the great king. Spite of their provincial bigotry, they were loyal subjects in the main. The little colony that now represented the dominion of ancient Israel could not safely bargain its allegiance, or play its part among the powers of the world. Its obscure foebleness was its safety. Its charter of existence

---

* In some part of this period, if anywhere, we are to insert the narrative of Esther (in the reign of Xerxes), and the apocryphal episode of Judith. (Judith iv. 8.) But the wreck of historical recollections, and the hopeless confusion of the names of the Persian kings, manifest in the Jewish traditions of this age, make it difficult to deal with these episodes as true matters of history. The worst insanity of despotic caprice would scarce have sanctioned the massacre of 75,000 subjects, under colour of self-defence against an irrepealable statute. (Esther viii. 11, ix. 16.)

it held by sufferance of a stronger will. The great
storms of conquest blew over Judah to spend their
strength elsewhere. The long struggle of Persian
and Greek, begun with the resentful invasion of Darius, and ending with the swift, broad conquests of
Alexander in the East, scarce disturbed the little
hierarchy that sheltered itself among the broken ramparts of Jerusalem. And when the friendly empire
is crushed under the resistless onset of the Macedonian, the petty Jewish state offers no resistance, but
yields itself, with easy deference, to be the prize of
the stronger arm.

The Jews in Babylon meanwhile kept up their religious estate and sympathies, with a line of sacred
descent parallel to that in Jerusalem. Ezra was their
" principal priest," — a man so devout that he was
" worthy to have been the author of the Law, if God
had not already given that dignity to Moses ; " so
learned in the Scriptures, that one tradition asserts
him to have written out the entire canon from memory, since Nebuchadnezzar had burned all the sacred
books. It was a signal service he rendered in the
interior development of Judaism. The attention of
Artaxerxes had been somehow called to the Jewish
colony, and Ezra was commissioned to be his envoy
to Jerusalem (B. C. 459). He was allowed to take
with him all who desired to join the colony (about
fifteen hundred men), and to carry rich gifts both
from his countrymen and from the royal treasury.
His spiritual rank in Babylon gave weight to his character as champion of the Law; and reports of the
new state of affairs would hasten his embassy of re-

form. "The good hand of his God was upon him;"
and so full of confidence in his divine mission, so full
of a prophet's faith and a reformer's zeal he set forth,
that he refused the royal guards, and passed through
the hazards of the desert march unarmed and safe.
"For I was ashamed," he says, "to require of the
king a band of soldiers and horsemen to help us
against the enemy in the way ; because we had spoken
to the king, saying, The hand of our God is upon all
them for good that seek him, but his power and his
wrath are against all them that forsake him. And
the hand of our God was upon us ; and he delivered
us from the hand of the enemy, and of such as lay in
wait by the way."

On a far narrower scale, yet with results almost as
signal and strongly marked, Ezra did for the hierarchy of Jerusalem what Hildebrand did long after
for that of Rome : that is, he gave it shape, coherency,
and a strenuous discipline, indispensable to its later
strength. His chief task of external reform, too, was
like Hildebrand's, — to correct the irregularity and
abuses that had sprung up through the " mixed mar-
riages " of priest and people. For the later colonists,
like the early conquerors, had broken the line of
rigid separation, and become considerably mingled
among the populations of the land. Their excuse
would doubtless be, that, as in many another case,
the colonists were mostly men, and must seek wives
where they might be found. No heresy in faith or
depravity of morals is related to have followed this
loosening of the bands of law ; but the popular conscience, trained to a ceremonial obedience, readily

took part with the reformer. The delinquents — a hundred and fourteen of their names are given — were forced to put away their wives and children. Politic and friendly alliance must yield to the rigour of the creed. The strict and exclusive Judaism of the later age had its seal and illustration in the ritual purity exacted by the zealous priest.

The later acts of Ezra are known to us only by distant tradition, more or less uncertain. It was he that completed the Hebrew canon; that wrote the books of Chronicles, as well as the brief sequel which bears his name; that introduced the square character of the Hebrew text, and made the inspired revision of every line or letter of the sacred books. The name Malachi, "my Messenger," writer of the latest prophecy, is currently held among the Jews to be a title of Ezra. Apocryphal legends tell of other visions and adventures, and his long conference with an angel touching the after fates of Zion.[*] Various reports of his death place it in extreme old age, — some, as late as a hundred and fifty years. It is his true merit and glory, that, by his reform of Jewish customs, and his labours on the written laws and records of his people, he more than any man was instrumental in giving shape and consistency to the later Judaism; or, as their saying is, in "setting a hedge about their law."

But the sudden reform of Ezra had provoked the anger of neighbouring districts, or local disasters had befallen from contentions among the greater powers, or the whole enterprise fell from the first behind its

* 2 Esdras.

hopes. " The remnant in the province were in great affliction and reproach ; the walls of Jerusalem were broken down ; its gates burned with fire ; " the people too few for their own defence. So the tidings came a few years later to Nehemiah, then the king's favourite and cupbearer in Susa. The Persian power had about this time suffered a series of reverses from the Athenian Cimon, terminating in a defeat at Salamis in Cyprus (just after his death), which left the Greeks masters of the Levant ; and the need of strengthening a loyal province on the exposed frontier may have favoured the expedition of Nehemiah. Under the king's commission he now entered on a course of vigorous administration, which continued near forty years. Roused by their new leader, the people rebuilt within two months their ruined fortifications,— a labour of constant peril, in which " every man with one of his hands wrought in the work, and with the other held a weapon." * And once more there was promise of a well-administered and defended peace.

But the people were poor, and distressed with dread of famine : many of them under debt to their richer neighbours to pay their current tribute to the government, and threatened with being sold as slaves. Nehemiah "was very angry when he heard their cry." " Will you even sell your brethren ? " he demanded of the usurers; " or shall I buy them of you ? " They had nothing to reply ; and in the great tide of public

---

* " Est igitur rarus, rus qui colere audeat, isque
Hac arat infelix hac tenet arma manu."
OVID, *Tristia*, v. 10, 15.

T

indignation he compelled them to restore the mort-
gaged lands and vineyards, and declared the general
abolishing of debt.   Drawn by his own generous
example, gifts flowed freely into the sacred treasury.
The deserted streets of Jerusalem were repeopled by
numbers from the surrounding country, who volun-
teered for the necessary defence.   The reform begun
by Ezra was sustained by the well-timed vigour of
his coadjutor, while his own labours on the law and
learning of the state found the advantage of securer
shelter and better aids.   The "great Synagogue" of a
hundred and twenty of the most devout and learned
Jews, — some of whom the vague chronology makes
extant a century later, — is related, with much probability and some fabulous exaggeration, to have shared
in this pious service.   The ritual law was now for-
mally established, or confirmed anew in its existing
shape ; the sacred books were publicly read by scribes ;
and such a celebration was had of the great festival
of Tabernacles as had not been " since the days of
Jeshua the son of Nun unto that day."

Returning to Susa when his work seemed well
accomplished, Nehemiah was again recalled to the
task that still required his vigorous and shaping
hand, and he scarcely relinquished it until his
death, at the age of seventy.

Among the later acts of his administration, his
strict and impartial discipline had banished several
of the most powerful of an opposition party.   Of
these was Manasseh, a man strong by position as
high-priest's son, and as son-in-law of the Samaritan
prince or governor.   His alliance had made a dan-

gerous entrance to Samaritan intrigue, to which his
exile put a sudden stop. His father-in-law, to avenge
more completely his defeat and damaged pride, built
a rival temple on Mount Gerizim, of which Manasseh
was made high-priest, that the line of regular descent, thus turned awry, might vex the religious
loyalty of the Jews. Some, it is said, were drawn
away, — those already discontented with the strict
rule of priest and governor, and coveting the laxity
of the half-gentile creed. But all the more ·bitter
was the resentment of the faithful. An angry strife
that would not be appeased sprang from the rivalry
of the two temples ; and the Jewish proverb of contempt classes among the unpardonable foes of God
"the foolish people that dwell in Sichem."* Manasseh, as the account proceeds, being of the high-
priest's family, had taken with him a copy of the
Hebrew law, which the Samaritans mangled and
corrupted to serve their claim of orthodoxy ;† so
that the war of the temples was further embittered
by controversy about the sacred books.

The next century offers us only one event of any
note, and that a tragic one. The high-priest Judah,
a generation after the reforms of Nehemiah, left two
sons, Jesus or Joshua, and John. The latter succeeding to his father's dignity, Joshua was suspected
of a plot with the Persian governor to get the office
for himself. John stabbed him in the temple ; and
personal resentment as well as public justice de-

* Ecclesiasticus l. 26.

† Particularly in Deuteronomy xxvii. 4, where the Samaritan text
substitutes Gerizim for Ebal.

manded vengeance from the Persian. (B. C. 366.)
To the horror of the Jews, the temple was now for
the first time profaned by Gentile feet; and the only
reply to their remonstrance was the stern question,
" Am I not purer than the murdered body ? "   Almost for the first time the imperial hand was felt for
chastisement instead of shelter, in the seven years'
penance imposed upon the city to expiate the sacrilegious fratricide.   A league with Egypt about this
time to throw off the Persian yoke is also spoken
of; and this, with the incident just told, may denote
the embittered party feeling, the religious degeneracy, and the decline of loyalty towards the decay-
ing empire, that probably marked this period of the
nation's life.

In five and thirty years that empire had fallen
under the Macedonian conquest, and Alexander the
Great was king in Babylon. (B. C. 331.)   The
Grecian arms had crushed the last great Oriental
dynasty.   An empire representing a more advanced
social condition, and a higher type of intellect, now
supplanted the perishing Asiatic despotism.   The
Eastern world was brought into new relations with
the West.   Grecian language, science, and cultivation came to explore and possess the fields once held
by the old theocracies of the East.   The process was
cruel and bloody; the result, auspicious and providential.   Free intercourse among populations long
hostile and estranged enlarged the domain of peaceable commerce.   It gave new and needed stimulus
to the advanced intelligence of the time.   It opened
in new forms the eternal questions of reason and

faith. It tempered by Grecian thought the vagueness of Oriental theology, while it gave fresh food to the religious imagination of the speculative and sceptic Greek. It assimilated by a subtile alchemy a thousand discordant elements. It established a tongue flexible beyond every other, and of infinite resources, as the common speech of the civilized world; and prepared the way of thought, as the Roman power prepared the way of empire, for the advent and swift conquests of a faith, claiming to be universal.

Results so vast in their bearing on human destiny were hidden from the eye of man, though clear in the great scheme of an historic Providence. Yet, in its own way, Jewish legend has symbolized this equal encounter of the two great forces, — the West with its victorious intellect and arms, the East with its victorious faith. When Alexander the Great, on the eve of his final conquest, had come to the country of the Jews, an enemy of their state accused their narrow and unjust policy, and besought him to reduce the insolent city to subjection. But as he approached, with his pomp of soldiers and his staff of mighty captains, the Jews hung their streets with holiday garlands, and formed a great procession, as for some religious festival, and went forth silently, clad all in white, the high-priest, with his richest robes of sacrifice, at their head, to meet the conqueror. Their eager enemies looked now to see them humbled and given up to them for vengeance. But Alexander, when he saw the form and apparel of the priest, gorgeous with purple, scarlet, and gold, and with the jewelled plate bearing the sacred name of God, went reverently forward and bowed before the priest, adoring that awful Name. Then, when his officers were astonished, and thought him mad, he answered them, that so in vision that form had appeared to him in Macedon, promising him victory in that name; and that his triumph in the approaching battle was now sure. Having so spoken, he entered the city, and performed the solemn rite of sacrifice; and confirmed to the Jews all their privileges, and granted them every favour that they desired. And so the majesty of Jehovah was once more manifest, not only in delivering the holy city from the vengeance of its enemies, but in receiving the willing adoration of the mighty conqueror of the Eastern world.

Twelve years later, Ptolemy, the half-brother of Alexander, having entered Jerusalem as if to take part peaceably in the Sabbath-sacrifice, made himself violently master of it. (B. C. 320.) Then followed the long struggles of ambition between Syria and Egypt, which, after twenty years, left Judæa for a century more a dependency of the latter power. A hundred thousand Jewish captives are said to have been removed to Egypt, where their descendants grew presently to a million, and made two fifths of the population in the splendid capital city, Alexandria. And, under the indulgent rule of the Ptolemies, each portion of the Hebrew stock was preparing to take the singular and important part assigned it in the great historic drama about to be unfolded.

X. THE MACCABEES.

THE annexing of Palestine to the realm of Ptolemy repeats, as it were, that event of the early history which transferred Israel and his fortunes to Egypt. As the old hierarchy of the Nile had been essential to the first stage of Hebrew development, so the Greek arms and culture that now displaced it gave force and direction to the last. And whether in Palestine or Egypt, the Jews began now to be powerfully affected by the new influences of the West. Their colony at Alexandria, favoured by an indulgent dynasty, had its own temple and independent worship; it was acted on, steadily and profoundly, by the mind of Greece that found there its adopted home; and, dwelling for three centuries in the intellectual capital of the world, brought about that extraordinary fusion of Greek and Oriental thought, which has acted so powerfully on the modern mind in the shape of the Catholic theology. The Palestinian branch, after long yielding to the encroachments of foreign custom, until seeming altered and degenerated to the very centre, was at length roused to a passionate reaction by the profane and implacable tyranny of its masters. Taking advantage of the disorder into which the Syrian power had fallen, it succeeded, under a line of heroic and able champions, in reviving the lost sovereignty of Judah. With the alliance, and under the cautious protection of Rome, its little monarchy endured the shocks of a century; and it still retained a native king, a population of zealous faith, a ritual unimpaired, and a temple of undiminished splendour, down to the death of Herod, almost exactly contemporary with the birth of Christ.

For about a century after its treacherous capture by Ptolemy, Judæa was embraced in the equivocal protectorate of Egypt. The stanch and united colony, now grown to be a populous little state, lay as a coveted prize on the Syrian border. At one time it became the basis of a diplomatic bargain, or the price of a family alliance; at another, the spoil of war. So bandied from hand to hand among the quarrelsome masters of the East, "like a ship in a storm (says Josephus), beaten about by the waves on both sides," it was exposed to the rudest invasion of that foreign influence against which its temper was so prudently jealous. The subtile intellect and secular culture of the Greeks were led, with their spreading maritime enterprise, towards the little theocratic state lying so near the great highways of empire; * while the victor's policy would work, by stealth or violence, to suppress the arrogant provincial creed, and enforce conformity with pagan ritual. Thus the integrity of the Jewish worship was perilled alike by flattery and fear. Among the changing fortunes of

---

* It is now that Grecian names, as *Palestine, Idumæa, Ptolemais, Scythopolis,* begin to predominate over Hebrew.

this period, the more strict and resolute Hebrew spirit was held as it were in abeyance, or became the property of a sect. Nothing in the previous course of things prepares us to expect the intense and sustained heroism of its reaction, or the inexhaustible resources of which it was able to take advantage.

Fortunately for the event, the period of Egyptian conquest had coincided with the ten years administration of Simon the Just, whom Jewish tradition makes a survivor of the " Great Synagogue," ascribing to him a part scarce inferior to Ezra in the revival of the Law. To quote the words of the son of Sirach, " he was as a morning star in the midst of a cloud, and as the moon at the full ; as the sun shining on the temple of the Most High, and as the rainbow beaming from the bright clouds." * His prudent forethought had strengthened, not only the spiritual fabric of the Law, but the outward defences of the sanctuary,† so as to prepare against the twofold invasion that was impending. His life was a revival of the better hope of Israel. His death was attended by omens of popular terror ; the scapegoat (that used to be " broken into bits when scarce half way down the precipice it was thrown from ") fled from the high-priest's hand, and was lost among the hills, or " eaten by the Saracens ;" the sacred fire and lamps refused to burn ; the shewbread of the temple failed.‡ And in the century succeeding, when the nation had rallied from its disasters,

---

* Ecclesiasticus l. 6, 7.

† Constructing, in place of the ruined aqueducts and imperfect fountains, a cistern or reservoir, " in compass as a sea."

‡ Lightfoot on Matthew iii. 7.

14

his eloquent eulogist enrolls him among the most sacred and honoured names of the elder history.

The little religious municipalities of Judæa were another safeguard in any obstinate struggle with heathenism. The colonists, as they dispersed among the hills of Palestine, carried everywhere the seeds of enterprise, personal independence, and religious loyalty. Each village (as we find it so clearly marked in the Gospel times) made in some regards an independent community. Each had its own synagogue, on the model of that in the metropolis, with its stated times of worship, and its reverent guardianship of the Law. Thus the fresh nationality fastened itself to the soil by a thousand roots at once. Palestine was a fortified country, bristling with religious garrisons, and defended by a drilled militia of veteran "saints."* The practice also of national feasts, religious pilgrimages to the temple at Jerusalem, and pious oblations, which gradually amassed surprising stores of wealth in the sacred treasury, made a constant counterpoise to the roving temper of this trader-race, and kept in check the tendency to merge and lose itself among gentile populations. The Palestinian Jews clung with a fervid and exclusive devotion about their own temple and city, however distant their commercial migrations, or however profaned the holy places might be by heathen invasion, impure rites, or fratricidal violence. Their first moment of complete sovereignty they improved to destroy the rival temple on Mount Gerizim ; and no " abomination of desolation " their capital might suffer from

* Chasidim.

infidel conquerors could excuse in their eyes the
sacrilege of dedicating to Jehovah another shrine in
Egypt. Thus something of the old Hebrew spirit,
in a narrower and intenser form, abode in Palestine
unimpaired ; and was strengthened alike to survive
the insidious undermining of Grecian scepticism, or
to drive the persecutor back with sharper weapons
than his own.

The busy and pervasive intellect of the Greeks,
already in its decline, began presently to invade this
stronghold of religious loyalty. The flattering favours of Ptolemy, who had bought at princely cost
the literary treasures of Hebrew Scripture, first
opened the way to something like equal intercourse
between the Jew and Greek. This was favoured on
one side by the wide dispersion of the Jews through
maritime and trading enterprise, and by alliances
and fancied consanguinities with foreign states ; * on
the other by the Grecian genius, at once organizing
and speculative, which began to remould the forms
of Oriental civilization, and to trace out the novel
elements of thought or faith in the Asiatic mind.

The intellectual compromise thus brought about
was manifest among the Jews chiefly in that phase of
doctrine known to us as *Sadduceeism*. The Sadducees
were in their origin a rationalizing or Hellenizing
sect, whatever they may afterwards have become as a
political party. As such, they were averse to the
intense intolerance of the Chasidim, or " saints," and
would be looked on in turn by them as little better

* As with the Parthians and Spartans. (See Josephus, XIV. 10, 22;
1 Macc xii. 21.)

than infidels or traitors. Their stronghold was a professed conservatism; adhering to the Mosaic law alone, which they rendered in their barren fashion, and denouncing the prophetic dreams, or foreign fables, which so won the enthusiasm of the more pious.

And so sectarian lines began to divide the nation. On one side, Babylonish theosophy and fable mingled with the tenacious ritualism of the more devout, to make the popular creed, and found the sect of Pharisees; on the other, new ideas and customs from the West gave something of a cosmopolite and aristocratic tone to their rationalist opponents. And while party lines were thus drawn, and party dissensions imbittered, many kept aloof from them all; and revolting from those who "made an art or trade of piety," withdrew to an ascetic, unsocial, and monastic life, to which certain Egyptian mystics already began to show the way,— substituting the ecstasies of devotion for the plainer practices of piety, repute as exhorters or wonder-workers for popular show or political intrigue, the spirit of a community or clan for patriotism, solitary penance or barren toils for home and social duties. And thus, in this century of political revolution, invading doubt, and intellectual compromise, we naturally find germs of the three well-known sects that afterwards divided the Jewish state, — the Pharisees, Sadducees, and Essenes.

Of the character of the Egyptian rule only a single illustration is given. The avarice or craft of Onias, the high-priest, had kept back for several years the tribute due to Ptolemy; and a corps of "farmers of

the revenue" were about to bid for the privilege of
legal pillage, — the old way of collecting government
taxes.   But a young man Joseph, sent as envoy to
Ptolemy, succeeds by his bold frankness in winning
the king's good humour, and carries his point by bidding twice as high as any other, naming the king
himself as his security.   With a retinue of armed
men to make the royal indorsement good, he puts to
death the wealthiest men of one or two refractory
towns, confiscating their estates; and for more
than twenty years succeeds not only in forwarding
the promised sum, but in bringing out the industry
and resources of the province, and so leaving the
people far more flourishing than he found them,
while he dies immensely rich.   But a violent family
feud breaks out after his death.   His youngest son,
Hyrcanus, is driven beyond the Jordan, where he
closes a career of marauding with death by his own
hand; and at the same time we find a powerful in-
clination among the Jews to revolt from Egypt, and
accept the conquering sovereignty of Syria.   The
Jews in Egpyt are threatened with indiscriminate
massacre, which they scarce escape ; and Antiochus
the Great wrests the whole district of Palestine from
the feebler grasp of Ptolemy, first winning the Jew's
good-will by many singular favours.* B. C. 205–198.
By this revolution Antioch became one of the most
important head-quarters of the Aramæan Jews, as
distinguished from the Hellenistic, whose metropolis
was Alexandria.

It is just here that the Republic of Rome begins to

* See the detail of them in Josephus, XII. 3, 4.

be powerful in the East, and its career of conquest
to be heralded by its presence as umpire in Asiatic
quarrels. Hannibal had just been overthrown at
Zama, and the unchallenged sovereignty of the Western world lay with the great Italian city. Alarm for
their own dominion began to be felt among the successors of Alexander. Antiochus leagued himself
with Philip of Macedon, and invited the exile Hannibal to his court. The league was broken by the defeat of Philip and the death of the two other allies.
But while Rome remained, in fact, arbiter of the
East, it was her prudent policy for yet another century to keep the balance of power there, and not lay
her grasp on the small, divided sovereignties which it
was more profitable to play off against each other.
Judæa was but the chance victim of a game between
Syria and Egypt, under the vigilant and wary sufferance of Rome.

Antiochus Epiphanes * — a name of eternal infamy
in history — was a young man, brave and handsome,
as his coins show him, and a true Greek in his love
of art; but frivolous and obstinate, sensual, cruel,
and superstitious. From his victories in Egypt, which
he was fast reducing to subjection, he was warned off
by the formidable voice of Rome, whose alliance was
sued by Ptolemy. But the same patient policy that
drove him from the Nile left him now unmolested in
Judæa; and it was not till a point of resistance was
already found in the indomitable temper of the people, that the career of his profligate tyranny was

* Epiphanes or Epimanes, — the glorious or the furious; for Greek
wit delighted in this play of names.

stayed, and Rome assumed a remote protectorate of Palestine.

A little before, Heliodorus, the treasurer of the Syrian king, being sent to seize the sacred treasures betrayed to him by one of the rival priests, had been driven off in deadly fright. " For there appeared a horse, with a terrible rider upon him, clad in complete harness of gold, and he ran fiercely and smote at Heliodorus with his fore feet: moreover two young men notable in strength, excellent in beauty, and of gorgeous apparel stood by him on either side, and scourged him with many sore stripes ; and Heliodorus fell suddenly to the ground, and lay speechless, without all hope of life." And so the sacrilegious plunder was prevented for a time.

But the king's rapacity was roused, and watchful of its opportunity. This was soon found in the party strifes and Hellenizing spirit among the ruling Jews themselves. Joshua (who, affecting Grecian fashion, called himself Jason) purchased from Antiochus, by a bribe of three hundred and sixty talents, his support as high-priest; and the most sacred dignity was thus openly set to sale, and bought of a foreign despot. The office got by his heathen alliance Jason administered in a way worthy of the bargain. The charges against him are sufficiently explicit, and very bitter. He "forthwith brought his own nation to the Greekish fashion;" he compelled young men to adopt a foreign dress; he established a gymnasium where the nude contests of the Greeks came in fashion, and unworthy Jews "made themselves uncircumcised;" he terrified the priests from the performance of sacred rites; he sent rich gifts to a shrine of Hercules, which the messengers, in terror at the sacrilege, "employed to the making of galleys." * Within two years Jason was outbid by his own envoy, Onias or Menelaus, who, for about the same space, played a like game of plunder and sacrilege, "increasing in malice, and being a great traitor to the citizens," till Jason, hearing a false rumour of Antiochus's death, " took at least a thousand men, and suddenly made an assault upon the city," which he entered and treated with merciless revenge. But Antiochus returning, baffled and in a rage, from his campaign in Egypt, retook the city with great violence and slaughter. It was on the Sabbath; and of the helpless, unresisting crowd, "forty thousand were slain in the conflict, and no fewer sold than slain."

Such was the course of tyrannous apostasy that now exposed the Jews to the horrors of a religious persecution. Antiochus took with him from Jerusalem the prodigious spoil of eighteen hundred talents, and left there, as governor, a man " for his country, a Phrygian, and for manners more barbarous than he that set him there," with the bloody commission to root out the Jewish religion at all hazards. Every injunction of the ritual was forbidden. Mothers who secretly performed the rite of circumcision were strangled with their infants in their arms. Under an edict of " uniformity," the Jewish was made to conform to the Pagan ritual. The temple at Jerusalem was dedicated to Zeus Olympius, as that on

* 2 Macc. chap. iv.

Gerizim had already been to Zeus, the strangers' god. Jews were forced to bear wreaths of ivy in Dionysiac festivities. The sacred books were hunted out everywhere and burned, those who hid them being put to death. As the bitterest insult to Hebrew custom, swine were slain on every altar; and Jews were compelled to sacrifice or eat the unclean flesh under penalty of the most frightful tortures.* Freethinkers and Greeks seemed completely victorious for a time. Antiochus had his party and his spies in Jerusalem; he " mocked at every god but Mars; " and his boast was that he had " abolished the deity of the Jews."

It was at this point,† when the long-brooding hostility between native faith and foreign innovation had come to a head, and nothing less than the very existence of the Jewish name and religion was at stake, that the reaction took place, astonishing alike for its desperate hardihood and its brilliant success, — a struggle which beat back the whole invading tide of heathenism, and gave immortal glory to the name of the Maccabees.

An old man, Mattathias, son of Asmonai, who lived in the hill-country of Judæa towards the sea, struck down an apostate Jew whom he saw offering a Pagan sacrifice. It was the signal of open resistance. Mat-

---

* See the tragical story of the mother and her seven sons, 2 Macc. chap. vii.

† To this period, most probably, belongs the composition of the "Book of Daniel," with its Messianic visions and its apocryphal additions; possibly, too, the Book of Enoch. We are also told of "Psalms of Solomon," a book deeply tinged with the same style of thought, in which the expression Χριστὸς κύριος occurs.

tathias roused a party of zealous religionists; attacked the royal troop, and drove them off with slaughter of several; and then fled with a large company of the bold and faithful to the caves and glens of the same mountain region that had sheltered the outlaw David.

The five sons of Mattathias — John, Simon, Judas, Eleazar, and Jonathan — became the bold, wary, and skilful leaders of the revolt. They all·died, one by one, by treachery or violence, but not before they had sustained the banner of Judah for more than thirty years. From their mountain retreat they now descended as they had opportunity upon the plains and villages. They overthrew pagan altars; slew their apostate countrymen; "what·children soever they found within the coast of Israel uncircumcised those they circumcised valiantly;" and held out with marvellous success and skill against every party despatched to hunt them down. Their followers were mostly of the sect known as Chasidim, — saints or purists — fanatic zealots of the law, with all the dauntless energy, the fierce enthusiasm, the implacable and resolute faith of the Covenanters, whom in position and fortune they so much resemble. Their creed did not suffer them to strike a blow in self-defence upon their Sabbath; and, seizing this advantage, their pursuers once smothered a thousand of them together in a cave. Then Mattathias urged the clear necessity to overbear the fatal scruple; and the loyal band were thereafter unconquerable. Dying in his fastness the following year, the stern old man gave his third son Judas, named the Maccabee, the charge of leader, and bade him " recompense fully the heathen, and take heed to the commandments of the Law." So Judas and his companions banded themselves anew, and " fought with cheerfulness the battle of Israel."

The war of defence was presently changed into one of attack by the bold and sagacious chieftain. The smaller parties sent against him he invariably cut to pieces at every odds. When a force of near fifty thousand was sent by Antiochus to capture his few hundreds, and a detachment of five thousand came to surprise him by night, Judas was beforehand with his assault, took the enemies' camp with great spoil, and put the whole host to flight; then the next year totally routed a much greater force, so that the whole southern region was in his possession. Now was the time to rescue and purify the sacred city. " Jerusalem lay void as a wilderness; there was none of her children that went in or out: the sanctuary also was trodden down, and aliens kept the stronghold; the heathen had their habitation in that place; and joy was taken from Jacob, and the pipe with the harp ceased. . . . And when they saw the sanctuary desolate, and the altar profaned, and the gates burned up, and shrubs growing in the courts as in a forest or in one of the mountains, yea, and the priests' chambers pulled down, they rent their clothes, and made great lamentation, and cast ashes on their heads, and fell down flat to the ground upon their faces, and blew an alarm with the trumpet, and cried towards heaven." The pious victors effected the purifying of the temple, and such repairs as were within their power ; and then, in the joy of their triumph, they established the great winter festival of Dedication. (B. C. 165.) The fortifications of the city were now restored, and the ancient capital, wrecked and dismantled by the shocks of its great convulsion, still gave shelter against any sudden assault.

The region in which Judas had won some degree of independence and security was blasted and desolate from its still fresh disasters, and his position was one of extreme hazard. Fortunately, Antiochus had drawn off his main strength in some schemes of conquest towards the east. He was defeated, and died on his return, — the Jewish account says, in the anguish of remorse at his atrocities. His treasury was empty, and little seems to have been dreaded from that quarter for some years, unless it were an act of treachery. But there were jealousies among neighbouring states to be guarded against, and hostilities to be suppressed by a marauding and border war. This Judas waged successfully for some five years. Dividing his force into three parties, and victorious both by the terror of his own name and the skill of his brother Simon, he reconquered almost the whole soil of Palestine. Hostile towns his troops laid waste with all the horrors of old Hebrew vengeance. Pagan temples he demolished with Jewish iconoclastic zeal. Combining his power as military commander with the high-priest's office, he ruled justly and humanely the people whose freedom his sword had won. He still further fortified himself by a strict alliance with the Romans, " hearing that they were mighty and valiant men, and such as would lovingly accept all that joined themselves unto them, and make a league of amity with all that came to them." This league seems to have been of no practical avail, except as it may have given more consequence to the position of the Jewish chieftain. A Syrian garrison was still unsubdued that commanded half the temple-hill; and an army of a hundred thousand, mustering the desert-hordes, assailed him on the south. Jerusalem was forced to surrender, on condition that the laws and customs of the nation should be unmolested; and again the sacred city suffered from the feuds occasioned by a false high-priest. One more desperate battle set the city free from its invaders, and left Judas a little longer master of the field. But in a Syrian attack that followed he was surrounded by a host of more than twenty thousand against three, deserted by the main part of his own force, enveloped in the wings of the army he had already in part discomfited, and killed fighting. Such was the life and fate of Judas the Maccabee.

His brother Jonathan succeeded to the high-priesthood and the chief command (B. C. 160). He was a man yet more subtle and wary in stratagem, and of infinite resource for the hazards of the long struggle that still had to be maintained, and for a time again by guerilla parties in the wilderness. The Roman alliance — in which he renewed the policy of Judas — was still of little service, except as giving moral weight to the Jews' declaration of independence. Something more practical and effective was found in bargaining with the rival heirs of Antiochus,

Demetrius and Alexander, from each of whom Jonathan got such terms of political recognition and immunity from tribute as to give him a real sovereignty. The terms of alliance recognized him as highpriest and ruler. It gave him the nominal jurisdiction of the fortress on a mound between Zion and Moriah, from which the citizens were still plundered and harassed, and which Judas was never able to subdue ; and released the Jews " from tribute, salt tax, crown tax, the third of seed-corn, the half of fruit, tithes, and tributes of their cattle." Jonathan proved himself a trusty ally, and once relieved the king from the terror of a formidable insurrection that had broken out at Antioch. It was in fear of his good faith that one of the royal officers, plotting a conspiracy against the king, entrapped him in a tower at Ptolemais, slaughtered the men of his guard, and afterwards murdered him, first taking the treasure and hostages sent for his ransom ; and his death was lamented " as far as Sparta and at Rome." (B. C. 143.)

John, the eldest brother, had already been captured and killed in an ambuscade. Eleazar had been crushed under the weight of an armed elephant which he had thrust through the belly with his sword in the great Syrian invasion of the south. Of the five brothers there now remained only Simon, the most prudent and able administrator of all. Him the people at once welcomed to the supreme command, " well pleased that Simon should be their governor and high-priest forever, until a faithful prophet [Messiah] should appear." His administra-

tion marks the era of returning prosperity and peace
to Israel. His alliance with the dominant party in
Syria gave him an unmolested rule. The hostile
fortress in Jerusalem, the monument of so much
disaster, was levelled to the ground, — the garrison
being first starved out, — and the hill it stood on
shorn to an even plain. As a mark of sovereign
power, Simon had the right granted him of striking
coin ; and silver shekels, with their Syriac inscription
betokening his wise and peaceful rule, are found in
cabinets of the curious at this day. " He took Joppa
for an haven, and made an entrance to the isles of
the sea; the law he searched out, and every contemn-
er of the law and wicked person he took away." In
his only struggles against foreign power he was fully
successful. At home, the regency and priesthood
were both made hereditary in his house. His three
grown sons were of ability to be intrusted with the
more remote and active enterprises, while he himself
maintained at home a prosperous and brilliant peace
for about eight years.

Although Simon, with two of his sons, followed the
fortune of his house in suffering a violent death, —
being treacherously murdered at a banquet, — a third
son, John Hyrcanus, survived him, and became father
of the brief line of " Asmonæan kings." His own
reign lasted almost thirty years. The military priesthood of the Maccabees had not only revived the old
heroic memories of the Hebrew race, but had rendered back to Israel the undisputed possession of the
Holy Land. Edom (hereafter better known by its
Greek name, Idumæa) was incorporated with Judah,

to be afterwards more closely identified with the Jewish fortunes, through the Herodian family. The vindictive jealousy of the Jews had its triumph in the complete destruction of the temple on Mount Gerizim, and the ruin of the beautiful " hill-city " of Samaria, which was not only dismantled and forsaken, but its abundant water-springs turned to make of its very streets an uninhabitable marsh. With security and quiet returned the arts of peace ; and as the day of persecution and conflict had stimulated afresh the people's quenchless patriotic or Messianic hopes, recorded in such books as Daniel, Judith, and Enoch, so now, in the last age of native Hebrew literature, we find the more calm, but no less characteristic compositions of the son of Sirach, with the pictorial and stirring narrative of the " Maccabees."

The victorious independence of Judæa gave new occasion also to the strife of native sects. All parties had become thoroughly nationalized in the long struggle ; and there is no longer on any side the profession of compromise with the Greeks. But the sect of Sadducees still retained its character of a certain exclusiveness, scepticism, and intellectual pride, — the qualities that had made it court the intellectual aristocracy of Grecian culture. They had never adopted, and they now thoroughly disowned, the Oriental theosophy, and the doctrines of " resurrection, angels, and spirits," which were welcomed so fondly by the more religious among the Jews ; and fell back on the code of primitive Mosaism (or what was received as such), as offering the simplest outline of religious thought, and the least hinderance to their Epicurean speculations and philosophical free-will. Their advantage and power lay in times of peace. In the century preceding the great convulsion, theirs had been the dominant party up to the threatened absorption of the national creed itself in the encroaching Hellenism.

But the period of struggle, which drew sharp the party lines, and committed every man either for or against his native land and ritual, had given ascendency to the stricter sect of Pharisees, represented by the indispensable and uncompromising bigotry of the Chasidim. The dynasty of the Maccabees, sprung from their stanch and indomitable loyalty, naturally looked to them for support; and John Hyrcanus, an intelligent and able constitutional prince, was identified with that party till near the close of his reign. But bigotry and spiritual pride are more profitable allies in a struggle at odds against a relentless despotism, than useful auxiliaries in an administration of peace. The Pharisees made affairs of state subordinate to ritual scruples and the petty policies of a sect, — cruel or lenient by turns, still seeking to be popular. Though apparently on friendly terms, a jealousy grew up between them and the government, till one of them, in phrase more broad than courteous, reproached John as low-born and no true heir, and bade him show his good faith as ruler by laying down his power. The Pharisee leaders would not allow this to be an act of treason; and, professing to be loyal themselves, they shielded the disloyalty of their associate. So John broke openly with them, and his rule found its natural support or ally in the rival sect.

With John Hyrcanus expired the priestly regency of this heroic family. In him were combined all the elements of a position of command; for, besides his birth and personal qualities, he was at once a king in sway, high-priest by office, and a prophet in the popular reverence. The Roman alliance gave him, too, the advantage of a citizen, in some sense, of the imperial city; while the dissensions at Rome, begun by the civil reforms of Gracchus, and resulting in the proscriptive massacres of Marius and Sylla, deferred for another generation the great spoils of ambition in the East. Thus, favoured both by the strength and weakness of its protector, the power of John descended without dispute to his sons, Aristobulus, and afterwards Alexander, the first to whom the title of king is usually given. Their authority rested on a different base from that of their heroic ancestry. It was not religious prestige or the priestly office or personal service to the state, but the claim of birth, the divine right of kings, which assumed a regal title, and held the diadem bestowed or allowed by Rome.

These Jewish princes* were as wide apart in character as in name from the house whose honours

---

* Called the Asmonæan kings. The genealogy of the house of Asmonai, better known by the heroic name of Maccabees, is as follows:—

1. Mattathias, son of Asmonai.

2. *Sons of Mattathias*, — John, Simon, Judas, Eleazar, Jonathan.

3. *Sons of Simon*, — John Hyrcanus, Judas, Alexander.

4. *Sons of John Hyrcanus*, — Aristobulus, Antigonus, Alexander Jannæus.

5. *Sons of Alexander*, — Hyrcanus (executed by Herod at the age of eighty) and Aristobulus (poisoned by partisans of Pompey).

6. *Sons of Aristobulus*, — Alexander and Antigonus (both executed by the Romans).

they inherited. Aristobulus, the bloody, in his reign of two years, starved in prison his mother, whom John had left as regent; and died in agonies of horror at learning the ghastly accident that had mingled his own blood with that of his brother Antigonus, slain by his order in the palace-court.

Alexander, named Jannæus, in a reign of five and twenty years, was mostly occupied in petty wars, — generally unsuccessful, but indefatigable to begin afresh. He signalized himself in successive revolts of his people, first by the barbarous slaughter of six thousand, then by a civil war of some six years, which cost ten thousand lives, and finally by crucifying eight hundred, whose wives and children were slaughtered before their eyes as they hung in death-agonies upon the cross. The people were so incensed against him, that they not only pelted him with citrons in the street, insulting him with opprobrious names, but the insurgents gloried in the tortures that revenged their enmity, and the only terms of peace they offered were that the tyrant should kill himself. A restless, dissolute, ambitious man, called the Thracian for his barbarities, his rule abhorred except for

Daughter of Hyrcanus, — Alexandra (married to Alexander, executed by Herod).

7. *Children of Alexander and Alexandra,* — Mariamne (wife of Herod) and Aristobulus (both put to death by Herod).

8. *Sons of Herod and Mariamne,* — Alexander and Aristobulus (both put to death by Herod).

9. *Son of Aristobulus,* — Herod Agrippa, who dies at Cæsarea. (Acts xii. 23.)

10. *Son of Herod Agrippa,* — King Agrippa, by whose death (A. D. 100) the family becomes extinct. His sisters were Bernice and Drusilla (the wife of Felix).

the comparative mercy he showed in the cities he had conquered, he died before the age of fifty, having done the one service of confirming the Jewish power upon the soil of Palestine.

Alexandra, his widow, by the aid of the more popular party of the Pharisees, ruled nine years longer, without failing either of the good will or contentment of the people, troubled only by the rebellion of her younger son, and died just after Herod the Great was born, — a man destined to be witness and agent of even greater changes than had yet befallen the state of Israel.

It was just after the death of Alexandra that family dissensions grew into a civil war, which was not ended until Herod, by Roman favour, had confirmed his power on the ruins of every rival. The two sons of Alexander were Hyrcanus and Aristobulus. Hyrcanus, feeble and irresolute, was not reluctant to divide the dignity, by accepting the peaceable honours of the priesthood, and giving up the cares of power, with the weight of it, to his abler brother. But when an old quarrel was revived, by some measures taken to punish those concerned in the massacres of Alexander, the struggle grew so violent that Antipater (or Antipas) the Idumæan, father of Herod, a bold and able officer of Alexander, easily persuaded Hyrcanus to put himself in his hands as rival king.

This was the occasion that brought the irresistible Roman power to bear practically on the affairs of Judæa. Hyrcanus had fled to Petra, where he won the alliance of an Arab chief, and commenced an assault on Jerusalem. In this assault the city was so fiercely divided that a holy man, Onias, was stoned because he would not pray for the ruin of either party; and when the besieged were in distress for want of victims to the sacrifice, the besiegers, promising to gratify their religious scruple, sent them swine, which were drawn up in baskets to the city walls, and then dashed down in horror, amid the scoffs and jeers of the pagan troop.* But Pompey, the great and favourite general of the Roman Senate, was now returning from the East in the full splendour of his conquest of Mithridates, and held his military court at Damascus. His general, Scaurus, ordered the hostilities of the Jews to cease, sent back the troop of Arabs, and summoned both competitors to plead before Pompey himself. They came, each with rich gifts; among them, from Aristobulus, a golden vine, valued at five hundred talents, wrought with wonderful art, exciting the amazement of the Romans at the wealth and skill of the obscure province. Aristobulus, resenting the arbitration, proceeded to fortify himself again in Jerusalem. But the city was quickly reduced by Pompey, the Roman works of siege being unmolested on the Sabbath, and Judæa lay at the mercy of its offended allies. (B. C. 63.)

Pompey, though insatiable of glory, was, by the

---

* According to a Jewish story, Hyrcanus furnished the regular victims to his brother at a fixed price, until some Greek in his camp convinced him that the city was impregnable so long as the sacrifices were duly fulfilled, and he was induced to send a hog in place of a ram, whereat all the land of Judæa trembled; whence the pious proverb, confounding in one curse those who hoist swine on windlasses with those who teach their sons the wisdom of the Greeks.

standard of antiquity, both enlightened and merciful.
His curiosity was stayed by no Jewish scruple from
penetrating as far as the secret shrine of the temple,
which had been violated before him by no Pagan;
and in this sacrilege Jewish superstition saw the reason of his speedy fall, and felt a sort of vindictive
triumph when, fifteen years later, his corpse was cast
out, headless and dishonoured, on the Egyptian shore.
But, more lenient than any other invader, he now
showed himself peaceable and friendly. Judæa had
only to surrender power as the price of peace. He
quieted the factions by which the country was mo-
lested, repaired the ruins of temple and city, and left
untouched the sacred treasure; only extending the
protectorate of Rome over the divided state, levying
a fixed tribute to the Roman treasury, and incorporating Judæa, as part of the province of Syria,
within the widening bounds of the Republic. Many
Jewish captives were carried to Rome, where they
afterwards obtained civil rights, and became an important part of the population. The boundaries of
Palestine were narrowed, and the system of ruling
and taxing the land by districts still further cramped
the power of Jerusalem. The Roman arm kept down
the rising insurrections among the chafing population. Aristobulus, and his sons Alexander and Antigonus, after long disputing the dominion, were at
length taken and put to death. A forced neutrality
was kept among the various factions, and — except
in such acts as the wanton pillage of the temple by
Crassus, who carried off, it is said, not less than ten
thousand talents — the foreign yoke was less disastrous than the native anarchy.

Under the powerful protection of Rome the real authority came altogether into the hands of Antipater, while the shadow of the regal dignity remained yet forty years with the incapable heir of the last native Jewish dynasty. Antipater was a popular and able governor; and when the great Julius passed, after Pompey's death, through Syria to his conquest of Egypt, he won by his prompt and valiant aid unusual favour from the Dictator, who made him a Roman citizen and Procurator of Judæa. He rebuilt the wall which Pompey had thrown down, restored quiet once more to the country, and established his two sons as local governors, Phasael at Jerusalem and Herod in Galilee.

The worst consequence of so many years of violence was now seen in troops of outlaws and bandits, who hid themselves in mountain glens and caverns, lived by plunder, and kept the land in perpetual alarm. It was in suppressing them that Herod, a young man of twenty-five, gave the first proof of that marked administrative ability which worthily won him the name of Great, while he roused a jealousy among the leading Jews nearly fatal to him at the very threshold of his career. Galilee was overrun and held in terror by a bold robber-chief, Hezekiah, who, after long holding out against every effort to capture him, was at length taken by Herod and immediately put to death, with all his troop. But the Sanhedrim, or great Council of Seventy, claimed to be the only tribunal with jurisdiction of life and death, and Herod was put on capital trial before them for his illegal stretch of power. His youth and fame, the

troops of his guard, with his brilliant equipment as
victorious chief, and the confessed need of the service
he had done, held the great council in check; and
while they paused, in doubt of using their authority
upon so formidable a subject, the seasonable inter-
vention of Sextus Cæsar brought him off in safety.
He escaped at night, by advice of Hyrcanus, and
submitted himself to the tribunal of Rome, which
was too politic not to spare its ablest Eastern ally.

From this time forth the career of Herod was as
uniformly successful as it was wary and adventurous.
Whether by politic boldness, or the persuasion of his
eloquence, or by his personal presence, he never failed
to be in favour with the dominant party in the long
struggles of the expiring Republic. By the party of
Cæsar he was made general of the Syrian army; by
Cassius, one of the governors of Syria, which gave him
power to avenge his father's and his brother's death;
by Antony, tetrarch, and by the Roman Senate, king.
When Phasael was taken prisoner by the Parthians,
and Antigonus was master of Judæa, he escaped with
imminent hazard of his life, and was once hardly
withheld from suicide; then, going to Rome to plead
the cause of his wife's young brother as heir of both
Asmonæan houses, Augustus and Antony united in
conferring the dignity on him. He never failed to
suppress sedition, rebellion, or hostile intrigue. His
bribes and persuasion made him a fast friend in Antony, when a deputation of a hundred Jews sought to
ruin him by their charges. Afterward, when Cleo-
patra, angry at his rejection of her flatteries, was
known to be his enemy, and eager to get his kingdom

for her own, he went, at the hazard of his life, and prevailed with Antony over the blandishments of the Egyptian queen herself.

The favour of the Jewish people he gained by interceding with the Roman commander, who won him possession of Jerusalem, not to desecrate the temple, or leave him " master of a desert instead of a city," and afterwards by restoring to them their temple and worship in all their ancient splendour. He freed the land from desperate bands of outlaws, whom he slew in their dens, letting down armed men in chests swung from windlasses above ; and thus made even the remoter districts comparatively safe. Unscrupulous and implacable where his own jealousy or vengeance was concerned, he knew when to be heroic in act and daring, when to be merciful and generous in administration. His taxes pressed lightly on the people in comparison with the weight of them elsewhere ; so that, to reconcile his munificence and economy, popular report gave him access to fabulous treasures said to have been hidden in David's sepulchre. The splendour of his royal abodes, the restored temple at Jerusalem, the sumptuous festivals and magnificent games, the new city Sebaste, or Augusta, on the site of Samaria, the strongly defended seaport of Joppa, the marble docks and palaces of Cæsarea, appealed powerfully to the people's religious or patriotic pride, and reconciled them for a time to the hated yoke of Edom. To allay the suspicions of the pious, the old temple was not demolished till the materials were all at hand for the new. The work was put in charge of priests, trained and clad as masons ; not the king himself would trespass on the boundaries of the sacred enclosure.*

But his theatres and games, his spectacles of wild beasts and fights of gladiators, were a heathenish innovation, " opposite to the Jewish notions," causing no small alarm and resentment among the people; which was further increased by his lavish gifts to Gentile cities at their expense, and his politic erecting or adorning of pagan shrines. His flatterers claimed for him that he was of Hebrew stock, born of a house that had shared the first captivity. But in the popular heart these things proved him no true Israelite. His name represents the traditional hate of Edom to the house of Jacob, and to this day he is execrated as the man who did more than all to betray his nation and its faith to heathenism.

Up to the moment of Antony's overthrow, Herod was his active and constant ally; and was only prevented by his positive orders, to keep the Arabs in check on his own frontier, from staking his fortunes with him in the fatal sea-fight at Actium. When the great battle of empire was decided, he went without hesitation or any mark of fear before Augustus, laid aside his diadem, professed freely his services and attachment to Antony, and put his claim to favour on the ground of that fidelity he had shown so well against him who was now master of his fortune and life. Augustus held it more prudent to secure the gratitude than the ruin of so sagacious and bold a

---

* According to the Jewish tradition, during eighteen months while it was in building, rain fell only at night, that the task might be undisturbed.

man. Admiring his frank courage, he not only restored to Herod his regal dignity, but added to his
dominion, making him free also of tribute, so that
he had almost the state and power of an independent prince. He was held by Augustus, says Josephus, second in love and honour only to Agrippa,
and by Agrippa second only to Augustus. His
skilful intercession procured for the Jews the degree of privilege which gave them afterwards so
much importance among the inhabitants of Rome.
His politic humanity saved numbers of them at his
private cost from starvation, after the great disaster of the earthquake at his return to power. And
his public administration shows, throughout, the
most consummate skill in all the arts and measures that could win at once the favour of his masters
and his subjects. Eight years he had ruled as regent,
or as most powerful among the chiefs of contending
factions ; and for thirty-seven years he reigned under
Augustus as undisputed king.

Such was the career of splendid and uninterrupted
success, often in the midst of the greatest personal
peril, which won for Herod the title of Great, — a
career darkly contrasted by his terrible domestic history. His private character was treacherous, passionate, and cruel. None were so near in blood or
affection as to be safe from his remorseless jealousy.
His own household was the scene of his guiltiest
ambition and his darkest crimes. The queenly Mariamne, granddaughter of both Hyrcanus and Aristobulus, unhappy heiress of her perished kindred, —
the beautiful, proud woman whose hand allied his

fortunes with the last royal house of Judah, — fell a victim to his insane suspicion, or else his jealous hatred of her race, at the very moment of triumph that crowned his long career of perilous adventure. He had married her during the hazards of his early struggle for power, — perhaps from policy, to divide the popular regard with his rival Antigonus, her uncle, — and professed a passionate love to her. But it was a passion wayward and fierce, like the wild Edomite blood that ran in his veins; and was turned to hate by the coldness she could not hide, and the jealousy that hunted all her family to death. Her brother Aristobulus he had made high-priest at the age of seventeen, — a youth of rare gentleness, grace, and beauty, and of no dangerous ambition, — and within a year had him treacherously drowned, in dread of the popular affection for his name. The old Hyrcanus himself, degraded from his priesthood, shorn of his ears by his nephew Antigonus, (which made him incapable of that dignity,) and living helpless among the female intrigues of Herod's court, he found occasion to put to death just at the moment when it was convenient to him to clear his ground of every rival, as he went to put his destiny in the hands of Augustus.

Mariamne alone remained of the priestly and heroic line, deprived even of her sons, who were taken from her charge by Herod, that they might be watched by his spies and bred in Roman ways. Twice, when his fortune and life were hazarded in his intricate game of ambition, he had left orders, that in case he failed she should be at once put to death, — from jealous love, as the historian pretends, lest they should be parted even in the grave. Each time the secret order was betrayed to her, and made her excuse for the coldness of her welcome and her answer to his lavish professions of affection ; and each time the officer who guarded her — once, Herod's own uncle — paid with his life for the indiscretion. His sister Salome, a woman no less skilful in her plots than bitter in her animosities, still urged him on by false charges and suspicions, till, " entangled between hate and love," in a sudden tempest of passion, he commanded that Mariamne should be beheaded, on an idle pretence that she had sought to poison him. Her womanly honour and queenly dignity were too proud and stainless to suffer the naming of any baser charge. So perished the last princess of the royal house of Judah, at the age of twenty-five, alone of all her kindred, forsaken and reproached at last even by her own mother, who had tempted her in vain to fly from the doomed and guilty house. In her death the last pure Hebrew blood of the Maccabees was shed, and the last bond of true loyalty was severed that might have united king and people. Deploring the fatal crime too late, with bitter and tempestuous remorse, Herod built for her monument a tower of stainless white marble, that made one of the strong defences of Jerusalem.

An avenging Destiny pursued the house of Herod. His father had died by poison, at the hands of a man whose life he had just preserved. One brother perished in captivity ; one was slain in battle ; a third, whom he had banished in a fit of rage, and then lamented bitterly when he died, he found was already conspiring to give him poison. His household was distracted with miserable female intrigues and fatal quarrels. In his own sister and his wife's mother, Alexandra, met the deadliest antipathies of race and creed. Suspicion and treachery, insane jealousies and false charges, — such that among his own kindred he could certainly know neither conspirators nor friends, — were the dreadful judgment that followed this career of distempered passion and unscrupulous ambition. Master of others' lives, he never felt his own was safe. Remorse and dread provoked him to fresh acts of violence. The entire Sanhedrim, all but one man, he slew as partisans of Antigonus. At Jerusalem he entrenched himself in the impregnable tower of Antonia, employed bands of spies, and walked the streets in disguise, to detect the lurking disaffection among his subjects ; and he built castles for retreat in various quarters, garrisoned and furnished against the too possible contingency of civil war. Of his ten wives, one only he seemed really capable of loving, and her he murdered. Of his many children, one only, the brutal and bad Antipater, he trusted through all the changing and bloody fortunes of his house, sacrificing to his false charge the two loyal and popular sons of Mariamne ; and him he found guilty of conspiracy, arrested him at landing on his return from Augustus's court, and, as his last act of royal authority, put him to death in prison, — the only unpitied victim of his rage. The Gospel narrative echoes the tone of history in ascribing to his suspicious tyranny the massacre of every infant child in Bethlehem ; and the Jewish story was, that, resolving there should be sincere mourning at his death, he shut up in prison many of the most eminent men of the nation, with the ferocious order, happily disobeyed, that they should be put to death as soon as he was gone. Consumed by passion, frenzy, remorse, and the most horrible distemper, he closed, at the age of seventy, his long, brilliant, most successful, and most tragical career.

With the life of Herod terminates the last chapter in the history of Israel as an independent power. We know henceforth only the petty principalities into which Palestine was divided by the Romans, and the dreary story of that oppression which ended in the utter ruin of nation and city. The sole interest which remains to the fallen fortunes of Judah is as an element in the great change impending in the religious destinies of mankind. For that political position which, through the fortunes of the Captivity, the theocratic colony, the desperate struggle of the Maccabees, and the glory and shame of the later monarchy, the Jews had been able to preserve, — surviving so many all but fatal shocks, and still bound by ties of ancient reverence and heroic memories to the soil of Palestine, — had not, as in so many other cases, saved from perishing a mere form or shell of national existence. But as the city of Jerusalem was itself a fortress, and guarded in its interior citadel the sanctuary and sacred treasures of the Hebrew faith, so the nation of the Jews preserved to the destinies and uses of humanity a treasure of which only the experience of ages should declare the value.

The religious enthusiasm and obstinate fidelity of the Jews themselves shaped their own interpretation of their mission and destiny as the chosen people. The religious hopes of each great Oriental race or creed have all, more or less vaguely, taken form in the expectation of some clear revealing of God in human life, or the advent of some glorified Messenger.* This expectation in the time of the earlier monarchy had found strong and fervent utterance in the Hebrew prophecy. It gave Isaiah the assurance of victory in the great impending invasion of the Assyrians. It comforted Jeremiah at the gloomy eve of the captivity he foresaw. It remained with the exiles of the Euphrates, and made the most sacred pledge among the scattered colonists of Judah. At every critical season of the later history it reappeared; now in the vivid visions of Daniel in time of terror and disaster, now in the calmer anticipation of sages and pious men in a season of peace, now in fanatic outbreak such as preceded the nation's final overthrow, now in the tone of reverence paid to a discreet . ruler, as Simon the brother of Judas and Simon the Just, now in the base flattery with which a later party were forward to welcome the yoke and court the imperial favour of Rome.

It is this that furnishes the thread of interior connection, and gives its vital significance to the later Hebrew history. The prophecy of ages cannot but work towards its own better interpretation and completer fulfilment. The culmination of the Roman power, its almost boundless empire and almost un-

* See Scholl, "Die Messias-Sagen des Morgenlandes."

broken peace, the new and near relations by which
Judæa found itself drawn towards the culture, enterprise, and customs of other nations, its helpless position in the arms of the great dominion, nay, that very
sceptic and destructive process in which the Grecian
intellect, preying upon itself, made more sensible the
want of a living and universal faith, — all were so
many stages of the preparation that led mankind to
welcome a world-wide rendering of the Hebrew hope,
and from the interior life of that ancient religious
polity evolved the germ of a divine revelation to all
ages.

This final office, yet held in reserve to the race
whose fortunes had been conducted through such
vicissitude, makes the single remaining point to be
regarded in the Hebrew history.   But meanwhile
another course of preparation for it has been going
on, by the intimate contact and blending of the mind
of East and West, — the interpretation of Jewish faith
in the light of Grecian philosophy.   No single element can effect the novel consummation.   The religious thought of humanity had had its nurture in the
porch and groves of Greece as well as among the hills
of Judah.   And the later richer chapter of man's
spiritual history might not be unfolded but by bringing together, in one living whole, all the separate
results of so large and various a culture.

15 *

XI. THE ALEXANDRIANS.

THE three centuries before the Christian era — included in the preceding review — are memorable in the history of opinion, as defining almost the precise boundaries of the second or middle period of Grecian philosophy. In this regard they offer, besides, a very important chapter in the development of Jewish thought, and an indispensable preparation for the new Religion that was to spring from the seed yet abiding in the Hebrew faith.

A glance, however slight, at the courses of speculation hitherto seems essential to a right understanding of the period at which we are now arrived.

Without concealing the deceptive character of such generalizations, to those who accept them instead of the facts they are meant to interpret, we may divide the whole history of Grecian philosophy into three pretty nearly equal periods. In the first it was mainly a theory of Nature and Thought, and was summed up in its completest form by Aristotle,. the teacher of Alexander. In the second it was mainly a theory of Life taught by the contending schools of Epicurus and Zeno, — the purely speculative element degenerating into an impotent scepticism. In the third it was mainly a theory of

Religion as taught by the later Platonists, springing from the same soil with the prevalent form of Christian doctrine, and for three centuries disputing with it the intellectual sovereignty of the empire. This last belongs to the era of Christian history, and need not be considered here. It is with the second period that we are chiefly concerned.

The history of free thought among the Greeks begins as early as that of free institutions. Thales, the "father of philosophy," was of the same age with Solon. (B. C. 600.) Among the disasters and troubles that befell the little Ionic league of states in their collision with the Persian monarchy, he took a citizen's share in the public defence, and his accurate observation of nature enabled him to forestall popular terror by predicting an eclipse. Although, in harmony with the mind of the age, the universe, as he regarded it, was "full of gods," he was yet sceptical as to that poetic creed which explained the groups of natural phenomena by its mythic genealogies; and vaguely but boldly he sketched the outline of a philosophy of nature, which made the point of departure of the famous Ionic school, that embraced the best intellect of Greece down to the time of Socrates. Almost contemporary with his protest, Pythagoras and Xenophanes took their departure from the dominant creed, each projecting in his own style a philosophy of thought. And thus, in the sixth century before Christ, among the earlier movements of the little Hellenic states and colonies, began the independent growth of speculation which accompanied the event-

ful course of Grecian political history in a parallel
but separate channel of its own.

The three original streams, scientific, mystic, and
dialectic, found their way to Athens in the time
of her short-lived empire, and were there blended
into one.   Anaxagoras, the illustrious friend of Peri-
cles, first indicated the great division-line among the
objects of philosophy, by marking the antithesis
of Mind and Matter.   Though the irritable suspicion of the popular faith denounced these novel-
ties, — though his own life was hardly spared, and
his pupil, Socrates, perished through the resentment
roused by his unsparing attack of prevailing fallacies
and superstitions, — yet peace was easily made with
the forces of a decayed mythology.   Plato followed
out unmolested, in his master's name, the minute
and weary analysis of his famous Dialogues, and
draped the baldness of his speculations in the fanciful garb of myths that charmed the Attic taste.
Aristotle, who came as a proud and sensitive boy to
learn in the school of this splendid aristocrat of
thought, speedily made himself master of all that
Greek science and speculation had accomplished
hitherto ; he extended prodigiously both the boundaries of observation and the scope of mental analysis ; and projected a " Philosophy of the Empire "
which the ancient world was never able to outgrow,
and which holds its mastery in modern schools, in
some regards, even to this day.

Such is a slight outline of what was effected in
rather less than three centuries, in the creative period of Grecian philosophy.   So far as a true theory

of Nature and Thought is concerned, Aristotle speaks
for us the last word of antiquity. The history of
pure speculation after his day shows a steady declen-
sion into the vanity of barren jargoning and the
helplessness of an intellectual scepticism. The special sciences of Mathematics and Astronomy were
cultivated, indeed, with brilliant success, in the later
schools of Greece. Euclid and Hipparchus rank
highest in a long list of eminent names that adorn
the Institute established by Ptolemy in his splendid
capital. But, besides this success in the analytic and
inductive sciences, the most marked intellectual feature of the second period was seen in the philosophy
of Life held by the sects of Epicureans and Stoics.
As these are both strongly characteristic of the age
we are now considering, — its moral as well as its
intellectual estate, — it will be well to set them forth
a little more in detail.* They are of the more interest to us, since the first conflict of intellectual Paganism with living Christianity took place when Paul the
Apostle being 'at Athens, " certain philosophers of
the Epicureans and of the Stoics encountered him."

When the search for Truth seemed to have been
exhausted, and there remained only the barren industry of analysis and erudition, the search next
instituted was for the " sovereign Good," or the right
practical philosophy of Life. The first consistent
answer was given by Epicurus, whose age falls immediately after that of Aristotle. The sovereign
good, he said, is Happiness. Pleasure is good : we
need not go behind it to ask why or how. Virtue is

* Taken partly from Ritter's excellent account.

good: for it adds to our sum total of enjoyment. Quietness and peace are good: for they put us out of the way of pain. So liberal is Nature, and so clearly does she exhibit this as the true end of life, that once remove the positive cause of pain and she finds the enjoyment of her own accord. With a bodily system in good repair, we may be passive recipients of her prodigal benevolence.

Not that we have the Author of Nature in especial to thank for this, he said. We do not deny that there is such a Being; we will not cross swords with the popular belief as to so remote a matter of mere speculation. But we cannot suppose that the Divine Being (one or many) can interest himself in the cares and destinies of men. He is apart and at peace with himself, — a type of that blissful unconcern which the wise man will seek to attain on earth. But the popular fear of God as an Avenger of guilt and Judge of men, or of the Future as a scene of retribution possibly capricious or vindictive, disturbs and harasses us. By all means the fears of Superstition should be done away. Did not Agamemnon, said Lucretius, sacrifice his own daughter to the Deity that withheld the prospering breeze?

" Tantum Relligio potuit suadere malorum ! "

The soul is but the finer essence or tissue of the bodily organization: it dissolves with the dissolving frame, or fleets away like mist.* Why should we fear Death? If it is annihilation, we shall not feel it; if a new mode of life, then it is not death. "If

* See Lucretius, *passim.*

we are, it is not; if it is, we are not; when it comes we feel it not, for it is the end of all feeling; and what can give no pain when it is here should give no dread when it is far off."

Meanwhile, it is a temperate and serene enjoyment the wise man will seek; not extravagant, violent, or injurious to others. The pleasures of the mind are far above those of sense. The wise man is superior to the shocks of fortune: in lingering sickness there is more to enjoy than suffer; in torture even, memory and hope may continue undisturbed. Luxury is not essential: there are limits to all things; pleasure must be economized; those most enjoy luxury who have least need of it. Why should a man quarrel with circumstances, or stand in fear of laws or men or destiny? In himself is the real source of happiness. His moral liberty has just this field of exercise: he can adapt himself to the state of things; he can acquiesce. Let him make the best of his lot. Let him seek the solace of private friendship: " a true friend can trust a true friend; " and in philosophy he will find " an activity that procures a happy life."

This pleasant and plausible style of ethics reflects well the average mind of an age when the state was crumbling and the ancient civilization verging towards decay; when foreign conquerors allowed no hope to political ambition; when the sacredness of antique Art was degraded, so as to minister to personal luxury instead of public reverence; when the circle of ancient knowledge and faith was run, and a pedantic scepticism had taken hold of the mind of studious men; when there was neither moral sympathy to comprehend the noble life and death of Socrates, nor intellectual grasp to retain the stores of thought treasured by his great disciples; when there was not as yet developed a religion of Life, that should gather up what was noblest of that thought, and make of it a doctrine of practical and vital goodness. In such a period of pause, of moral degeneracy and intellectual decline, Epicurus lived out, on the whole, worthily and well the precepts of his code,—harmless, prudent, reasonable, praiseworthy in comparison with the dull or ferocious level of a vulgar life; but destitute of faith or living energy, "having no hope, and without God in the world." He taught it from boyhood up, and lived by it to old age. It gave him such resource and solace as he craved. He gathered about him attached and affectionate friends. His school was a proverb for goodwill and harmony; his writings a great bulk of easy, good-humoured exposition of his very superficial views of nature, mind, and morals, plain to understand, provoking no debate; and he died at upwards of seventy, bequeathing his pleasant gardens as the school to teach his cheerful theory of life to all coming time. But the school dishonoured the master. The inevitable tendency became a notorious fact. The garden of Epicurus is better known to us by its stern Miltonic designation of "Epicurus' sty."

It was from his contemporary, Zeno, that the antagonistic school of Stoics, or the Porch, began. He was a man of feeble health, austere manners, severe and melancholy temper, who sought consolation in philosophy for the utter wreck of his fortune at an early age. His stern, practical aim was to set the mind above the risk and change of life, upon the impregnable heights of Virtue. The two schools were developed side by side, and kept pace with one another through all the succeeding generations of pagan thought. The statement of Epicurus, that happiness is the whole aim of life, including virtue, was met by Zeno with the nobler counter statement, that virtue is the whole aim of life, including happiness. It was a severe and masculine morality he taught. Not love or pity, any more than fear or enjoyment, did he suffer to be a wise man's motive, — no love but that high, unimpassioned love to be bestowed alike on friends and enemies. Virtue, he said, is inexorable law, — law as strict as that followed by the stars in their courses, or in the growth of plants. Duty is the distinguishing and noble instinct of man. It is a sentiment primitive, inexplicable, inalienable, as much as the instinct of hunger or the care of its young in every creature. We cannot go behind it; we may not go against it. All wisdom he would reduce to virtue, all philosophy to a practical and religious common sense.

The great thought of God as universal Law lay at the bottom of his creed of ethics; of God as the life-giving * and indwelling Word of his system of physics. Man's happiness, he said, is in the free unfolding of his mental life, the primitive instinct of right being developed according to reason and conscience. There is a crisis in the interior life, — a moment when the

* σπερματικός.

dim reason awakes and asserts its supremacy, and thenceforward there can be no neutrality. A moral antithesis, inherent in the very nature of things, brings the strict alternative. A man chooses right or wrong, honour or baseness, good or ill; and the whole of his life afterwards is but the acting out of the choice of that moment. Hence, morally speaking, all men are ranked in two great classes. There is no middle ground. All virtues are on one level; all vices and crimes on another level. No allowance for human weakness, none for the pressure of circumstance. The one problem of life is to make the divine Reason paramount and supreme. " Lead me," said Cleanthes, " where I am commanded of thee to go, that I may follow without backwardness; but though, becoming base, I should not consent, yet none the less shall I follow thee." " He is a bad soldier," said Seneca, " who follows his general reluctantly : let us receive our leader's commands with cheerfulness, and execute them with alacrity; and never desert the path marked out for us because perplexed with difficulties. He has a truly great mind who surrenders himself wholly to God." " God "— so runs the Stoic doctrine — " is the eternal Reason that governs the universe and pervades all things; the beneficent Providence that taketh care of all as well as of each; the foundation of that natural Law which commands the right and forbids the wrong. He punishes the violation of the law, and rewards the right; he is perfect in himself, and possessed of perfect blessedness."

The practical doctrine of the Porch was equally

austere and high. " The duty we owe to others is to love all, even our enemies. A good man will love his neighbour from his heart, and take pleasure in protecting and serving him. He will not think himself born for himself alone, but for the common good of all; and will be good to all according to his opportunity. The consciousness of well-doing is ample reward for him; though he have no witness of his deeds, and receive no applause or recompense. He will relieve the sick, aid the shipwrecked, protect the stranger, or supply the hungry with food; but with a cheerful countenance, disdaining all sorrow arising from sympathy, as well as that from personal suffering. The poor, weak, and slaves are his special charge. The wise man alone is free, or rich, or of a sound mind; in truth, the only sovereign."

The noblest phrases of Christian ethics are borrowed from the Stoics. St. Paul before the Areopagus quotes one of their religious hymns. There is no exceeding their maxims of severe, uncompromising virtue. They taught them earnestly too. Cleanthes toiled by night in drawing water and grinding meal, that he might be at liberty to teach by day. Carneades seized the occasion of an embassy to Rome to plant the doctrine in what would be the capital of the world. Seneca insisted on its precepts in the court of Nero, in language which, for earnest morality and intelligent piety, is rarely excelled: and it has been a favourite opinion with many, and not unlikely, that he was secretly a disciple of the Apostle Paul.

Such, in its nobler aspect, was the character of that celebrated protest against the degeneracy of ancient thought and life. But as a means of really escaping from the degradation it deplored, it was lame and ineffectual. It had no visible centre and rallying-point of faith ; no organization of the sentiment of virtue. It had no word of mercy to those "that labour and are heavy laden ;" no deliverance to offer men from the base condition it assumed them to have freely chosen. Manual toil it scorned as slavish, except what was barely needful to maintain the higher life ; all care for health as effeminate and base. All tender charities it forgot or crowded out of sight. It laid no broad hold upon the sympathies of men, but remained the exclusive possession of a few, — aristocrats and monopolists of virtue. With these, the boastful love of all the world, friends and enemies alike, would most likely dwindle to a sterile philanthropism. It demanded an impossible flight to regions of airy excellence, to which it pointed the way, but furnished no motive force.

With many it thus became a vain theory and barren declamation, — the mere heroics and rhodomontade of virtue.* There was no attempt to reconcile the empty and vague ideal with obstinate fact. Hence the theory itself became arbitrary and capricious. All the extravagances which Antinomian fanatics have permitted to the Elect the Stoics said could belong harmlessly to their perfect man. For him, no need of the distinction of virtues and crimes. In his soul was the transmuting principle that rendered all alike holy : he could innocently do what by the common measure would be gross wickedness, —

* As in Cicero's hollow "Paradoxes."

an assertion harmless only because impracticable, since none could hope to reach that state. Such a theory was but an impotent and vain protest against an aggressive moral scepticism, a frail barrier against a tide of dissoluteness and sophistry. It grew to a stern and deepening gloom in the sincere, to empty rhetoric in more artificial and superficial minds. It is a dreary commentary on this ethically noblest philosophy of the pagan world, that the founder of it himself, and three whose names stand high as any among his followers, died by their own hands.* Contempt of death was the final refuge of Stoic virtue, — not that which strengthens a man to endure life to the uttermost, and keep to the last the post which Providence has assigned, but that which overleaps unshrinking the awful brink, to brave the unsolved secret of Eternity.

For about three hundred years the two philosophic creeds, or theories of life, were on trial before the world. Whatever we have found plausible in one or noble in the other, they lent but a treacherous foundation to any positive system of truth or practical style of morals. The speculative philosophy, meanwhile, characteristic of the period, is that of a complete and absolute Scepticism, — sometimes daintily eclectic, as with the "New Academy" of dilettante Platonists, sometimes bald and unqualified in its dogmas of uncertainty. Its creed was, that "Nothing can be certainly known, either by sensation or reflection." Its

---

* Zeno, Cleanthes, Cato, Brutus. "The wise man lives while he ought, not while he can," says Seneca. (Epist. lxx., which argues at length the pros and cons of suicide.)

maxim was, " I must assert nothing, not even this,
that I assert nothing ; " and that " to every assertion
one may be opposed of equal weight, *as it seems to
me.*" This phrase must qualify every proposition.
All science is unsettled by a universal If. The corresponding practical doctrine was absolute indiffer-
entism, and universal compromise. Common sense
revenged itself on the founder of this insolent and
mocking creed by inventing tales of his absurd consistency with it in practice ; saying that his friends
had to rescue him from being run over by what he
would regard as phantom-carriages, and to snatch
him from plunging over the brink of precipices which
his theory ignored. But thought was too far divorced
from life to seek or demand consistency. Pyrrho
himself was a priest of the faith he undermined ; and
lived in honour and esteem to a great old age.

Indeed, scepticism at this period was not so much
a fault of intellect or will, as the symptom of a chronic
mental malady. The harvest of ancient metaphysics
was reaped, and yielded no bread-corn to the hungry
mind.

> " The intellectual power through words and things
> Went sounding on, — a dim and perilous way."

The studious toil of centuries had availed to lay no
impregnable foundation of truth. Natural science
was still in its early rudiments. It could neither
grasp the universe as a whole, nor check the vagaries
of speculation, nor suggest to the philosopher a consistent theory of life on the basis of unalterable fact.
The conception of law was but an impotent general-
ization, a sterile name. The ancient belief in the

sovereign sway of gods had become the doctrine of a
fatal and blind Destiny.* A vague religious instinct
protested vainly against the blank of unbelief. As
the fortunes of the world were drawn more and more
within the embrace of one gigantic Empire, all the
more deeply was felt the craving for a unity of belief,
for one philosophic and religious creed, to define the
faith of the future. The general growth of mind,
and the loss of enterprise and stimulus in the pur-
suits of life, made the religious want more deeply
felt just when it was farthest from being satisfied.
Metaphysical speculation had done its utmost ; but,
spell-bound as it were, and held by a sort of fatality,
it but plunged into deeper darkness at every step.
It became at best a dreamy transcendentalism, a barren sublimation of thought, hair-splitting dialectics
about the divine nature and spiritual things, — which
Oriental mysticism tended more and more to separate from the natural world as impure and base.
The great problem of existence, human and divine,
was solved by limitless negation ; and the human
mind confessed itself incompetent to meet with a resolute affirmative the simplest question as to morals
or belief or destiny.

From Scepticism so radical and entire the natural
reaction at once, and the readiest escape, is Mysticism, — its "positive phase," as it has been called.†
This cuts the knot of negation, and assumes the point
of view of faith. A speculative answer to the great

---

* This alteration in the old mythology is best set forth by Comte,
"Philosophie Positive," Vol. V. pp. 277 – 279.

† Zeller.

Doubt that now invaded the ancient mind might well be despaired of: a religious answer alone could meet the malady at the root. Philosophy had already set the Deity at a distance from the system of things as conceived by the intellect; and the conscience, moved by the degradation of the time, took pleasure in magnifying this distance,—insisting on man's inability to know Him without a mediator, or maligning the world of matter which His hand had wrought. A positive and vital faith once given, to blend with the intellectual material so richly stored, one way of refuge seemed open from the doom to which the most cultivated intellect of the age was hastening. Such was the motive by which the ever busy and inquiring sagacity of the Greeks was drawn towards those Oriental systems of belief, which at this precise point of time offered themselves in Alexandria. A chapter of extraordinary interest is. thus opened in the history of the human mind. Two separate courses of religious speculation present themselves,—one, developed into the New Platonism, which was an euthanasy of the expiring beliefs of paganism; the other taking the direction which we have now to follow.

When Alexander the Great founded his stately capital on the Delta, it was with the political and commercial view of making it the imperial city of the world. Ptolemy, who in the fourfold division received this southern portion of his empire, sought further to make it "the metropolis of science, the asylum of letters, and sanctuary of light." Alexandria became "the great Hellenic city, centre of the commerce of three continents, the common shelter

of letters and the arts," — "the crown of all cities."
When Physco passed his decree of exile, says Athe-
næus, he "filled cities and islands with grammarians,
philosophers, geometers, musicians, painters, teachers,
doctors, and many other professions." From Alexandria, it was said, are all teachers among Greeks
and barbarians. Every population and every faith
was free to share its ample and cosmopolitan domain.
Both Grecian and Egyptian gods had been honoured
with temples by its founder. Oriental mysticism and
Western culture met in the equal hospitality of its
schools.* As the political power of Greece declined,
her intellectual eminence continued undisputed here;
and long after Christianity ruled the world from the
imperial throne of Byzantium, the stately temple of
Serapis remained, as the last citadel of the perishing
culture and creed of Paganism.

In this splendid Grecian capital, that spread its
broad crescent on the Mediterranean shore, the ancient faith of Israel came once more in contact with
remote and strange elements; and here, as in Babylon, while retaining its own strong vitality, it lost
something of its intrinsic character, and adopted the
tone of foreign thought. In the saying of the Jews,
their nation was dispersed in three "Captivities."
Babylon, Palestine, and Egypt were three several
centres or homes, having each its spiritual chief, its
own style of culture, and a development of the religious tradition peculiar to itself. While the Babylonian Jews were busied with the eccentric frivolities
afterwards embodied in the Talmud, while those of

---

* See Simon, also Matter, "Histoire de l'École d'Alexandrie."

16

Palestine were defending their hard-won independence, or nourishing political ambitions and dreams
of vengeance, the Alexandrians were eager to enjoy
the advantage of the great metropolis of Western
thought. While with the first the Hebrew Messianic
hope was overwrought with fables of a fantastic Paradise, — while with the second it became the goad
of enterprises as vindictive and fierce as they were
fruitless, — with the last it was blended with the nobler speculations, and interpreted in the philosophic
phrases of the Grecian schools. Loyal as ever in their
national belief, they clung to the persuasion that theirs
was from of old the one chosen people and interpreter
of God to the whole earth. Their sacred books they
held to be the peculiar and direct gift of God. However alien from the old Hebrew faith their new style
of interpretation, they followed without suspicion of
heresy the fashion of the day, in their metaphysical
refinements and allegorical fancies. Heretics and
aliens by the jealous judgment of those who ruled the
synagogue at Jerusalem and in the estimate of modern Jews, they doubtless regarded themselves as the
true and orthodox expounders of the Old Testament
creed. To the angry horror of those who held that
there could be only one centre of worship, and that
Zion was the true religious home of every pious
Hebrew, these latitudinarian dissenters embraced in
good faith the regal hospitality tendered them. To
the number of at least a million, they became naturalized in the soil of Egypt. They had their own
temple at Leontopolis, — a deserted shrine of Bubas-
tis, granted them, not without a heathen's jest at the

transfer, by Ptolemy. They had their own Sanhedrim of seventy " elders," for whom " seventy golden arm-chairs " were set in the great synagogue at Alexandria; they had their independent religious literature, and their own Greek version of the sacred Scriptures.

This last — the celebrated version of the Seventy — was their peculiar religious treasure, and was looked on through a halo of marvellous tradition, that made it of equal sanctity and authority with the Hebrew original, which indeed few of them could read.* Its preparation, it was said, was intrusted to seventy learned men, — or seventy-two, six to represent each tribe, — who were sent in sacred embassy from Jerusalem at the king's express command.† To save noise and interruption in their task, they were placed on a little island, where they might be in presence of " those elements only whose creation they should describe," and where nothing might be heard save the solemn murmur of the sea; and here each in a separate room, or groups of seven each, prepared a copy of the entire Scripture, which was completed in seventy-two days. And so manifest was the Divine hand in this work, that when the seventy copies came to be compared, not a word or syllable was found to vary.‡

* Philo, it is well known, argues on the significance of Hebrew names from Greek roots.

† About B. C. 280.

‡ Among the characteristic variations of the LXX. from the Hebrew text are the following: The substitution of "Lord" for "Jehovah" throughout, generally followed in the modern versions ; " God *perceived* that he had made man, and *considered*" (Gen. vi. 6) ; "I appeared to Abraham, etc., *as their God*" (Ex. vi. 3) ; "The elders saw *the place* where the God of Israel stood " (Ex. xxiv. 10); " He set the bounds

Thus early were the numerous colonists from Judæa naturalized in Egypt, making it the adopted home of their religion, long before the time when the Jews of Palestine were engaged in their life-and-death struggle with Antiochus. In the main, though at first forced colonists, they were treated with favour and indulgence. They occupied two of the five municipal districts of Alexandria, and in Cyrene made the predominant part of the population. It was a saying, that " he who has not seen the synagogue at Alexandria has not seen that which is most beautiful." So vast was the size of it, that " during service it was necessary to appoint a special officer, who, by the raising and waving of a banner, should at the proper time give a signal to the congregation to respond."

With that cosmopolitan feeling which in exiles often takes the place of a narrower patriotism, the Jews of Alexandria craved intercourse and instruction in the literary and philosophic schools of the Greeks. The celebrated Museum, or Institute, founded by the enlightened Ptolemy Philadelphus, did

---

of the nations according to the number of *his angels* " (Deut. xxxii. 8), —these being supposed to be seventy, and the Law proclaimed on Sinai being divided into as many voices and tongues; "From his band went forth *angels with him* " (Deut. xxxiii. 2); " The Gods of the nations are *Dæmons* " (Ps. xcvi. 5),—a favourite argument of the Alexandrians, in their interpreting between Greek and Jewish thought. Of twelve *theophanies* of the Old Testament, eight are so translated as to disguise the visible appearance of Jehovah, while the rest may be taken as vision or allegory. The Messiah, as a pre-existing divine power, (Dan. vii. 13,) is easily made the Revealer of the Old Testament. See Gfrörer ("Philo," etc.) and Dähne. Respecting the value of this version to the Grecian public, see an Essay of De Quincey on the "Word signifying Eternal."

not admit them on equal terms to its privileges ; but excepting this, there was no bar to the most liberal interchange of thought. The Greeks, following the fashion of the day, eagerly sought among Oriental races signs of that sacred tradition, a purer religious light, whose home to their fancy lay in the far East; and the Jews on their part were both delighted and astonished at the novel speculations of the Greeks as to the divine order of the universe, the Kosmos, and the inscrutable nature of the Deity. The infinite and unchangeable One, the perfect Good, the essential Reason, the divine and universal Life, they were not slow to identify with the Jehovah revealed in their own sacred books. They readily seized on the traditions current among the 'philosophical sects, to prove that Pythagoras and Plato, who were said to borrow their doctrine from the East, must have found it in the Hebrew Scriptures, and that Moses was the true father of Grecian philosophy.

The Old Testament, especially the Pentateuch, was interpreted into an enormous scheme of symbolism, or allegory, "the natural fruit of a mental revolution." The "Word of Jehovah," which in the Hebrew writings expresses, with a vague sublimity, the active agency of the Creator, was identified with the indwelling or "seminal" reason of the Stoics,*— in whose stern protest against effeminacy the Jews found many points of attraction and sympathy, as formerly in the austere ritual

---

* "The Stoics teach an *essential*, the Alexandrian Jews and Neo-Platonists only a *dynamic* immanence of God in the world." — Zeller, "Philosophie der Griechen," Vol. III. p. 493.

of the Persians. This divine Reason, or living Word of God, was spoken of as God's own Son, and as Father or Creator of the Universe.* The Jews were a nation of priests, agents, and interpreters of the Divine Word, intercessors with the Almighty in behalf of the creation.† The high-priest in his prayers interceded for the elements; and his sacred robes were a symbol of the visible universe.‡ The Divine Word, they held, is a perpetual Mediator, through whom the world is continually reconciled to God. It is "the first of angels, the Archangel of many names;" the first-born Son of God; the atoning Mediator, or High-priest, in behalf of mankind; present in the creation from the beginning, but first revealed to the Jews through Moses.§ Adopting the doctrine of the Platonists, they further identified the Divine Word with the realm of eternal Ideas, existing from the beginning in the mind of God; and hence, as his executive Agent in the work of creation, — the three advocates with God being the Divine mercy, the piety of the Fathers, and repentance.

Such is the somewhat vague and undiscriminated circle of theological ideas got by blending the con-

---

* The personal view of the Logos was earlier in Alexandria, says Gfrörer, than the philosophical; and the term was introduced as the masculine equivalent of the feminine Sophia, or Wisdom. (Compare Prov. viii. 30.)

† Dorner, "Lehre von der Person Christi," Vol. I., Introduction.

‡ Wisdom of Solomon xviii. 24. So Philo says: "The high-priest is the Word, which putteth on the world as a garment." — *De Profugis*, p. 466 (Frankfort folio of 1691).

§ Philo, *Quis Hæres,* p. 509; and *Confusio Linguarum*, p. 341.

ceptions of several Grecian schools, especially the
Platonist and Stoic, with the religious language of
the Old Testament. It is the longing for a universal
religion, expressed in the terms of a limited and peculiar creed. It is a style of thought often incon-
sistent with itself, still more often unintelligible or
incoherent to a modern mind; yet highly characteristic of that age, and indispensable to be known in
studying, not only the "preparations of the Gospel,"
but the gradual development also of the Christian
doctrine itself.*

The first traces of this blending of two elements
seemingly so incongruous are found as early as in
the Alexandrian version of the Seventy. Of Aristobulus (B. C. 150), a Jew of considerable eminence,
we know little more than that he first directly as-
serted the Hebrew origin of Greek philosophy; and
that his exposition of Homer and the Orphic poets,
as well as the Old Testament, was in violent conformity with this idea.†   And it was in the hands of
Aristeas, a little later, that the miracle of the Septua-
gint came into its present and popular form.

The "Wisdom of Solomon," an apocryphal book
of uncertain date, is the most complete and interesting exhibition of this colouring of Jewish by Grecian
thought. God (to quote the new religious phrase-

---

* For the several contributions to that development, Stoic, Platonist, and Jewish, see Vacherot, "Histoire Critique de l'École d'Alexandrie."

† See Zeller and Gfrörer. The following specimen of his theology
is preserved to us : "God never ceases to create; but as it is the
nature of fire to burn and of snow to be cold, so of God to create, and
much more, since he is the source of activity to all."

ology) is "the lover of souls, whose incorruptible spirit is in all things." His spirit "filleth the world, and that which containeth all things hath knowledge of the voice." His "almighty Word leaped down from heaven, out of his royal throne, as a fierce man of war." Wisdom is "a breath of the power of God, a pure influence flowing from the glory of the Almighty; in all ages, entering into holy souls, she maketh them friends of God, and prophets." "God created man to be immortal, and made him to be an image of his own eternity. . . . . . The souls of the righteous are in the hand of God, and there shall no torment touch them; for though they be punished in the sight of men, yet is their hope full of immortality." "The thoughts of mortal men are miserable, and their devices but uncertain; for the corruptible body presseth down the soul, and the earthly tabernacle weigheth down the mind that museth on many things: " but "incorruption maketh us near to God." *

This style of thought shows already traces of an asceticism quite foreign to the true Hebrew doctrine, and most nearly allied whether to the practices of the far East, or to the sentiments of the Stoics. It is as if the language of their protest were taken in good faith, and made the practical rule of life among some sects that now appear on this Egyptian soil, so fertile in all extravagances of religious doctrine. Of these, the most noted are the *Therapeutæ*, a body of Jewish monks, — men sharing the religious and mental cul-

---

* Wisdom of Solomon, xi. 26; xii. 1; i. 7; xviii. 15; vii. 25, 27; ii. 23; iii. 1, 4; ix. 14, 15; vi. 19.

ture of the time, but devoted to the most rigid austerity of celibate and monastic life.* In each dwelling
was a private chapel or "monastery." Their religious exercises were frequent; their Sabbath scrupulously kept. Their only common worship was a
banquet and sacred dance on the seventh day, — a
dramatic commemoration of the Passover and passage of the Red Sea.† Their food was of bread, salt,
and herbs, their drink only water, like the later
Christian monks, with frequent fasts of three or
even six days. Slavery among them was held to
be "against nature," and strictly forbidden. Their
name, which signifies Healers, or attendants on the
sick, denotes either their religious charities, or their
office of healing the diseases of the soul. The body
they regarded as a prison, and the ground of all
evil they held to reside in Matter. A visionary and
impassioned ecstasy was their way of access to divine
energies, and their method of prophetic inspiration.
Hence their maceration and austerities; and hence
the fervours of their mystical piety. They carried to
its greatest extent the new doctrine of mediation
through the divine Spirit, or living Word of God,
and of the ministration of angels, whose names they
said were revealed as a sacred mystery. Their doctrine of mediating spirits exposed them to the charge
of magical ceremonies; and many of their opinions
and practices they shared with the sect of pagan
Mystics, who claimed to be the new disciples of
Pythagoras.

One eminent writer — so eminent that he is often

---

* Philo, *De Vita Contemplativa.* † Gfrörer.

regarded as the true founder of the New-Platonic school, that obstinate rival of the Christian Church — represents to us in its completest proportions the blending of Jewish and Grecian thought that took place gradually during the three centuries before Christ. Philo the Jew was of a priestly family, rich and honourable, and was thoroughly instructed in the religious traditions of his people. His birth was we know not how many years before that of Jesus, — probably as many as twenty. The most marked event of his life was his being sent at the head of an embassy to intercede with Caligula (A. D. 40) in behalf of the Jews, then suffering under a cruel and wanton persecution from Flaccus, the governor of Alexandria, because they would not worship the emperor as a God. He was then already well advanced in years, being the oldest of the legation. One tradition makes him acquainted with the Apostle Peter, if not his convert, as if to account for his extraordinary anticipation of Christian forms of thought; but the saying, "Plato Philonizes, or else Philo Platonizes," gives, no doubt, the truer story.

In his voluminous writings are found all the various characteristics and opinions which have been ascribed to the Jewish philosophy of the period, — not set forth in an orderly manner, but floating at random in an interminable flood of paraphrase and comment of the Pentateuch. One is at a loss to know how far he accepts the Hebrew tradition as fact, or how far he uses it as a veil to his own fond fancies. As with the Church Fathers, much of his exposition is in the form of homily, and reads like oral discourses, not always wanting in pulpit eloquence, taking some sacred legend for the text. The narrative is treated with the utmost freedom, to square it with the prevalent style of religious speculation. "None but a fool would think the world was made in six days, or in any given period of time;" since it is the Divine nature to act always, and creation is eternal. Adam is the intellectual nature, and woman is formed from the necessity of joining with it the sensual and material: that she was taken literally from his side, "who can believe it? the tale is mythical." The river of Paradise is wisdom; which being "parted into four heads" becomes the four cardinal virtues.* Cain and Abel are rival principles; and since evil is self-destructive, it follows that Cain kills himself, not his brother.

The patriarchs are living intercessors with "the God of the living." Abraham, Isaac, and Jacob represent three styles of religious illumination, — innate knowledge, culture, and practical discipline. Again, Abraham is intellect, and Sarah virtue, whose marriage is wisdom. Again, Abraham routs the banded kings and delivers his allies, — that is to say, the five senses and the four affections. It is in a phantom shape, not a real body, that the Word (not Jehovah) appears to him in Mamre. His migration is emancipation from the body, and is attended by angels; "for he who follows God necessarily has for his attendants those Words of his which we call angels." His offering of Isaac is the sacrifice of pleasure or delight, which belongs to God alone.

* So Josephus; also Augustine, *De Civitate Dei*, XIII. 21.

His change of name was from "lofty father," to "elect father of the Voice."

The angels of the sacred books are equivalent to the Dæmons or Heroes of the Greek mythology. Noah is the same as Deucalion ; the builders of Babel are compared with the Titans who heaped Pelion on Ossa ; and the fabled Atlantis finds its place in the exposition of Jewish legend. Moses when a child refused all childish sports ; and while at the court of Pharaoh, his teachers were brought "from the remotest parts of Egypt and Greece." The burning bush signifies that the righteous "shall not perish by the fury of their foes." Not God himself, but his Word, was present in the pillar of cloud that led the desert march.* Moses is the "prophet Word ; " "Balaam (the empty vulgar) holds discourse with his ass, — that is, the brutish way of life that every fool rides on." The high-priest entering the sanctuary is no longer a man, but represents "the Word, which putteth on the universe as a garment." And of Manna, "what is sweeter than honey, or whiter than snow ? that bread which is the word of God." † Such are specimens of this novel rendering of the Hebrew books, taken at random from the wide expanse of Philo's commentaries.

Of particular doctrines are the following : —

Of God and his Worship. — " We may know that God is, but not what God is." The divine powers or

---

* Compare 1 Cor. x. 4.

† See the treatises, *De Abrahamo, De Temulentia, De Migratione Abrahami, De Confusione Linguarum, De Vita Mosis,* pp. 509, 613, *De Nobilitate, De Profugis,* p. 466.

attributes are segments of Deity; the names " Lord "
and " God " are significant of might and goodness,
whose reconciler is the Word. This is Philo's trinity. God is " the God of Abraham," etc., that is, the
relative for the absolute, since God has no need of
name. " God governs not as a tyrant, but as a mild
and lawful king, whose most fit name is Father."
He gives blessings to the evil and unthankful, to
stimulate them to goodness. Spirit is that which is
breathed into the soul by God. To receive the divinity, one must be as in Corybæan ecstasy, as a child
without speech or consciousness. " The mind when
it purely serves God is not human, but divine; but
when it turns to any human thing, descending from
heaven, rather falling upon the earth, it goes forth,
even though it remain in the body." " Nothing so
rouses the mind to liberty as to become a fugitive and
suppliant to God." " What should be true sacrifice
but the worship of a pious soul? whose homage is
everlasting, written on tablets before God, to last as
long as sun and moon and universe." The only fit
sacrifices are " those of the soul that brings as its
offering mere and only truth." " God finds no worthier temple than the mind." *

---

* Philo, *De Abrahamo, De Providentia, Quod Deterior Potiori invidet,*
p. 159, *De Lege Allegoriæ, Quis Rerum Divinarum Hæres,* p. 492, *De
Vita Mosis, De Nobilitate.*

Compare Apollonius of Tyana (quoted by Zeller, Vol. III. p. 305):
" Thus, as I think, should one render the most fit service to the Divinity, and thence find him merciful and propitious, and thus only: if
to God (of whom we have first said that he is One, apart from all,
and whom it is needful for all to search out), he neither offer sacrifice
nor kindle fire nor have recourse to anything at all of sensible things;

Of the Divine Word. — God having determined to make the world, first (as the builder of a city) made an intellectual image or model, — the Logos or Word, which is the *intelligible world* (κόσμος νοητός), idea of ideas, and image of God; mediator among the divine attributes; "helmsman and ruler of all things." "If no one is worthy to be called son of God, at least share the glory of the Word." "To the archangel and most ancient Word the Father, who hath begotten all things, gave the choice gift, that, standing as Mediator, he should judge the Maker's work. He is Advocate of the mortal with the Eternal, an Envoy of the Ruler to his subjects. He rejoices in his office, and fulfils it, saying, I am come between the Lord and you, being neither unborn as God nor born as you, but midst of the two extremes, and hostage to both, — with the Creator, as assurance that he will never wholly destroy or forsake his offspring; and with the Creature, as a pledge that the merciful God will never overlook his own work. For I announce peace from him that knoweth how to put an end to war, — God the Guardian of peace." *

It is not the particular opinions he held, or the fond fancies that garnish his writings, but rather the

---

—for He needs nothing, not even from those better than we; nor is there a plant which the earth puts forth, or a creature which the air supports, to which there adheres not some taint; — but uses always towards him the *better discourse* alone, — I mean not that which passes through the lips, but from the fairest of beings seeks the best things by what is fairest in us; and the mind requires no organs. Thus by no means should we offer sacrifice to God, who is great and above all."

* Philo, *De Cherubis*, p. 114, *De Confus. Ling.*, p. 341, *Quis Rerum Divin. Hæres*, 509.

style of thought, making him a representative of his era, and preparing the way for later schemes of Christian doctrine, that gives interest and value to Philo's speculations. In them we find, not clearly or consistently set forth, but assumed as part of the texture, that doctrine of the Divine Word so remarkably expanded afterwards in the Alexandrian theology. It is hardly too much to say, that in the various treatises of Philo almost every cardinal point of the later school of Christian dogmatics is clearly anticipated or reproduced ; at least, a groundwork is prepared for it in the style of thought and language which they helped to make familiar. We find in him already the Word as the second Divinity,* the first-born Son, the Image, Messenger, and executive Agent ($\H{v}\pi\alpha\rho\chi o\varsigma$) of God, the Light of the world, the Advocate, Mediator, Intercessor, Mediatorial High-Priest, the Refuge and Physician of souls, Shepherd of the flock, Ordainer of all things, Type of the creation,† Seal of testimony, Fountain of wisdom, and sinless Saviour from sin.‡ We find the doctrine of Ransom or Redemption, of spiritual blessedness, of repentance and faith as the source of good works and the ground of justification ; of the Holy Spirit and the sacred Triad. How important the service .rendered in advance by this rich circle of ideas, this complete system of religious symbolism, to those who strove to interpret to the succeeding generation the life and ministration and·spiritual offices of Christ !

---

* $\Theta\epsilon\acute{o}\varsigma$, but not $\acute{o}$ $\Theta\epsilon\acute{o}\varsigma$.

† Compare Coloss. i. 15, 16.

‡ See Bryant, " Sentiments of Philo concerning the Logos."

But it is not the service rendered in this one direction alone that we owe to these religious schools of Alexandria. Another spectacle so interesting, so solemn in its significance, is scarcely presented in the whole history of human thought, as this confluence of the two main streams of the spiritual life of antiquity. However fantastic or arbitrary the particular form into which they ran, the point of chief moment yet remains, — that this confluence was actually brought about, and at such a time and in such a way as to render the most needed service to humanity. The ripe fruit of ancient culture, the loftiest results attained by an elaborate metaphysics, were gathered before the root they sprang from was wholly perished, — before the intellectual life of the time was altogether wasted and destroyed by scepticism. The grand and earnest faith of the old Hebrew people was the element required to restore life and vigour to the effete metaphysics of the West; while it was saved from a technical and vain provincialism by blending itself with the richer culture developed on the soil of Europe. Each was needful to the other ; and their union was brought about at the precise point of time that made it of the greatest possible avail in the new religious era about to be inaugurated.

Still, great and transcendently important as was the service thus effected, it was but a service of preparation, — " a spectral and visionary *fata morgana* appearing on the horizon where Christianity was about to dawn." * The material was prepared, and

* Dorner.

the way was open; but the breath of life had yet to be breathed from another source. The Word as the immanent Reason and Life of things, as the divine and creative Energy, made part of men's philosophic creed, and was ready to be ingrafted in due season on their theology. But the same Word was yet to be recognized as "manifest in the flesh and dwelling among men," before the Alexandrian speculations could become fruitful in men's religious life, or the final task of Israel could be done. That which had been developed as Philosophy was to be seized and appropriated as Faith. This was a revolution for which the world had yet to wait.

Nothing in the tone of the writings we have been now considering is more striking to the Christian reader than their complete unconsciousness of any symptoms of the great change already impending, — their utter inability to apprehend their own moment and value as an element in the spiritual regeneration of the race. The glorious "almost Christian" thoughts of Philo, so vivid in their new relations as symbolic drapery of the living form of divine Truth and Love, appear but feebly and at random in the confused detail of allegoric interpretations by which he was eager to recommend his religious traditions to the sceptic and subtile Greek. They have to be painfully sought and carefully traced out by an eye already familiar with them in their new garb and colouring. And what the Jewish philosopher but casually betrays in the undertone of allusion, exposition, or appeal, becomes, if so regarded, significant of the most momentous revolution that has ever been wrought in the intellectual history of mankind.

This unconscious testimony, this betrayal at unawares of a form of thought destined to have so profound an influence in the coming generation, is what gives its deepest interest, and even a certain pathos, to the history of these religious exiles of Alexandria. The sacred treasure of their tradition, twice violently transferred from the soil where its growth was native, they held with a jealous reverence ; and proved their fidelity by incorporating it with the best they could learn or share of the rich intellectual heritage of their adopted country. Standing on the verge of their expiring fortunes as a people, and destined within another generation to be dispersed in a far more remorseless "Captivity" than any they had known as yet, their patient zeal lent itself to the task of interpreting to the world the oracles of their holy Word. The world received them ; yet in another than the intended sense. And long after the Hebrew remnant was shattered and dispersed, and its very name had become a mockery and reproach, these very words and phrases, by which it signified the identity of its own tradition with the loftiest of the world's cultivated thought, were emblazoned on the victorious Creed of Christendom.

XII. THE MESSIAH.

FROM the death of Herod the Great to the siege of Jerusalem by Titus is a period of rather more than seventy years. To the Jews it was, almost from first to last, a time of despairing struggle and hopeless suffering. The destiny foredoomed in the fate of the last native line of kings came steadily on, like the cloud which the prophet saw rising from the west, till it overwhelmed state and people in one ruin. A single spot of comparative calm exhibits the advent of the new and higher Faith that sprang from the perishing stock of Israel; all else shows only a protracted and disastrous effort to ward off the impending doom, animated by the nation's obstinate hope of its coming Deliverer and King.

The history of this final period turns therefore upon the Jewish expectation of the Messiah, — the fanatical attempts to realize it, and "take the kingdom of heaven by violence," together with the fulfilment of it in a revolution which burst the bands of the ancient creed, threw down "the middle wall of partition," and shared the hope of Israel among all the families of the earth. In this regard, it is not only the catastrophe of a nation that we are to consider, but a crisis momentous above every other in the

spiritual destinies of mankind: The three leading
forms of antique civilization were now come to their
final term of development. The way of thought had
been prepared for the new religion by a fusion between the Hebrew and Grecian mind as complete as
the elements might admit; the way of empire was
now laid open by the conquests of that great city
whose history is henceforth, for fifteen hundred
years, the history of the world. As Rome came to
embrace in its dominion the circuit of the Mediterranean, " the coast-line of Judæa was the last remote
portion which was needed to complete the fated cir-
cumference." *   Israel — in the person of its afflicted
people, and of One who represents at this period its
highest and truest life — was the last victim offered
up on this altar of the world, that nations might
be reconciled in a common empire, and minds in a
common faith.

Such is the spiritual aspect of this period, taken as
a whole, and its place in the history of the world.
As a portion of the life of the Hebrew people, its
interest is almost wholly tragical. A destiny, inexpiable and horrid, like that of the Greek heroic
drama, broods over it, growing more black and
gloomy towards the close. The nation's doom throws
its shadow far back upon the past. Rome, in the
flush of her triumph over Hannibal, had marked the
contests of the petty Asiatic states, and her powerful
word of recognition had upheld the Jewish commonwealth in the struggle by which its last liberties were
won. Now the same dread and domineering power

---

* Conybeare's " St. Paul."

began to invade those liberties, and to crush out the
nation's life.

Edom, in the language of Jewish mystics, is the
Scripture type of Rome: the reign of Herod made it
also the historical type. It was by a Roman lord that
he was thrice made master of the destinies of Israel.
It was the model of Roman dominion that this powerful and unscrupulous Idumæan chief laboured to
establish. It was as a conqueror, or (in the old
Greek sense) a tyrant, that he ruled, — one whose
might was his only right; and the nation never professed him its allegiance. His merciless suspicion
had destroyed every one of the only Hebrew family
which the national hope could oppose to him, so as
even to undermine his own authority by the murder
of his Maccabæan wife. If he had nearly won the
people's good-will by restoring their religious privilege, and reinstating their ritual in far more than its
ancient splendour, he roused their passionate grief
by the treachery that destroyed their young and
royal priest on the evening of their high festival;
and tempted their deadliest suspicion by the foreign
manners with which he invaded their national character and faith. The stately temple, glittering with
marble front and gilded roof, displayed on its portal
the imperial golden eagle, and was flanked by the
impregnable fortress Antonia, named by Herod for
the most profligate of the Romans. A theatre within
the walls exhibited the Greek plays and dances; an
amphitheatre without, the bloody spectacles of Rome.
Cæsarea, with its spacious port and marble colonnades,
"a habitation of princes," was a Roman town; bear-

·ing, like Sebaste or Augusta, the Roman emperor's name.　In strict accordance with the centralizing policy of the empire, Herod thus sapped the characteristic life of his own people, and provoked the first outbreak of that " frightful Messianic tempest " which raged with little intermission for more than half a century, and ceased not but with the total ruin of the Jewish state.

While his two sons, Archelaus and Antipas, were disputing their claim before Augustus, the revolt (which had already begun in an assault on the gold eagle of the temple) first took a distinct and threatening shape.　With no royal or priestly line . about which the hopes of all might rally, Palestine was for a few years a prey to aimless bursts of frenzy, and the feuds of as many pretended kings as there were ambitious rebel chiefs.　Judas, son of the old Galilæan bandit Hezekiah, Simon, a former slave of Herod, who destroyed many royal palaces, and the giant shepherd Athronges, are named in quick succession as candidates for the perilous honours of royalty ; and a pretender, in the name of·Alexander son of Mariamne, received homage and royal gifts from the Jews in Crete and Rome, till Augustus, looking at his hands, which were strong and coarse, exposed the imposture, and made him a rower in the imperial galleys.　" Thus did a great and wild fury spread itself over the nation, because they had no king to keep the multitude in order," and because the troops sent to quell the sedition cared less for the public peace than for plunder and revenge.　"Judæa was full of robberies ; and as the several companies of rebels lit upon any one to head them, he was created a king immediately."

This horrible disorder was stayed by Varus, the Syrian governor,—mercifully and temperately, it should seem, by the standard of provincial rule, but at the cost of crucifying some two thousand of the guiltiest. The Jews sent to Rome to beg such liberties as the imperial state might grant. Loudly and bitterly they accused the recent tyranny of Herod, who "had put upon them such abuses as not a wild beast upon the throne would have done;" they entreated "to be delivered from kingly and the like forms of government;" and prayed to be put under the more just rule of the Syrian governor, whoever he might be. But Herod's three sons, Archelaus, Antipas, and Philip, were confirmed as rulers of three districts of Palestine, till ten years later, when the popular complaint of "barbarous and tyrannical usage" reached Augustus's ears, and Archelaus was sent into banishment to Gaul.

Now for the first time Judæa was enrolled as a Roman province, and the celebrated "taxing" took place under Cyrenius (or Quirinus), governor of Syria. (A. D. 7.) Not all were prepared to submit peaceably to this surrender of the last forms of independence. A formidable revolt under Judas the Gaulonite began that systematic opposition to the Roman rule — now latent, now open and furious — which took presently the final and fatal form of the sect of Zealots. "The nation was infected with this doctrine to an incredible degree;" whence resulted, says Josephus, robberies and murders innumerable, with famine and the dreadful desolation that came at last. But the object which Roman policy had aimed at so long was now secured. Judæa by its own choice had become a portion of the conquering empire. Steadily and irresistibly pressed the remorseless Roman rule, aggravated, no doubt, by the scorn felt towards the race and faith.* Coponius Ambivius and Antonius Rufus filled with their brief administrations the last seven years of Augustus. Tiberius during all his reign (A. D. 14 – 37) sent only two, Valerius Gratus and Pontius Pilate, — a merciful relief to the impatient rapacity of those whose term of legal plunder was brief and must be improved. The reason Tiberius gave is characteristic of the Roman rule generally, as well as of his own cold and scornful temper : — he would not drive away the flies that were already well gorged with feeding on the " sick man's " bruises and sores, and so admit a fresh, hungry swarm.

The reign of Tiberius, so full of the sullen terrors of tyranny at home, was accordingly a time of comparative repose to Palestine. The north was ruled by Herod Antipas ; the east by the milder Philip ; Gratus and Pilate sharing successively the domination of the south. Roman policy spared such national customs, and religious beliefs or rites, as did not openly challenge Roman supremacy in the state. In secular affairs Cæsar claimed his own ; in spiritual, no conscience was forbidden to " render to God

---

* " Vile damnum," says Tacitus, speaking of a few thousand Jews expelled from Rome, who perished in the savage island of Sardinia. (Annals, II. 85.)

the things that are God's." Neither of the Procurators under Tiberius exceeded the average of provincial peculation and cruelty; both probably came short of it. As long as the national hope remained a barren doctrine, — nay, even when it took the form of a strong popular enthusiasm (as in the case of Jesus), yet without directly menacing the imperial rule, — it was the cautious policy of Pilate not to interfere. Experience, indeed, had made him wary, and suspicion made him cruel, as in the case of the Galilæans whose blood he "mingled with their sacrifices," — a temper which the Jews easily wrought upon to procure a Galilæan prophet's condemnation;* and one is tempted to assign a diplomatic motive, rather than humane, to his long parleying with them in the Judgment Hall, as if he would commit them in advance against any Messianic insurrection. Gaining this, he safely insulted the nation's hope by the mocking inscription on the cross. Once he ventured so far as to bring the emperor's image on the Roman ensigns within the sacred city; but when the Jews offered themselves, without resistance, to be massacred by the troops rather than endure the sacrilege, he yielded, and carried the images back to Cæsarea.† Once a popular revolt was threatened, when he undertook to build an aqueduct of some twenty-five miles from the funds of the temple treasury; but a party of his guards, mingling in the crowd, despatched no few of them

* Luke xiii. 1; xxiii. 6.

† Or the imperial shields, as Philo says, which he removed at Tiberius's command.

with hidden daggers, and "quickly put an end to that sedition."

In this last brief period of the nation's life, some show of independence was still preserved. The governor's head-quarters were at Cæsarea on the sea-coast. Jerusalem was the religious capital of the district, and was left mainly under native rule. A spiritual power, resting on the sacred tradition, and administered by Rabbins* (interpreters, or doctors of the Canon-Law), had gradually grown up since the Captivity, and for practical purposes had nearly supplanted the priesthood itself. This learned body had now acquired an extraordinary sanctity. "The voice of the Rabbi is the voice of God," was the Jewish saying; and the Almighty himself was pictured, by a coarse and irreverent fancy, as the ideal or archetypal Rabbi, — his robes of authority and his daily customs being those of this "spiritual police." † Where there are ten who have knowledge of the Law, there must be a Synagogue with its stated service; if fewer assemble, the Lord will say, Wherefore am I called and none are here? With each synagogue was connected a school for the instruction in the Law; in Palestine, it was said, were five hundred such schools, the least containing five hundred pupils; Rabbi Gamaliel alone had no less than a thousand, of whom half studied Jewish and half Gentile learning. In

---

* The title Rabbi is said to have been first given to Simeon, — the same who took up the infant Jesus in the temple.

† Three hours a day, they said, he renders judgment, three hours he contemplates the Law, three hours he feeds his creatures, and three he plays with Leviathan. (Job xli. 5.)

Jerusalem alone were four hundred and sixty syna-
gogues. "To multiply schools and put a hedge
about the Law," was the Rabbinic maxim. Such a
system of public instruction by degrees gathered the
real religious power into the hands of this body ; and
more than all else prepared the name and faith of
Israel to survive the annihilation of temple, priesthood, and the nation's life.

At the head of this system of spiritual jurisdiction
was the Sanhedrim, or great Court of Seventy. Tradition fondly traced it by direct descent from the
"elders" appointed by Moses in the wilderness. It
was now in its highest eminence and splendour, with
power supreme in religious affairs, and civil authority
little short of life and death. While the Temple was
shorn of its ancient glories, — deprived of the Divine
fire, ark, and holy oracle, the Shekinah or visible
Presence, and the consecrating oil, — a share of its
diminished sanctity fell to this great ecclesiastical
Court. Pilate himself was practically powerless to
rescue Jesus from its condemnation ; and the death-
sentence of the first Christian martyr was delayed for
no formal sanction of procurator or king. "To each
state its own religion," was the maxim of Roman
rule ; * and among the Jews civil and religious matters were so intimately blended, that in virtue of it
no small degree of popular liberty still survived. A
style of thought had gradually grown up, and was
prevalent now, as characteristic and strongly marked
as at any former period of Hebrew history. As being
(so to speak) the last expression of the Hebrew mind,

* Cicero, Pro Flacco, c. 28, in express reference to the Jews.

and as forming that soil of Judaism in which the
religion of Christ had its first planting and nurture,
it becomes one of the most important features of the
age we are now considering.

While the Jews of Egypt were slowly transforming
the faith of their fathers into the likeness of Grecian
wisdom, among those in Palestine had grown up a
system of belief more deeply tinged with Oriental
notions, — far more characteristically and exclusively Jewish. The speculations they shared with their
brethren in the remoter East became sacred mysteries,
hidden by the cipher of which Rabbinic tradition only
held the key. They became scholiasts of Holy Writ;
explaining it "by anagram, riddle, and acrostic,"
by cabalistic play of numbers,* by a system of casuistry marvellously and hopelessly minute.† The Scriptures, in such a system, are easily made the source
and summary of all wisdom. Not "a jot or a tittle"
could pass from the law;‡ to every letter was as-

* Thus, taking the *numerical equivalent* of "Ethiopian" (Numbers xii. 1),
they explained that Moses married a woman of "fair countenance," so
acquitting him of the guilt of an uncanonical marriage. The numerical
value of *David* is 14 (Matthew i. 17); of *Balaam son of Beor*, 666
(Revelation xiii. 18); and *Shiloh*, by the same interpretation, is made
equivalent to *Messiah*.

† A celelebrated Rabbi says that there are at least eight hundred
volumes which he must have "at his fingers' ends," to meet cases
of daily practice. "How should he have time for Gentile learning?"

‡ Illustrated, in Jewish fashion, thus: The letter Jod fell on its face
before God, and said, O eternal Lord! thou hast taken me away from
the name of that holy woman! (in the change from *Sarai* to *Sara*);
but the blessed God answered, Hitherto thou hast been but in the name
of a woman, and that at the end; hereafter thou shalt be in the name
of a man, and at the beginning. And for four hundred years the letter

signed its place and traditionary size in the sacred scroll; * and the mightiest miracles are wrought by the hidden virtue of the letters which spell the name Jehovah. †

The dominant sect of Pharisees had an equal jealousy at the allegorical fancies of the Mystics, and that whole style of learning which they comprehensively termed "wisdom of Javan." "Is it not written in the Law," said a Rabbi to his scholar, "that thou shalt meditate therein day and night? whatever hour, therefore, thou canst find belonging neither to the day nor night, in that thou mayest study Grecian wisdom." In the interpreting of Scripture, Prophecy itself is set far below that oral Tradition which was given by Moses to the Seventy, and from them descended to Ezra, by whom it was embodied in the doctrines of his school.‡ It was even a question whether the Law itself or the tradition were the holier; " The words of the Law are weighty and light, but the words of the Scribes are all weighty," was a saying

Jod did not cease to importune, until Oshea the son of Nun was born, whom the Lord called Joshua.

* Thus the full form *toledoth* ("generations") occurs only in Ruth iv. 18: by its six letters, say the Rabbins, it is shown that in Messiah shall be restored the glory of man, length of days, stature, fruits of earth, fruits of trees, and light of heaven. The letter *Nun* is twice reversed; signifying once the turning of Jehovah to his people, and once their turning back from him. It is an argument for the stability of Scripture, that a diminished *Heth* has not vanished entirely.

† The *Shem hamphorash* ("explained name"), by the stolen knowledge of which, say the Rabbins, the miracles of Jesus were wrought.

‡ Since Malachi, they said, the Urim and Thummim have ceased in Israel; in place of which is granted the andible omen, or Bath-kol, "daughter of the Voice," — a reverential and beautiful belief, to which several allusions occur in the Christian Scripture.

among the Jews, — one which must have been vehemently contested until the dispute was compromised by affirming that both, if not absolutely eternal, at least existed in Paradise before the world was.

That storehouse of Jewish fancy, anecdote, custom, tradition, and canon-law, the Talmud, was in great part gathered in its present form a century or two later, but was already in substance the popular creed and the staple learning of Jewish schools. Its body of doctrine may have owned a Babylonish parentage; but the garb it wore was woven of Scripture threads. All is taught in detail, and by specification. Thus pre-existence and transmigration are signified in the dogmatic formula that all men have sinned in Adam, and in him a covenant was made with them long before their birth. From the dim cloud-land, *Goph*, the limbo of pre-existent spirits, each child is before its birth led by an angel to hell and paradise, whereof all after knowledge is but a faint reminiscence. The federal head of the human race is Adam Kadmon the primal Man, male-female,* from whom all souls are emanations; or, by another opinion, his spirit is the image of God incarnate afterwards in Enoch, Noah, Jacob, and the Messiah.† Elijah is identical with Phinehas, Melchizedek, and Shem; Laban still carries on his strife with Israel in the person of Balaam and of Cushan-Rishathaim the first invader. The

---

* Genesis i. 27.

† So some of the early Christians held that Jesus was clothed in Adam's body, and crucified upon the spot of his grave. See in Sir John Mandeville the beautiful legend of the Cross, wrought of four kinds of trees, — the cedar for strength, the cypress for fragrance, the palm for victory, and the olive for peace.

seven dukes of Edom " before there was any king in
Israel" signify seven preadamic worlds, which were
"without form and void" previous to the existing
creation.   And the phrase " day one" (instead of
" first day "), in the story of the Creation, has a mysterious reference to the unity of all things in God.
" A man does not hurt his finger on earth but it is
decreed in heaven," was the proverbial form of the
doctrine of predestination ; "a little bird is not taken
without the will of Heaven ; how much less the soul
of a man."

Well known to us, through the New Testament, are
the doctrines of Dæmons, descended from the " sons
of God and daughters of men," as the cause of many
maladies ; of Beelzebub their prince, and their desert-
haunts ; of Satan the chief Adversary, whom the Messiah must overcome in personal encounter, so as to
expiate his people's sin ; of guardian spirits and the
hierarchy of the Angels ; of sin before birth, and
disease the penalty of parents' guilt ; as well as the
scrupulous casuistry of the rules respecting Sabbath,
fasting, alms, and prayer.*   The extraordinary fables

---

* As an instance of Jewish scruple, when a poor scholar asked if it
were lawful for cheapness to write on pigskin parchment, the reply was,
"Is it not written, The words of this Law shall be *in thy mouth* and in
thy heart?" whence it was ingeniously gathered that they might be
written on the skins of such beasts only as may be eaten.   One prayer
of the Jews was recited in Syriac, lest the angels, who are ignorant of
that tongue, should overhear it, and envy the Jews the blessings it
besought.   The rules of the Sabbath are curiously quibbling and
minute.   The wretched Jewish exiles from the Spanish Inquisition,
starving on the African shore, would not gather with their hands on the
Sabbath the grass which was their only food, but stooped and plucked
it with their teeth.

respecting the terrestrial Paradise in Messiah's kingdom ; of Behemoth, a beast so huge as to cover "a
thousand hills," and Leviathan, slain and salted from
of old for the everlasting banquets of the elect ;
vineyards, of which each cluster shall yield a year's
store of wine, and each grape be clamorous to be
gathered before its fellow ; and the prodigious stature
of the primal Adam,* are the grotesque exaggeration
and travesty peculiar to the later style of Judaism.

The two grand pivots of this system of doctrine are
" Moses, the ideal of the past, and Messiah, the ideal
of the future," between whom ran an elaborate
dogmatic parallelism.

Moses is made almost a divinity, — "a prophet
(says Josephus) such as never was known ; so that
whatever he spake one would think he heard the
voice of God himself." The miracle of crossing the
Red Sea was magnified by supposing twelve separate
channels in the waves for the twelve tribes of Israel ;
and even by asserting that the people crossed dry-
shod, walking upon the waters. At the giving of the
Law, Mount Sinai was lifted up to heaven ; and the
Israelites, thus "baptized in the cloud and in the
sea," were washed free from all stain of original sin.
The mysterious expression, that they " saw the light-
nings and the noise of the trumpet," was interpreted
into the startling fancy that the trumpet-voice became "cloven tongues of fire," which proclaimed the
Law in the seventy languages of the earth ; so that
each nation, summoned by the same trump to judg-

* A phantom man ninety-six miles high; his terrestrial representative reaching a hundred and twenty-five feet.

ment, shall be righteously judged by the same law, "without which there can be no sin." When the time drew near for Moses to depart, the Lord thrice sent Sammael the death-angel to bring away his soul, which he would yield to none other but God himself, who received it with a kiss; he was taken up to heaven in a cloud, in the presence of his grieving companions; and Michael the archangel, the celestial champion of Israel, strove with Satan for his body.*

Whatever wonders had attended the old dispensation were greatly magnified in the anticipation of the new. That prayer, say the Jewish writers, is not a prayer, which does not make mention of the kingdom of God. The coming of that kingdom in the person and triumph of the Messiah had been the old prophetic hope, which was elaborated now into a doctrine full and positive enough to make for two generations the goad of the people's struggle and the final crisis of the nation's life. A prevalent belief among the Jews fixed the duration of the world at seven thousand years, of which six were nearly expired, — the remaining thousand being the Messiah's destined triumphant reign. In the calamities of the time, it was felt that "the whole creation groaned and travailed in pain" for the birth of the coming One; † and the "seventy weeks" predicted in the Book of Daniel were by the general interpretation just fulfilled. "Through the whole East," says Suetonius, "an old and constant opinion had spread that the

---

* See Epistle of Jude v. 9.

† Romans viii. 22. Compare the expression ἀρχὴ τῶν ὠδίνων, Matt. xxiv. 8.

17 *

destined rulers of things should come about this time from Judæa." "When you bury me," said a dying Jew, "put shoes on my feet and a staff in my hand, that I may be ready when Messiah cometh." Many a man, "just and devout was waiting (like Simeon) for the consolation of Israel ; " many a mother hoped in her heart that her new-born child should be the expected one. And the belief was no doubt encouraged, and moulded to their own purpose, by men who had no hearty share in it; who were too willing to profit by the popular faith as a point of resistance to Roman tyranny, or to enhance the price of their own discretion, while they left the multitude a prey to the frenzies and oppressions which such a doctrine' must provoke.

The details of the Messianic hope at this period were peculiarly the property and shaping of the religious schools ; vague and incoherent as it doubtless was, yet modelled in the main after a common type. A most disastrous hope it proved in the form now given it, " more fatal to them than any pestilence ; a faith to which they sacrificed myriads of their stoutest youth." The fruit at first of a pure religious patriotism, the solace of deep calamity, the stay against impending ruin, it had grown to be a vindictive and passionate confidence of triumph and revenge. A hope long deferred it was ; and Jewish subtilty was exhausted to devise the conditions of its fulfilment. The Messiah would come, they said, if the Sabbath should be perfectly observed twice or thrice ; or if for a single day all Israel should heartily repent. " Open to me the way of repentance as the eye of a needle,"

they said, "and I will open to you a passage for chariots." The coming deliverance must be preceded
by great disasters. Corruption and depravity should
overspread the earth, with desertion of the law, followed by dreadful judgments of heaven in calamity
of many kinds, — drought, famine, and tempest, pestilence and war, with the horrors so powerfully reflected in the apocalyptic warning given to the followers of Jesus.* "Galilee shall be destroyed, and
the men of Galilee shall go from place to place, and
shall find no pity."

These calamities, drawn too truly from the fact,
were no arbitrary infliction, nor a mere retributive
judgment on the people; but in the Jewish view had
a direct propitiatory value. Not only, by their doctrine of expiation, did the faith of Abraham and the
patriarchs atone in advance for their descendants' sin,
but all death, especially one of violence, and all suffering, especially that which befalls the innocent, has
the same effect.† Moved, therefore, not so much by
compassion as by the legal expiation of their guilt,
God should bring his people to a season of repentance, and Israel should be once more redeemed by
the merit of the saints. For, they held, miraculous
degrees of virtue and superhuman holiness among
the chosen few are a better passport to Divine favour
than the more moderate and equal virtue of the
whole; it is for the elect's sake that the world is pre-

---

* Matthew, chap. xxiv.; Luke, chap. xxi.

† See John xi. 50. Hence the execution of criminals at the time of
Passover; and the abuse and vilifying of the condemned, in the merciful hope of alleviating their torments in another world.

served and redeemed ; it is the sacrificial efficacy of their merit, or their suffering, that wins the blessing from above.

That blessing should be granted at length, in the voluntary manumission of captive Jews among all nations, in preparation for the reign of peace. Under a mysterious impulse from God, or by the invisible guidance of his Word, the ransomed captives should throng at once to Palestine. Then should be a season of prosperity and gladness to the chosen land. Cities should be built, and the ancient realm of Israel restored to far more than its former splendour. Then, heralded by the star of Jacob, the victorious Warrior and just Prince should come, and inflict a bloody vengeance on the enemies of his people. His coming should be as a thief in the night; being manifested first " in Galilee and the parts of Joseph, because Galilee was first led captive." In him (to quote the vague and various opinions of the Jews) shall be incarnate the spirit that was in Moses and Elias; he shall be the second Adam, to restore the ruins of the first ; the prophet, like to Moses, whose name is Comforter; the ideal or official representative of the Hebrew people; the prophet, priest, and king, to fulfil the purpose of the elder dispensation; the Son of Man, who shall sit in judgment over men and angels ; the embodiment of the pre-existing wisdom or Word of God ; the Son of David, who shall restore the kingdom to Israel; the Son of God, born of no human father, but of the Divine Spirit: the breath of his mouth shall be a flame to slay the wicked. The ten lost tribes shall be restored from their long exile, to rejoin their brethren in the Holy Land. Kings shall bring their gifts; all nations shall either be subdued or peaceably submit. All war and crime shall cease, and all ravage of wild beasts. Children and kindred shall throng in every house, and none shall die before their time. Jerusalem, its palaces decked with gold and jewels, shall spread from the sea coast to Damascus, — its length, breadth, and height all equal.* The river of life shall flow from the temple; the tree of life grow for the faithful. No blind, lame, or leper shall be found there; the pious dead shall be restored to die no more; " and all shall be gathered in Paradise, with fulness of delight all the days of the world, fed with bread from heaven; and Messiah shall give his people peace."

Still another form of belief was that the Messiah should come twice, — once as the Son of Joseph (or representative of the ten tribes) to expiate by his death the sin of Israel in the division of the kingdom; who should lead the nation victoriously as far as the gates of Jerusalem, but be defeated there, and perish at the hands of his foes: and again, as the Son of David, to represent the branch and reward the fidelity of Judah; who should ride, as peaceful sovereign, the same ass that Abraham and Moses rode, and die at length in peace, leaving the restored kingdom to his children.

Four distinct elements are more or less confusedly blended in the popular expectation as thus described: the general prophetic conception of a political Deliverer, most frequent and popular of all; the super-

* See Revelation xxi. 16.

human Presence described in Daniel * as " the Son
of Man coming in the clouds of heaven ; " the divine
Word (of the Alexandrians), or Adam Kadmon (of
the Cabbalists), in whom the divine image should be
restored to man ; and the " Prophet, like to Moses," †
who should complete the purpose of the Law, and make
a transfigured or heavenly Israel the spiritual sovereign of all people ; — while other features were added,
as a capricious fancy devised, or as some fresh disaster or disappointment required fresh interpretation.

Thus, derived from many sources and suited to
every variety and extravagance of men's desire, the
Messianic hope of the age was the more passionate
and intense the less it was capable of consistent statement or clear analysis. Its diversity of ingredients
political and religious, gave room to all latitude
of exposition. The desperate patriotism of the Zealots would make it the incitement to revolt, and enterprises of fierce and hardy daring ; and would
almost welcome any calamity or personal suffering
that made its fulfilment seem more near. The Herodian, finding security only in a strong government
at home, and seeing but too clearly the impregnable
strength of Rome, would pretend that in the brilliant
and sagacious rule of Herod it had all the fulfilment
the time made possible. The cautious and sceptic
Sadducee would treat it as a popular delusion, and
regard the fancies bound up in it as an heretical
fable, with no foundation in the books he counted
holy. The Pharisee would secretly indulge the hope,
develop it into doctrine, expand and inculcate it as a

---

* Chap. vii. 13, 14.   † Deuteronomy xviii. 15.

popular creed; but in his place of power and advantage would shrink from the practical result it led to, and challenge, with a jealous fear and brooding hate, the claim of any who should win too warm tokens of the popular zeal.

One small sect, or religious Order, among the Jews was better prepared to interpret the national hope in its purely religious sense. The Essenes were a community numbering in all some four thousand. Keeping remote from the corruption of great towns, they dwelt mostly in the wild country near the Dead Sea, some in solitary places, some in the smaller villages. If they took any share at all in the national observances, it was to protest against the bloody sacrifice and the ritual formalism. By penitence and prayer, by pious austerities and humble labour, it was their creed that the favour of heaven should be won. In doctrine they were closely allied with the Egyptian mystics, the Therapeutæ, of whose name their own is an exact translation, — being Healers or Physicians, either in the literal or moral sense. Their practice of praying towards the East, (also found in the early Church,) their doctrine of angels and of the Divine Spirit, their asceticism and general abstinence from marriage, their mystic festival of communion, their voluntary poverty, and the simple regimen that enabled many of them to live more than a hundred years, — all liken them to those monastics of the Nile. Of all the Jews, their morality was most simple and austere; their Sabbath most strictly kept; their doctrine most remote from ritual or tradition; their reliance on Providence most implicit, amounting to a strict religious fatalism; their faith in a life to come most ardent; their temper most unshaken under persecution. Speculation and logic, says Philo, they leave to word-hunters; their study is holiness, justice, and love. Oaths they refrained from, except the sacred vow of their Order, not to divulge their sacred books or the mysterious names of the angels. A long probation was exacted, through three preliminary grades, before the candidate could be initiated in the interior or highest circle. Whatever secret doctrine or practice may have been taught, it was their religion outwardly to heal the sick, support the weak, and venerate the old. Frugal and benevolent, they refused all use of money, subsisting on the scanty product of their husbandry. For as living in a " holy land " their task was agriculture, instead of the petty handicrafts by which the Egyptian monastics throve. Neither wealth, personal indulgence, nor worldly honour could be their portion, but sadly to bewail and expiate their nation's sin. No evil would they ascribe to God, neither would they shed in sacrifice the blood of any creature. It was a mystical and symbolic sacrifice they rendered; the body itself was their " sin-offering," which they might not anoint with oil,*— the prison of the soul, whose burden they might not augment by any luxury, or delight of sense. Spiritual gifts were the reward of their austerities; a new line of prophets had risen among

---

* Levit. v. 11. The tree of life, according to these mystics, was the Olive; as the tree of knowledge was the Vine.

them, dating as far back as the age of the Maccabees ; and their superior sanctity was acknowledged
among the sects that now divided the faith of Israel.

Such was the community or sect of Essenes, as
reported by writers of the period. Its real history,
and especially its relation to the great religious
revolution now impending, are matters of vague,
perhaps hopeless conjecture. By many a religious
affinity it seems allied with what we know of the
early Christian Church, especially the sects of Ebionites and Nazarenes ; and the Catholic hierarchy has
even been held to be derived from its religious
orders. On the other hand, the utter silence of the
Christian records, save in a few doubtful allusions,*
makes it quite impossible to trace the degrees of that
alliance, and leaves an unlimited space to theory and
guess. Both ancient and modern surmise has identified these pious recluses with the first Jewish Christians. Some of the Greek fathers made their name †
equivalent to " Society of Jesus ; " and, a little
altered,‡ it stands among the earliest in the obscure
list of Christian heresies. A favourite rationalistic
hypothesis has regarded Jesus himself as the confidential emissary of an " Essenian Lodge ; " while a
more recent argument maintains that this was a
secret society into which the Christians of Palestine

---

* As, for example, the mode of journey and voluntary poverty
enjoined on the apostles (Matt. x. 9) ; the doctrine of spiritual aid and
guidance (v. 20) ; the commendation of celibacy (xix. 10 ; compare
xxii. 30) ; and discredit of riches (xix. 21, 23) ; together with the censure of the Pharisees and the temple service.

† Ἐσσαῖοι, or Ἰεσσαῖοι. Epiphanius, Hæres. I. 2, 4, 5.

‡ Ὀσσαῖοι. Ibid.

z

resolved themselves a few years before the downfall of Jerusalem, to shelter their doctrine from persecution, or to save it from being overwhelmed and confounded in a political frenzy.* The whole matter remains one of the riddles of history, — ever tempting a solution, and still unsolved.

In its relation to the Christian doctrine, what Judaism was to the world this community seems to have been to the other Jewish sects.† As the Christion monastic orders were a "church within the Church," so to these pious Hebrews it may have been given to guard the interior shrine of their nation's faith, from which the new spirit should proceed; — "every good gift and every perfect gift" descending, through whatever channel, from a common source.

As a little secluded sect, indeed, they could only helplessly deplore the fanaticism and error that had clustered around the nation's hope, or the people's sin that kept the Divine purpose from being fulfilled, — possibly, afford the soil out of which a better faith might spring, or in which it might be nurtured. But the Divine gift itself is something quite aside from the formula or the mechanism of any sect. For any real agency in the coming "regeneration," they would have been as thoroughly inefficient as the Alexandrians, but for the inspiration of a more positive purpose, and the blending of their ethical austerity with

* See De Quincey, Historical and Critical Essays, Vol. I. The decisive answer to which seems to be the familiar mention of the Essenes by Philo, who could hardly have written later than A. D. 50.

† See Gfrörer, "Jahrhundert des Heils."

a popular faith. Compelled by their whole style of
life and thought to give the Messianic hope a mystical sense, — to make the religious life a " spiritual
building," and the promised kingdom a reign of holiness, — their existence was an organized but vain
protest against the wild and headlong frenzy into
which their countrymen were ready to be plunged.
And so it must remain aloof from popular sympathies, and powerless to any larger end, until the energies spent in holding this frail dike against the torrent
rent should be absorbed in the allegiance rendered
to an inspired and guiding mind.

It is at least plausible to associate with this ascetic
and devout community the earlier training, if not the
particular commission, of that Forerunner, who from
a child " was in the deserts until the day of his shew-
ing unto Israel." The water of Baptism, by which
according to long custom aliens were admitted to religious fellowship with Jews, became the symbol of
the repentance preached by John. His stern and
resolute temper, unsoftened during his orphan youth
by the gentle disciplines and sympathies of home,
likened him to the elder prophets, whose worthy successor the popular reverence at once declared him.
His voice, crying in the wilderness, found a quick
response from priests that served in the temple, and
from the multitudes that thronged the banks of Jordan. "Art thou he that should come," they were
all ready to ask, "or look we for another?" John
the Baptist was no reed shaken with the wind; no
courtier clad in soft raiment; but a man equal to the
best and bravest of woman born; one to confront the

crafty and sensual Herod with the open charge of
guilt ; one to forfeit his head in prison rather than
withhold or withdraw where conscience marked the
way ; a man noble and dauntless, yet of a temper too
strict and narrowly austere to comprehend the real
want of the time. He "came neither eating nor
drinking, and men said, He hath a devil." The
larger sympathies, the profounder and gentler life
that marked the true Messiahship, he recognized but
by anticipation and in part in the greater One that
followed : and long after his death, a little sect still
bore his name, and echoed his herald-call to repentance, without even asking whether the Hebrew hope
was not already fulfilled.

In Jesus of Nazareth the popular heart acknowledged its rightful King. Doubtless he shared those
patriot hopes and longings, those thoughts, beliefs,
and sacred associations, that made not only the national heritage but the public religious education of
the Jews. His home and his heart were among the
people. "Galilee of the nations" was the nurse of
world-wide sympathies and thoughts, as well as centre
of the political fervour and religious zealotry that
survived so many wrecks and changes of the state.
With a lingering and patriotic fondness the son of
Mary clung to the phrasing of those popular hopes
which his clearer foresight must renounce, while his
true Hebrew sympathy should make them the germ
of nobler human hopes : it is as one sharing in the
nation's heroic memories and religious life that he
laments the ruin which cannot long be stayed from
the beloved Jerusalem.

That Jesus himself, in his interior consciousness, was lifted to apprehend the dread and solitary grandeur of his historic destiny, that he fully conceived the true and legitimate hope of his nation to be consummated in himself, — that hope created by ages of prophecy, sustained through centuries of disaster, and now expanding to embrace the spiritual destinies of all mankind, — is not only the clear and evident reading of his life, it is the one thing without which that life can receive no intelligible interpretation. Imperatively disclaiming the assumption of personal merit or holiness as the ground of his authority, he as distinctly exalts the official dignity of the Messiahship, while asserting it for his own. Knowing well the fate to which it leads him, and that the Son of Man must be made " perfect through suffering," he never once abates that claim or wavers in it. The heavenly omens of his nativity, and a childhood watched by fond, motherly hopes, had nurtured this overwhelming conviction of his vocation and destiny, as Son of God and Deliverer of his people, which made so thoroughly a part of his maturer manhood.* That if he chose he might even have been such a Deliverer as they madly looked for, he seems to have

---

* The struggle by which the popular Jewish hope was transformed in him into a purely spiritual purpose is shown symbolically in the scene of the Temptation, which is the Messianic encounter with the Adversary of Israel; as the celestial sense in which the ancient Hebrew faith was reproduced is symbolized in the Vision that shows him transfigured upon the mount with Moses and Elias.

Again, what an appeal to the national memories of the Jew, recalling the pastoral youth of David and traditions of Jacob and Moses, lay in the story of the Messiah's birth among the shepherds of Bethlehem !

The " Visit of the Wise Men " may have some connection (obscured

believed, and hinted more than once, especially towards the mournful close of his ministry. And it was a clear and voluntary and noble sacrifice in which he laid down his life as the price of that "atonement" in which the heart of man should be reconciled to the truth and providence of the Father.

Yet we may easily believe it to have been — as we find it in fact — with a certain reluctance and misgiving that Jesus first directed the Messianic expectations of the people upon himself. He forbore to stimulate in them what was at best a false and vindictive, and what proved a bitterly pernicious and fatal, hope. When they would "take him by force and make him a king," he withdrew to the solitude of mountain or wilderness; he stilled the insane or eager clamour of demoniacs, or the grateful homage of those he healed of hopeless malady, by commanding "that they should not make him known." But the hope was firmly embedded in the religious life and language of the day. It could not be contradicted or evaded : it might perhaps receive a higher and juster interpretation. The phrase "kingdom of heaven" he set himself, therefore, steadily to disengage from all the vindictive and fantastic images of Jewish fancy ; to make it mean to others what his clearer understanding and finer spiritual apprehen-

---

in the present form of narrative) with the school of Magi or false prophets believed to have been established in the East by Balaam, the "Archimage ;" who, recognizing by magical arts the star of Jacob, predicted by their founder (Numbers xxiv. 17. See p. 65), had nearly compassed the Messiah's death in his cradle. (Gfrörer.) In the Talmud, Jesus (son of Mary Magdalen) is a great magician and wonderworker, who has stolen his magic formula from Egypt.

sion discerned in it; to sketch, as it were, its boundaries in the realm of the moral life. When one
asks him if the kingdom shall immediately appear,
he answers by saying that it comes not with observation; that men cannot say, Lo here! or Lo there!
for it is within. It is for the meek, the merciful, the
peacemakers, the poor in spirit, the pure in heart.
It is like leaven, like seed sown in a field, like a hidden pearl, like the impartial wages of labourers in a
vineyard, like the return for a faithful use of money,
like a marriage feast open by proclamation to all
that are worthy and willing to enter, — like anything
rather than what they hoped and craved. Whatever
of the images or notions more familiar to the popular
conception are adopted in his discourse, they are subdued to that main purpose, they but bridge the interval between the common thought and his.* In
numberless ways he set himself thus to stem the swift
and turbulent stream of his countrymen's desire, and
teach the true meaning of the hope of Israel.

His own name he would not at first suffer to be
used in too near connection with that hope, or announced as the Messiah of the coming kingdom;
yet assured as he was that the true culmination and
completion of the Hebrew prophetic history were
in himself, his claim became by degrees more public
and explicit; and when he distinctly foresaw his
own death as decreed and inevitable, he no longer
scrupled to declare, in the most open manner, that
he was the true Son of God, the Prophet foretold by

---

* Unless one should except the parables and discourses recorded
about the time of his triumphant entrance into Jerusalem.

Moses, the expected Man. His death, he knew, when nothing else could do it, would break the spell of that charmed thought, that false hope, which stimulated the worst passion of the people, while it fettered their best religious life. "It was expedient that he should go away;" since then and not before "another Comforter" might come, the spirit of Truth, and those who believed in him for his own sake might be guided to a better apprehension of the Unseen. During his lifetime he could be to them, at best, only the leader of a religious reform, the sincerest and best of Jewish teachers, the messenger (they trusted) of a deliverance daily and passionately longed for. It was after his departure that he became to them a spiritual Presence, the living manifestation of the Word of God, and the Saviour of the world. Once granting his Messianic claim, all the rest would follow in time of its own accord.

But early associations lost their hold very slowly. To the first generation of believers the clearest notion of Christ's kingdom seems to have been, that he would presently reappear "in the clouds with power and great glory" as in the visions of Daniel; and that the dazzling but incoherent imagery of the Hebrew dreams would yet be literally fulfilled in him. As surely as he was the true Messiah and the hope of Israel, so surely his Messianic work on earth was still unfinished. The vagueness of the Future made good the deficiency and disappointment of the Past. The historical lineaments of Jesus were pieced out with the features of the genuine Hebrew type of the Messiah. These superadded features were held in reserve against the supposed immediate future ; and were made objective to the disciples' minds in the angelic declaration, " This same Jesus, which is taken up from you into heaven, shall so return in like manner as ye have seen him go into heaven," and in the apocalyptic imagery in which his coming is vaguely foretold in the doom impending over Israel. The spiritual office of the Messiah having been discharged, there remained the temporal, which could not be long delayed. Such was the early hope of the Jewish Christians, certified to their mind by the resurrection of their Lord. It served a temporary but most important use, as a stay or scaffolding to their imperfect faith in the spiritualized and risen Christ, for the space of perhaps a generation, — when it fell, with the utter ruin of the Jewish state. Then, and not till then, Christianity was released from the narrowness of Hebrew forms, and became an independent faith.*

Meanwhile two distinct influences were at work in the Church, to bring this primitive form of Christian belief round to that with which we are historically familiar : first, the practical demand of the Christian organization, which continually thrust aside the fanatic anticipation of the future, in obedience to the instant claim of the present, — so constantly exhibited in the writings of Paul, composed during the first generation of believers ; and,

---

* The bitterness with which this change was resisted, and the obstinacy of the protest against the Pauline doctrine, are put in abundant relief in some of the early Petrine writings, the " Clementines," which make Simon Magus a parody, or a mythical pseudonyme, of St. Paul.

18

secondly, the spontaneous development of a Christian philosophy within the Church, with the instinctive effort to assimilate its tone and terminology with the intellectual habit of the age, — so conspicuous in the writings of the second generation, especially in those ascribed to John. Hence the gentle and (as it were) unconscious transition from the style of representation found in the first three Evangelists to that given in the fourth; as afterwards, in successive phases, in the later Alexandrian schools, — by Clement in the second century, Sabellius in the third, and Athanasius in the fourth. Thus the Church doctrine was gradually brought into a shape to match the most arrogant forms of Gentile philosophy, though without yielding the point of generic difference which makes one a subtile scheme for the understanding, and the other a religion profoundly practical in the life. The Christology of the second and third centuries was run easily into the mould prepared for it by the entire development of Greek and Oriental thought, — from which it was taken, almost without a flaw, by the Nicæan Council, in the form at once adopted by the Latin Church.

By these stages of transition, and in strict accordance with historical conditions already found for it, the Hebrew Messianic hope was transformed into a doctrine which has had perhaps a profounder influence on human life and thought than every other, — the doctrine, namely, that God did descend upon earth and dwell among men in the person of Jesus of Nazareth; whose word was the authoritative foundation of belief, and his death the literal sacrifice for the world's salvation. The religious need of the time was satisfied by a faith embracing these conditions: that it was faith in a divine Person, whom an increasing reverence identified at length with the Supreme Being himself; that it was engrafted on a tradition, conceived according to a pre-existing type, and made part of an already living faith; and that it was finally cast in a form that harmonized it with the religious speculations of the cultivated world.

Still further, this faith became the centre and rallying-point of a powerful organization of the religious life. The Church polity, first inherited from the Hebrew synagogue, and borrowing many a feature from Jewish models, became the regulating power of men's religious life and discipline. It grew in time to be the nucleus of a powerful hierarchy, that for a thousand years guided the destinies of civilization. It formed the bridge across the dark gulf of barbarism between the empire of Rome and the states of Christian Europe. Not only the customs of the Synagogue, but the elaborate order of the Jewish Priesthood, was adopted in the Christian Church.* Thus the new religion allied itself with the still powerful traditions and institutions of antiquity; and the ecclesiastical foundation borrowed from Judæa sustained a structure, aptly enough termed Catholic, in which Etruscan ritual and Roman discipline, blended with a philosophy wrought out by Grecian intellect, gave new and powerful embodiment to the faith of Galilee.

* For the impulse given to the growth of the hierarchy by the thronging of the Jewish Christians to Rome, after the destruction of Jerusalem, see Gfrörer, Eccl. Hist., Vol. I. pp. 253 – 277.

So fruitful and profound, in its influence on the after destinies of mankind, beyond every other element of antiquity, was this final form taken by the old Hebrew faith. Historically regarded, Jesus is uplifted on the great wave formed by the confluence of three main courses of ancient life and thought, — the Hebrew, Oriental, and Greek, — all embraced in the imperial sway of Rome. His life, as the fulfilment of Hebrew Messianic prophecy, becomes the central and pivotal fact in the annals of mankind. However it be interpreted, the doctrine of the Church remains, that in it met all the separate threads of human development: so that, religiously regarded, it becomes the great revelation of God in human life; and, historically, the isthmus of two great continents, — the connecting link between the ancient and modern world.

The historical significance of the Hebrew race and faith is therefore now exhausted. It becomes an undistinguishable element in a structure far more rich, various, and comprehensive. The history has henceforth only the dreary and tragic interest that attends the catastrophe of a people's life. For a few years, by favour of Caligula, Herod Agrippa, grandson of Mariamne, was king of united Palestine (A. D. 37 – 44). From the crazy young despot, whose intimate companion he had been in the vices and pleasures of the capital, he won for his people the repeal of an edict to worship the emperor's statue, and so deferred a little longer the last struggle of the

Jews' despair.   Though sensual and vainglorious, and prompt to lift his hand in persecution of the Church, he inherited enough of Hebrew feeling along with his Maccabæan blood to make his reign a time of general contentment and prosperity, until his sudden death in Cæsarea,* when the line of Roman governors returned, and violence began anew.

The revolt of Theudas was provoked by the rigorous policy of Cuspius Fadus, which offered too sharp a contrast to the indolent indulgence of Agrippa (A. D. 44).   Theudas was one of the "false Christs and false prophets," who from this time forth arose to deceive many.   Promising his followers a miraculous passage of the Jordan and certain victory, he was surprised by a company of soldiers, and beheaded.   Some relics of old sedition were rooted out also by Tiberius Alexander, — an apostate Jew, nephew of the Alexandrian Philo, — the patriot sect of Galilæans beginning (it appears) to be formidable once more.   Under his successor, Cumanus, a systematic course of insult to the Jewish faith, aggravated by a quarrel at the Passover, and the "accidental" death of some twenty thousand, led towards the last desperate revolt.   Cumanus fell into disgrace by his misconduct in a revival of the old feud between Samaritans and Jews; and the freedman Felix, "husband of three queens," ruled for nine years, with "the authority of a king and the disposition of a slave" (A. D. 52 – 61).   "The affairs of the Jews now grew worse and worse continually; again the country was filled with robbers and impostors, who led the multitude astray."   Patriotism,

* See Acts xii. 21 – 25.

now in its last extremity, took the form of an organized conspiracy. Bands of Sicarii, or secret and pledged Assassins, made an invisible Committee of Public Safety, and by a system of Terrorism headed the popular hate towards Rome. Daily executions did not stay the course of public disorder. An adventurer from Egypt led four thousand men * into the wilderness, and then escaped, leaving them a prey to Roman vengeance. Feuds between Jew and Gentile grew more bitter, until Felix too was recalled. Festus died in office, too soon to achieve the reconciliation he sought. Under Albinus, matters fast grew worse. Besides old complaints, there were now miserable contentions and oppressions among the priesthood, of whom the lower orders most likely shared too deeply in the dangerous temper of the populace. Many of the inferior Levites, it is said, actually perished of destitution, their superiors withholding their slender benefices. The people were clamorous at the loss of civil rights, the result of bloody riots in Cæsarea ; and troops of robbers were set loose by Albinus, out of recklessness or else revenge, when the general complaint got him removed from Palestine. So all was ripening for the great revolt.

The last envoy whom Nero sent to vex the rebellious province was Florus (A. D. 64), a man so meanly and sordidly rapacious, that some carried a basket, asking " alms for the beggar ; " and the crowd insulted him openly in the streets by name, hate casting out fear. He took a malignant delight in exasperating the popular passion that should give

* Or thirty thousand, says Josephus.

ampler sweep to Roman revenge, which his soldiers seconded by studious mockery of the Jewish ritual.* With ostentatious contempt and cruelty, he mocked the embassies of peace sent him by the city, and made their humble remonstrance the occasion of fresh massacres. When Agrippa and his sister Bernice, son and daughter of the late king, besought him mercy, he answered by the scourging and beheading of their countrymen before their very eyes. Agrippa, the last inheritor of Jewish royal blood, — endowed by the Romans with the regal title, and an outlying district of territory as well as the protectorate of the " holy places," — staked all his popularity in a last eloquent but fruitless appeal to the citizens, whom tyranny had driven frantic. They listened patiently as he represented the overwhelming force of Rome and the hopelessness of revolt, till he spoke of submission for the time to Florus; when at that name his voice was drowned in the angry clamour. Forced to withdraw, he left the misruled and misguided city to its fate.

Though some were still for compromise, and followed Agrippa's counsel to observe the forms of customary homage, yet the bolder party suddenly found themselves in power. They ventured the decisive step of refusing the customary sacrifice in Cæsar's name, thus renouncing their allegiance in the most offensive way possible. They sent and surprised the garrison at Masada, which was Herod's stronghold in

* Especially by mimicking the sacrifice of a sparrow for leprosy, an insult calling to mind the old tradition of the uncleanness of the race.

extremity, near the Dead Sea; and by an unhoped-
for success, inspiring a fatal confidence, they routed
the provincial forces of Gallus, who had nearly taken
possession of Jerusalem. Even the more cautious
now saw that the hope of peace was past. Unless
open traitors, they must win by the sword any future
terms of safety. Ananus the high-priest became pro-
visional Dictator. The city was strongly fortified,
the country divided into military districts. Galilee
— the most strongly intrenched in natural defences
and the vehement patriotism of its people — must
expect the first brunt of attack. Its governor and
chief-captain was Josephus the historian, a man now
thirty years of age. He had belonged to the peace
party hitherto, and after one campaign he surrendered, and sided again heartily with the Romans,
testifying no small animosity against the new chiefs
of the sedition. But for once he showed himself a
skilful and bold commander. The two months' siege
of Jotapata exhausted the resources of Jewish ingenuity, backed by an unconquerable hate: its fall,
soon followed by that of Tiberias and Gamala, sealed
the doom of all Palestine.

The revolt had been found so serious that Vespasian, the ablest general of the empire, was sent to
quell it with an army of sixty thousand men, — such
a force as Rome had employed only against the most
powerful kingdoms. The life had to be crushed from
the ill-fated province drop by drop; and at so formidable cost that Vespasian fell back, to let dissension and famine do his work, rather than assault
the walls and towers of Jerusalem. The two years'

partial respite given by the disorders at Rome that followed the death of Nero were employed by the Romans in securing the remoter districts; by the Jewish chiefs only in bitter strife among themselves, and wanton ravage, that made the defence more hopeless. When Vespasian, now emperor, sent his son Titus to the siege, the temple, the sacred court, and the city were held each as a separate fortress by three armed factions, each at deadly war with both the others, uniting only to cut off the last hope of peace by the massacre of the priestly body. Only in the utmost peril was party hate changed to emulous boldness, in manning the breach or fighting in the trenches.

Throughout the siege, the sacrifice at the great altar went on daily undisturbed, amidst the terrible storm of engines, and in courts that flowed with the blood of victim, priest, and worshipper, in a common stream. Starving wretches that crept out to pluck roots and weeds were forced back or slain; if they had gathered anything, it was snatched from them by violence; or, escaping to the camp, some were torn open by the savage Arabs to hunt for gold and jewels they had swallowed, others crucified by Titus, as many as five hundred in a day, till "there was no wood for the crosses, or space to plant them." The glens below were rank with unburied corpses, hurled from the walls, — a horrible but needful order of the military police. A mother, driven crazy by the barbarity of the plunderers and the rage of famine, killed and devoured her own child "secretly, for her utter want." Every tree within twelve miles of

Jerusalem was cut down for military engines, and not an olive, say the Jews, was left in all the land.

Starvation, murder, pestilence, torture, assault, — all were endured for a ghastly period of eight months, and still the Zealot faction would not yield. To the last they looked for that "sign from heaven" which, when the measure of calamity was full, should bring victory and revenge. It was treason as well as infidelity to despair of the altar and holy city.

At length * the walls were broken down, the strong towers seized or undermined, the streets filled with the slaughter of the populace, the temple set on fire in the blind fury of the soldiery. Jerusalem was no more. A ploughshare was passed over the foundation. The site of city and sanctuary was sown with salt. Such sacred vessels as escaped the flames were brought to Rome by Titus, where their mouldering forms still decorate his arch of triumph. A hundred thousand captives were sent to the slave market or amphitheatre; and for every captive, more than fifteen are said to have perished in the war, — upwards of a million in Jerusalem alone. All Palestine was set to sale by Vespasian. The two shekels of temple-money paid by every Hebrew man must go to rebuild the shrine of Jupiter of the Capitol; and no Jew might visit the sacred ruins on pain of death.

Of the Zealots, some fled to the strong fortress Masada, where, after a short resistance, they set fire to the tower, and perished with their families in the flames; some made their way to Alexandria and

* October, A. D. 70.

Cyrene, with the vain hope of holding out the contest a little longer ; but most were slaughtered with their chiefs, — even women and children smiling in the midst of torture, and defying the Gentile conqueror with their indomitable faith. Such as had taken no share in the great rebellion, together with the little sect of Christians,* still remained in possession of the villages ; and when the storm of war was blown past, remained there unmolested. The Sanhedrim, through its ten "flittings" from place to place, like the Ark at the ruin of the first temple, lost little of its former dignity or authority. The line of Rabbins was continued in Tiberias for many years, under the "Patriarch of the West," who still held spiritual headship over a dispersed and exiled nation. In touching memorial of the desolation, an ornament of turrets and battlements, called the "golden city," was worn by Jewish women as a head-dress, in mourning for Jerusalem, — perhaps as a pledge that it should be restored.

Such was the issue of the false and fatal hope which had grown out of the Divine promise of the Messiah. After many transmutations, it came at last to be a mere political frenzy. The tendencies that might have held it in check were drawn away by the Christian society. To the loyal Jew, of whatever sect, there was left no hope but in the independence of his native land. Nothing but a powerful fanaticism could have sustained the audacity of that hope. " Even the most peaceful mystic, who

---

* Ebionites or Nazarenes, including, as is probable, the relics of the Essenes.

expected from his Adam-Logos the renewal of Paradise, still had in his eye the fall of the Roman power. There was the particular grief that touched them all. But how resist the arms of Rome? What a distance between the legions of the world-empress and the petty forces of a population of some few millions, crowded in a corner of Asia! The Jewish scribes and Levites had in the Sanhedrim, almost to the outbreak of the war, a certain share of administration in state affairs. Political power has always been the school of political wisdom. One can never better learn men than in ruling them. May there not have been among these Jews in power some who saw that the Messianic hopes of their nation rested on a groundless fantasy, and pointed to an impossibility? Certainly there were such. Not only the records of their faith, but the history itself shows it. . . . . . These priests would play the city and sanctuary into the hands of the Romans, to save both; for they despaired of the future issue of the war. They hoped not at all, at least not heartily, in the future. Still they helped to spread the delusion among their people. Doubtless it was to save the nationality, more and more menaced by Rome, the devourer of nations, and to hold up *in terrorem* to the successors of Cæsar the fiercely kindled popular hope. But, as is so often the case with a priesthood, they did not themselves believe in what they preached. When the storm broke forth, and their great possession was in peril, they fell back like cowards. Hence the sword of the determined Zealots justly struck their guilty heads. One should not play with a nation's enthusiasm! The division between chiefs and priest-hood inflicted the heaviest damage on the Jews, and most contributed to the fatal result of the war. Had the Levites and their adherents thrown their whole weight into the scale, to recognize a bold warrior from the popular ranks as the Messiah, all would have submitted to him, and the chosen one might have carried the united strength of the nation against the foreign foe, — instead of as many Messiahs rising up as there were ambitious leaders, who conflicted with each other to the greatest injury of all, adding the miseries of internal feud to those of foreign war. Had the Jews under Vespasian acted with the same united energy as in the revolt under Hadrian, the struggle would have been a formidable one ; and their Messiah might perhaps have been for imperial what Hannibal was for con-sular Rome." *

After the thorough and systematic uprooting by Vespasian, there was no more a visible centre and home of the Jewish nationality ; yet in its several dispersions or " captivities " the scattered Israel re-tained something of the same slumbering fire. Be-fore the dreadful tempest swept over Judah, like dis-aster had befallen the colonists in Babylonia and Egypt.† In Rome, in Cyrene, in Antioch, there were

---

* Gfrörer, " Jahrhundert des Heils," Vol. II. pp. 439 – 441.

† The recorded massacres of the Jews at the commencement of the wars were, in Babylon, 50,000, in Alexandria, 50,000, in Cæsarea, 20,000, in Ascalon, 2,500, in Ptolemais, 2,000, in Scythopolis, 13,000, in Damascus, 10,000, besides that of their chief men in Tyre, Hippo, and Gadara, and of uncertain numbers in other Syrian towns.

but various degrees of the same wanton cruelty. And long after Jerusalem was desolate, "so that one would not even know where its forts and walls had been," flashes of desperate resistance broke forth, such as to renew the ancient terror of the Hebrew name.

The policy of Trajan, statesmanly and severe, was to guard well the boundaries of the empire, — now beginning to be seriously threatened by barbarians, — and reduce it at home more thoroughly to a uniform central rule. Provoked by fresh cruelties, and a conflict in which, it is said, every Jew in Alexandria was slain, a furious outbreak took place in Cyrene (A. D. 115). The Jews slaughtered of their fellow-colonists no less than two hundred and twenty thousand; and, with savage instincts stimulated by the fanatic interpretation of old prophecy,* devoured fragments of the flesh, stained their faces with the blood, and wore the bleeding entrails as trophies upon their shoulders. In Cyprus the slaughter was even greater; and the insurrection was only quelled by the destruction of half a million Jews. These atrocities took place just when the Roman Empire was in its meridian splendour, under, perhaps, the ablest of its rulers, in what has been called the golden period of human welfare. Now it was resolved to root out the last remnant of the invincible and hated faith. Not even in case of shipwreck could a Jew set foot in Cyprus, on pain of death. Circumcision, the Sabbath worship, and reading of the Law were forbidden; and a Roman colony, with a temple to Jupiter, was to occupy the sacred heights of Zion.

* Zechariah ix. 15.

Hadrian, "by turns an excellent prince, a ridiculous sophist, and a jealous tyrant,"* visited Judæa in his imperial journey of curiosity and reform (A. D. 131). His sceptic temper was not likely to respect the remnants of Jewish " superstition " still assiduously cherished there, nor his wary statesmanship to overlook the perilous fanaticism lurking under it. The very next year, the last great revolt broke out with the obstinate intrepidity of despair. Avoiding now too late the fatal error of the former war, the sacred college at Tiberias, with Rabbi Akibah, their noblest and saintliest,† unanimously recognized as Messiah the young disciple whose energy and religious zeal placed him at the head of the insurrection, — Simon, whose mystic title was Bar-cochab, " Son of the Star."‡ Once more the horrors of war and religious persecution raged through Palestine. The unhappy remnant of Jewish Christians suffered miserably : — a little heretic sect, scorned by Christians as still holding Jesus to have been a man, hideously tortured by fanatic Jews as followers of the Nazarene, and confounded by the Romans in one ruin with their rebellious countrymen. For a time the sudden fury of the storm swept everything before it. Bar-cochab assumed the public title of Prince of Judah, and coined money bearing the device of his Messianic reign. He even seized and garrisoned the capital,

---

* Gibbon.

† His fame was attested by no less than 24,000 pupils. " For forty years he had been an illiterate peasant, forty years he gave to the study of the Law, and forty years he ministered to Israel." The accounts of his death are various.

‡ Numbers xxiv. 17. See page 65.

holding it for two years against the Romans. It was not till (according to the story) five hundred and eighty thousand had fallen, armed and fighting, — among them the false Messiah himself, and the aged Akibah, who served as his shield-bearer, — that the fury of the revolt was stayed.* Jerusalem, with the title Ælia Capitolina, was made a Roman town. Strange edifices crowned the sacred heights, and the localities of ancient story were utterly lost. Nothing but the site and name, the everlasting hills and the Syrian sky, remains to the sacred capital of Judah.

Since the last dispersion, the name of Israel is lost to human history. A scattered and long-suffering remnant, a people of zealous and indomitable faith, more tenacious than ever of traditions and rites that set them apart from all; the traders and slave-merchants of Barbaric times, outcasts from the Feudal System, first victims of the Crusades and the Inquisition, clinging still through long centuries to the hope that once and again had plunged them in so deep disaster,† — they have lived on, a singular and death-

---

* The Jews say of the slaughter at Bitter, the last stronghold of Bar-cochab, that the horses waded in blood up to their nostrils; there were slain 400,000 in a day, and Hadrian walled a vineyard of sixteen miles about with dead bodies to a man's height; the brains of three hundred infants were dashed upon one stone, and the torrent of blood floated the bodies of the slain down to the sea, a distance of forty miles. Thousands were sold, "cheap as horses," under the terebinth-tree that stood by Abraham's tent; and Akibah (who at the tribunal of the victor forgot not the hour of prayer) was barbarously flayed alive.

† Of many impostors assuming the title of Messiah, the last of any note, Sabbathai-Sevi, appeared in Smyrna in 1648, where he figured for eighteen years. At length he was brought before the Sultan, who, in the prompt way the Turks have of convincing infidels, offered him

less monument of the Life that had its home of old in Palestine. Hate, persecution, contempt, suffered from Christian and Mussulman alike; the cruelties of sovereign or priesthood safely spent on a victim helpless and cursed already by the popular odium; the tortures of a rapacious exchequer and the tortures of a holy Inquisition, — all combined have not been able to destroy or alter this hidden stream of a religious nationality. In its solitary channel it has continued to flow on, strangely unaffected by events that have remoulded, once and again, the entire face of the civilized world. Untouched by political changes, uncaring for Gentile culture and erudition, unmingled in the thousand cross-currents that intersect it, steadily and mysteriously this stream of a people's life flows on. The nation of Israel lies, as it were, latent and diffused among the populations of the earth, — still known by its visible marks of separation, and still, to trust its own declaration, prepared, when the summons shall come, to throng to the banner of Judah, and see the fulfilment of its ancient prophecy in the restoring of its dominion under its long-promised and still-expected Messiah.

This also the Jews have recorded in the peculiar manner of their tradition. When Rabbi Akibah, say their writers, was once passing with some of his scholars near the broken walls of Jerusalem, they saw a fox which ran out from the most holy place,

the choice of an ordeal of three poisoned arrows, death, or conversion. He discreetly chose the last, and became a Mussulman; but his followers, accepting his assurance that the Messiah must be "numbered among the transgressors," clung to their belief in him, which subsists, it is said, in one Jewish sect even to this day.

and hid among the ruins; and his scholars wept, but Rabbi Akibah laughed. And they asked him, " Shall we not weep when we see the desolation of the city, and all the calamity which our prophets have foretold?" But he replied, " And shall I not rather laugh when I see these things? for while those words were not yet fulfilled which foretold the destruction of our people and our holy temple, we might doubt if they came from God; but now we know that they are true, and that the God of Israel liveth, and his people shall be redeemed."

CHRONOLOGICAL OUTLINE OF THE LATER MONARCHY.

[Ewald's dates. Events marked † are found only in Chronicles.]

B. C. *Judah.*	B. C. *Israel.*
985. REHOBOAM (17 y.) Return of Levites. Shishak's invasion. Fortified cities.	985. JEROBOAM (22 y.) Royal cities built. Golden calves, at Dan and Bethel.
968. ABIJAM (8 y.) † Disastrous war with Israel.	
965. ASA (41 y.) Reform. Fortifications and equipments; † army of 580,000.	Ahijah's warning.
	963. NADAB (2 y.) Murdered by
	961. BAASHA (24 y.)
Wars between Israel and Judah.	
Treasures sent to Damascus. † Rout of 1,000,000 Ethiopians.	Attack of Syrians. Ramah deserted.
† Asa suppresses idolatry in Israel.	
† Great religious festival.	987. ELAH (2 y.) Murdered.
† Warning of *Hanani* against Syrian alliance.	931. OMRI (12 y.) Samaria built.
	919. AHAB (22 y.) Baal-worship.
917. JEHOSHAPHAT (25 y.) Reforms. Peace with Ahab. Viceroy in Edom. Commerce. † Military and religious establishment.	[Acts of *Elijah.*] Siege of Samaria by Benhadad. Defeat of Syrians. Fresh invasion, east of Jordan.
Alliance against Syrians. Ahab slain.	
† Attack of Moab, etc., repulsed with great slaughter.	897. AHAZIAH (2 y.) Revolt of Moab. Killed by a fall.
893. JEHORAM (8 y.) Revolt of Moab. † Invasion of Arabs, &c.	895. JEHORAM (12 y.) Idolatry suppressed. Devastation of Moab.
885. AHAZIAH (1 y.) Murdered by	[Acts of *Elisha.*]
883. ATHALIAH (6 y.) Baal worship established.	883. JEHU (28 y.) Massacres. Golden calves retained.
877. JOASH (40 y.) Repairs of temple. Joash bribes Hazael, who devastates Gilead, &c.	
Dissensions with priests. † Murder of Zechariah. Joash slain by conspiracy.	855. JEHOAHAZ (17 y.) Deliverance from the invasion.
837. AMAZIAH (29 y.) Conquest of Edom. † Army of 300,000.	839. JEHOASH (16 y.) Death of *Elisha.* Invasion of Moabites. Victories over Syrians.

Judah.   Israel.

† Amaziah rejects alliance of Israel, who smite 8,000 cities.
Challenges Jehoash. Jerusalem pillaged.
[Prophecies of *Joel*, in time of Amaziah.]

Amaziah slain by conspiracy.	823. JEROBOAM II. (41 y.) Restores
808. UZZIAH (52 y.) Recovers Elath.	former bounds of Israel. Recov-
† Victories over Arabs, &c. ;	ers Damascus. [*Amos, Hosea.*]
tribute from Ammon ; building	770. ZACHARIAH and SHALLUM,
of towers; army 807,500.	murdered.
Dissensions with priests.	769. MENAHEM (10 y.) Barbarities.
[Visions and early prophecies	Assyrian invasion of Pul.
of *Isaiah.*]	759. PEKAHIAH (2 y.) Murdered by
757. JOTHAM (16 y.) Victories over	757. PEKAH (20 y.) Conquest of
Ammonites. Fortifications.	Galilee by Tiglath Pileser.

Judah threatened by league of Pekah with Rezin.

740. AHAZ (16 y.) Idolatries. [Messianic predictions of *Isaiah.*]
Invasion of Pekah and Rezin ; loss of Elath.
† 120,000 slain; 200,000 captives restored.
Ahaz bribes Assyrians, who invade Damascus.

724. HEZEKIAH (29 y.) Abolishes	728. HOSHEA (9 y.) Invasion of
idolatry.	Shalmanezer. Tribute to him.
[*Micah.* Prophecies and polit-	Conspires with Egypt. Three
ical influence of *Isaiah.*]	years' siege of Samaria.

719. *Captivity of Ten Tribes. Samaritan Colony.*

Invasion of Judah by Sennacherib; his host destroyed.
Hezekiah's sickness. Embassy from Babylon.
Public works. † Solemn purification of temple.

695. MANASSEH (55 y.) Idolatry and persecutions.
† Taken captive to Babylon. His repentance.

640. AMON (2 y.) His idolatry; death by conspiracy.

638. JOSIAH (31 y.) Repair of temple. Finding of the Law.
Inroad of Scythians. Josiah slain at Megiddo.
[*Zephaniah, Obadiah, Habakkuk, Jeremiah.*]

608. JEHOAHAZ (3 m.) dies a captive in Egypt.
JEHOIAKIM (11 y.) Tributary to Pharaoh. Conquered by Nebuchadnezzar. Revolts. Chaldee invasion.

597. JEHOIACHIN (3 m.) taken to Babylon with 10,000 captives.

596. ZEDEKIAH (11 y.) Revolts. Invasion of Nebuchadnezzar.
Siege of Jerusalem. [*Jeremiah.*] Jerusalem taken. Gedaliah
assassinated. Flight of many Jews to Egypt.

586 – 536. THE CAPTIVITY IN BABYLON.

AFTER THE CAPTIVITY.

B. C.

636. Edict of Cyrus. Return of the Jews from Babylon.
616. Dedication of the Temple.
459. Mission of Ezra.
445. Administration of Nehemiah.
366. Murder of Joshua.
832. Alexander in Jerusalem.
820. Conquest of Judæa by Ptolemy.
300. Administration of Simon the Just.
230. Joseph the Tax-gatherer.
205–198. Antiochus the Great in Judæa.
176. Antiochus Epiphanes. Heliodorus.
170. Persecutions of Antiochus Epiphanes.
186. Judas the Maccabee.
160. Jonathan.
143. Simon.
135. John Hyrcanus.
107. Aristobulus.

B. C.

106. Alexander Jannæus.
79. Alexandra.
70. Hyrcanus and Aristobulus.
63. Jerusalem taken by Pompey
48. Administration of Antipater
37–4. Herod the Great.
20 to A. D. 50. *Philo of Alexandria*

A. D.

6. Judæa a Roman Province.
26. Administration of Pontius Pilate.
80. Crucifixion of Jesus.
37–44. Reign of Herod Agrippa.
64. Administration of Gessius Florus.
66 Jewish Revolt.
68. Subjugation of Galilee.
70. Siege of Jerusalem by Titus.
115. Jewish Revolts in Cyrene and Cyprus.
132. Revolt under Bar-Cochab.
185. Jerusalem destroyed.

INDEX.

THE END.

Cambridge : Stereotyped and Printed by Welch, Bigelow, & Co.

MARCH, 1861.

CATALOGUE

OF THE MOST

RECENT PUBLICATIONS

OF

WALKER, WISE, & CO.,

245 Washington Street, Boston.

Hymns for Mothers and Children. Selected and edited by one of the compilers of "Hymns of the Aged." Printed on delicately tinted paper, and adorned by an appropriate title-page and frontispiece, and six exquisite vignettes by Billings. Square 16mo. $1.25.

"The collection is unexceptionable of its kind, and one of the best ever made. Pure taste, true feeling, and good judgment have brought together poems that for finish and sentiment must be accepted as lyric treasures in every nursery and parlor." — *Boston Journal.*

"There is not a commonplace or an inferior piece in the whole selection : a beautiful design, carried out with excellent judgment and taste, and consummated with the daintiest skill of printer, engraver, and binder." — *N. Y. Independent.*

"It will be a charming companion in the homes of the land, or wherever the English tongue is spoken." — *Gospel Banner.*

"The more it becomes known, the greater will be its popularity. Pure taste, true feeling, and excellent judgment have worked together in compiling this volume." — *Lowell Courier.*

"Full of rare gems of song and verse, which give beautiful expression to many of the holiest feelings which can fill the heart." — *New Englander.*

"A remarkable success." — *New York Tribune.*

Recent Inquiries in Theology. By eminent English Churchmen: Dr. TEMPLE, ROWLAND WILLIAMS, BADEN POWELL, JOWETT, &c. Being "ESSAYS AND REVIEWS," reprinted from the Second London Edition. Edited, with an Introduction, by Rev. Dr. HEDGE. 12mo. Price, $1.25. Second American Edition. With an Appendix, containing a Note on the "Phalaris Controversy" by Dr. HEDGE, and Dr. TEMPLE'S Sermon on "The Present Relation of Science to Religion," &c. 12mo. $1.25.

"A decisive proof of the progress made by free thought, sound scholarship, and liberal opinion, in matters theological." — *Christian Reformer.*

"The candor and good temper which shine on every page win the reader's sympathy, not less than the profound learning and acumen of the author command his respect." — *The Century.*

"It is a most significant fruit of modern scholarship and of robust courage given to the treatment of the issue between the old traditionary faith and the new knowledge. Dr. Hedge has furnished an Introduction to this American edition, in which he shows how thoroughly he masters the whole scope of its contents, and how gratefully he recognizes the noble vigor and spirit of its writers." — *Christian Examiner.*

"A book which will bear careful reading and study. Thoughtful, scholarly, reverent, earnest, and manly in its tone, it is destined to create no little sensation in the religious world." — *Rochester Union.*

" The writers are evidently men who have discovered that reason was given them to be used, and not to be trifled with ; and that the highest problems in religious philosophy and cosmogony are not to be settled by the literal sense of the Apocalypse or the Book of Genesis." — *Monthly Religious Magazine.*

" The social and official position of the authors, their learning, their abilities, and their sincerity, courage, and earnest, reverential spirit, as attested by their joint publications, entitle them to an unprejudiced and considerate hearing." — *Westminster Review.*

Historical Pictures Retouched. A volume of Miscellanies. In Two Parts : Part I. STUDIES ; Part II. FANCIES. By Mrs. C. H. DALL, Author of " Woman's Right to Labor." 16mo. $1.00.

" Probably no book written to advance the cause of ' Woman's Rights ' can approach this in the number of names adduced in proof of the intellectual ability of women." — *Boston Transcript.*

" They are full of tender sentiment and a delicate imagination, and on subjects that must interest a wide circle." — *Christian Register.*

" Mrs. Dall writes with an earnestness and candor that cannot fail to make an impression, even on the most obdurate opponent of her theory. We find, too, in the volume evidences of a kind and gentle heart, with a spirit of firmness and patience that marks the author as no common woman." — *Home Journal.*

Struggle for Life. By the author of several brilliant papers in the *Atlantic Monthly*, — " The Queen of the Red Chessmen," " Sunshine," and others. 12mo. $1.00.

" It is a warm, lovable book, — a human ' Struggle for Life.' " — *New York World.*

" It teaches good lessons, is an interesting narrative, and may be read with pleasure and profit." — *Boston Recorder.*

" A series of sharply-drawn pictures from real life, which it is safe to prophesy will attract thousands of eyes, and touch thousands of hearts." — *Salem Gazette.*

" Animated in style, genial in spirit, and bright with delineations both of healthful and loving home service, and of unselfish efforts for the ignorant and degraded poor." — *Dover Gazette.*

" Decidedly a readable book : a story which one feels the better for having read." — *Christian Freeman.*

A Practical Illustration of Woman's Right to Labor ; being an Autobiographical Letter. By Dr. MARIE ZAKRZEWSKA, late of Berlin, Prussia. Edited by Mrs. C. H. DALL. 16mo. 63 cents.

" Absorbing in its interest as a romance ; and is as much more suggestive and instructive than a formal discussion of the principles involved could be as life is more powerful than words." — *Christian Review.*

"The story is unaffectedly told, and affords a striking example of success under difficulties, where ordinary perseverance would have failed." — *Lawrence American.*

"We have never read the narrative of a heroic and manly (womanly) and triumphant struggle with difficulties, that interested us more than this." — *Zion's Herald.*

"Has the charms of romance, but is of higher value than the best work of that character, since it is an unvarnished tale of heroic efforts, Christian patience, and true success." — *New Bedford Mercury*

Kormak : an Icelandic Romance of the Tenth Century. In Six Cantos. 16mo. 75 cents.

"There is much that is attractive and exciting in these old Sagas, and the anonymous author of this Poem has woven them into his verse in an agreeable manner." — *Salem Gazette.*

"Rich in interesting adventure, and the wild romance with which the history of the Northmen is filled." — *Christian Freeman.*

"It abounds in beautiful and strong passages. . . . We think it will take rank among the best specimens of American poetry." — *Zion's Herald.*

"A romance unique, instructive, and interesting. Opening the book at the title-page, we could not leave it till we had read to the closing line." — *Gospel Banner.*

Sawyer's Translation of the New Testament. New, revised, and improved edition. 12mo. Cloth, $1.00 ; morocco, $1.25. Eleventh thousand.

"The translation is singularly accurate, and evinces careful, conscientious, and diligent scholarship." — *New York Evangelist.*

"Should all Christians have this book on their table, they would have many an ancient difficulty made easier by it, and many an antiquated error corrected." — *Philadelphia Evening Journal.*

Sawyer's Translation of the Old Testament, Vol. II., containing the Hebrew Prophets. 12mo, to match *Sawyer's Translation of the New Testament.* Cloth, $1.00 ; morocco, $1.25.

Ten thousand copies of the *New Testament* have already been sold ; and the demand for the Old Testament, as testing the translator's principles of translating, has been constantly increasing. The publication of this volume will materially advance the cause of a new version of the Holy Scriptures ; and, as an aid in understanding the meaning of the sacred writers, these volumes should be in every family where the Bible is read at all.

"We have in these volumes the best efforts of a devoted man, of varied ability, of ripe scholarship, and of an eminently catholic spirit, to *improve* in translation, not to supplant our old family Bible." — *Congregational Quarterly Journal.*

Ninety Days' Worth of Europe. Memoranda of Travel, and Familiar Letters to Friends at Home. By Rev. E. E. HALE. With numerous illustrative sketches on wood. 16mo. 75 cents.

"Mr. Hale inherits the use of a facile pen, wide bearings of learning, and preserves in these rambling references much of the quick evolutions of his talk. It has one positive element of worth; it has not been studiously collated with 'Murray,' as the journeymongers are wont." — *Boston Correspondent New York World.*

Pictures and Flowers for Child-Lovers. 18mo. Illustrated. 50 cents.

"This is really a charming selection of the good things said about children by poets and prose-writers the past three centuries. The modest volume is a mine of rich 'brilliants' from the best British and American poets, and must be an acceptable present to any member of a home-circle." — *Boston Transcript.*

"Parents and sympathizers with children's sorrows and joys have only to know how many good things there are in its pages, to create a demand which a hundred thousand copies will not satisfy." — *Norfolk County Journal.*

Katherine Morris. An Autobiography. By the Author of "Step by Step, or Delia Arlington," and "Here and Hereafter." 12mo. $1.00.

Without any loud pretensions, or attempts at creating a sensation, this thoroughly good book has noiselessly made its way into the hands of appreciative readers and critics. Even the *London Athenæum* gives it a hearty commendation for its spirit and execution.

"Among the excellent religious tales which exhibit in so attractive form many phases of the popular Christianity, we are glad to call special attention to one of the latest, and, it seems to us, one of the best." — *Christian Examiner.*

"Pervaded by a fine religious spirit, it leaves the best impression which this kind of literature is capable of producing." — *Religious Magazine.*

"The earnest piety of a true Christian is constantly manifest, and the moral of the tale is well inculcated." — *Saturday Evening Gazette.*

The Boy Inventor. A Memoir of Matthew Edwards, by the Author of "The Age of Fable." Illustrated. 16mo. 50 cents.

Rarely does a little book make its way so rapidly. The first edition (one thousand copies) sold in about six weeks. Hundreds of critical notices could be appended, indicating the favor with which it has been received by the press. The burden of all is, that the volume is invaluable as a stimulation to patient industry, and improvement of opportunities. Every boy in the land should read it.

The Church of the First Three Centuries ; or,
Notices of the Lives and Opinions of some of the Early Fathers, with special Reference to the Doctrine of the Trinity, illustrating its Late Origin and Gradual Formation. By ALVAN LAMSON, D. D.   8vo. $ 1.75.

" In this erudite work, an exposition is given of the early theology of the Christian Church, as exemplified in the opinions of Justin Martyr, Clement of Alexandria, Origen, and Eusebius." — *New York Tribune.*

" Dr. Lamson's careful habits of inquiry, sagacious discernment, candid moderation, familiarity with ancient learning, and lucid and direct style, have produced a work full of entertaining information, which can be depended upon for its accuracy, and attractive by its literary execution." — *Christian Register.*

" We conceive this to be a highly valuable publication. It shows the human origin of the doctrine of the Trinity, and traces its gradual growth, and incorporation into the Christian Church." — *Christian Ambassador.*

In addition to other forcible testimony on this side the Atlantic, the London Critical Journals bear witness to Dr. Lamson's scholarly ability and fairness.

Disquisitions and Notes on the Gospels. — Matthew. By Rev. JOHN H. MORISON, D. D. Second Edition, revised and improved. 12mo. $ 1.25.

This important work, which has been long in preparation, and upon which the accurate and accomplished author has bestowed great labor and thought, will, it is believed, meet a decided want in this department of knowledge. The publishers invite public attention to it.

" The object of this work is to assist in the interpretation of the Gospels. It does not seek to go beyond the authority of Jesus. It does not undertake to show what the Evangelists ought to have said, and to force their language into accordance with it." — *Extract from the Preface.*

" The author has done his work well, and the book will prove a most interesting and useful help to students of the New Testament." — *Boston Advertiser.*

" The 'Notes' evince a thorough knowledge of the Scriptures, an extensive acquaintance with ancient and modern commentators, and strong native powers of analysis." — *Saturday Evening Gazette.*

" We cannot refrain from heartily commending the spirit in which this work is conceived and expressed. The attitude of the author, and the one into which he seeks to lead his readers, is that of a reverent student of the words of Christ, placing perfect faith on all his teachings, and seeking only, by freeing the mind from the trammels of prejudice and preconceived opinions, to arrive at the true meaning of those teachings. This loving and reverential spirit, united to ripe scholarship, abundantly fits the author for his task, and makes his work a valuable guide to students of the Bible." — *Boston Journal.*

𝕿𝖍𝖊 𝕾𝖎𝖑𝖛𝖊𝖗-𝕻𝖊𝖓𝖓𝖞 𝕾𝖊𝖗𝖎𝖊𝖘.

Patty Williams's Voyage.

The Story of the Princess Narina and her Silver-feathered Shoes.

Nobody's Child; and other Stories. Edited by the Author of "Violet," "Daisy," "Noisy Herbert," &c.

Sunny-eyed Tim, the Observant Little Boy. By the Author of "Faith and Patience," &c.

Theda and the Mountain. By the Author of "Summer with the Little Grays."

Juthoo and his Sunday School. A Tale of Child-Life in India. By the Brahmin, J. G. Gangooly.

These little books are to be published in an attractive manner, at the low price of *twenty-five cents each*, to meet the demand for good but cheap Juveniles.

"They possess the rare merit of being written in a style easily comprehended by those for whom they are designed, and on themes that combine interest with instruction." — *Burlington Sentinel.*

"The whole series are of a character unexceptionable in every point, and admirably suited for the home or the Sunday School." — *Syracuse Courier.*

FRED. FREELAND; or, The Chain of Circumstances. 75 cents.

"We cordially recommend this finely written and instructive tale." — *Philadelphia National Argus.*

"Exceedingly interesting and instructive." — *Dover Gazette.*

"Cannot fail to interest and improve." — *Burlington Sentinel.*

"Attractive in style, and unexceptionable in matter." — *Woodstock Spirit of the Age.*

"Well conceived and happily executed." — *Boston Christian Era.*

"An excellent volume." — *Greenfield Gazette.*

"We can, with much pleasure, commend it." — *Fall River News.*

"A good book." — *Haverhill Banner.*

"Inculcating an excellent moral." — *Peterson's Magazine.*

"Quite spirited, and will be read with interest." — *Northampton Gazette.*

"The general tendency of the book is wholesome." — *Salem Observer.*

ALL THE CHILDREN'S LIBRARY.

NOISY HERBERT, and other Stories for Small Children.
50 cents.

The R. B. R.'s : My Little Neighbors. 50 cents

BESSIE GRANT'S TREASURE. 50 cents.

A SUMMER WITH THE LITTLE GRAYS. 50 cents.

FAITH AND PATIENCE. A Story — and something more — for Boys.
75 cts.

MODESTY AND MERIT. 75 cents.

All fully and finely illustrated, and tastefully bound.

"These books may be unreservedly recommended." — *Daily Advertiser.*

"We cordially recommend them." — *Sunday School Gazette.*

"This charming Library, for variety and adaptation to meet the wants of the various ages of a family group, is certainly unsurpassed." — *Christian Register.*

"For lessons of truth, honesty, generosity, courtesy, and all of manliness (not more) that should be found in the ingenuous boy, — and these lessons, not in a didactic form, but insinuated in the natural course of a graceful and charming story, — we have seldom seen 'Faith and Patience' paralleled, never surpassed, in juvenile literature. Its morality is that of the Sermon on the Mount, and it is redolent throughout of the spirit of the Divine Teacher." — *North American Review.*

ALICE'S DREAM. A Tale of Christmas-Time. Two exquisite Illustrations by Billings. 50 cents.

A charmingly written Christmas Story, worthy the perusal of old and young.

"A tone of practical common sense and piety pervades 'Alice's Dream,' and we strongly recommend it." — *Saturday Express.*

"The story is pleasantly told, and conveys a fitting Christmas lesson of true, unselfish charity." — *Boston Journal.*

"Calculated to exercise a good and refining influence upon the hearts of the young." — *Essex County Democrat.*